Tyranny of the Mind

SELF-RULE & THE COMMON AMERICAN UPRISING

JULIE A. FRAGOULES

χάος Publishing

ISBN: 978-0-9987403-7-9

Xaos Publishing, United States of America

www.xaospublishing.us

"Liberty of conscience and of the press cannot be cancelled,"

- James Madison, December 21, 1798 [1]

Also by Julie A. Fragoules
The Serpent Underneath

Table of Contents

Foreword

Helen and Catherine

Amidst rural landscapes, the hustle of turn-of-the-century cities and shaped by America's tumultuous history, my family's journey blends dreams, sacrifices, and the steadfast pursuit of opportunity and improvement. The children of immigrants on one side and migrant pickers on the other, my parents used hard work and sacrifice to achieve the American Dream of creating a better life for themselves and their children. Our family story stands beside countless others across this nation as evidence of the attainability of that dream, at least at the time. The bedrock American ideals of individual liberty and personal responsibility, however imperfectly applied, greatly improved the human condition even for most of its poorest and ill-treated residents.

MY FATHER'S SIDE

American Immigration

My dad's mother, Catherine, was born to Austrian immigrants. Her mother, Helen, fled rural poverty in Galicia, Austria-Hungary, arriving in the U.S. alone in 1901 when she was 16, though some records suggest a year later. It was a harrowing journey, leaving her family to travel across the Atlantic in the steerage section of a massive steam-powered, steel-hauled ocean liner. Steerage was usually a temporary passenger section partitioned off from the cargo hold; a cramped but livable space accessed by narrow ladders[2], most often with open, dormitory style quarters. In good weather, even that made for a decent seven to twelve day trip, especially for lines crossing North Atlantic.

Unfortunately, the route was also known for vicious storms that rolled and pitched ships, tossing their passengers relentlessly. Seasickness was common, saturating the damp, musty holds with a repulsive stench that poor ventilation and inattentive crew often made unbearable.[3] She was just one of some 25 million Europeans to make a similar trip in the late 19th and early 20th Century. As time went on, immigration from around the world became more common and, of course, slave ships and other forms of involuntary travel occurred here beginning long before the founding of the United States.

Isolated from everyone and everything she knew, not speaking the language and alone in a foreign country, Helen settled in Chicago where she likely worked as a housekeeper. Domestic servants were the leading occupation for women in the city then and most lived with the families they served. Helen sent money back to her family until her mother and nine of her siblings were able to come over. Her mother arrived in 1910 but her father died in Austria. Two years after her arrival, Helen married Benedict, who was a few years older than her and also from Austria. Records show Benedict was a merchant in the candies industry. Tragedies quickly began to accumulate for the family.

Helen and Benedict had a son named Joseph who lived only a year and a second son that survived one day. My dad's mother, Catherine, was their first of four daughters that would come next. Helen's youngest was born in 1913, her sixth pregnancy in only seven years. Her difficult young life took a serious toll. With three other young daughters to care for, Benedict handed the newborn to others so that Helen could "rest", as they said back then. Most likely dealing with post-partum depression, Helen was placed in the Chicago State Hospital, which was used for the treatment and care of the insane. Her stay was brief and heartbreaking.

Previously known as the Dunning asylum, it was a place area parents threatened to send their children to if they did not behave. A special train car that transported some inmates to the facility was known locally as "the crazy train". The multistory, red brick structure could have been the setting of the most terrifying horror movies, with bars on the windows, little heat and crawling with vermin. Always overcrowded, it was known for neglect, corruption and infested food, along with a nauseating putrid smell.

Women inmates, Chicago State Hospital, 1910

When the state took over the facility the year before Helen was admitted, conditions were improving, but inmates were still ragged and unclean, locked away or wandering the grounds like extras from The Walking Dead. There were several cemeteries, and as the facility expanded over the years, new buildings constructed on top of unmarked graves. There was an outbreak of typhoid fever that year and even though a vaccine was developed some years earlier, it likely wasn't available to Helen. A bacterial infection that today is only common in third world countries, typhoid was probably caused by contaminated water supply. Helen died at 28, just five months after giving birth to her fourth daughter. Benedict remarried a year later.

My dad's mother Catherine, the oldest daughter, was only five when her mother died. Catherine described unpleasant conditions as the young daughters adapted to the now favored, new family. In time, they would work at the Greek restaurant and night club owned by their step-sister's husband, located on the north side of the city, not far from Lake Michigan. This is where Catherine met my dad's father, Themistocles, who worked as a cook. Helen's daughters would all find happiness, but, like her mother, Catherine's life took a tragic turn when my dad was only ten.

Out of Greece:

Sharing his name with a great Athenian general known as the father of naval warfare, my dad's father Themistocles "Tom," was born in the small village of *Ano Achaia* near Patras, Greece. His mother died when he was very young, possibly during the birth of his sister. With the family struggling and war with Turkey on the horizon, his older brother, Gust, traveled alone to America in 1907. Themistocles followed, also alone, two years later, arriving on April 19, 1909. Public records show Gust was 16 and Themistocles 15, though the brothers told us they were even younger when they came here and had to lie about their ages to do so.

Themistocles traveled aboard a six-thousand-ton ocean liner, aptly named the *S.S. Themistocles.* He was one of 1,500 third class passengers making the journey in the ship's steerage section. Conditions for crossings that originated in the south of Europe were worse than the northern routes and amenities even fewer. When the ship docked along the way in the Mediterranean, my grandfather told that he and other boys were tasked with knocking the rats off the anchor lines as they tried to board. Upon his arrival in New York, they met with quarantines and various inspections before release.

Despite the daunting experience, reaching New York was only the beginning of his story. Like his brother before him, Themistocles served as an indentured servant for one year to pay for the cost of his travel. Living in contracted servitude, Themistocles was a shoeshine boy in New York City. When he was finally set free on his own in turn of the century America, he headed west in search of his brother. They left word for each other as they traveled, hopping trains, living in improvised encampments and finding work in railroad construction and logging camps.

Themistocles is second from left

Both became cooks, eventually reuniting in Chicago. I once heard a Greek immigrant who came over around the same time say he was told the streets in America were paved with gold, but when he arrived he found the streets weren't even paved, and the immigrants were expected to pave them.

Themistocles and Gust

My grandfather said something similar, but there was opportunity and peace, which was better than they had at home. At one point, they both worked in the restaurant of the hotel that Al Capone used as his base of operations. Themistocles recalled delivering room service to Capone and his men, their Thompson submachine guns, or Tommy guns, propped up against the table, smoke drifting up. The brothers were also familiar with a doctor who was slaughtered in the Saint Valentine's Day massacre along with six unarmed members of the George "Bugs" Moran gang. It was the height of Chicago's gang wars between Capone and Moran as the roaring twenties collided with the Great Depression. Restaurant work, at least, kept them employed. The brothers were never able to return to Greece or see their family again, but Gust sent money back for as long as he lived.

Settling in Michigan

My dad's parents, Catherine and Themistocles, married in 1921. The couple saved money and bought a farmhouse in southwest Michigan at the end of the 1920's, but lost that property in the economic travails of the Great Depression. Starting over, Themistocles maintained multiple jobs, including work at a steel mill. They eventually bought another farmhouse on forty acres in the small Michigan town of Bangor where my dad and his brother grew up.

Catherine and my dad, Bangor

My dad was only 11 when his mother, Catherine, died from Aplastic Anemia, caused by exposure to materials in her job at an electronics factory, the same ailment, curiously, that caused the death of Eleanor Roosevelt and Marie Curie. Catherine was just 41. The company paid the family a stipend until my dad turned 18, which helped them barely make ends meet.

Themistocles and son

His brother George, older by ten years, joined the Navy during World War II for the "duration of the war", which, fortunately, ended before he left the base in Hawaii. My dad and his father worked the farm, living off what the rich Michigan soil could produce. Eventually, they bought a tractor, though my dad rode the back to make the horse-drawn implements function. Themistocles was determined to keep my dad with him.

MY MOTHER'S SIDE

Rural Arkansas

My mother's parents, Vernon and Pearl, grew up in the on the rural farmland of White County in Central Arkansas along the Little Red river. Vernon was one of eight children, five boys and three girls, born to William and Lillie May, who were married in 1906. The family relocated to the Arkansas King Ranch in the town of Providence - which memories cast as reminiscent of TV's Yellowstone, albeit on a smaller scale, and mercifully devoid of the orchestrated mayhem. William served as ranch foreman and blacksmith. He was a gruff looking man in one photo, a pipe dangling from his lips.

William's ancestry has been traced back to the War of 1812, where a father and son served, one as sergeant and the other a private. Several of the men in his family line were blacksmiths, including one that served as such in the Civil War. My mom said her grandfather William was a harsh taskmaster to his diminutive but resilient wife, Lillie May. When asked why he ordered her around, he would repeat the saying, "You don't buy a dog and do your own barking." Vernon was a teenager on the ranch when he met Pearl.

Gladys, Wesley (left), Vernon, Pearl (right), Pearl's

My mom's mother, Pearl, was the daughter of southern farmers, Wesley and Gladys. Wesley grew up working on his parents' farm where his father also served as blacksmith. Gladys was born in Oklahoma but relocated with her family to nearby Judsonia, Arkansas when she was a baby. Timber harvesting, cattle ranches and farms covered the flat to hilly landscape.

Wesley was 22 when he married 16-year-old Gladys in 1917. The next year, my grandmother Pearl was born, but only a couple of months later Wesley left his teenaged wife and new baby behind for World War I, where he served in the army. After he returned from the war, they bought a farm and had seven more children. Economic conditions were strained in rural Arkansas even before the stock market crash of 1929 hurled the nation into the Great Depression. Floods ravaged the state in 1927, followed by a devastating drought three years later that caused the price of cotton to plummet and made other crops unprofitable. Wesley and Gladys lost their farm and were forced into the role of tenants, navigating the harsh reality of sharecroppers. They also picked fruit. The strawberry industry thrived in the area, even during the depression.[4]

The Great Migration

My mom's parents, Vernon and Pearl, married in 1935 when he was 17 and she 16. While the ranch that his father ran had been less affected by the economic downturn, now the young couple struggled. They worked as migrant pickers, harvesting strawberries in the sticky, humid 100 degree heat of Arkansas summers and then following the crop seasons north into Michigan each year. My mother was born in Michigan while they were there to pick cherries. They continued to travel back and forth with the seasons, living in primitive migrant housing. They had two more daughters in Arkansas before Vernon took a job at a Michigan steel mill in the early 1940s and they relocated permanently. Like millions of others across the country, they were part of the Great Migration of Americans from depressed rural areas looking for jobs in the cities.

Vernon, Pearl, Marvel, Ramona and my mother

Though disparaged as "dumb hillbillies" and "dirty migrant," they worked and saved. Vernon and Pearl had two sons but had to bury my mother's younger sister, Marvell. Her life was snuffed out within a

Vernon (right) putting up the sign for the auto trim shop

day from an infection at the age of five. Finally, the couple opened a paint and wallpaper business called the Village Color Shop in Benton Harbor that Pearl and her sister Hope operated. Hope's husband opened an auto trim shop in the back, skills he learned from his father, who was retired from General Motors. Vernon and Pearl later opened an upholstery business and moved to Bangor, where they bought a home and farm. My parents would learn upholstery from them.

OUR FAMILY

Bangor, Michigan

My dad and mom, Constantine "Dean" and Norma Jean, were high school sweethearts who graduated in 1955 and married three years later. My mom sewed her own clothes growing up and said she learned to use patterns in her Home Economics class. This turned out to be valuable in their own business later.

Constantine "Dean" and Norma Jean

My dad was a high school basketball star and state champion, but had to forgo college to care for his father. By 1965, my parents and their three boys moved into the farmhouse where my dad grew up. Though there was room, Themistocles wanted to give them space so Dean and Jean built a separate house for him on the property using reclaimed wood. As with many things in life, they learned how as they went. The home has since been added onto and is still inhabited today.

Relocating to Arkansas

A couple years after Themistocles passed of natural causes, my family turned their sights on Arkansas in search of better economic opportunities and warmer weather. The type of business they started and work they could do fit well into the local environment and its bourgeoning industries. North Central Arkansas is beautifully natural, an isolated landscape of limestone mountains, deep lakes and pristine rivers. It became a recreational mecca as the 20th Century progressed for those willing to drive for hours on a tangled, scattering of two-lane roads from the closest city or commercial airport.

Two hydroelectric dams were built here in the years leading up to World War II on the White and North Fork rivers, drowning small communities beneath vast reservoirs and changing the area's fortunes forever. Jobs came with the construction and then from the growth of tourism as little resorts, shops and boat docks grew up to service the fishermen, watersport enthusiast and other vacationers and retirees willing to hazard the rugged terrain to enjoy its natural wonders. Wages and cost of living were low. Young people's first jobs when I grew up tended to be at factories or food service. The area would become the center of the bass boat industry for many years.

Norfork dam postcard, 1940s

My parents, Dean and Jean, moved here in 1968, carrying with them their three young sons and only those belongings they could cram into the used school bus they bought for the move. I was born a couple of years later. They started an upholstery business with one used sewing machine, working out of the bus until it sold. They then worked out of a tent until moving into a small concrete block building they built themselves. At first, they repaired anything from car seats and old furniture to diesel-covered tarps used by big trucks to cover their loads, all often nasty, difficult work.

First block shop building, late 1960s

Some years later they had a larger metal building built and kept adding to it over the years. Though they still did custom work, they also started building marine products, including seats and covers for many boat companies, among them Champion Boats, Ranger, Bass Cat and a long list of others, that either briefly or consistently relied on my family's business for design and production. Their work became legendary in the bass boat industry. They built a new home behind "the shop," which is how we always referred to the business. My mom sewed from home as she watched me and then started bringing me to the shop with her.

I remember, when I was little, going to see my dad who would still be toiling away at a sewing machine late into the night in an otherwise deserted building. My three brothers and I all worked there when we got older. The house I grew up in was a kit ordered from a magazine that included all of the materials for construction and was dried in by hired workers. My parents finished much of the interior themselves over time. Along the way, if they needed to know how to do something - electric, plumbing, construction - they researched it.

We always accomplished more as a family helping each other than any of us ever could have done alone, perhaps inheriting some of those hands-on blacksmithing skills from our ancestors. Had we been forced to hire everything done, we could never have afforded it, nor could we have started a business. My parents were never afraid of hard work and always strove to do what was right and provide a quality product. They would spend more to buy materials locally or regionally because small businesses succeed by supporting each other.

Over many years, through effort and sacrifice, their business grew, putting two children through college and starting the other two as successful small business owners. At the same time, they employed thousands of people and contributed to the growth and advancement of the community. My parents celebrated their 65th wedding anniversary in 2023 before my mom passed that September after a long, torturous struggle with the effects of strokes. She was 86. My dad still lives next door to me today. The business my parents built stayed in the family – on the same property, using the

First metal building (left) 1977, late 1980's (right). By 2023, it almost doubled the buildings visible here.

same phone number – for over 45 years before being sold. There are many in America with darker stories but also many brighter ones. I certainly had a better quality of life than my parents and certainly much better than their parents.

Growing Up

Grandpa Vernon and Julie

I was raised in the rural south of Arkansas in the 1970's and 1980's with my family as my role models, supporters and protectors. The traditional family unit definitely made a difference in my life. Our community was safe and quiet. I learned about our unique and exceptional nation and the ideals built into its founding documents at school.

I was also taught about our nation's troubled past, including slavery, civil war, segregation and, finally, the civil rights movement. Arkansas figured notably in the death of the old order as Democrat Governor Orval Faubus infamously attempted to prevent black students from entering Little Rock Central High School during desegregation. Having emerged from this dark past, however, a nation designed for liberty and justice, had finally applied those ideals and rights to all under law. Despite its flaws, our nation and its people were viewed as basically good and striving to be better.

I was idealistic and, like most youth, more than a little naive. My family succeeded on hard work and determination, overcoming various difficulties and personal tragedies. They had no advantages or privileges, more or less than many other rural or immigrant poor. Greeks were not considered "white" when my grandfather came to this country as an indentured servant and migrant pickers and sharecroppers were little regarded, whatever their skin color. If race was a benefit, it wasn't much. As a nation, we can't deny the dark parts of our history, but that doesn't diminish the positives that made this country stand apart from the rest of the world. Yet, how a nation that offered the opportunities of the American Dream to so many, arrive at its current state? Plagued by violence, our debt skyrocketing, wars raging and equal justice under the law beyond reach, our nation's positive trajectory has clearly cratered. I began to understand *why* over the years of research I put into this book.

This book began as my personal investigation into the relationship between religion and liberty in the establishment of this nation and the true intent of its founders, determined to make sense of apparent contradictions in the accounts and, at the same time, discover whether my nonconforming beliefs were intended to be equally protected under its authority or merely tolerated. What I discovered was not likely to fully please either side of the debate, but it exposed a greater battle. It was a conflict was waged across the millennia between those ambitious to gain power over others and those desperate to make their own way and think for themselves. The battle between these competing desires was evident during the establishment of the United States and, in fact, can be traced back to the very beginning of western civilization. It continues at the heart of our political conflicts today, where we see that a religiously held ideology need not include a god to be beyond the authority of civil government to promote or serve as a tool for state control. Our nation, based on the ideal of individual freedom, limited only by the equal freedom of others, was unlike every other nation in history and, though imperfect, marked a tremendous victory in the fight against tyranny.

We are often told that Americans are more divided than ever, but I disagree. I have spent the last twenty years working and living around the country, responding to national disasters, helping people recover and learn how to reduce future losses through hazard mitigation. I've met people from all walks of life, all shades, histories and political leanings, and have come to believe that the vast majority of Americans, regardless of political party, are on the same side and share the same natural sense of justice and morality. Though constantly manipulated to fight against each other, to dehumanize and demean our opponents, we share a common foe that has corrupted the establishment of both sides, put racism and injustice into the system designed to fight against it, and indoctrinated our institutions.

I believe the vast majority of Americans are compassionate, level-headed people who just want a safe environment for their families and a fair shot at life. I believe the Americans agree on far more than they disagree and are willing to compromise on even the most contentious issues. Honest compromise, however, does not serve the interests of those in power. To survive as a nation, we need to look beyond the distortions that separate us, that convince half of the country that the other half is evil or ignorant. It is time to redefine the political spectrum in order to accurately separate the totalitarians from the humanitarians, those who value people for their intrinsic worth and those who assess their worth only as pawns to be sacrificed for their own ambitions. We need a clear to see past the platitudes, propaganda and indoctrination our domestic enemies produce.

I had no idea what conclusions this book would reach or the changes that would affect our nation by the time I finished it. I also failed to predict how significant this era in our history would be. Our republic and our people face grave peril, and it is a hazard we have failed to mitigate against. This last decade or two, however, aptly demonstrates the forces at play and the tools being used to control the people. The story of this battle started many centuries ago.

"So the restraints of religion are thrown off, by which alone kingdoms stand."

– Pope Gregory XVI

Chapter 1

By Which Kingdoms Stand

Starting with the family and then the clan, the father or eldest father commonly led from inherent authority. As humans began to live in larger concentrations, leaders claimed the authority of the gods and, in the common era, the authority of the father in the form of a God.

> Pope Leo XIII, On the Christian Constitution of States, 1885: "In civil society, God has always willed that there should be a ruling authority, and that they who are invested with it should reflect the divine power and providence in some measure over the human race. They, therefore, who rule should rule with evenhanded justice, not as masters, but rather as fathers, for the rule of God over man is most just, and is tempered always with a father's kindness."[5]

It was not merely that powerful leaders claimed the favor of gods, but it was understood that these leaders would not have attained their positions of authority had the gods not chosen and ordained them in those roles. This idea can be seen from our earliest leaders to the relatively modern practices of Trial by Ordeal[6], where people were subjected to often deadly experiences where survival determined innocence, and Trial by Battle, in which God's providence was seen to assure the person in the right prevailed. That mindset was then used for much of western history to justify anything leaders chose to do. It was might makes right, success makes right, regardless of justness or reason. Some committed sacrifices. All manners of violence and oppression were justified in the name of God or gods, comprising the accepted rationale for many thousands of years. Over time, governments, laws and religions would be instituted to maintain order and guide behavior.

Origins of Western Law

Civilizations and written language arose roughly 5,500 to 4,500 years ago (3,500 to 2,500 B.C.E), according to current estimates, among the peoples across the world, from Mesopotamia, Egypt, China, India, Mediterranean Europe to Mesoamerica. A case can be made that there may have been a civilization around the world far earlier than official estimates[7], but we can only speak with any confidence on those cultures whose languages were recorded in a durable fashion, such as carved into stone, and since translated. Western civilization can be traced back to the Middle East.

The Sumerians of Mesopotamia represent the earliest known civilization and writing system. Their origin and ethnicity are unknown. Mesopotamia refers to the fertile lands between the Tigris and Euphrates rivers in the currently sand choked region of the Middle East now known as Iraq. The Sumerians established great city-states that would eventually be conquered by the Akkadians, a Semitic people from regions farther south on the Arabian Peninsula. The Sumerian culture, however, remained dominant and would prove exceedingly influential on our history. The Sumerians worshiped multiple gods, including a creator god, in a polytheistic religion typical of many early cultures.[8] They also left legends and poems which would form the basis of the Epic of Gilgamesh, a precursor to the Hebrew stories of Adam and Eve in the Garden of Eden and of Noah and the flood. These tales would later be expanded upon by an Assyrian king, and later yet rewritten to feature the Hebrew god, all referring to prehistoric events.[9]

The first known legal code came from a Sumerian leader named Urukagina, from around 2,350 B.C.E., though it was believed to have been reforms of existing laws. Urukagina's Code included death by stoning as a punishment for theft or adultery and the first known record of the concept of liberty.[10] Like so many laws that would follow, this code declared that the king was appointed by the gods. A few hundred years later, a more complex legal framework called Ur-Nammu's Code was developed by the Sumerian King of Ur around 2,050 B.C.E., which provided for judges, testimony under oath and punishments in proportion to crimes. Written in Cuneiform during a revival of Sumerian culture, the code would directly influence Babylonian laws to follow.[11] An upright stone slab (known as a Stele), dating to about 1790 B.C.E. has been found that featured the laws of the Babylonian King Hammurabi, known as Hammurabi's Code.

Discovered in 1901, the Stele is now on display at the Louvre museum in Paris.[12] It includes a variety of laws related to theft and damages due to dishonesty or carelessness, protecting the rights of property (including slaves as property) and prohibitions against false imprisonment (the inherent contradiction there apparently escaping them).

While laws were developed around the world, western laws and governmental systems can be traced directly from these early examples to the Roman Republic and the Greek city-states of roughly 500 B.C.E. The harsh legal codes of a Greek citizen named Draco in 621 B.C.E. would form the first written laws of Greece and put the term "Draconian" into the English lexicon. Draco's laws were more than strict, as most offenses were punishable by death. The laws that laid the foundation of western constitutional law and democracy came at roughly 500 B.C.E. when an Athenian named Solon worked to rewrite the laws of his Greek city-state in order to eliminate those injustices found in existing Draconian law, retaining the punishment of death only for the crime of murder. The Constitution of Solon[13] would also inspire a sort of bill of rights for the citizens of the neighboring Roman Republic.

Philosophy and logic as we know it emerged in Greece under the teachings of Socrates, born 469 B.C.E., who was known primarily through the writings of his students, particularly Plato. He is credited with the method of inquiry known now as the Socratic Method, a debate technique intended to encourage critical thinking, and for his ideas of ethics and justice. A proponent of conscience, Socrates was eventually tried by a jury and put to death by poison in 399 B.C.E., having been convicted of corrupting the minds of the young people of Athens and of not believing in the its gods.[14] Inspired by the Greeks, the Romans introduced a legal code called The Twelve Tables.[15] This came during the emergence of the Roman Republic, established in about 500 B.C.E., and provided for trial procedures, rights of property, the awarding of damages, punishment, parental rights, due process, the right to trial in capital cases, and prohibitions of a variety of acts, including 'speaking false witness', theft and murder.

The Roman Republic, which rose and fell before the advent of Christianity, established an advanced legal system with professional judges and lawyers in an era known as the Classical period of Roman law. Meanwhile, Greece's Alexander the Great united an empire that drew together Greek, Egyptian and Persian law. The Greek, or Hellenic, cultural influence on Roman culture was substantial and Greek remained the common language throughout the Roman lands. All this then laid the foundation for western law as we know it today. The Roman Republic lasted about 500 years before transitioning into an Empire, its republican institutions substantially diminished, at about time of Jesus.

According to religious scholars, the commandments of the Hebrew god given to Moses and the people of Israel were believed to have occurred, based on historical references in the Bible, sometime between 1600 to 1300 B.C.E. They were not believed to be introduced to the world outside of Jewish society until after the advent of Christianity, beginning around 20 C.E. and, some argue, did not become prominent even in that faith until after the Protestant Reformation.[16] The story of Abraham leaving Ur to found a new nation in Canaan is dated to around 2000 B.C.E. or later. The Old Testament represented a collection of stories, a blend of historical record, parable and philosophy, many traceable to Sumer, Ur and Babylon in Mesopotamia.

The legal concepts in the old testament had its foundations, ultimately, in the Sumerian Civilization to which virtually all western law can trace its origins. The Ten Commandments are ancillary to western law. Reference to the justice of "an eye for an eye, tooth for a tooth" is first found in the Sumerian inspired Hammurabi's Code, which would have already been in effect before Abraham's departure from that culture. Also, like early Sumerian law, theft, murder and adultery were condemned in the Hebrew commandments as punishable offences. These ideas were not unique but were instead directly influenced by earlier legal thought. What was unique among western religions was the idea of a one and only god of monotheism.

It has been suggested that monotheism developed first in Egypt. It can be found in the ancient Egyptian civilization with the god Aten as promoted by the Pharaoh Akhenaten, who ruled at roughly the same time as Moses was supposed to have lived in Egypt. The Egyptians also thought humans, if judged positively on the actions of this life, would in death be met with punishment or join the divine and become eternal. However, any connection between Egyptian and Jewish monotheism is speculative. Other cultures also developed the idea of a superior or supreme deity which ruled over other gods, but it was the concept of a one and only god which would set the Jewish religion and its progeny apart.

By a couple of decades after the death of Jesus, his religious reforms began to spread into non-Jewish communities and then across the Roman Empire, facilitated by a common language and the mobility enabled by

Roman roads. A wide range of religious beliefs and rituals, including multiple gods and the religions of conquered peoples, coexisted in the Roman Empire until the influx of Christianity changed the dynamic. What made Christianity different was that it required followers to renounce all other gods. This made non-Christians fear that other gods would be offended and bring harm to their lives and fortunes as a result. This led to widespread, violent mistreatment of Christians. By the end of the 3rd Century, Christians faced extensive persecution, forced to denounce their beliefs, flee or face horrifying methods of execution.

Seeing the persecution of Christians and perhaps the potential of this religion in political terms, Roman Emperors finally made moves to stop its oppression. First by Emperor Gaius Galerius in the Edict of Toleration in 311 C.E. and then in the Edict of Milan[17] presented by the Western Emperor Constantine and Eastern Emperor Licinius Augustus in 313 C.E., tolerance was granted to all religions, specifically directing protections for Christians. Numerous different interpretations of the scripture developed throughout this time, particularly about the nature of Jesus as human, God or something other.

A few decades into the 4th Century, a Christian convert named Constantine I, called together Christian Bishops from the Empire as the Council of Nicaea to consolidate the widely varying beliefs and practices of Christian churches into a single doctrine while separating out all that they considered heretical. The First Council of Nicaea in 325 C.E. presented a statement of belief and list of policies and revisions of canon law that would represent the official faith of the Roman Catholic Church. This did not end differences of opinions within the religion, as various sects with conflicting interpretations continued, but it blazed the path of the "one true faith" under the Roman Catholic Church for many centuries to come.

"They will suffer... the punishment of our authority which in accordance with the will of Heaven we shall decide to inflict."
- Edict of Thessalonica

It was this version of Christianity which was declared by Emperor Theodosius I as the official religion of the Roman Empire fifty-five years later, leaving non-Christians to face punishment for not sharing the chosen faith. The tables had turned. Perhaps even more significant in the many centuries to follow, a doctrine of Christianity was established that would tolerate no deviation. A compilation of dictates by Christian Emperors since 312 C.E. was published throughout the Empire by 438 C.E. as the Edict of Thessalonica. Among the dictates:

> Edict of Thessalonica, Emperor Theodosius, 380 C.E.: "According to the apostolic teaching and the doctrine of the Gospel, let us believe in the one deity of the Father, the Son and the Holy Spirit, in equal majesty and in a holy Trinity. We authorize the followers of this law to assume the title of Catholic Christians; but as for the others, since, in our judgment they are foolish madmen, we decree that they shall be branded with the ignominious name of heretics, and shall not presume to give to their conventicles the name of churches. They will suffer in the first place the chastisement of the divine condemnation and in the second the punishment of our authority which in accordance with the will of Heaven we shall decide to inflict."[18]

Reflective of the changing religious perspective in the empire, the dictates asserted the privileges for holding the chosen faith and outlined punishments for dissenters. Roman law was conforming to canon law as it eagerly strove to take the opportunity of sinning away from dissenters, and failing that, taking their property or life.

"It is necessary that the privileges which are bestowed for the cultivation of religion should be given only to followers of the Catholic faith."
- Constantine Augustus

> Constantine and Constans Augusti:
> "It is decreed that in all places and all cities the temples should be closed at once, and after a general warning, the opportunity of sinning be taken from the wicked. We decree also that we shall cease from making sacrifices. And if anyone has committed such a crime, let him be stricken with the avenging sword. And we decree that the property of the one executed shall be claimed by the city, and that rulers of the provinces be punished in the same way, if they neglect to punish such crimes."
>
> Constantine Augustus:
> "It is necessary that the privileges which are bestowed for the

> cultivation of religion should be given only to followers of the Catholic faith. We desire that heretics and schismatics be not only kept from these privileges but be subjected to various fines."
>
> Gratian, Valentinian, and Valens Augusti:
> "The ability and right of making wills shall be taken from those who turn from Christians to pagans, and the testament of such an one, if he made any, shall be abrogated after his death."
>
> Valentinian and Valens Augusti:
> "Whenever there is found a meeting of a mob of Manichaeans, let the leaders be punished with a heavy fine and let those who attended be known as infamous and dishonored, and be shut out from association with men, and let the house and the dwellings where the profane doctrine was taught be seized by the officers of the city."[19]

Any semblance of religious liberty in the empire had come to an end. Our second President, John Adams, reflected on this freedom.

"That wise and humane toleration which does so much honor to the Romans, and reflects disgrace on almost every Christian nation." - President John Adams

---

> John Adams, The Defence, speaking of ancient Roman law, 1851:
> "In private, every family were free to worship the gods in their own way; and in public, though certain forms were required, yet there was not any penalty annexed to the omission of them, as the punishment of offences in this matter was left to the offended god.' This, probably, was the source of that wise and humane toleration which does so much honor to the Romans, and reflects disgrace on almost every Christian nation."[20]

The civil authority of the empire stepped fully into the role of enforcing church doctrine and eradicating heretical influences. Beginning in 528 Emperor Justinian collected and codify existing Roman law in his Corpus Juris Civilis (Code of Justinian), thoroughly incorporating Christianity and increasing the punishments for any who rejected the faith.[21] These legal codes and the canon law of the church became the basis of the legal system moving forward for much of Europe.

"We definitely state that it is not allowable for anyone to produce another faith." - Third Council of Constantinople

---

The nature of monotheism proved inherently amenable to the despotic aims of those then most inclined to leadership. Both the exclusionary nature of the doctrine and its inherent obligation toward the propagation of the faith made for an irresistible influence toward tyranny over the Roman Empire, Medieval Europe, and Muslim lands. When people believed in multiple gods, each asking different manners of reverence, a division of thought was common and generally acceptable. When, on the other hand, there was only one god and only one truth, the power of the religion became concentrated in whoever most successfully established themselves as the holders of that truth.

> Third Council of Constantinople, 681 C.E.:
> "So now that these points have been formulated by us with all precision in every respect and with all care, we definitely state that it is not allowable for anyone to produce another faith, that is, to write or to compose or to consider or to teach others; those who dare to compose another faith, or to support or to teach or to hand on another creed to those who wish to turn to knowledge of the truth, whether from Hellenism or Judaism or indeed from any heresy whatsoever, or to introduce novelty of speech, that is, invention of terms, so as to overturn what has now been defined by us, such persons, if they are bishops or clerics, are deprived of their episcopacy or clerical rank, and if they are monks or layfolk they are excommunicated."[22]

To be excommunicated was to be condemned to hell. Along with eternal consequences, it also meant cutting one off from society and any civil rights. For the good of the people, and their eternal souls, dissention would not be tolerated.

"Therefore all those who dare to think or teach anything different... that they be suspended if they are bishops or clerics, and excommunicated if they are monks or lay people." - Second Council of Nicaea

---

> Second Council of Nicaea, 787 C.E.:
> "The Lord has removed away from you the injustices of your enemies, you have been redeemed from the hand of your foes. The Lord the king is in your midst, you will never more see evil, and peace will be upon you for time eternal. Therefore all those who dare to think or teach anything different, or who follow the accursed heretics in rejecting ecclesiastical traditions, or who devise innovations, or who spurn anything entrusted to the church (whether it be the gospel or the figure of the cross or any example of representational art or any martyr's holy relic), or who fabricate perverted and evil prejudices against cherishing any of the lawful traditions of the catholic church, or who secularize the sacred objects and saintly monasteries, we order that they be suspended if they are bishops or clerics, and excommunicated if they are monks or lay people."[23]

As the Roman Empire declined in power, the Roman Catholic Church and feudalism rose, and darkness ensued. The era of Classical Antiquity, with all of the knowledge, thought and culture of the Greeks and Romans faded from memory, leaving a world where only the elite and well-connected had access to knowledge or any real degree of liberty. The books of Christianity were kept from the people. At the same time in neighboring lands, Muslim powers flourished and battles between the two continued. The early period of the Middle Ages in Europe was long known as the Dark Ages because of an apparent lack of published thought and literature, though many scholars today reject the attribution, pointing at cultural and intellectual activity that did continue. The true darkness came from centuries of war and persecution under the civil and ecclesiastical authorities, creating something far worse than just a slowdown in art and literature.

As the former Roman Empire was divided up by conflicting powers, the bloody and oppressive tendencies of the early church continued to emerge. Viciousness was praised when used to maintain control of the populous who were seen as sheep to be herded.

"I glorify you for having maintained your authority by putting to death those wandering sheep who refused to enter the fold... A king need not fear to command massacres, when these will retain his subjects in obedience." - Pope Nicholas I

> Pope Nicholas I in a letter to the King of Bulgaria in 860 C.E.:
> "I glorify you for having maintained your authority by putting to death those wandering sheep who refused to enter the fold; and you not only have not sinned, by showing a holy rigour, but I even congratulate you on having opened the kingdom of heaven to the people submitted to your rule. A king need not fear to command massacres, when these will retain his subjects in obedience, or cause them to submit to the faith of Christ; and God will reward him in this world, and in eternal life, for these murders."[24]

In these dark times, the remission of sins and entry into heaven, as offered below, must have even made certain death attractive. If the fight seemed just and in response to enemy aggression, that would surely only reinforce the religious rewards used to encourage it.

"All who die... in battle against the pagans, shall have immediate remission of sins. This I grant them through the power of God with which I am invested."- Pope Urban II

> Pope Urban II's address at the Council of Clermont, France, 1095:
> "[The Turks and Arabs] have killed and captured many and have destroyed the churches and devastated the empire. If you permit them to continue thus for awhile with impurity, the faithful of God will be much more widely attacked by them. On this account I, or rather the Lord, beseech you as Christ's heralds to publish this everywhere and to persuade all people of whatever rank, foot-soldiers and knights, poor and rich, to carry aid promptly to those Christians and to destroy that vile race from the lands of our friends. I say this to those who are present, it meant also for those who are absent. Moreover, Christ commands it. All who die by the way, whether by land or by sea, or in battle against the pagans, shall have immediate remission of sins. This I grant them through the power of God with which I am invested. O what a disgrace if such a despised and base race, which worships demons, should conquer a people which has the faith of omnipotent God and is made glorious with the name of Christ!"[25]

The vast, positive influence of Christianity in Europe grew in parallel as the ruling authority of the Roman Catholic Church also strove to assert its supremacy over all civil powers, stretching tentacles into the treasuries and command structures of many kingdoms.

"It is absolutely necessary for salvation that every human creature be subject to the Roman Pontiff." - Pope Boniface VIII

> Pope Boniface VIII, Papal Bull Unam sanctam, 1302 "Hence we must recognize the more clearly that spiritual power surpasses in dignity and in nobility any temporal power whatever, as spiritual things surpass the temporal. This we see very clearly also by the payment, benediction, and consecration of the tithes, but the acceptance of power itself and by the government even of things. For with truth as our witness, it belongs to spiritual power to establish the terrestrial power and to pass judgement if it has not been good. Thus is accomplished the prophecy of Jeremias concerning the Church and the ecclesiastical power: 'Behold to-day I have placed you over nations, and over kingdoms' and the rest... We declare, we proclaim, we define that it is absolutely necessary for salvation that every human creature be subject to the Roman Pontiff." [26]

As the head of the Roman Catholic Church, the Pope presumed absolute authority over the true and proper faith of his subjects, working in concert with the civil rulers or, when opposing, toward their ruin. The application of civil and ecclesiastical dominion under the banner of Christianity provided authority to the good but also to the powerful and power hungry, justifying their deeds under godly pretense. Despite the better capacities of mankind and the positive and attractive philosophy of the Christian faith, oppressors and brutal despots gained the upper hand for most of the Christian era. Monotheism set the world aflame, and Christianity was its unlikely accelerant. In other lands, the Muslim version of monotheism took root, labeling opponents Infidels and working with equal relish to extinguish the embers of dissent.

This had nothing to do with Christianity itself, which persevered even in the darkest of times and gave rise to a great advancement of western civilization. It can be difficult to separate the corruptions and darker parts of history from their religion and faith, but criticism of the former is not meant as an attack on the latter.

Set the World in Flames

Different teachings and sects existed throughout the history of Christianity and they were all seen as a threat to the authority and supremacy Roman Catholic Church. Attempts to suppress heresy, though, had less to do with truth or the teachings of Jesus than with power and submission: controlling the people by controlling speech, publication, thought and action. It labeled opposing ideas as heresy and a threat to the established order, often countered in the most brutal and tyrannical ways. Not all of Europe, nor all of the world, fell under the thumb of the Roman Catholic Church, but not for lack of ambition or effort.

The persecution of heretical depravity took an even darker turn in 1184 when Pope Lucius III defined heresy as treasonous and created an investigation to root it out, primarily in the south of France. Other Popes followed up with Papal Bulls further defining procedures for investigating and eliminating heresy. Along with various crusades, there were also numerous versions of inquisitions authorized by multiple popes, each one broader and crueler than the last. The Catholic Church turned into a totalitarian force, with the papacy doing everything it could to submit each nation to its rule.

Pope Innocent called the Fourth Lateran Council in an effort to establish the supremacy of the Papacy over the entire religion and secular authorities through a variety of canon laws. The declaration of heretics produced by this council also furthered a climate of terror, where the people were pressured to turn on each other to escape accusations against themselves.

> Fourth Lateran Council, 1215, Constitutions, On Heretics: "We add further that each archbishop or bishop, either in person or through his archdeacon or through suitable honest persons, should visit twice or at least once in the year any parish of his in which heretics are said to live. There he should compel three or more men of good repute, or even if it seems expedient the whole neighbourhood, to swear that if anyone knows of heretics there or of any persons who hold secret conventicles or who differ in their life and habits from the normal way of living of the faithful, then he will take care to point them out to the bishop. The bishop himself should summon the accused to his presence, and they should be punished canonically if they are unable to clear themselves of the charge or if after compurgation they relapse into their former errors of faith."[27]

In 1229, Pope Gregory IX established the Medieval Inquisition, which came to be used primarily in France and Italy. The use of torture was authorized by Pope Innocent IV in 1252 (the irony of his name clearly lost) and then in 1256 Pope Alexander IV gave inquisitors the authority to absolve each other of their deeds during inquisitions so that they could directly commit despicable acts without a risk to conscience or eternal punishment.[28] In 1478, Pope Sixtus IV authorized the Spanish monarchs to establish the Spanish Inquisition, which would spread to Africa, Asia and the Americas.

The Catholic monarchs of Spain used the inquisition against Muslim and Jewish influences and used it, inevitably, toward their own political ends. There was some common history between these religions but a common Judeo-Christian culture did not yet exist and their interactions were most often adversarial. The interrogations and punishments became ever darker. Torture was applied to elicit confessions and heretics who were convicted for a second offense or who failed to confess despite evidence of guilt were sentenced to burn at the stake at the hands to the secular authority. The added advantage was that the possessions of those convicted of serious heresy would be confiscated, allegedly to defer the cost of their prosecution. The Spanish Inquisition expanded in scope over the years and did not end until 1834, more than half a century after the declaration of American independence.[29]

"Punishment... for the public good in order that others may become terrified." - Inquisitor General Nicholas Eymerich

---

The Roman Inquisition was established in the 16th Century by Pope Paul III in response to the growth of Protestantism. It extended, in time, as earlier Inquisitions had done, to widely aim at all manner of dissent, from heresy to witchcraft, blasphemy and immorality. Published for the Spanish Inquisition and again in Rome in 1578, a prominent manual for inquisitors described its purpose:

> Directorium Inquisitorum, 1376 by Inquisitor General Nicholas Eymerich:
> "Punishment does not take place primarily and per se for the correction and good of the person punished, but for the public

> good in order that others may become terrified and weaned away from the evils they would commit."[30]

It was terrorism. Only a fraction of those investigated by the Inquisition were put to death, but that fraction was still enough to send untold thousands, or hundreds of thousands, to their graves and enough to keep the flock under control. Throughout much of their history, the inquisitors were able to "keep their hands clean" by turning the convicted heretic over to civil authorities for the infliction of the prescribed punishment. In time and under the direct authority of the Pope, the Inquisitors themselves became especially skilled in the application of torments. Methodologies were developed over time, including various detailed in instructional manuals.[31] Even when the Catholic Church outwardly prohibited the spilling of blood, the reality of the times was unequivocally brutal.

"Among other works well pleasing to the Divine Majesty... that barbarous nations be overthrown and brought to the faith itself."
- Pope Alexander VI

The inquisitions also suppressed advancements in science and knowledge that diverged from the accepted faith, such as in the case of Galileo Galilei and his teachings about the Copernican Theory, that the earth revolved around the sun. Galileo was convicted of heresy by the Roman Inquisition. For a lenient sentence (house arrest), Galileo signed a statement denouncing the science described, professing belief and complete submission to church doctrine, and promising to also report any heretics he encountered to the Holy Office.[32] Along with bringing the inquisition in the Americas, the forcible conversion of natives was approved by the Catholic Church for some time.

> Pope Alexander VI, The Bull Inter Caetera, May 4, 1493:
> "Among other works well pleasing to the Divine Majesty and cherished of our heart, this assuredly ranks highest, that in our times especially the Catholic faith and the Christian religion be exalted and be everywhere increased and spread, that the health of souls be cared for and that barbarous nations be overthrown and brought to the faith itself."[33]

"The king has every right to send his men... to demand their territory from these idolaters." – Judge Martin Fernandez de Encisco

---

This Papal Bull was used to justify war on any natives of the Americas who refused to convert to Christianity or to give up their land and wealth. A Spanish Judge in the Americas wrote in defense of these actions.

> Judge Martin Fernandez de Encisco, 1509:
> "The king has every right to send his men to the Indies to demand their territory from these idolaters because he had received it from the pope. If the Indians refuse, he may quite legally fight them, kill them and enslave them, just as Joshua enslaved the inhabitants of the country of Canaan." [34]

There were differences in tone and substance, from one Pope to another. In a contradictory statement 28 years later, Pope Paul III declared American Indians should not be stolen from or enslaved. Unfortunately, this perspective seems to have been the exception in practice.

"The said Indians... are by no means to be deprived of their liberty or the possession of their property, even though they be outside the faith of Jesus Christ." - Pope Paul III

> Pope Paul III, Sublimus Dei, 1537:
> "We, who, though unworthy, exercise on earth the power of our Lord and seek with all our might to bring those sheep of His flock who are outside into the fold committed to our charge, consider, however, that the Indians are truly men and that they are not only capable of understanding the Catholic Faith but, according to our information, they desire exceedingly to receive it. Desiring to provide ample remedy for these evils, We define and declare by these Our letters, or by any translation thereof signed by any notary public and sealed with the seal of any ecclesiastical dignitary, to which the same credit shall be given as to the originals, that, notwithstanding whatever may have been or may be said to the contrary, the said Indians and all other people who may later be discovered by Christians, are by no means to be deprived of their liberty or the possession of their property, even though they be

> outside the faith of Jesus Christ; and that they may and should, freely and legitimately, enjoy their liberty and the possession of their property; nor should they be in any way enslaved; should the contrary happen, it shall be null and have no effect."[35]

The church also excelled at censorship. The printing press, coming in about 1440, facilitated the propagation of contrary ideas and led to the creation of a forbidden books list by the Catholic Church. Book burnings were conducted to stamp out opposing opinions and all manner of heretical thought. Another way the church maintained their control was to restrict the common people's access to knowledge and history, especially the texts of the Bible, so that the church remained the sole authority. For this reason, these texts were printed in Latin, a language then unknown to most of Europe. This helped the Catholic Church secure its authority and its version of the truth. These texts were thought to be beyond the capacity of the common people to comprehend without their guidance.

> Pope Gregory XVI, Inter Praecipuas, On Biblical Societies, 1844: "Among the special schemes with which non-Catholics plot against the adherents of Catholic truth to turn their minds away from the faith, the biblical societies are prominent. They were first established in England and have spread far and wide so that We now see them as an army on the march, conspiring to publish in great numbers copies of the books of divine Scripture.

"Indeed, what is even more absurd and almost unheard of, they do not exclude the common people of the infidels from sharing this kind of a knowledge." - Pope Gregory XVI

> "These are translated into all kinds of vernacular languages for dissemination without discrimination among both Christians and infidels. Then the biblical societies invite everyone to read them unguided. Therefore it is just as Jerome complained in his day: they make the art of understanding the Scriptures without a teacher 'common to babbling old women and crazy old men and verbose sophists,' and to anyone who can read, no matter what his status. Indeed, what is even more absurd and almost unheard of, they do not exclude the common people of the infidels from sharing this kind of a knowledge...

> "Moreover, regarding the translation of the Bible into the vernacular, even many centuries ago bishops in various places have at times had to exercise greater vigilance when they became aware that such translations were being read in secret gatherings or were being distributed by heretics. Innocent III issued warnings concerning the secret gatherings of laymen and women, under the pretext of piety, for the reading of Scripture in the diocese of Metz. There was also a special prohibition of Scripture translations promulgated either in Gaul a little later or in Spain before the sixteenth century. But later even more care was required when the Lutherans and Calvinists dared to oppose the changeless doctrine of the faith with an almost incredible variety of errors.
>
> "They left no means untried to deceive the faithful with perverse explanations of the sacred books, which were published by their adherents with new interpretations in the vernacular. They were aided in multiplying copies and quickly spreading them by the newly invented art of printing. Therefore in the rules written by the fathers chosen by the Council of Trent, approved by Pius IV and placed in the Index of forbidden books, we read the statute declaring that vernacular Bibles are forbidden except to those for whom it is judged that the reading will contribute 'to the increase of faith and piety.' Because of the continued deceptions of heretics, this rule was further restricted and supplemented by a declaration of Benedict XIV: for the future the only vernacular translations which may be read are those which 'are approved by the Apostolic See' or at least were published 'with annotations taken from the holy Fathers of the Church, or from learned and Catholic authors.'"[36]

A change in thought began to emerge in England regarding the rights of citizens and their capacity for self-rule. Reforms came with the adoption of the Magna Carta in 1215, which introduced the supremacy of the rule of law over kings and the establishment of individual liberties and immunities of free citizens.[37] The use of unfathomably brutal methods of punishment and execution, though, continued for hundreds of years to come. While the use of torture to attain information was technically illegal in England during this period, no restrictions were noted to the methods of punishment and execution. [38] This meager attempt to secure the rights of the people, however, was met with condemnation by king and pope. These rights were in direct opposition of church doctrine. Pope Innocent III issued a papal bull to annul the Magna Carta, which he said was forced on King John "by such violence and fear as might affect the most courageous of men," in a document the pope called "illegal, unjust, harmful to royal rights and shameful to the English people."[39] The Magna Carta was reissued many years later.

"The chain of authority was broken, which restrains the bigot from thinking as he pleases, and the slave from speaking as he thinks."
- David Gibbon

Though the Catholic Church long enjoyed the ability to determine the "correct" doctrine and declare heresy, the same claims in time would be made by other leaders of the reformation, each convinced that theirs was the one true faith. Opposing sects had always existed but the church was able to put them down through various murderous campaigns and tyrannies. But, after more than a thousand years of dominion over Christian thought and belief, the religion became irreparably splintered. The efforts of religious reformers Martin Luther, John Calvin and others established the Protestant branch of Christianity in the 1500's, rejecting much of the doctrine and structure established by the Catholic Church, while continuing the practice of violent intolerance. Historian David Gibbon, whose massive work on Roman history is still admired today.

"Each Christian was taught to acknowledge no law but the scriptures, no interpreter but his own conscience." - David Gibbon

---

> David Gibbon, "The Decline and Fall of the Roman Empire": "The chain of authority was broken, which restrains the bigot from thinking as he pleases, and the slave from speaking as he thinks; the popes, fathers, and councils were no longer the supreme and infallible judges of the world, and each Christian was taught to acknowledge no law but the scriptures, no interpreter but his own conscience. This freedom, however, was the consequence, rather than the design, of the Reformation. The patriot reformers were ambitious of succeeding the tyrants whom they had dethroned.

> They imposed with equal rigour their creeds and confessions; they asserted the right of the magistrate to punish heretics with death...
>
> "The nature of the tiger was the same, but he was gradually deprived of his teeth and fangs... Since the days of Luther and Calvin, a secrete reformation has been silently working in the bosom of the reformed churches; many weeds of prejudice were eradicated; and the disciples of Erasmus[40] diffused a spirit of freedom and moderation. The liberty of conscience has been claimed a common benefit, an inalienable right... I am sorry to observe that the three writers of the last age, by whom the rights of toleration have been so nobly defended, Bayle, Leibnitz, and Locke, are all laymen and philosophers."[41]

While Northern Europe was dominated by reformed versions of the faith, Southern Europe remained mostly Catholic, leading to religious wars that would rage for more than a hundred years. Meanwhile, religious leaders on both sides saw the common people as being incapable of thinking for themselves. In 1521 the German reformer Martin Luther was condemned as a heretic by the Pope.

"...should not deceive the multitude of the simple by their lives and their deceitful devices." - Pope Leo X

> Pope Leo X, Papal Bull on Martin Luther, Jan. 3, 1521:
> "Through the power given him from God, the Roman Pontiff has been appointed to administer spiritual and temporal punishments as each case severally deserves. The purpose of this is the repression of the wicked designs of misguided men, who have been so captivated by the debased impulse of their evil purposes as to forget the fear of the Lord, to set aside with contempt canonical decrees and apostolic commandments, and to dare to formulate new and false dogmas and to introduce the evil of schism into the Church of God—or to support, help and adhere to such schismatics, who make it their business to cleave asunder the seamless robe of our Redeemer and the unity of the orthodox faith.
>
> "Hence it befits the Pontiff, lest the vessel of Peter appear to sail without pilot or oarsman, to take severe measures against such men and their followers, and by multiplying punitive measures and by

> other suitable remedies to see to it that these same overbearing men, devoted as they are to purposes of evil, along with their adherents, should not deceive the multitude of the simple by their lives and their deceitful devices, nor drag them along to share their own error and ruination, contaminating them with what amounts to a contagious disease...

"We would protect the herd from one infectious animal, lest its infection spread to the healthy ones." - Pope Leo X

> "We prescribe and enjoin that the men in question are everywhere to be denounced publicly as excommunicated, accursed, condemned, interdicted, deprived of possessions and incapable of owning them. They are to be strictly shunned by all faithful Christians.... We would make known to all the small store that Martin, his followers and the other rebels have set on God and his Church by their obstinate and shameless temerity. We would protect the herd from one infectious animal, lest its infection spread to the healthy ones."[42]

While the German theologian Martin Luther was credited with initiating the Protestant Reformation, he did not differ from the previous establishment in denouncing liberty and the reliance on human reason to discover knowledge. His anti-Semitism and elitism were prevalent in his works.

"Faith must trample underfoot all reason, sense, and understanding." - Martin Luther

---

> Martin Luther, Table Talk:
> "For reason is the greatest enemy that faith has; it never comes to the aid of spiritual things, but - more frequently than not - struggles against the divine Word, treating with contempt all that emanates from God." [43]
>
> Martin Luther, "Works", Vol. 12:
> "There is on earth among all dangers no more dangerous thing than a richly endowed and adroit reason, especially if she enters into

> spiritual matters which concern the soul and God... For it is more possible to teach an ass to read than to blind such a reason and lead it right; for reason must be deluded, blinded, and destroyed. Faith must trample underfoot all reason, sense, and understanding, and whatever it sees must be put out of sight and... know nothing but the word of God." [44]

"This fool wishes to reverse the entire science of astronomy." - Martin Luther

---

> Martin Luther's Last Sermon in Wittenberg:
> "But the devil's bride, reason, the pretty whore comes in and thinks she is wise, and what she says, what she thinks, is from the Holy Spirit. Who can help us then? Not jurist, physician, nor king, nor emperor, for she is the Devil's greatest whore." [45]

> Martin Luther, 1539:
> "People gave ear to an upstart astrologer [Copernicus] who strove to show that the earth revolves, not the heavens or the firmament, the sun and the moon.... This fool wishes to reverse the entire science of astronomy; but sacred scripture tells us that Joshua commanded the sun to stand still, and not the earth." [46]

Though considered by many at the time to be responsible for the peasant uprising, Luther stood with their oppressors, placing obedience of the people to the established authority above all else. In his pamphlet "Against the Heavenly Prophets" Luther said that the penalties of sword and law restrained the people from error and to obedience in the same way that "wild beasts are held in check by chains and bars, in order that outward peace may prevail among the people; for this purpose the temporal authorities are ordained, and it is God's will that they be honoured and feared."[47] In the beginning oppression under the direction of Luther was little different to that which preceded the Reformation.

"Just as one must slay a mad dog, so, if you do not fight the rebels, they will fight you, and the whole country with you." - Martin Luther

---

> Martin Luther, "Against the Peasants", 1525:
> "It is right and lawful to slay at the first opportunity a rebellious person, who is known as such, for he is already under God's and the emperor's ban. Every man is at once judge and executioner of a public rebel; just as, when a fire starts, he who can extinguish it first is the best fellow. Rebellion is not simply vile murder, but is like a great fire that kindles and devastates a country; it fills the land with murder and bloodshed, makes widows and orphans, and destroys everything, like the greatest calamity. Therefore, whosoever can, should smite, strangle, and stab, secretly or publicly, and should remember that there is nothing more poisonous, pernicious, and devilish than a rebellious man. Just as one must slay a mad dog, so, if you do not fight the rebels, they will fight you, and the whole country with you."[48]

"We condemn, reprobate, and reject completely each of these theses or errors as... offensive to pious ears or seductive of simple minds."
- Pope Leo X

Pope Leo X published a list of errors supported by Martin Luther, condemning them, and at the same time revisiting the belief that the common people were simple and easily seduced by errors. They believed the greatest virtue was obedience.

> Pope Leo X, Exsurge Domine, 1520:
> "No one of sound mind is ignorant how destructive, pernicious, scandalous, and seductive to pious and simple minds these various errors are, how opposed they are to all charity and reverence for the holy Roman Church who is the mother of all the faithful and teacher of the faith; how destructive they are of the vigor of ecclesiastical discipline, namely obedience. This virtue is the font and origin of all virtues and without it anyone is readily convicted of being unfaithful... We condemn, reprobate, and reject completely each of these theses or errors as either heretical, scandalous, false, offensive to pious ears or seductive of simple minds, and against Catholic truth."[49]

Religious reformer John Calvin of France, though also breaking from the Catholic Church and further spurring the Christian Reformation, expressed distrust in the individual intelligence. He also believed that the fear of God was required for morality, a perspective that would continue to be common to the Christian traditions of Europe and America.

"For without the fear of God, men preserve no equity and love among themselves." - John Calvin

---

> John Calvin, Calvin's New Testament Commentaries: A Harmony of the Gospels:
> "That in order to our being properly qualified for becoming his disciples, we must lay aside all confidence in our own abilities, and seek light from heaven; and, abandoning the foolish opinion of free-will, must give ourselves up to be governed by God. Nor is it without reason that Paul bids men become fools, that they may be wise to God, (1 Corinthians 3:18;) for no darkness is more dangerous for quenching the light of the Spirit than reliance on our own sagacity [intelligence]."[50]

> John Calvin, the Institutes of the Christian Religion, 1536:
> "It is in vain, therefore, to boast of righteousness without religion; as well might the trunk of a body be exhibited as a beautiful object, after the head has been cut off. Nor is religion only the head of righteousness, but the very soul of it, constituting all its life and vigour; for without the fear of God, men preserve no equity and love among themselves."[51]

These leaders were still willing to extinguish the lives of those who disagreed with their version of the truth. Despite an earlier work in favor of tolerance[52], Martin Luther also called for the extermination of heretics. While he acknowledged a freedom to believe as one chooses, Luther strongly opposed freedom of speech and religious expression, as these might lead others to heresy. Though the Catholic Church had for so many centuries keep down opposing Christian sects and ideologies by war, inquisition and sometimes massacres[53], it found the Reformation and, eventually, the Enlightenment, beyond its ability to suppress.

King Henry VIII left the Catholic Church and established the Church of England in 1534 with himself at its head, burning as heretics any who professed opposing doctrines. He was the first of Europe's leaders to break from the Catholic Church, though his motives were bound in his desire to escape an undesirable marriage which the church refused to annul. Over

Henry's reign the numbers of men, women and children executed has been estimated in the tens of thousands, with countless others tortured. After Henry's death, his son Edward would make the Church of England a Protestant institution, as opposed to the independent church his father established, but he and his reign were short-lived.

His older sister Mary took power and returned the country to the Catholic faith. Known to history as Bloody Mary, she married King Phillip II of Spain, a country well embroiled in the Inquisition. She sent hundreds of men, women and children to the flames for the crime of not being sufficiently Catholic, often in mass burnings that spread the aroma of searing flesh for miles around. It was a deliberate and torturous death, but the pain inflicted prior to burning was often even more hideous. Mary killed all of the top Protestant Bishops and a long list of others who contradicted her faith or threatened her rule.[54] Only later, under the rule of her sister Queen Elisabeth, did England begin to put that religious motivated violence behind them.

While the Reformation led to alternative interpretations of Christianity and even to reforms within the Catholic Church, it led also to violent conflict across the continent between the newly divided factions, darkly enhancing an already brutal landscape. Peace finally came in the middle of the 1600s and, as a result, Catholicism, Lutheranism and Calvinism were identified as religions available for leaders to declare as their State religion. Christians were also granted the right to practice these religions even if it was not the religion of their State. For large parts of Europe, freedom of religion was established, though only within the primary Christian faiths. Pope Innocent X opposed the agreement and refused to acknowledge it, as it greatly reduced his financial base and domain of control.

Despite the splitting of authority, the appetite for the blood of people holding differing beliefs remained insatiable; fueled by the intoxication of power on the one hand and religious fervor on the other. Though the Roman Church continued to battle the Protestant heresy, it also pointed its investigations at witchcraft. Witch trials that originated in France in the 14th Century would continue well into the 18th, killing tens of thousands, if not more, for some manner of imagined sorcery. As with the Inquisition, the point was terror and control.

The Catholic Church denied the existence of witchcraft until the early 1300s, then influenced in part by the widespread death from the Black Plague. In the following centuries, Christian leaders and followers imagined all manner of evil infesting everyday life, again, like a contagion to which people might unwittingly fall prey. Even as the Catholic Church lost its singular dominion over Christianity, the totalitarian nature of the religion's leaders continued. The thoughts, beliefs and practices of the people in Europe were strictly monitored and controlled, with the notion of tolerance truly unimaginable. Souls were at stake.

> James Howell, Historiographer Royal to King Charles II, 1646:
> "We have multitudes of witches among us; for in Essex and Suffolk there were above two hundred indicted within these two years; and above the half of them executed.... I speak it with horror! God guard us from the Devil! For I think he was never so busy upon any part of the earth that was lightened by the beams of Christianity."[55]

Under the law of the time, those convicted of heresy and who refused to recant would be burned at the stake by the secular authority. Hundreds were simultaneously burned in public executions.[56] The hysteria over any hint of heresy, demons or witchcraft was like adding an accelerant to fire. In time, though, the religion would shed its atrocities and corruptions.

Emerging from History

Humanity's advancement toward liberty was painfully slow. England led the charge by limiting the power of the King. Their Glorious Revolution of 1688 led to the ouster of King James II and the passage into law of the English Bill of Rights in 1689, which created a Constitutional Monarchy. Under this structure, the power of the monarch was limited and the authority of Parliament was elevated. Despite the history of bloodshed, the morality that persisted at the heart of Christianity had a profound effect on the west, especially our nation's founders. Many extracted a benevolent morality from the religious texts, while rejecting much of what made Christianity, in the words of President John Adams, quoted farther below, "the most bloody religion that ever existed."[57] Adams described the tyranny of the previous millennia and the need to restrain the powers of leadership.

> President John Adams, Dissertation on the Canon and Feudal Law in 1763:
> "Since the promulgation of Christianity, the two greatest systems of tyranny that have sprung from this original are the canon and the feudal law. The desire of dominion, that great principle by which we have attempted to account for so much good and so much evil, is, when properly restrained, a very useful and noble movement in

the human mind. But when such restraints are taken off, it becomes an encroaching, grasping, restless, and ungovernable power.

"They even persuaded mankind to believe, faithfully and undoubtingly, that God Almighty had entrusted them with the keys of heaven" - President John Adams

---

"Numberless have been the systems of iniquity contrived by the great for the gratification of this passion in themselves; but in none of them were they ever more successful than in the invention and establishment of the canon and the feudal law.

"By the former of these, the most refined, sublime, extensive, and astonishing constitution of policy that ever was conceived by the mind of man was framed by the Romish clergy for the aggrandizement of their own order. All the epithets I have here given to the Romish policy are just, and will be allowed to be so when it is considered, that they even persuaded mankind to believe, faithfully and undoubtingly, that God Almighty had entrusted them with the keys of heaven, whose gates they might open and close at pleasure; with a power of dispensation over all the rules and obligations of morality; with authority to license all sorts of sins and crimes; with a power of deposing princes and absolving subjects from allegiance;

"All these opinions they were enabled to spread... by reducing their minds to a state of sordid ignorance and staring timidity, and by infusing into them a religious horror of letters and knowledge." - President John Adams

---

"with a power of procuring or withholding the rain of heaven and the beams of the sun; with the management of earthquakes, pestilence, and famine; nay, with the mysterious, awful, incomprehensible power of creating out of bread and wine the flesh and blood of God himself. All these opinions they were enabled to spread and rivet among the people by reducing their minds to a state of sordid ignorance and staring timidity, and by infusing into them a religious horror of letters and knowledge. Thus was human nature chained fast for ages in a cruel, shameful, and deplorable servitude to him, and his subordinate tyrants, who, it was foretold, would exalt himself above all that was called God, and that was worshipped.

"In the latter we find another system, similar in many respects to the former; which, although it was originally formed, perhaps, for the necessary defence of a barbarous people against the inroads and invasions of her neighboring nations, yet for the same purposes of tyranny, cruelty, and lust, which had dictated the canon law, it was soon adopted by almost all the princes of Europe, and wrought into the constitutions of their government. It was originally a code of laws for a vast army in a perpetual encampment. The general was invested with the sovereign propriety of all the lands within the territory. Of him, as his servants and vassals, the first rank of his great officers held the lands; and in the same manner the other subordinate officers held of them; and all ranks and degrees held their lands by a variety of duties and services, all tending to bind the chains the faster on every order of mankind.

"Liberty, and with her, knowledge and virtue too, seem to have deserted the earth, and one age of darkness succeeded another." - President John Adams

---

"In this manner the common people were held together in herds and clans in a state of servile dependence on their lords, bound, even by the tenure of their lands, to follow them, whenever they commanded, to their wars, and in a state of total ignorance of every thing divine and human, excepting the use of arms and the culture of their lands. But another event still more calamitous to human liberty, was a wicked confederacy between the two systems of tyranny above described. It seems to have been even stipulated between them, that the temporal grandees should contribute every thing in their power to maintain the ascendency of the priesthood, and that the spiritual grandees in their turn, should employ their ascendency over the consciences of the people, in impressing on their minds a blind, implicit obedience to civil magistracy.

> "Thus, as long as this confederacy lasted, and the people were held in ignorance, liberty, and with her, knowledge and virtue too, seem to have deserted the earth, and one age of darkness succeeded another, till God in his benign providence raised up the champions who began and conducted the Reformation. From the time of the Reformation to the first settlement of America, knowledge gradually spread in Europe, but especially in England; and in proportion as that increased and spread among the people, ecclesiastical and civil tyranny, which I use as synonymous expressions for the canon and feudal laws, seem to have lost their strength and weight.

"The struggle between the people and the confederacy aforesaid of temporal and spiritual tyranny... It was this great struggle that peopled America." - President John Adams

---

> "The people grew more and more sensible of the wrong that was done them by these systems, more and more impatient under it, and determined at all hazards to rid themselves of it; till at last, under the execrable race of the Stuarts, the struggle between the people and the confederacy aforesaid of temporal and spiritual tyranny, became formidable, violent, and bloody. It was this great struggle that peopled America. It was not religion alone, as is commonly supposed; but it was a love of universal liberty, and a hatred, a dread, a horror, of the infernal confederacy before described, that projected, conducted, and accomplished the settlement of America."[58]

Still, the religious violence of Europe did spread to the New World, most famously in the Salem Witch Trials, where one man was pressed to death in 1692 after refusing to enter a plea and dozens of others were hung or died in prison. That year a special court was established to judge cases of witchcraft. The methods of investigating and prosecuting witchcraft developed in England were employed in the Colonies, though on a much smaller scale.

"To deny the possibility, nay, actual existence of witchcraft and sorcery is at once flatly to contradict the revealed Word of God."
- Sir William Blackstone

> William Poole, Librarian of the Chicago Public Library:
> "The New-England colonists had no views concerning witchcraft and diabolical agency which they did not bring with them from the Old World. The prosecutions in England were never carried on with a blinder zeal and more fatal results than during the first twenty years after Governor Winthrop and his company landed in Boston."[59]
>
> Sir William Blackstone, English Judge, Commentaries on the Laws of England, 1753:
> "To deny the possibility, nay, actual existence of witchcraft and sorcery is at once flatly to contradict the revealed Word of God in various passages in both the Old and New Testament; and the thing itself is a truth borne testimony, either by examples seemingly well attested, or by prohibitory laws, which at least suppose the possibility of commerce with evil spirits."[60]

Thus, religious tyranny continued in the New World even in the time of change and social advancement, just as other forms of tyranny also survived. Even under the authoritarian rule of church and state, a core of morality and an innate desire to learn, reason and create emerged. The Renaissance led to a rediscovery of Classical culture and a creative awakening, both supported and restricted by the church. The stage was then set by the scientific revolution of the 17th Century for the emergence of the Enlightenment. Along with the underlying nature of Christianity, the Enlightenment was the most direct and easily demonstrated antecedent to the ideals identified with our American Republic and expressed in our founding documents.

It was a movement in which reason and individual intelligence, liberty, republicanism, democracy and religious tolerance were embraced. Religion and heresy were subjected to reason. The Enlightenment was a driving force of western philosophy, as well as intellectual, scientific and cultural life. The movement broke from the idea that kings had a divine right to rule and the traditional collusion of the church and civil authority, suggesting instead that rulers gained their authority from the consent of the governed and that individuals were capable of making their own religious decisions without the need of civil enforcement.

No longer did the common man accept without question the authority of his religious or civil leaders. The Enlightenment was in distinct contrast to established religious and feudal traditions. It was daylight to a world too long darkened by dogma and oppression. It promoted freedom and reason, engaging fervently in the critical questioning of some traditional institutions, customs and principles, while often retaining a belief in Christianity which remained at the center of western culture. There was a rational reassessment of the world, relying on the accumulated knowledge of the past, long suppressed, and a belief in the value of every individual. Just as Christianity was reborn through the reformation, the capacity of mankind was renewed and rekindled in the Enlightenment.

It included the belief that humans were both equal by nature and equally capable of enlightenment. The movement saw humanity moving from superstition to reason and from slavery to freedom, believing the individual could seek knowledge independently, rather than being told what to think by the established authorities. To the idea of logic embraced by the Greeks, the Enlightenment added a depth of reason, common sense and observation, entwined with the morality of natural law and Christianity. They imagined the individual was responsible for his own fate and fortune and drew on the philosophers and systems of the past to inform their conclusions about the manner of government most likely to be successful and practical.

While the horror of the French Revolution also came from the Enlightenment, the English and American movements furthered the advancement of mankind, the former being more atheistic while the latter embraced belief in God. Enlightenment thinkers often replaced the belief in revealed religion and the supernatural with a deist view of a god: a being one could infer through the logical construction of the world, though Christianity was still embraced. Enlightenment thinkers shared a belief that the universe was accessible to human reason, even if never entirely understood by it, and that humans were capable of ruling themselves.

They supported tolerance but these men were a product of their time and many, including the influential John Locke, believed in liberty and tolerance only to a point, excluding Catholics and atheists, for instance. A belief in divine providence also persisted among many, including our founders, harkening back to the justifications of previous eras.

Nonetheless, the progress of liberty during the Enlightenment was substantial. John Locke, an English philosopher and physician, was perhaps the single most influential mind among the Enlightenment thinkers affecting our founders and the establishment of our nation. He was referred to by them often. Locke believed in government by the consent of the governed, separation of civil and ecclesiastical powers and that governments should be limited.

> John Locke, Second Treatise on Government, 1690:
> "The beginning of politic society depends upon the consent of the individuals to join into and make one society, who, when they are thus incorporated, might set up what form of government they thought fit."[61]

"The end of law is not to abolish or restrain, but to preserve and enlarge freedom." - John Locke

---

> John Locke, Second Treatise on Government, 1690:
> "For law, in its true notion, is not so much the limitation as the direction of a free and intelligent agent to his proper interest, and prescribes no farther than is for the general good of those under that law: could they be happier without it, the law, as an useless thing, would of itself vanish; and that ill deserves the name of confinement which hedges us in only from bogs and precipices. So that, however it may be mistaken, the end of law is not to abolish or restrain, but to preserve and enlarge freedom."[62]

> John Locke, 'A Letter Concerning Toleration', 1689:
> "Now that the whole jurisdiction of the magistrate reaches only to these civil concernments, and that all civil power, right and dominion, is bounded and confined to the only care of promoting these things; and that it neither can nor ought in any manner to be extended to the salvation of souls, these following considerations seem unto me abundantly to demonstrate.

"No man can so far abandon the care of his own salvation as blindly to leave to the choice of any other." - John Locke

---

> "First, because the care of souls is not committed to the civil magistrate, any more than to other men. It is not committed unto him, I say, by God; because it appears not that God has ever given any such authority to one man over another as to compel anyone to his religion. Nor can any such power be vested in the magistrate by the consent of the people, because no man can so far abandon the care of his own salvation as blindly to leave to the choice of any other, whether prince or subject, to prescribe to him what faith or worship he shall embrace. For no man can, if he would, conform his faith to the dictates of another...
>
> "And further, things never so indifferent in their own nature, when they are brought into the Church and worship of God, are removed out of the reach of the magistrate's jurisdiction, because in that use they have no connection at all with civil affairs. The only business of the Church is the salvation of souls, and it no way concerns the commonwealth, or any member of it, that this or the other ceremony be there made use of. Neither the use nor the omission of any ceremonies in those religious assemblies does either advantage or prejudice the life, liberty, or estate of any man."[63]

Other Enlightenment thinkers also greatly influenced our nation's founders and the remarkable turn of civilization that culminated in our American Republic, as I often refer to the United States of America. The idea of the social contract was a key concept.

> Jean-Jacques Rousseau: The Social Contract 1762:
> "We must grant, therefore, that force does not constitute right, and that obedience is only due to legitimate powers... What man loses by the social contract is his natural liberty and an unlimited right to everything he tries to get and succeeds in getting; what he gains is civil liberty and the proprietorship of all he possesses. If we are to avoid mistake in weighing one against the other, we must clearly distinguish natural liberty, which is bounded only by the strength of the individual, from civil liberty, which is limited by the general will; and possession, which is merely the effect of force or the right of the first occupier, from property, which can be founded only on a positive title... We might, over and above all this, add, to what man acquires in the civil state, moral liberty, which alone makes him truly master of himself; for the mere impulse of appetite is slavery,

> while obedience to a law which we prescribe to ourselves is liberty."[64]

Europe was changing into an era where many of the chains of established authorities were loosened and, in some cases, broken. To the Roman Church, liberty of conscience, religious expression, speech, press, and reason, were foolish errors that undermined its authority and influence, and that of the civil leaders with which they were in league. To trust one's own reason above the established authority, or to have a direct connection to God without their guidance, was an outrageous arrogance. The dictates of Popes below provide a glimpse into the church's view on the ideals central to the Enlightenment and our American Republic. In their minds, rejecting establishment was equivalent to rejecting all civil and divine authority.

> Encyclical of Pope Pius VI, Sec. 7, December 25, 1775:
> "When they have spread this darkness abroad and torn religion out of men's hearts, these accursed philosophers proceed to destroy the bonds of union among men, both those which unite them to their rulers, and those which urge them to their duty.

> "That society accordingly is a crowd of foolish men who stupidly yield to priests who deceive them and to kings who oppress them"
> - Pius VI

> "They keep proclaiming that man is born free and subject to no one, that society accordingly is a crowd of foolish men who stupidly yield to priests who deceive them and to kings who oppress them, so that the harmony of priest and ruler is only a monstrous conspiracy against the innate liberty of man. Everyone must understand that such ravings and others like them, concealed in many deceitful guises, cause greater ruin to public calm the longer their impious originators are unrestrained. They cause a serious loss of souls redeemed by Christ's blood wherever their teaching spreads, like a cancer; it forces its way into public academies, into the houses of the great, into the palaces of kings, and even enters the sanctuary, shocking as it is to say so."[65]

As the 18th century turned into the 19th, the Catholic Church played a different role, not only having to share power and influence with Protestant branches of the faith, but facing a new nation that forbade any religious establishment at all, something unheard of in the Christian world. The encyclical below addresses the view of the church with respect to liberty and obedience to authorities.

> <u>Encyclical of Pope Gregory XVI, August 15, 1832:</u>
> "5. Our Roman See is harassed violently and the bonds of unity are daily loosened and severed. The divine authority of the Church is opposed and her rights shorn off. She is subjected to human reason and with the greatest injustice exposed to the hatred of the people and reduced to vile servitude. The obedience due bishops is denied and their rights are trampled underfoot. Furthermore, academies and schools resound with new, monstrous opinions, which openly attack the Catholic faith; this horrible and nefarious war is openly and even publicly waged.

"The restraints of religion are thrown off, by which alone kingdoms stand." - Pope Gregory XVI

> "Thus, by institutions and by the example of teachers, the minds of the youth are corrupted and a tremendous blow is dealt to religion and the perversion of morals is spread. So the restraints of religion are thrown off, by which alone kingdoms stand. We see the destruction of public order, the fall of principalities, and the overturning of all legitimate power approaching...

The church specifically targeted religious liberty and freedom of speech.

> "13. Now We consider another abundant source of the evils with which the Church is afflicted at present: indifferentism. This perverse opinion is spread on all sides by the fraud of the wicked who claim that it is possible to obtain the eternal salvation of the soul by the profession of any kind of religion, as long as morality is maintained... 'without a doubt, they will perish forever, unless they hold the Catholic faith whole and inviolate...'

"Experience shows, even from earliest times, that cities renowned for wealth, dominion, and glory perished as a result of this single evil, namely immoderate freedom of opinion." - Pope Gregory XVI

> "14. This shameful font of indifferentism gives rise to that absurd and erroneous proposition which claims that liberty of conscience must be maintained for everyone. It spreads ruin in sacred and civil affairs, though some repeat over and over again with the greatest impudence that some advantage accrues to religion from it. 'But the death of the soul is worse than freedom of error,' as Augustine was wont to say. When all restraints are removed by which men are kept on the narrow path of truth, their nature, which is already inclined to evil, propels them to ruin. Then truly 'the bottomless pit' is open from which John saw smoke ascending which obscured the sun, and out of which locusts flew forth to devastate the earth. Thence comes transformation of minds, corruption of youths, contempt of sacred things and holy laws -- in other words, a pestilence more deadly to the state than any other. Experience shows, even from earliest times, that cities renowned for wealth, dominion, and glory perished as a result of this single evil, namely immoderate freedom of opinion, license of free speech, and desire for novelty.

The censorship of books was justified as a way to protect the people from error. They also rejected the argument that bad speech can best be countered by more speech.

"That harmful and never sufficiently denounced freedom to publish any writings whatever and disseminate them to the people." - Pope Gregory XVI

> "15. Here We must include that harmful and never sufficiently denounced freedom to publish any writings whatever and disseminate them to the people, which some dare to demand and promote with so great a clamor. We are horrified to see what monstrous doctrines and prodigious errors are disseminated far and wide in countless books, pamphlets, and other writings which,

though small in weight, are very great in malice. We are in tears at the abuse which proceeds from them over the face of the earth. Some are so carried away that they contentiously assert that the flock of errors arising from them is sufficiently compensated by the publication of some book which defends religion and truth. Every law condemns deliberately doing evil simply because there is some hope that good may result. Is there any sane man who would say poison ought to be distributed, sold publicly, stored, and even drunk because some antidote is available and those who use it may be snatched from death again and again?

"16. The Church has always taken action to destroy the plague of bad books. This was true even in apostolic times for we read that the apostles themselves burned a large number of books...

"'We must fight valiantly,' Clement XIII says in an encyclical letter about the banning of bad books, 'as much as the matter itself demands and must exterminate the deadly poison of so many books; for never will the material for error be withdrawn, unless the criminal sources of depravity perish in flames.' Thus it is evident that this Holy See has always striven, throughout the ages, to condemn and to remove suspect and harmful books. The teaching of those who reject the censure of books as too heavy and onerous a burden causes immense harm to the Catholic people and to this See. They are even so depraved as to affirm that it is contrary to the principles of law, and they deny the Church the right to decree and to maintain it.

"Those who, consumed with the unbridled lust for freedom, are entirely devoted to impairing and destroying all rights of dominion." - Pope Gregory XVI

"17. ...both divine and human laws cry out against those who strive by treason and sedition to drive the people from confidence in their princes and force them from their government.

"19. These beautiful examples of the unchanging subjection to the princes necessarily proceeded from the most holy precepts of the Christian religion. They condemn the detestable insolence and improbity of those who, consumed with the unbridled lust for

> freedom, are entirely devoted to impairing and destroying all rights of dominion while bringing servitude to the people under the slogan of liberty.

"They preach liberty of every sort... and pluck authority to pieces." - Pope Gregory XVI

> "20. Nor can We predict happier times for religion and government from the plans of those who desire vehemently to separate the Church from the state, and to break the mutual concord between temporal authority and the priesthood. It is certain that that concord which always was favorable and beneficial for the sacred and the civil order is feared by the shameless lovers of liberty.
>
> "21. But for the other painful causes We are concerned about, you should recall that certain societies and assemblages seem to draw up a battle line together with the followers of every false religion and cult. They feign piety for religion; but they are driven by a passion for promoting novelties and sedition everywhere. They preach liberty of every sort; they stir up disturbances in sacred and civil affairs, and pluck authority to pieces.
>
> "22. ...It is the proud, or rather foolish, men who examine the mysteries of faith which surpass all understanding with the faculties of the human mind and rely on human reason which by the condition of man's nature, is weak and infirm."[66]

The Catholic church at that time reviled these ideas of liberty and the separation of church and state that were so crucial to our founders, who sought a separation of civil and ecclesiastical authorities, not a separation of the people from God or religion. Pope Leo XIII openly derided the notion that a nation's people could rule themselves or be permitted freedoms of the mind. This fight for self-rule constituted an insurrection against the established powers.

"A State becomes nothing but a multitude which is its own master and rule." - Pope Leo XIII

Pope Leo XIII, Immortale Dei, Nov. 1, 1885:
"5. ...To despise legitimate authority, in whomsoever vested, is unlawful, as a rebellion against the divine will, and whoever resists that, rushes willfully to destruction. 'He that resisteth the power resisteth the ordinance of God, and they that resist, purchase to themselves damnation.' To cast aside obedience, and by popular violence to incite to revolt, is therefore treason, not against man only, but against God.

"6. ...So, too, is it a sin for the State not to have care for religion as a something beyond its scope, or as of no practical benefit; or out of many forms of religion to adopt that one which chimes in with the fancy; for we are bound absolutely to worship God in that way which He has shown to be His will...

"That everyone has unbounded license to think whatever he chooses and to publish abroad whatever he thinks." - Pope Leo XIII

"25. The authority of God is passed over in silence, just as if there were no God; or as if He cared nothing for human society; or as if men, whether in their individual capacity or bound together in social relations, owed nothing to God; or as if there could be a government of which the whole origin and power and authority did not reside in God Himself. Thus, as is evident, a State becomes nothing but a multitude which is its own master and ruler. And since the people is declared to contain within itself the spring-head of all rights and of all power, it follows that the State does not consider itself bound by any kind of duty toward God.

"26. And it is a part of this theory that all questions that concern religion are to be referred to private judgment; that every one is to be free to follow whatever religion he prefers, or none at all if he disapprove of all. From this the following consequences logically flow: that the judgment of each one's conscience is independent of all law; that the most unrestrained opinions may be openly expressed as to the practice or omission of divine worship; and that every one has unbounded license to think whatever he chooses and to publish abroad whatever he thinks.

"The unrestrained freedom of thinking and of openly making known one's thoughts is not inherent in the rights of citizens."
- Pope Leo XIII

> "35. From these pronouncements of the Popes it is evident that the origin of public power is to be sought for in God Himself, and not in the multitude, and that it is repugnant to reason to allow free scope for sedition. Again, that it is not lawful for the State, any more than for the individual, either to disregard all religious duties or to hold in equal favor different kinds of religion; that the unrestrained freedom of thinking and of openly making known one's thoughts is not inherent in the rights of citizens, and is by no means to be reckoned worthy of favor and support...
>
> "37. In the same way the Church cannot approve of that liberty which begets a contempt of the most sacred laws of God, and casts off the obedience due to lawful authority, for this is not liberty so much as license, and is most correctly styled by St. Augustine the 'liberty of self-ruin'...
>
> "42. Especially with reference to the so-called 'liberties' which are so greatly coveted in these days, all must stand by the judgment of the apostolic see, and have the same mind. Let no man be deceived by the honest outward appearance of these liberties, but let each one reflect whence these have had their origin, and by what efforts they are everywhere upheld and promoted.
>
> "47. Hence, lest concord be broken by rash charges, let this be understood by all, that the integrity of Catholic faith cannot be reconciled with opinions verging on naturalism or rationalism, the essence of which is utterly to do away with Christian institutions and to install in society the supremacy of man to the exclusion of God."[67]

To the contrary of that last statement, the great majority of those clamoring for liberty were Christian and believers in God, though opposed to the authority of religious establishments and the Roman Catholic Church as it had long existed.

"Superstition sets the whole world in flames; philosophy extinguishes them." - Voltaire

> Voltaire, aka François-Marie Arouet, a Philosophical Dictionary, 1764:
> "I defy you to show me a single philosopher, from Zoroaster down to Locke, that has ever stirred up a sedition, - that has ever been concerned in an attempt against the life of a king, - that has ever disturbed society; and, unfortunately, I will find you a thousand votaries of superstition, from Ehud down to Kosinski, stained with the blood of kings and with that of nations. Superstition sets the whole world in flames; philosophy extinguishes them.... Nearly all that goes farther than the adoration of a supreme being, and the submission of the heart to his eternal orders, is superstition."[68]

For fifteen hundred years the collusion of ecclesiastic and civil establishments created a state of overarching tyranny, where violence and the threat of violence were used to constrain speech and the printed word, to restrict education and to suppress earlier philosophies and conflicting interpretations. A benevolent philosophy was used so that the few in power could oppress the many. The horrors of medieval times were expressions of evil beyond comprehension, and while blame for the millennia of torture and executions that preceded our nation's founding rests entirely on the individuals who committed those acts, were it not for supernatural fears, oppressors might have found society far less receptive and permissive to the atrocities human reason innately rejects.

Virtually every method employed in the inquisitions and witch trials stand in stark contrast to the laws and rights later declared in the American Constitution and Bill of Rights. Where America had freedom of the press, the church had an index of forbidden books. Where America protected freedom of thought and belief, the church used fear and torture to conform all to its one 'true' belief. Where America had free speech, saying the wrong thing in these times of religious dominion could get one killed in the most brutal of ways.

> Historian Edward Gibbon, History of the Decline and Fall of the Roman Empire:
> "The influence of the clergy, in an age of superstition, might be usefully employed to assert the rights of mankind; but so intimate

> is the connection between the throne and the altar, that the banner of the church has very seldom been seen on the side of the people."[69]

For many in power, the individual's ability to reason and think independently was so dangerous that any means of its suppression was justified. The fear of ideological contagion was stronger than the horror employed in its eradication. The church and the civil authority at its disposal did not invent torture or terror, but its methods of investigation and oppression were honed under the leadership of many tyrants in the pursuit of the control and conformity during those dark times. The established church in all its forms evolved and religious expression flourished in the new world where none were established civilly.

The religious and cultural traditions that preceded the Enlightenment and our American experiment in self-rule were, by overwhelming majority, based on the belief that man was not trusted to rule himself or come to the "correct" conclusions on his own. Submission to civil and ecclesiastical authority was unquestioned, as both ruled by the authority of God. The common man must be controlled for his own good. The utility of religious belief in the oppression of the people has proven especially pervasive, but examples of unfathomable totalitarian and authoritarian regimes that denounced theistic belief have also emerged, namely in communism and related ideologies. Though they professed very different beliefs, their opinions of the common people were identical. It isn't a belief in god that they had in common, but a belief in tyranny.

"We have seen the mere distinction of colour made in the most enlightened period of time, a ground of the most oppressive dominion ever exercised by man over man."

– President James Madison

Chapter 2

Evil of Colossal Magnitude

Christopher Columbus, an Italian acting on the dime and direction of the Spanish monarchy, set off to find a western route to the far east and landed instead in the Bahamas in 1492. His arrival marked the beginning of European exploration and exploitation of the western hemisphere, primarily at the hands of Spanish and Portuguese, who's combined empires at their height covered virtually all of the Americas. The English, though having spread their dominion around the world, had far less holdings there. Pope Alexander VII divided much of the new world between Portugal and Spain, as if it was his to give, so that Portugal took what became Brazil and Spain claimed virtually everything else in the western hemisphere, eventually claiming most of central and north America. Much later the French and the English expanded in North America, though both were and are still minorities in the hemisphere.

Slavery itself was common practice around the world, even in America before the arrival of Europeans. Natives committed their own atrocities among themselves, including human sacrifice, but this behavior was not isolated to the Americas. Still, the natives faced the horrors of not only war, rape and enslavement, but plagues from invaders. The arrival of the conquistadors, with advanced weaponry, forced labor and foreign diseases, decimated native populations, leaving insufficient labor to work the fields and mines of their newly acquired lands. Millions of Africans were taken and transported to the Americas because not enough of the indigenous people survived the Europeans' arrival to enslave.

As the numbers of the natives plummeted, African slaves became their laborers and servants. Most Africans were trafficked into the Americas under the control of the Spanish and Portuguese empires and, to a much smaller extent, the settlements of the Dutch, French and English. The English colonies, and then the United States, were also guilty of importing African slaves and of warring against and ultimately devastating the way of life of American natives. The history of the expansion of the United States over north America was often times just as unfathomably brutal to our modern mind.

Human history is replete with similar atrocities and examples of nations invading, slaughtering, enslaving and oppressing others. It doesn't justify anything but it adds perspective. Even more blacks were taken from Africa at the same time as slaves to serve eastern powers. Nothing that happened in America was isolated or unique. It also does not lessen our nation's accomplishments to acknowledge and learn about the darkest parts of our history, because we must learn from our mistakes or we will most definitely repeat them. At least we have continued to strive for better. Unfortunately, such horrific acts around the world are not limited to the past.

More recently, the Communist Chinese took complete control over a region to their northwest called Xinjiang. America no longer makes slaves pick cotton, but China does.[70] The Uyghurs, a predominantly Muslim ethnic minority, had lived in that area for a thousand years before being subjected to Chinese rule. Today more than a million Uyghur people are being held in concentration camps the communists still call "re-education centers", and are subjected to forced labor and other horrors that the international community has called crimes against humanity and genocide. The government and people responsible for the ongoing atrocities have yet to be held accountable.[71] This is but one example.

Certain terrorist factions and governments have also continued vicious inhuman practices, like burning people alive and decapitating children. America does not entirely escape this as we passively condone human trafficking across our borders and all of the assault and abuse that comes with it. Even if America and the West have substantially, though not completely, left such barbarism behind, the world has not. The savagery with which many natives in the Americas and imported slaves were subjected to was unfathomably vile and that is even in comparison to the

American natives who cut the beating hearts out of living victims in ritual sacrifices.[72] Humanity's past is particularly dark.

Columbus is revered by many, but not because of the destruction that came with him. History has a way of separating out the accomplishments from the man and from the nature of the times. The original invaders devastated the civilizations of the Americas not just by accident but by purposefully destroying the native culture, language and writings, because they were outside of the Roman Catholic faith. They saw it as a part of the civilizing mission of Christians, morally obligated to destroy and murder if it might bring these barbarians to God.[73]

The church revered Columbus for having brought Catholicism to the New World, as if the wanton destruction and the massive death that ensued were somehow justified. Should Catholicism, or Christianity in general, be detested because the religion was used as an excuse to plunder and enslave large parts of the Americas? Of course not. Most Latin Americans are still Catholic today, so that doesn't seem to be the case. Latin America has apparently forgiven Catholicism for its European roots and its role in their history. They have separated the good from the bad of their past, as have we all.

> Encyclical of Pope Leo XIII, the Columbus Quadricentennial, July 16, 1892:
> "By his toil another world emerged from the unsearched bosom of the ocean: hundreds of thousands of mortals have, from a state of blindness, been raised to the common level of the human race, reclaimed from savagery to gentleness and humanity; and, greatest of all, by the acquisition of those blessings of which Jesus Christ is the author, they have been recalled from destruction to eternal life... he saw in spirit a mighty multitude, cloaked in miserable darkness, given over to evil rites, and the superstitious worship of vain gods. Miserable it is to live in a barbarous state and with savage manners: but more miserable to lack the knowledge of that which is highest, and to dwell in ignorance of the one true God."[74]

The conditions under which humans were enslaved in this darkest of crimes existed across cultures and times. Slaves were the spoils of war, taken by conquering forces as an accepted consequence of victory. Sometimes criminals or political adversaries were offered up as slaves. "More-civilized" peoples enslaved "less-civilized" peoples, at least by their own definitions. The whole world condoned and engaged in it. Slaves in

Europe were often members of different religions, pagans or heretics of all manner. Muslims enslaved large numbers of Christians and vice versa. Christians enslaved Christians of other nations.

Over time, though, ideas about slavery finally began to change. The Church no longer favored Christians enslaving other Christians and reasons were searched for to justify the continuation of slavery even of non-Christians. Bringing nonbelievers to Christ served that purpose for a time as new peoples and lands were discovered. Later, new distinctions would be imagined.[75] Though Christianity was used as a reason for their actions in the Americas, this religion was at the same time responsible for a change in European society, for the first time in history, to turn against the practice of slavery and the conquerors' behavior.

The Portuguese were the first to begin sourcing slaves from Africa to Europe and then to the Americas[76], followed by the Dutch, Spanish, French and British, as colonialism spread across the hemisphere. It was the Spanish who began the mass importation of African slaves as labor for its vast empire in the Americas.[77] It is estimated that, from the 1500s to the mid-1800s, some 12.5 million African people were transported across the Atlantic, of which 10.7 million survived the trip. The vast majority of these went to South America, Central America and the Caribbean, with only a fraction, under 400,000, debarking in North America.[78]

Even under the influence of the Enlightenment and the positive moral doctrine of Christianity, the traffic and practice of human slavery continued after our nation's founding. Slavery had been an accepted part of society and law throughout human history, part of an ever-shifting social hierarchy. It would take a polar shift for humanity to escape its use. It took our nation 77 years to abolish slavery. For most countries, it took thousands of years. That it could have been sanctioned in our society to the modern mind is unfathomable. That our founders didn't fight for its elimination tooth and nail is equally incomprehensible, given their commitment to liberty and justice. But it was a different world and changing it would take time. The state of affairs preceding our revolution was not one of widespread liberty and, unfortunately, equal liberty did not become reality just because the U.S. Constitution was signed or the Bill of Rights approved.

Society had a long way to go to live up to the ideals upon which our nation was built and yet it was far ahead of other nations. The U.S. banned the South African slave trade in 1808, though slavery continued with its self-sustaining population. There were just under four million people enslaved here by the time the vile institution was finally abolished. Great Britain banned the trade in 1807 and outlawed slavery in 1833. The Atlantic slave trade continued elsewhere until the 1860s.[79]

A Distinction of Color

Even though our founders were born into a world still ordered by privilege and artificial hierarchy, a world where slavery not only existed but had endured as far back as history existed, they did recognize its evil and hoped to see it ended. There is no justification or defense of slavery. It can't be ignored, though, that it was practiced and condoned across the world and across time almost universally. The societies that didn't practice it were by far the exception. Today, it is hard to comprehend how anyone could have considered the ownership of other human beings as just. It was certainly opposed to every ideal our nation would embody.

"We have seen the mere distinction of colour made... a ground of the most oppressive dominion ever exercised by man over man."
- President James Madison

> John Adams letter to William Tudor, Jr., 1819:
> "Negro Slavery is an evil of Colossal Magnitude.—Mr Walsh in his late Scourge of the British Reviewers, has given such a picture of the Guilt, and Hypocrisy of the People of Europe, especially in England that little or nothing is to be expected from that side of the Water in relation to this Traffic—The United States therefore ought to persevere in the example they have begun, and hitherto continued to discountenance, and totally abolish it—it is a gangreene which thretens Mortality."[80]
>
> James Madison, Popular Election of the First Branch of the Legislature, 1787:
> "We have seen the mere distinction of colour made in the most enlightened period of time, a ground of the most oppressive dominion ever exercised by man over man."[81]

"I brought in a bill to prevent their further importation [of slaves]. this passed without opposition... leaving to future efforts its final eradication." - President Thomas Jefferson

---

Slavery would not be easily ended here. Jefferson described its known history.

> Thomas Jefferson, Autobiography, 1821:
> "The first establishment in Virginia which became permanent was made in 1607. I have found no mention of Negroes in the colony until about 1650. the first brought here as slaves were by a Dutch ship; after which the English commenced the trade and continued it until the revolutionary war. that suspended, ipso facto, their further importation for the present, and the business of the war pressing constantly on the legislature, this subject was not acted on finally until the year '78, when I brought in a bill to prevent their further importation. this passed without opposition, and stopped the increase of the evil by importation, leaving to future efforts its final eradication."

Of our early Presidents, Thomas Jefferson, James Madison and George Washington owned plantations or farms with slaves, though each expressed a desire to see the practice abolished. President John Adams never owned a slave. Benjamin Franklin, an elder statesman and founder who started a Pennsylvania anti-slavery society, freed his domestic slaves, as did John Jay. Jay was a New York politician who wrote the state's first constitution, helped negotiate the end of the Revolution, wrote some of the Federalist papers and was a founder who served in numerous national offices, including as the first Chief Justice of the U.S. Supreme Court.[82] Among other leading founders, Alexander Hamilton, our first Secretary of the Treasury, joined with Jay in working with the New York Manumission Society, another anti-slavery group.

"[The British King] ... violating its most sacred rights of life & liberty in the persons of a distant people who never offended him, captivating & carrying them into slavery in another hemisphere." - First Draft of the Declaration of Independence

---

Jefferson owned slaves, but the initial draft of the Declaration of Independence he wrote condemned the trade as a moral outrage. That first draft was conceived by a committee of five (which included John Adams, Thomas Jefferson, Benjamin Franklin, Roger Sherman[83] and Robert Livingston[84]), written in Jefferson's hand and presented to Congress. Among the parts from that original that were cut out by Congress, was the following grievance against the English King (emphasis his):

> "He has waged cruel war against human nature itself, violating its most sacred rights of life & liberty in the persons of a distant people who never offended him, captivating & carrying them into slavery in another hemisphere, or to incur miserable death in their transportation thither. This piratical warfare, the opprobrium of INFIDEL powers, is the warfare of the CHRISTIAN king of Great Britain. Determined to keep open a market where MEN should be bought and sold, he has prostituted his negative for suppressing every legislative attempt to prohibit or to restrain this execrable. And that this assemblage of horrors might want no fact of distinguished die, he is now exciting those very people to rise in arms among us, and to purchase that liberty of which he has deprived them, by murdering the people upon whom he also obtruded them; thus paying off former crimes committed against the LIBERTIES of one people, with crimes which he urges them to commit against the LIVES of another."[85]

Jefferson made note of the decision by Congress to leave out the part opposing the enslaving of Africans, writing that pressure came from the south and some northern members who still did some dealing in the trade. In the letter below, John Adams described the Declaration's first draft.

> John Adams Letter to Timothy Pickering, Aug. 6, 1822: "I was delighted with its high tone and the flights of oratory with which it abounded, especially that concerning negro slavery, which, though I knew his Southern brethren would never suffer to pass in Congress, I certainly never would oppose... Congress was impatient, and the instrument was reported, as I believe, in Jefferson's handwriting, as he first drew it. Congress cut off about a quarter of it, as I expected they would; but they obliterated some of the best of it, and left all that was exceptionable, if any thing in it was. I have long wondered that the original draught has not been

published. I suppose the reason is, the vehement philippic against negro slavery."[86]

"Slavery is such an atrocious debasement of human nature, that its very extirpation... may sometimes open a source of serious evils."
- Benjamin Franklin

Benjamin Franklin owned slaves but in later years became an advocate for their emancipation by founding, along with Benjamin Rush, the Pennsylvania Society for Promoting the Abolition of Slavery. He believed slavery was an evil, but also believed great care would be needed so that the freed people could become employed and independent, not because of their race or nature but because of how they had been treated and the cruel life to which they had been subjected.

> Public Address, Benjamin Franklin, President of the Pennsylvania Society, 1789:
> "Slavery is such an atrocious debasement of human nature, that its very extirpation, if not performed with solicitous care, may sometimes open a source of serious evils. The unhappy man, who has long been treated as a brute animal, too frequently sinks beneath the common standard of the human species. The galling chains, that bind his body, do also fetter his intellectual faculties, and impair the social affections of his heart. Accustomed to move like a mere machine, by the will of a master, reflection is suspended; he has not the power of choice; and reason and conscience have but little influence over his conduct, because he is chiefly governed by the passion of fear. He is poor and friendless; perhaps worn out by extreme labor, age, and disease.
>
> "Under such circumstances, freedom may often prove a misfortune to himself, and prejudicial to society. Attention to emancipated black people, it is therefore to be hoped, will become a branch of our national policy; but, as far as we contribute to promote this emancipation, so far that attention is evidently a serious duty incumbent on us, and which we mean to discharge to the best of our judgement and abilities. To instruct, to advise, to qualify those, who have been restored to freedom, for the exercise and enjoyment of civil liberty, to promote in them habits of industry, to furnish them with employment suited to their age, sex, talents, and other

> circumstances, and to procure their children an education calculated for their future situation in life; these are the great outlines of the annexed plan, which we have adopted, and which we conceive will essentially promote the public good, and the happiness of these our hitherto too much neglected fellow-creatures."[87]

"I wish from my Soul that the Legislature of this State could see the policy of a gradual abolition of Slavery." - President George Washington

---

Slavery's long history does help explain how such a horror could have been continued by people who could clearly see its injustice. Our first president, George Washington, became a slave owner at age 11 when his father died. Washington expressed his desire to see slavery end but believed that it should be ended through legislation rather than by violent revolt or activist groups operating outside of the law. He also believed, like several others, that they should be freed through a deliberate process. Though today we cannot imagine any end of slavery being worse than the continuing of it, clearly abolition in that age was far easier believed in than accomplished. Washington made efforts to improve the living conditions of his slaves by building new living quarters during the early 1790s. Whatever weakness or justification he had for not freeing them while he lived, Washington did free his slaves in his will when he died in 1799.

> George Washington letter to the Marquis De Lafayette, May 10, 1786:
> "The benevolence of your heart, my dear Marquis, is so conspicuous upon all occasions, that I never wonder at any fresh proofs of it; but your late purchase of an estate in the colony of Cayenne, with a view of emancipating the slaves on it, is a generous and noble proof of your humanity. Would to God a like spirit would diffuse itself generally into the minds of the people of this country. But I despair of seeing it... To set them afloat at once would, I really believe, be productive of much inconvenience and mischief; but by degrees it certainly might, and assuredly ought to be effected; and that too by legislative authority."[88]

"There is not a man living who wishes more sincerely than I do, to see a plan adopted for the abolition of [slavery]." - President George Washington

---

> George Washington to nephew Lawrence Lewis, 1797: "I wish from my Soul that the Legislature of this State could see the policy of a gradual abolition of Slavery; It might prevt much future mischief."[89]
>
> George Washington letter to Robert Morris, Apr. 12, 1786: "I give you the trouble of this letter at the instance of Mr. Dalby of Alexandria, who is called to Philadelphia to attend what he conceives to be a vexatious lawsuit respecting a slave of his, whom a society of Quakers in the city, formed for such purposes, have attempted to liberate... I hope it will not be conceived from these observations, that it is my wish to hold the unhappy people, who are the subject of this letter, in slavery. I can only say that there is not a man living who wishes more sincerely than I do, to see a plan adopted for the abolition of it; but there is only one proper and effectual mode by which it can be accomplished, and that is by Legislative authority; and this, as far as my suffrage will go, shall never be wanting.
>
> "But when slaves who are happy and contented with their present masters, are tampered with and seduced to leave them; when masters are taken unawares by these practices; when a conduct of this sort begets discontent on one side and resentment on the other, and when it happens to fall on a man, whose purse will not measure with that of the Society, and he loses his property for want of means to defend it; it is oppression in the latter case, and not humanity in any; because it introduces more evils than it can cure."[90]

"I have through my whole life held the practice of Slavery in such abhorrence–that I have never owned a Negro or any other Slave." - President John Adams

---

President John Adams was the primary author of the Massachusetts Constitution, by which slavery was abolished there in 1781. He opposed slavery, calling "negro slavery" a "foul contagion in the human character". He was also aware of Jefferson's involvement with his own slave and called it a blot on his character.[91] Like Washington, Adams thought slavery should be ended through a gradual process that would not involve violence or leave slaves worse off than they already were.

> John Adams letter to Robert J. Evans, 1819: "I have through my whole life held the practice of Slavery in such abhorrence—that I have never owned a Negro or any other Slave—tho I have lived for many years in time when the practice was not disgracefull when the best men in my Vicinity—thought it not inconsistant with their Character and when it has Cost me thousand's of dollars for the Labour and Subsistence of free men which I might have saved by the purchase of negros at times when they were very Cheap."[92]

"The condition, of the common Sort of White People in Some of the Southern States... is more oppressed, degraded and miserable than that of the Negroes." - President John Adams

---

> John Adams letter to George Churchman, 1801:
> "Although I have never Sought popularity by any animated Speeches or inflammatory publications against the Slavery of the Blacks, my opinion against it has always been known, and my practice has been so conformable to my Sentiment that I have always employd freemen both as Domisticks and Labourers, and never in my Life did I own a Slave. The Abolition of Slavery must be gradual and accomplished with much caution and Circumspection. Violent means and measures would produce greater violations of Justice and Humanity, than the continuance of the practice. Neither Mr Mifflin nor yourselves, I presume would be willing to venture on Exertions which would probably excite Insurrections among the Blacks to rise against their Masters and imbue their hands in innocent blood.
>
> "There are many other Evils in our Country which are growing, (whereas the practice of Slavery is fast diminishing,) and threaten to bring Punishment in our Land, more immediately than the oppression of the blacks. That sacred regard to Truth in which you

and I were educated, and which is certainly taught and enjoined from on high, Seems to be vanishing from among Us. A general Relaxation of Education and Government. A general Debauchery as well as dissipation, produced by pestilential phylosophical Principles of Epicures[93] infinitely more than by Shews and theatrical Entertainment. These are in my opinion more Serious and threatening Evils, than even the Slavery of the Blacks, hatefull as that is. I might even Add that I have been informed, that the condition, of the common Sort of White People in Some of the Southern States particularly Virginia, is more oppressed, degraded and miserable than that of the Negroes. These Vices and these Miseries deserve the serious and compassionate Consideration of Friends as well as the Slave Trade and the degraded State of the blacks."[94]

Though he also wished to see slavery end, our third president, Thomas Jefferson, did not end it in his own home. He also failed to foresee a future where both races could exist under the same government, after all that had transpired between them, arguing instead for deportation of slaves back to the native land from which they were taken. Jefferson acknowledged that the slaves should be free and that a failure to achieve that end quickly would entail most dreadful outcomes, foretelling the Civil War, the continued oppression of blacks and consequences for our nation for many years thereafter. Though all of the northern states abolished slavery by the early 1800s, the trade continued in the south. Jefferson here describes a proposed Virginia bill respecting slavery and his thoughts on it.

"Nothing is more certainly written in the book of fate than that these people are to be free." - President Thomas Jefferson

---

Thomas Jefferson, Autobiography, 1821:
"The bill on the subject of slaves was a mere digest of the existing laws respecting them, without any intimation of a plan for a future & general emancipation. It was thought better that this should be kept back, and attempted only by way of amendment whenever the bill should be brought on. The principles of the amendment however were agreed on, that is to say, the freedom of all born after a certain day, and deportation at a proper age. But it was found that

> the public mind would not yet bear the proposition, nor will it bear it even at this day.
>
> "Yet the day is not distant when it must bear and adopt it, or worse will follow. Nothing is more certainly written in the book of fate than that these people are to be free. Nor is it less certain that the two races, equally free, cannot live in the same government. Nature, habit, opinion has drawn indelible lines of distinction between them. It is still in our power to direct the process of emancipation and deportation peaceably and in such slow degree as that the evil will wear off insensibly, and their place be pari passu filled up by free white laborers. If on the contrary it is left to force itself on, human nature must shudder at the prospect held up."[95]

Despite their stated opposition to it, our founders failed to implement any plan to end the scourge of human enslavement nationwide, even as the years continued to pass.

"The mere circumstance of complexion cannot deprive them of the character of men." - President James Madison

---

> James Madison, Speech in Virginia Convention, regarding slaves, 1829:
> "It is due to justice: due to humanity: due to truth; to the sympathies of our nature: in fine, to our character as a people, both abroad and at home, that they should be considerd, as much as possible, in the light of human beings; & not as mere property. As such they are acted upon by our laws; and have an interest in our laws. They may be considered as making a part, tho a degraded part of the families to which they belong. If they had the complexion of the Serfs in the North of Europe, or of the villeins formerly in England in other terms, if they were of our own complexion, much of the difficulty would be removed. But the mere circumstance of complexion can not deprive them of the character of men."[96]

Alexander Hamilton, our first treasury secretary, like several others, became a member of an organization aimed at the legal emancipation of slaves.

"... a commerce so repugnant to humanity." - Alexander Hamilton

> Alexander Hamilton, A Full Vindication of the Measures of the Congress, 1774:
> "Were not the disadvantages of slavery too obvious to stand in need of it, I might enumerate and describe the tedious train of calamities, inseparable from it. I might shew that it is fatal to religion and morality; that it tends to debase the mind, and corrupt its noblest springs of action. I might shew, that it relaxes the sinews of industry, clips the wings of commerce, and introduces misery and indigence in every shape."[97]
>
> In March of 1786, Alexander Hamilton signed a petition to the New York legislature calling for the end of slavery. The petition called the slave trade "a commerce so repugnant to humanity, and so inconsistent with the liberality and justice which should distinguish a free and enlightened people."[98]

Much has in modern times been made of this partial representation of slaves in the Constitution, as if it meant to equate black people as only proportionately human, making the document intrinsically racist. It was rather a question of apportioning representation to slave states. Also, the distinction that did exist was between slave and free, with no reference in the constitution to race or national origin. Even at our founding there were free blacks who could vote. To count slaves toward the representation in Congress, but then not let them vote, would give an excess of representation in government to those states with slavery. When it came to the drafting of our Constitution and given the established existence of slavery, they had to consider how slaves would be counted in terms of representation and taxation. A compromise was found.

Of note, Gouveneur Morris wrote the Preamble to the U.S. Constitution.

> During the debates, Federal Convention, 1787, as reported by James Madison:
> "Mr. GOUVERNEUR MORRIS moved to insert 'free' before the word 'inhabitants.' Much, he said, would depend on this point. He never would concur in upholding domestic slavery. It was a nefarious institution. It was the curse of heaven on the states where it prevailed. Compare the free regions of the Middle States, where a rich and noble cultivation marks the prosperity and happiness of

> the people, with the misery and poverty which overspread the barren wastes of Virginia, Maryland, and the other states having slaves... Upon what principle is it that the slaves shall be computed in the representation? Are they men? Then make them citizens, and let them vote. Are they property? Why, then, is no other property included?
>
> "The houses in this city (Philadelphia) are worth more than all the wretched slaves who cover the rice swamps of South Carolina. The admission of slaves into the representation, when fairly explained, comes to this,–that the inhabitant of Georgia and South Carolina, who goes to the coast of Africa, and, in defiance of the most sacred laws of humanity, tears away his fellow-creatures from their dearest connections, and damns them to the most cruel bondage, shall have more votes, in a government instituted for the protection of the rights of mankind, than the citizen of Pennsylvania or New Jersey, who views, with a laudable horror, so nefarious a practice."

He added that such a situation would encourage the southern states to bring in more slaves because it would mean being able to send more representatives to Congress. The same situation occurs today as illegal immigrants are counted in the census from which representatives are proportioned even though they cannot legally vote. This gives greater representation to states that provide sanctuary to illegal immigrants like California. Madison's relation of the comments during the debates continued, noting that a U.S. Constitution that outlawed slavery would not pass in the southern states:

> "Mr. SHERMAN was for leaving the clause as it stands. He disapproved of the slave trade; yet, as the states were now possessed of the right to import slaves, as the public good did not require it to be taken from them, and as it was expedient to have as few objections as possible to the proposed scheme of government, he thought it best to leave the matter as we find it. He observed, that the abolition of slavery seemed to be going on in the United States, and that the good sense of the several states would probably by degrees complete it. He urged on the Convention the necessity of despatching its business."

"Every master of slaves is born a petty tyrant. They bring the judgment of Heaven on a country." – Col. George Mason

---

> "Col. Mason: This infernal traffic originated in the avarice of British merchants. The British government constantly checked the attempts of Virginia to put a stop to it. The present question concerns not the importing states alone, but the whole Union... Every master of slaves is born a petty tyrant. They bring the judgment of Heaven on a country."

"If slavery be wrong, it is justified by the example of all the world... In all ages, one half of mankind have been slaves."
- Charles Pinckney

> "Mr. ELLSWORTH, as he had never owned a slave, could not judge of the effects of slavery on character. He said, however, that if it was to be considered in a moral light, we ought to go further, and free those already in the country. As slaves also multiply so fast in Virginia and Maryland, that it is cheaper to raise than import them, whilst in the sickly rice swamps foreign supplies are necessary, if we go no further than is urged, we shall be unjust towards South Carolina and Georgia. Let us not intermeddle. As population increases, poor laborers will be so plenty as to render slaves useless. Slavery, in time, will not be a speck in our country. Provision is already made in Connecticut for abolishing it. And the abolition has already taken place in Massachusetts. As to the danger of insurrections from foreign influence, that will become a motive to kind treatment of the slaves."
>
> "Mr. PINCKNEY: If slavery be wrong, it is justified by the example of all the world. He cited the case of Greece, Rome, and other ancient states; the sanction given by France, England, Holland, and other modern states. In all ages, one half of mankind have been slaves. If the Southern States were let alone, they will probably of themselves stop importations. He would himself, as a citizen of South Carolina, vote for it. An attempt to take away the right, as proposed, will produce serious objections to the Constitution, which he wished to see adopted."

> "Mr. WILLIAMSON said that, both in opinion and practice, he was against slavery; but thought it more in favor of humanity, from a view of all circumstances, to let in South Carolina and Georgia on those terms, than to exclude them from the Union."[99]

In the Federalist papers, James Madison presented the argument from the point of view of southern representatives in support of the partial count of slaves in order to justify the plan. This was a difficult thing for Madison and the others who wrote the Federalist papers because they greatly opposed slavery, yet wanted the constitution to pass. The compromise made, that both northern and southern states were willing to accept, was sold as a way to balance between the slaves being counted for representation and as property to be taxed. It did not reference race but only the condition of servitude.

> The Federalist Number 54, February 12, 1788, Madison Papers: "But does it follow from an admission of numbers for the measure of representation, or of slaves combined with free citizens, as a ratio of taxation, that slaves ought to be included in the numerical rule of representation? Slaves are considered as property, not as persons. They ought therefore to be comprehended in estimates of taxation which are founded on property, and to be excluded from representation which is regulated by a census of persons. This is the objection, as I understand it, stated in its full force. I shall be equally candid in stating the reasoning which may be offered on the opposite side.
>
> "We subscribe to the doctrine, might one of our southern brethren observe, that representation relates more immediately to persons, and taxation more immediately to property, and we join in the application of this distinction to the case of our slaves. But we must deny the fact that slaves are considered merely as property, and in no respect whatever as persons. The true state of the case is, that they partake of both these qualities; being considered by our laws, in some respects, as persons, and in other respects, as property. In being compelled to labor not for himself, but for a master; in being vendible by one master to another master; and in being subject at all times to be restrained in his liberty, and chastised in his body, by the capricious will of another, the slave may appear to be degraded from the human rank, and classed with those irrational animals, which fall under the legal denomination of property.

"The constitution... regards them as inhabitants, but as debased by servitude below the equal level of free inhabitants, which regards the slave as divested of two fifths of the man." - The Federalist No. 54

> "In being protected on the other hand in his life and in his limbs, against the violence of all others, even the master of his labour and his liberty; and in being punishable himself for all violence committed against others; the slave is no less evidently regarded by the law as a member of the society; not as a part of the irrational creation; as a moral person, not as a mere article of property. The federal constitution therefore, decides with great propriety on the case of our slaves, when it views them in the mixt character of persons and of property. This is in fact their true character. It is the character bestowed on them by the laws under which they live; and it will not be denied that these are the proper criterion; because it is only under the pretext that the laws have transformed the negroes into subjects of property, that a place is disputed them in the computation of numbers; and it is admitted that if the laws were to restore the rights which have been taken away, the negroes could no longer be refused an equal share of representation with the other inhabitants.
>
> "This question may be placed in another light. It is agreed on all sides, that numbers are the best scale of wealth and taxation, as they are the only proper scale of representation. Would the Convention have been impartial or consistent, if they had rejected the slaves from the list of inhabitants when the shares of representation were to be calculated; and inserted them on the lists when the tariff of contributions was to be adjusted? Could it be reasonably expected that the southern states would concur in a system which considered their slaves in some degree as men, when burdens were to be imposed, but refused to consider them in the same light when advantages were to be conferred? ...Let the compromising expedient of the constitution be mutually adopted, which regards them as inhabitants, but as debased by servitude below the equal level of free inhabitants, which regards the slave as divested of two fifths of the man.[100]

Our Constitution referred to those enslaved as "other persons", "such persons as any of the states now existing shall think proper to admit" and a "person held to service or labor in one state, under the laws thereof."[101] Our founding document did not limit its protections to men, whites or even property owners. There has been a frightening amount of racism in this nation over time, but it was not made a part of our founding documents. Slavery was obviously contrary to the idea of equal justice under the law and the inalienable rights to life and liberty. While they felt it was not possible to get the Constitution approved by all the states had it included the abolition of slavery, by establishing the ideals in the Bill of Rights, our founders made the equality of all under the law possible, even inevitable. The founders may or may not have foreseen women's suffrage or the successful integration of blacks into American society, but they made it possible, nonetheless, by establishing the Constitution and Bill of Rights without qualification as to gender or race.

The Constitution addressed slavery in Section 9: "the Migration or Importation of such Persons as any of the States now existing shall think proper to admit, shall not be prohibited by the Congress prior to the Year one thousand eight hundred and eight, but a Tax or duty may be imposed on such Importation, not exceeding ten dollars for each Person." In legislation promoted by then President Thomas Jefferson, Congress prohibited the importation of slaves in an 1807 act that became effective the next year, the first year allowed under the Constitution. This prevented more slaves from being brought into the country but did not address reproduction of those already in servitude, through which the slave trade continued to expand.

A man named Edward Coles wrote Jefferson, urging him to "eradicate this most degrading feature of British Coloniel policy, which is still permitted to exist, notwithstanding its repugnance as well to the principles of our revolution as to our free Institutions."[102] The 71-year-old former President's response below expressed in some detail his views, good and bad. Some might call this racist, but his opinions were reflective of the time and his experience. While his argument against the blending of the freed slaves into their society might be indefensible today, he always held that slavery should be ended.

"It is a mortal reproach to us that they should have pleaded it so long in vain." - President Thomas Jefferson

---

Thomas Jefferson letter to Edward Coles, 1814: "Your favor of July 31. was duly recieved, and was read with peculiar pleasure. the sentiments breathed thro' the whole do honor to both the head and heart of the writer. mine on the subject of the slavery of negroes have long since been in possession of the public, and time has only served to give them stronger root. the love of justice & the love of country plead equally the cause of these people, and it is a mortal reproach to us that they should have pleaded it so long in vain, and should have produced not a single effort, nay I fear not much serious willingness to relieve them & ourselves from our present condition of moral and political reprobation. from those of the former generation who were in the fulness of age when I came into public life, which was while our controversy with England was on paper only, I soon saw that nothing was to be hoped. nursed and educated in the daily habit of seeing the degraded condition, both bodily & mental, of those unfortunate beings, not reflecting that that degradation was very much the work of themselves & their fathers, few minds had yet doubted but that they were as legitimate subjects of property as their horses or cattle.

"the quiet & monotonous course of colonial life had been disturbed by no alarm, & little reflection on the value of liberty. and when alarm was taken at an enterprise on their own, it was not easy to carry them the whole length of the principles which they invoked for themselves. in the first or second session of the legislature after I became a member, I drew to this subject the attention of Colo Bland, one of the oldest, ablest, and most respected members, and he undertook to move for certain moderate extensions of the protection of the laws to these people. I seconded his motion, and, as a younger member, was more spared in the debate: but he was denounced as an enemy to his country, & was treated with the grossest indecorum. from an early stage of our revolution other and more distant duties were assigned to me, so that from that time till my return from Europe in 1789. and I may say till I returned to reside at home in 1809. I had little opportunity of knowing the progress of public sentiment here on this subject.

"I had always hoped that the younger generation, recieving their early impressions after the flame of liberty had been kindled in every breast, and had become as it were the vital spirit of every American, that the generous temperament of youth, analogous to the motion of their blood, and above the suggestions of avarice, would have sympathised with oppression wherever found, and proved their love of liberty beyond their own share of it. but my intercourse with them, since my return, has not been sufficient to ascertain that they had made towards this point the progress I had hoped. your solitary but welcome voice is the first which has brought this sound to my ear; and I have considered the general silence which prevails on this subject as indicating an apathy unfavorable to every hope. yet the hour of emancipation is advancing in the march of time. it will come; and whether brought on by the generous energy of our own minds, or by the bloody process of St Domingo, excited and conducted by the power of our present enemy, if once stationed permanently within our country, & offering asylum & arms to the oppressed, is a leaf of our history not yet turned over.

"For men, probably of any colour, but of this color we know, brought up from their infancy without necessity for thought or forecast, are by their habits rendered as incapable as children of taking care of themselves." - President Thomas Jefferson

---

"As to the method by which this difficult work is to be effected, if permitted to be done by ourselves, I have seen no proposition so expedient on the whole, as that of emancipation of those born after a given day, and of their education and expatriation at a proper age. this would give time for a gradual extinction of that species of labor and substitution of another, and lessen the severity of the shock which an operation so fundamental cannot fail to produce. the idea of emancipating the whole at once, the old as well as the young, and retaining them here, is of those only who have not the guide of either knolege or experience of the subject. for, men, probably of any colour, but of this color we know, brought up from their infancy without necessity for thought or forecast, are by their habits rendered as incapable as children of taking care of themselves, and are extinguished promptly wherever industry is necessary for raising the young. in the mean time they are pests in society by their idleness, and the depredations to which this leads them. their amalgamation with the other colour produces a degradation to which no lover of his country, no lover of excellence in the human character can innocently consent.

"We should endeavor, with those whom fortune has thrown on our hands, to feed & clothe them well, protect them from ill usage, require such reasonable labor only as is performed voluntarily by freemen."
 - President Thomas Jefferson

"I am sensible of the partialities with which you have looked towards me as the person who should undertake this salutary but arduous work. but this, my dear Sir, is like bidding old Priam to buckle the armour of Hector 'trementibus aevo humeris et inutile ferrum cingi.' no. I have overlived the generation with which mutual labors and perils begat mutual confidence and influence. this enterprise is for the young; for those who can follow it up, and bear it through to it's consummation. it shall have all my prayers, and these are the only weapons of an old man. but in the mean time are you right in abandoning this property, and your country with it? I think not.

"my opinion has ever been that, until more can be done for them, we should endeavor, with those whom fortune has thrown on our hands, to feed & clothe them well, protect them from ill usage, require such reasonable labor only as is performed voluntarily by freemen, and be led by no repugnancies to abdicate them, and our duties to them. the laws do not permit us to turn them loose, if that were for their good: and to commute them for other property is to commit them to those whose usage of them we cannot controul. I hope then, my dear Sir, you will reconcile yourself to your country and it's unfortunate condition; that you will not lessen it's stock of sound disposition by withdrawing your portion from the mass. that, on the contrary you will come forward in the public councils,

> become the Missionary of this doctrine truly Christian, insinuate & inculcate it softly but steadily thro' the medium of writing & conversation, associate others in your labors, and when the phalanx is formed, bring on & press the proposition perseveringly until it's accomplishment."[103]

As a nation we were not innocent, but Americans today are no more responsible for the actions of our predecessors than the Aztec descendants are responsible for theirs. We can work to improve things now, but cannot do so justly if it involves doing injustice to others. Trying to keep score over the generations, or blaming a particular race for the actions of some of their predecessors, is anything but rational. Overall, it is an ugly history, both unjustifiable and irreparable today, but at the same time there were great advancements to the human condition, even for peoples previously brutalized. Our founders were flawed and our nation, like every other, was flawed, but was still a vast improvement from its predecessors. Our Constitution failed to abolish slavery, an evil and ancient institution clearly opposed to the principles of our nation's founding, but also so ingrained in our history as to make its elimination one of humanity's most difficult tasks. We are still far from eliminating slavery from this world. Though the practice is technically illegal in most countries today, it is often either condoned by governments or allowed to continue in the shadows. Today, it is estimated that over 45 million people live in modern slavery (a term which includes human trafficking, forced labor, sexual exploitation and debt bondage) in 167 countries as of 2016.[104] It has only gotten worse. It's happening here because we let it. Our attention is kept elsewhere.

Liberty of Conscience

Our founders spoke of religious freedom as liberty of conscience and saw it as fundamental to all other freedoms. Its restriction was thought as evil as slavery itself. It is the liberty of thought and belief that the established powers of Europe so reviled and this religious persecution was hard to stop. Thomas Jefferson, who was governor of Virginia during the Revolutionary War, described in some detail during the early years of our independence, the evolution of religious freedom in America, presenting an enlightening reflection on an issue that would greatly motivate our founders. It was not quite the circumstances generally believed today, but the revolution was the turning point.

"They cast their eyes on these new countries as asylums of civil and religious freedom; but they found them free only for the reigning sect." - President Thomas Jefferson

The Works of Thomas Jefferson, Chapter XVII, published 1904: "The first settlers in this country were emigrants from England, of the English church, just at a point of time when it was flushed with complete victory over the religious of all other persuasions. Possessed, as they became, of the powers of making, administering and executing the laws, they shewed equal intolerance in this country with their Presbyterian brethren, who had emigrated to the northern government. The poor Quakers were flying from persecution in England.

"They cast their eyes on these new countries as asylums of civil and religious freedom; but they found them free only for the reigning sect. Several acts of the Virginia assembly of 1659, 1662, and 1693, had made it penal in parents to refuse to have their children baptized; had prohibited the unlawful assembling of Quakers; had made it penal for any master of a vessel to bring a Quaker into the state; had ordered those already here, and such as should come thereafter, to be imprisoned till they should abjure the country; provided a milder punishment for their first and second return, but death for their third; had inhibited all persons from suffering their meetings in or near their houses, entertaining them individually, or disposing of books which supported their tenets.

"If no capital execution took place here, as did in New-England, it was not owing to the moderation of the church, or spirit of the legislature, as may be inferred from the law itself; but to historical circumstances which have not been handed down to us. The Anglicans retained full possession of the country about a century. Other opinions began then to creep in, and the great care of the government to support their own church, having begotten an equal degree of indolence in its clergy, two thirds of the people had become dissenters at the commencement of the present revolution. The laws indeed were still oppressive on them, but the spirit of the one party had subsided into moderation, and of the other had risen to a degree of determination which commanded respect.

"At the common law, heresy was a capital offence."
- President Thomas Jefferson

"The present state of our laws on the subject of religion is this. The convention of May 1776, in their declaration of rights, declared it to be a truth, and a natural right, that the exercise of religion should be free; but when they proceeded to form on that declaration the ordinance of government, instead of taking up every principle declared in the bill of rights, and guarding it by legislative sanction, they passed over that which asserted our religious rights, leaving them as they found them. The same convention, however, when they met as a member of the general assembly in October 1776, repealed all acts of parliament which had rendered criminal the maintaining any opinions in matters of religion, the forbearing to repair to church, and the exercising any mode of worship; and suspended the laws giving salaries to the clergy, which suspension was made perpetual in October 1779. Statutory oppressions in religion being thus wiped away, we remain at present under those only imposed by the common law, or by our own acts of assembly.

"If a person brought up in the christian religion denies... the scriptures to be of divine authority, he is punishable on the first offence by incapacity to hold any office or employment... on the second... by three years imprisonment, without bail." - President Thomas Jefferson

---

"At the common law, heresy was a capital offence, punishable by burning. Its definition was left to the ecclesiastical judges, before whom the conviction was, till the statute of the 1 El. c. 1. circumscribed it, by declaring that nothing should be deemed heresy but what had been so determined by authority of the canonical scriptures, or by one of the four first general councils, or by some other council having for the grounds of their declaration the express and plain words of the scriptures. Heresy, thus circumscribed, being an offence at the common law, our act of assembly of October 1777, c. 17 gives cognizance of it to the general court, by declaring that the jurisdiction of that court shall be general in all matters at the common law. The execution is by the writ De hæretico comburendo.

"By our own act of assembly of 1705, c. 30, if a person brought up in the christian religion denies the being of a God, or the trinity, or asserts there are more Gods than one, or denies the christian religion to be true, or the scriptures to be of divine authority, he is punishable on the first offence by incapacity to hold any office or employment ecclesiastical, civil, or military; on the second by disability to sue, to take any gift or legacy, to be guardian, executor or administrator, and by three years imprisonment, without bail. A father's right to the custody of his own children being founded in law on his right of guardianship, this being taken away, they may of course be severed from him and put, by the authority of a court, into more orthodox hands. This is a summary view of that religious slavery under which a people have been willing to remain who have lavished their lives and fortunes for the establishment of their civil freedom."

"It does me no injury for my neighbor to say there are twenty gods, or no god. It neither picks my pocket nor breaks my leg." - President Thomas Jefferson

---

Jefferson goes on to describe the consequence of this religious slavery and the justification for complete liberty, a goal they struggled toward.

"The error seems not sufficiently eradicated, that the operations of the mind, as well as the acts of the body, are subject to the coercion of the laws. But our rulers can have authority over such natural rights, only as we have submitted to them. The rights of conscience we never submitted, we could not submit. We are answerable for them to our God. The legitimate powers of government extend to such acts only as are injurious to others.

"Reason and free inquiry are the only effectual agents against error."
- President Thomas Jefferson

"But it does me no injury for my neighbor to say there are twenty gods, or no god. It neither picks my pocket nor breaks my leg. If it be said his testimony in a court of justice cannot be relied on, reject it then, and be the stigma on him. Constraint may make him worse by making him a hypocrite, but it will never make him a truer man. It may fix him obstinately in his errors, but will not cure them.

"Reason and free inquiry are the only effectual agents against error. Give a loose to them, they will support the true religion by bringing every false one to their tribunal, to the test of their investigation. They are the natural enemies of error, and of error only. Had not the Roman government permitted free inquiry, christianity could never have been introduced. Had not free inquiry been indulged, at the æra of the reformation, the corruptions of christianity could not have been purged away. If it be restrained now, the present corruptions will be protected, and new ones encouraged. Was the government to prescribe to us our medicine and diet, our bodies would be in such keeping as our souls are now. Thus in France the emetic was once forbidden as a medicine, and the potatoe as an article of food.

"It is error alone which needs the support of government. Truth can stand by itself. - President Thomas Jefferson

---

"Government is just as infallible, too, when it fixes systems in physics. Galileo was sent to the inquisition for affirming that the earth was a sphere; the government had declared it to be as flat as a trencher, and Galileo was obliged to abjure his error. This error however at length prevailed, the earth became a globe, and Descartes declared it was whirled round its axis by a vortex. The government in which he lived was wise enough to see that this was no question of civil jurisdiction, or we should all have been involved by authority in vortices. In fact the vortices have been exploded, and the Newtonian principles of gravitation is now more firmly established, on the basis of reason, than it would be were the government to step in and to make it an article of necessary faith. Reason and experiment have been indulged, and error has fled before them. It is error alone which needs the support of government. Truth can stand by itself.

"Millions of innocent men, women and children, since the introduction of Christianity, have been burnt, tortured, fined, imprisoned."
- President Thomas Jefferson

"Subject opinion to coercion: whom will you make your inquisitors? Fallible men; men governed by bad passions, by private as well as public reasons. And why subject it to coercion? To produce uniformity. But is uniformity of opinion desireable? No more than of face and stature. Introduce the bed of Procrustes then, and as there is danger that the large men may beat the small, make us all of a size, by lopping the former and stretching the latter. Difference of opinion is advantageous in religion. The several sects perform the office of a Censor morum over each other. Is uniformity attainable? Millions of innocent men, women and children, since the introduction of Christianity, have been burnt, tortured, fined, imprisoned: yet we have not advanced one inch towards uniformity. What has been the effect of coercion? To make one half the world fools, and the other half hypocrites. To support roguery and error all over the earth.

"Let us reflect that it is inhabited by a thousand millions of people. That these profess probably a thousand different systems of religion. That ours is but one of that thousand. That if there be but one right, and ours that one, we should wish to see the 999 wandering sects gathered into the fold of truth. But against such a majority we cannot effect this by force. Reason and persuasion are the only practicable instruments. To make way for these, free inquiry must be indulged; and how can we wish others to indulge it while we refuse it ourselves. But every state, says an inquisitor, has established some religion. "No two, say I, have established the same." Is this a proof of the infallibility of establishments?

"Our sister states of Pennsylvania and New York, however, have long subsisted without any establishment at all. The experiment was new and doubtful when they made it. It has answered beyond conception. They flourish infinitely. Religion is well supported; of various kinds indeed, but all good enough; all sufficient to preserve peace and order: or if a sect arises whose tenets would subvert morals, good sense has fair play, and reasons and laughs it out of doors, without suffering the state to be troubled with it. They do not hang more malefactors than we do. They are not more disturbed with religious dissentions. On the contrary, their harmony is unparalleled, and can be ascribed to nothing but their unbounded tolerance, because there is no other circumstance in which they differ from every nation on earth. They have made the happy discovery, that the way to silence religious disputes, is to take no notice of them. Let us too give this experiment fair play, and get rid, while we may, of those tyrannical laws.

"It is true we are as yet secured against them by the spirit of the times. I doubt whether the people of this country would suffer an execution for heresy, or a three years imprisonment for not comprehending the mysteries of the trinity. But is the spirit of the people an infallible, a permanent reliance? Is it government? Is this the kind of protection we receive in return for the rights we give up? Besides, the spirit of the times may alter, will alter. Our rulers will become corrupt, our people careless. A single zealot may commence persecuter, and better men be his victims. It can never be too often repeated, that the time for fixing every essential right on a legal basis is while our rulers are honest, and ourselves united.[105]

Our fourth President, James Madison, described the state of religion in American in a letter written to his lifelong friend William Bradford, an attorney and judge from Philadelphia who became our nation's second Attorney General. The letter came in the wake of the Boston Tea Party, where tea was dumped into the harbor, and also Philadelphia's act of turning a British ship carrying tea away from its shores.

James Madison to William Bradford, Jr., Jan. 24, 1774:
"I congratulate you on your heroic proceedings in Philadelphia with regard to the tea. I wish Boston may conduct matters with as much discretion as they seem to do with boldness. They seem to have great trials and difficulties by reason of the obduracy and ministerialism of their Governor. However, political contests are necessary sometimes, as well as military, to afford exercise and practice, and to instruct in the art of defending liberty and property.

> I verily believe the frequent assaults that have been made on America (Boston especially) will in the end prove of real advantage.

"That diabolical, hell-conceived principle of persecution rages among some." - President James Madison

---

> "I want again to breathe your free air. I expect it will mend my constitution and confirm my principles. I have indeed as good an atmosphere at home as the climate will allow; but have nothing to brag of as to the state and liberty of my country. Poverty and luxury prevail among all sorts; pride, ignorance, and knavery among the priesthood, and vice and wickedness among the laity. This is bad enough, but it is not the worst I have to tell you. That diabolical, hell-conceived principle of persecution rages among some; and to their eternal infamy, the clergy can furnish their quota of imps for such business. This vexes me the worst of anything whatever.
>
> "There are at this time in the adjacent country not less than five or six well-meaning men in close jail for publishing their religious sentiments, which in the main are very orthodox. I have neither patience to hear, talk, or think of anything relative to this matter; for I have squabbled and scolded, abused and ridiculed, so long about it to little purpose, that I am without common patience. So I must beg you to pity me, and pray for liberty of conscience to all."[106]

The Colonies were settled by Christians of different creeds, each hoping to establish a society based on their own religious beliefs, but most were no more tolerant of dissention than their predecessors. It was a battle, as it always had been, between force and will, between tyranny and liberty.

> John Adams, The Works of John Adams, vol. 1, Life of the Author, 1856:
> "The question between the Church of Rome and all the reformers, was essentially a question between liberty and power; between submission to the dictates of other men and the free exercise of individual faculties. Universities were institutions of Christianity, the original idea of which may, perhaps, have been adopted from the schools of the Grecian sophists and philosophers, but which were essential improvements upon them. The authority of the Church of Rome is founded upon the abstract principle of power.

> The Reformation, in all its modifications, was founded upon the principle of liberty.

"The principal achievement of the reformers, therefore, was to substitute one form of human authority for another." - President John Adams

---

> "Yet the Church of Rome, claiming for her children the implicit submission of faith to the decrees of her councils, and sometimes to the Bishop of Rome, as the successor of Saint Peter, is yet compelled to rest upon human reason for the foundation of faith itself. And the Protestant churches, while vindicating the freedom of the human mind, and acknowledging the Scriptures alone as the rule of faith, still universally recur to human authority for prescribing bounds to that freedom.
>
> "It was in universities only that this contentious question between liberty and power could be debated and scrutinized in all its bearings upon human agency. It enters into the profoundest recesses of metaphysical science; it mingles itself with the most important principles of morals. Now the morals and the metaphysics of the universities were formed from the school of Aristotle, the citizen of a Grecian republic, and, perhaps, the acutest intellect that ever appeared in the form of man. In that school, it was not difficult to find a syllogism competent to demolish all human authority, usurping the power to prescribe articles of religious faith, but not to erect a substitute for human authority in the mind of every individual. The principal achievement of the reformers, therefore, was to substitute one form of human authority for another; and the followers of Luther, of Calvin, of John Knox, and of Cranmer, while renouncing and denouncing the supremacy of the Romish Church and the Pope, terminated their labors in the establishment of other supremacies in its stead."[107]

The authoritarian vestiges of established religion still suppressed conflicting beliefs. In the colonies, the rights of speech and publication were restricted in an attempt to suppress heresy and resist Satan. The bringing of these diverse colonies together to the single task of resisting English tyranny was a spectacular feat orchestrated by our founders, including many more than those I reference here, an achievement both inspired and made possible by the emergence of the Enlightenment. Our second President described the challenge they faced.

> John Adams letter to H. Niles, 1818:
> "The colonies had grown up under constitutions of government so different, there was so great a variety of religions, they were composed of so many different nations, their customs, manners, and habits had so little resemblance, and their intercourse had been so rare, and their knowledge of each other so imperfect, that to unite them in the same principles in theory and the same system of action, was certainly a very difficult enterprise. The complete accomplishment of it, in so short a time and by such simple means, was perhaps a singular example in the history of mankind. Thirteen clocks were made to strike together–a perfection of mechanism, which no artist had ever before effected."[108]

As in the case of slavery, the religious liberty our founders professed would take time to be equally applied to all. It would not be until after the Civil War that the U.S. Constitution would be amended to apply the Bill of Rights and its immunities and protections of citizenship to all levels of the government.[109]

"In most countries of Europe [blasphemy] is punished by fire at the stake, or the rack, or the wheel." - President John Adams

---

In one of his last letters to Thomas Jefferson, January 23, 1825, John Adams lamented the religious intolerance which survived as the lingering influence of the old order, even at that late date, when he and Jefferson were both old men and most of their fellows gone. The prohibition against establishment then did not yet apply to the states.

"Books that cannot bear examination certainly ought not to be established as divine inspiration by penal laws." - President John Adams

---

> The Works of John Adams, Volume 10, published 1856:
> "We think ourselves possessed, or, at least, we boast that we are so, of liberty of conscience on all subjects, and of the right of free inquiry and private judgment in all cases, and yet how far are we

from these exalted privileges in fact! There exists, I believe, throughout the whole Christian world, a law which makes it blasphemy to deny or to doubt the divine inspiration of all the books of the Old and New Testaments, from Genesis to Revelations. In most countries of Europe it is punished by fire at the stake, or the rack, or the wheel. In England itself it is punished by boring through the tongue with a red-hot poker.

"In America it is not much better; even in our own Massachusetts, which I believe, upon the whole, is as temperate and moderate in religious zeal as most of the States, a law was made in the latter end of the last century, repealing the cruel punishments of the former laws, but substituting fine and imprisonment upon all those blasphemers upon any book of the Old Testament or New. Now, what free inquiry, when a writer must surely encounter the risk of fine or imprisonment for adducing any argument for investigation into the divine authority of those books? Who would run the risk of translating Dupuis?

"But I cannot enlarge upon this subject, though I have it much at heart. I think such laws a great embarrassment, great obstructions to the improvement of the human mind. Books that cannot bear examination certainly ought not to be established as divine inspiration by penal laws. It is true, few persons appear desirous to put such laws in execution, and it is also true that some few persons are hardy enough to venture to depart from them. But as long as they continue in force as laws, the human mind must make an awkward and clumsy progress in its investigations. I wish they were repealed."[110]

Adams and Jefferson both died the following year on the 50th anniversary of the signing of the Declaration of Independence. Adams was 90 and Jefferson 81. In an earlier letter to Jefferson, John Adams described an assembly of the young men of the city of Philadelphia, whose diversity reflected the nation.

John Adams to Thomas Jefferson, 28 June 1813:
"Who composed that army of fine young fellows that was then before my eyes? There were among them Roman Catholics, English Episcopalians, Scotch and American Presbyterians, Methodists, Moravians, Anabaptists, German Lutherans, German Calvinists, Universalists, Arians, Priestleyans, Socinians,

> Independents, Congregationalists, Horse Protestants, and House Protestants, Deists and Atheists; and 'Protestans qui ne croyent rien' [Protestants who believe nothing]. Very few, however, of several of these species; nevertheless, all educated in the general principles of Christianity, and the general principles of English and American liberty."[111]

It is likely only because they were from such a variety of sects that the prohibition against establishment was even possible. Though their ideals were not fully realized in their lifetimes, our founders established a nation where a great variety of faiths, races and opinions could coexist.

Chapter 3

Unbridled Lust for Freedom

The individual religious beliefs of these founders were not as relevant to the country they founded as their commitment to liberty, that everyone should have the equal liberty to think, believe and express those beliefs without cowering to government or religious oppression. There is no doubt these founders believed in God and valued religion. Still, they also understood the effects of the religious intolerance and oppression and, as such, were motivated to take an exceptional step toward liberty by creating this nation free of religious establishment. What they thought about religion and government was unprecedented and vital to understand today as a new tyranny has begun to take its place.

Religion has flourished here even without the sanction of government, expressed in many forms, including the sects that were once oppressive in their application. The new tyranny we face today is not centered on a god, but mingles government with education, private enterprise and organizations to change how we think and live based on ideologies just as dangerous when given the force of government. Just as religious oppression in the past was not about Christianity but control, this new type of religion is not about justice or the environment or what's best for our children. It too is about control. The answer is equal liberty and personal responsibility.

So vital was liberty that the signers of the Declaration of Independence risked and often lost their lives and their fortunes in its quest, and the fight for it, united Americans of all religions and nationalities.

> George Washington address to the inhabitants of Canada during our Revolution:
> "The cause of America and of liberty is the cause of every virtuous American Citizen Whatever may be his Religion or his descent, the United Colonies know no distinction, but such as Slavery, Corruption and Arbitrary Domination may create. Come then ye generous Citizens, range yourselves under the Standard of general Liberty, against which all the force and Artifice of Tyranny will never be able to prevail."[112]

The colonies rejected taxation by Britain without representation and sought independent self-rule. In his famous speech, Patrick Henry, an attorney and twice a governor of Virginia, spoke of liberty in no uncertain terms.

> Patrick Henry to the Second Virginia Convention, 1775:
> "If we wish to be free-- if we mean to preserve inviolate those inestimable privileges for which we have been so long contending-- if we mean not basely to abandon the noble struggle in which we have been so long engaged, and which we have pledged ourselves never to abandon until the glorious object of our contest shall be obtained--we must fight... The millions of people, armed in the holy cause of liberty, and in such a country as that which we possess, are invincible by any force which our enemy can send against us... I know not what course others may take; but as for me, give me liberty or give me death!"[113]

Unlimited liberty, however, was never their intent as it would equate to anarchy and the complete lack of morality and law. Their ideal was liberty bound only by the equal liberty of others. They believed the people were thought capable of political and religious self-rule, a revolutionary idea.

> Thomas Jefferson letter to Archibald Stuart, 23 December 1791:
> "I would rather be exposed to the inconveniences attending too much liberty than those attending too small a degree of it."[114]

"Rightful liberty is unobstructed action according to our will within limits drawn around us by the equal rights of others."
– President Thomas Jefferson

Thomas Paine, 1795, Dissertation on First Principles of Government:
"He that would make his own liberty secure, must guard even his enemy from oppression; for if he violates this duty, he establishes a precedent that will reach to himself." [115]

Thomas Jefferson letter to Isaac H. Tiffany, 1819:
"Of liberty I would say that, in the whole plenitude of its extent, it is unobstructed action according to our will. But rightful liberty is unobstructed action according to our will within limits drawn around us by the equal rights of others. I do not add 'within the limits of the law,' because law is often but the tyrant's will, and always so when it violates the right of an individual." [116]

The ideal of equal rights and equal liberty is a founding principle of American morality, but religious liberty met with opposition from old-world influences and religious leaders in America at the time.

John Adams letter to Thomas Jefferson, June 28, 1813:
"It is very true that the 'denunciations of the priesthood are fulminated against every advocate for a complete freedom of religion. Comminations, I believe, would be plenteously pronounced by even the most liberal of them, against atheism, deism', against every man who disbelieved or doubted the resurrection of Jesus, or the miracles of the New Testament. Priestley himself would denounce the man who should deny the Apocalypse, or the prophecies of Daniel. Priestley and Lindsey have both denounced as idolaters and blasphemers all the Trinitarians and even the Arians. Poor weak man! When will thy perfection arrive? Thy perfectibility I shall not deny, for a greater character than Priestley or Godwin has said, 'Be ye perfect.' For my part, I cannot 'deal damnation round the land' on all I judge the foes of God or man."

Religion of Our Founders

Scholars have long debated the religion of some of our most prominent founding fathers and it is easy to find quotes from them praising Christianity and God. Surprisingly, it is just as easy to find quotes in which some our leading founders were critical and even derisive of Christianity. Taken out of context, this could give two very different views of these men and what they believed. In context, their words reflect a deep appreciation for the morality of Christianity, an unwavering belief in god and trust in every individual's ability to reason and come to their own conclusions. Even so, questions remain, because they considered their personal beliefs irrelevant to anyone but themselves. Many others intimately involved in our founding were, no doubt, traditional Christians, but I focused my research on the leaders, especially our first four presidents.

The United States of America was peopled almost entirely by Christians, but some of its founders might be more accurately described as deists or theists, those believing in a creator god whose existence is evident by reason and nature but who discard many of the supernatural aspects of revealed religion. Deism gained some prominence during the Age of Enlightenment. While deists commonly held that god created the universe and then left it and us to our own devices, these founders instead often expressed a belief in Providence, a god that intervened in the lives of its creations and acted in support of their efforts. This variation is called theism but they didn't use that term. They publicly and privately praised the general principles of Christianity and Jesus, while their personal correspondence provides further insight into those beliefs.

"No People can be bound to acknowledge and adore the invisible hand... more than the People of the United States."
- President George Washington

George Washington was not only our first president but also led our Continental Army and our nation during in its struggle for Independence. He was a singular force in the founding of America. Some of Washington's contemporaries said he attended various churches but did not participate. Perhaps he just didn't want to openly support any particular Christian faith, but respect all of them. While he seldom spoke in terms exclusive to Christianity, he did refer often to the influence of Divine Providence on his endeavors and the country, given the improbability of its success.

> George Washington to John Armstrong, 1792: "I am sure there never was a people who had more reason to acknowledge a divine interposition in their affairs than those of the United States; and I should be pained to believe that they have forgotten that agency which was so often manifested during our Revolution—or that they failed to consider the omnipotence of that God who is alone able to protect them."[117]

George Washington's "First Inaugural Address", April 30, 1789: "It would be peculiarly improper to omit in this first official Act, my fervent supplications to that Almighty Being who rules over the Universe, who presides in the Councils of Nations, and whose providential aids can supply every human defect, that his benediction may consecrate to the liberties and happiness of the People of the United States, a Government instituted by themselves for these essential purposes: and may enable every instrument employed in its administration, to execute with success, the functions allotted to his charge. In tendering this homage to the Great Author of every public and private good, I assure myself that it expresses your sentiments not less than my own; nor those of my fellow-citizens at large, less than either: No People can be bound to acknowledge and adore the invisible hand, which conducts the Affairs of men more than the People of the United States."

George Washington to the Grand Lodge of Pennsylvania, 1792: "I request you will be assured of my best wishes and earnest prayers for your happiness while you remain in this terrestial Mansion, and that we may hereafter meet as brethren in the Eternal Temple of the Supreme Architect."[118]

George Washington to the Savannah, Ga., Hebrew Congregation, June 14, 1790:
"I rejoice that a spirit of liberality and philanthropy is much more prevalent than it formerly was among the enlightened nations of the earth; and that your brethren will benefit thereby in proportion as it shall become still more extensive. Happily the people of the United States of America have, in many instances, exhibited examples worthy of imitation—The salutary influence of which will doubtless extend much farther, if gratefully enjoying those blessings of peace which (under favor of Heaven) have been obtained by fortitude in war, they shall conduct themselves with reverence to the Deity, and charity towards their fellow-creatures.

"May the same wonder-working Deity, who long since delivering the Hebrews from their Egyptian Oppressors planted them in the promised land—whose providential agency has lately been conspicuous in establishing these United States as an independent nation—still continue to water them with the dews of Heaven and to make the inhabitants of every denomination participate in the

> temporal and spiritual blessings of that people whose God is Jehovah."[119]

Washington was a Free Manson, a group that referred to god in such terms as Great Author or Architect of the Universe."[120] When he spoke to a Freemason lodge, as above, he used that terminology but similar terms appeared elsewhere in his writings. Freemasonry is described as an oath-bound society, devoted to fellowship, moral discipline, and mutual assistance, a non-Christian organization that started as a guild of stone masons and continues today. Requirements for memberships were being male and believing in a god.[121] I found few writings revealing Washington's private thoughts on religion. Most references come from public addresses where he was always magnanimous. Some of his contemporaries questioned his conformity to traditional Christianity but evidence is spare.

> George Washington speech to the Delaware Indian Chiefs, May 12, 1779:
> "You do well to wish to learn our arts and ways of life, and above all, the religion of Jesus Christ. These will make you a greater and happier people than you are."[122]
>
> George Washington to Lafayette, 1787:
> "Being no bigot myself to any mode of worship, I am disposed to endulge the professors of Christianity in the church, that road to heaven which to them shall seem the most direct plainest easiest and least liable to exception."[123]

By no means conclusive, but curious, is the following entry Thomas Jefferson made in his journal a few weeks after Washington's death. This account was in Jefferson's handwriting.

> Thomas Jefferson notes of conversation with Benjamin Rush, February 1, 1800:
> "Dr. Rush tells me that he had it from Asa Green that when the clergy addressed Genl. Washington on his departure from the govmt, it was observed in their consultation that he had never on any occasion said a word to the public which showed a belief in the Xn religion and they thot they should so pen their address as to force him at length to declare publicly whether he was a Christian or not. They did so. However, he observed the old fox was too cunning for them. He answered every article of their address particularly except that, which he passed over without notice.

> "Rush observes he never did say a word on the subject in any of his public papers except in his valedictory letter to the Governors of the states when he resigned his commission in the army, wherein he speaks of the benign influence of the Christian religion. I know that Gouverneur Morris, who pretended to be in his secrets & believed himself to be so, has often told me that Genl. Washington believed no more of that system than he himself did." [124]

Benjamin Franklin was one of the very few involved in our nation's founding to actually identify himself as a deist, though he held no animosity toward traditional faiths. He also had some supernatural beliefs. He was a leading figure in the American Enlightenment, an author, scientist, U.S. Ambassador to France and Governor of Pennsylvania. A colorful character, to be sure, Franklin was also a newspaper editor and printer in Philadelphia, among other roles and wide-ranging accomplishments too plentiful to recount here. He was much older than most of the other men involved in our nation's founding and very influential.

"I soon became a thorough deist." - Benjamin Franklin

> Autobiography of Benjamin Franklin (published 1895):
> "Some books against deism fell into my hands; they were said to be the substance of the sermons which had been preached at Boyle's lectures. It happened that they wrought an effect on me quite contrary to what was intended by them. For the arguments of the deists, which were quoted to be refuted, appeared to be much stronger than the refutations; in short, I soon became a thorough deist." [125]
>
> Benjamin Franklin to his sister Jane Mecom, July 28, 1743: "You express yourself as if you thought I was against Worshipping of God, and believed Good Works would merit Heaven; which are both Fancies of your own, I think, without Foundation. I am so far from thinking that God is not to be worshipped, that I have compos'd and wrote a whole Book of Devotions for my own Use: And I imagine there are few, if any, in the World, so weake as to imagine, that the little Good we can do here, can merit so vast a Reward hereafter. There are some Things in your New England Doctrines and Worship, which I do not agree with, but I do not

therefore condemn them, or desire to shake your Belief or Practice of them."[126]

"As to Jesus of Nazareth... I think the system of morals and his religion as he left them to us, the best the world ever saw." – Benjamin Franklin

---

Benjamin Franklin, a month before his death, in letter to Ezra Stiles, March 9, 1790:

"You desire to know something of my religion.... Here is my creed: I believe in one God, creator of the universe. That He governs it by his providence. That he ought to be worshipped. That the most acceptable Service we can render to him, is doing good to his other children. That the soul of man is immortal, and will be treated with Justice in another life respecting its conduct in this. These I take to be the fundamental principles of all sound religion, and I regard them as you do, in whatever sect I meet with them.

"As to Jesus of Nazareth, my opinion of whom you particularly desire, I think the system of morals and his religion as he left them to us, the best the world ever saw, or is likely to see; but I apprehend it has received various corrupting changes, and I have with most of the present dissenters in England, some doubts as to his divinity: tho' it is a question I do not dogmatise upon, having never studied it, and think it needless to busy myself with it now, when I expect soon an opportunity of knowing the truth with less trouble....

"My opinions, indeed, on religious subjects ought not to be of any consequence to any but myself." – President John Adams

---

"I have ever let others enjoy their religious sentiments, without reflecting on them for those that appeared to me insupportable and even absurd. All sects here, and we have a great variety, have experienced my good will in assisting them with subscriptions for building their new places of worship, and as I have never opposed any of their doctrines, I hope to go out of the world in peace with them all." [127]

Our second President, John Adams was a Massachusetts delegate to the Continental Congress. Adams lost re-election to Thomas Jefferson after a bitter campaign. The two became close friends again later in life and wrote each other often. Most of Adams writings regarding religion were in private correspondence, having concluded in a letter to Samuel Miller in 1820: "My opinions, indeed, on religious subjects ought not to be of any consequence to any but myself."[128] His beliefs, particularly later in life, were not very traditional, rejecting some supernatural aspects of Christianity.

> John Adams letter to Hannah Adams, March 16, 1804: "No inconsiderable portion of my Life for fifty years has been passed in the Society of Skepticks Atheists and Deists. I have heard their Reasonings, Ridicule, Scoffs and Sarcasms... I am pretty well apprised of all their Objections and Difficulties, which have been so well answered, that I entertain no doubt of the Truth and Excellence of the Christian Religion. On the contrary I believe it to be the best Religion in the World. The profoundest System of Phylosophy and Policy. The best adapted to the intellectual, moral, Social, and Physical Constitution of Man and the World, and far beyond the reach of human Genius and Invention."[129]

"There is... but one being who can understand the universe, and that it is... wicked for insects to pretend to comprehend it." - President John Adams

---

> John Adams letter to Thomas Jefferson, Sept. 14, 1813:
> "God has infinite wisdom, goodness, and power; he created the universe; his duration is eternal, a parte ante and a parte post. His presence is as extensive as space. What is space? An infinite spherical vacuum. He created this speck of dirt and the human species for his glory; and with the deliberate design of making nine tenths of our species miserable for ever for his glory. This is the doctrine of Christian theologians, in general, ten to one. Now, my friend, can prophecies or miracles convince you or me that infinite benevolence, wisdom, and power, created, and preserves for a time, innumerable millions, to make them miserable for ever, for his own glory? Wretch! What is his glory? Is he ambitious? Does he want promotion? Is he vain, tickled with adulation, exulting and triumphing in his power and the sweetness of his vengeance?

"Pardon me, my Maker, for these awful questions. My answer to them is always ready. I believe no such things. My adoration of the author of the universe is too profound and too sincere. The love of God and his creation—delight, joy, triumph, exultation in my own existence—though but an atom, a molécule organique in the universe—are my religion... It has been long, very long, a settled opinion in my mind, that there is now, ever will be, and ever was, but one being who can understand the universe, and that it is not only vain but wicked for insects to pretend to comprehend it."[130]

Adams strongly supported the principles and moral teachings of Christianity without the supernatural tenets of the faith, what he called rational Christianity. In private, he even expressed derision for what he and Thomas Jefferson saw as the corruptions of the religion.

"How has it happened that millions of fables, tales, legends, have been blended with both Jewish and Christian revelation that have made them the most bloody religion that ever existed?" - President John Adams

---

John Adams, letter to Thomas Jefferson, June 20, 1815:
"The question before the human race is, whether the God of nature shall govern the world by his own laws, or whether priests and kings shall rule it by fictitious miracles?"

John Adams to Thomas Jefferson, Nov. 4, 1816:
"We have now, it seems, a national Bible Society, to propagate King James's Bible through all nations. Would it not be better to apply these pious subscriptions to purify Christendom from the corruptions of Christianity than to propagate those corruptions in Europe, Asia, Africa, and America? ...Conclude not from all this that I have renounced the Christian religion, or that I agree with Dupuis in all his sentiments. Far from it. I see in every page something to recommend Christianity in its purity, and something to discredit its corruptions."[131]

"His system is founded in the hopes of mankind, but they delight more in their fears." - President John Adams

---

John Adams, letter to FA Van der Kamp, December 27, 1816:
"As I understand the Christian religion, it was, and is, a revelation. But how has it happened that millions of fables, tales, legends, have been blended with both Jewish and Christian revelation that have made them the most bloody religion that ever existed?"

John Adams to Thomas Jefferson, May 29, 1818, Speaking of Jesus:
"His system is founded in the hopes of mankind, but they delight more in their fears. When will man have juster notions of the universal, eternal cause? Then will rational Christianity prevail." [132]

John Adams letter to John Taylor, Apr. 15, 1814:
"The priesthood have, in all ancient nations, nearly monopolized learning. Read over again all the accounts we have of Hindoos, Chaldeans, Persians, Greeks, Romans, Celts, Teutons, we shall find that priests had all the knowledge, and really governed all mankind. Examine Mahometanism, trace Christianity from its first promulgation; knowledge has been almost exclusively confined to the clergy. And, even since the Reformation, when or where has existed a Protestant or dissenting sect who would tolerate a free inquiry? The blackest billingsgate, the most ungentlemanly insolence, the most yahooish brutality is patiently endured, countenanced, propagated, and applauded. But touch a solemn truth in collision with a dogma of a sect, though capable of the clearest proof, and you will soon find you have disturbed a nest, and the hornets will swarm about your legs and hands, and fly into your face and eyes."[133]

Adams seemed more orthodox in his earlier years. He and Thomas Jefferson both saw Christianity as natural law rather than revealed religion.

John Adams letter to Thomas Jefferson, July 16, 1814:
"I am bold to say that neither you nor I will live to See the Course which 'the Wonders of the Times' will take. Many years, and perhaps Centuries must pass, before the current will acquire a Settled direction. If the Christian Religion as I understand it, or as you understand it, Should maintain its Ground as I believe it will; yet Platonick Pythagoric, Hindoo, and cabballistical Christianity which is Catholic Christianity, and which has prevailed for 1500 Years, has recd. a mortal Wound of which the Monster must finally

die; yet So Strong is his constitution that he may endure for Centuries before he expires."[134]

"Whatever may have been the private sentiments of Mr. Madison on the subject of religion, he was never known to declare any hostility to it." - Episcopal Bishop William Meade

---

Our fourth President, James Madison, has been seen as the primary author of the Constitution and the Bill of Rights, though by no means the only significant contributor. He was a leading proponent of religious liberty and of the limitation of the power of the new republic to protect the rights of the individual against the majority. He was a primary advisor and speech writer for President Washington,[135] author of many of the Federalist Papers, along with Alexander Hamilton and John Jay, and advanced religious freedom legislation in his home state of Virginia. Madison's actual religious views were something he did not disclose.

> Episcopal Bishop of Virginia, William Meade, as published in 1886:
> "Whatever may have been the private sentiments of Mr. Madison on the subject of religion, he was never known to declare any hostility to it. He always treated it with respect, attended public worship in his neighborhood, invited ministers of religion to his house, had family prayers on such occasions--though he did not kneel himself at prayers." [136]

> James Madison to William Bradford, Sept. 25, 1773: "I cannot however suppress thus much of my advice on that head that you would always keep the Ministry obliquely in View whatever your profession be. This will lead you to cultivate an acquaintace occasionally with the most sublime of all Sciences and will qualify you for a change of public character if you should hereafter desire it. I have sometimes thought there could not be a stronger testimony in favor of Religion or against temporal Enjoyments even the most rational and manly than for men who occupy the most honorable and gainful departments and are rising in reputation and

> wealth, publicly to declare their unsatisfatoriness by becoming fervent Advocates in the cause of Christ."[137]

In a letter, John Adams described how both Madison and Jefferson were often accused of being atheists because of their advocacy for separating church and state. Adams thought both had been wronged by Alexander Hamilton who had more traditional views.

> John Adams to Benjamin Rush in September of 1812: "The pious and virtuous Hamilton, in 1790 began to teach our Nation Christianity, and to commission his Followers to cry down Jefferson and Madison as Atheists, in league with The French Nation, who were all Atheists. Your 'British Federalists,' and your 'Tory Federalists,' instantly joined in the clamour; their Newspapers and their Pulpits, at least in New England have resounded with these denunciations now for many years. At the Same time, Great Britain has been represented as the Bulwark of civil Liberty and the Protestant Religion. All the pious Souls in the World are in England and America...
>
> "At the Same time, how Shall We vindicate our Friends Jefferson and Madison? You and I know that they very early read and Studied Fournaux's Controversy with Blackstone, and Priestleys Controversy with Blackstone, on the Subject of Ecclesiastical Establishment. They read also Blackburnes Confessional. From these and Lock and Price &c they adopted a System, which they had influence enough to introduce into Virginia. They abolished the whole Establishment. This was enough to procure them the Characters of Atheists, all over the World. I mean among the fanatical Advocates for Establishment, and these have been almost universally the fashionable Advocates, till very lately all over the Christian World."[138]

Whereas Madison wrote little on his religious views, his friend and fellow Virginian, Thomas Jefferson, left no doubt to his beliefs as expressed in private correspondence. Our third president, Jefferson had an immeasurable influence on the ideas embodied by our government and was the primary author of the Declaration of Independence. He had strong opinions about Christianity, good and bad, and it was clear that he opposed the orthodoxy, despite his religious upbringing.

"To the corruptions of Christianity, I am indeed opposed; but not to the genuine precepts of Jesus himself." - President Thomas Jefferson

---

> Thomas Jefferson to Dr. Benjamin Rush, Apr. 21, 1803 (emphasis his):
> "Christian religion was sometimes our topic; and I then promised you, that one day or other, I would give you my views of it. They are the result of a life of inquiry & reflection, and very different from that anti-Christian system imputed to me by those who know nothing of my opinions. To the corruptions of Christianity I am indeed opposed; but not to the genuine precepts of Jesus himself. I am a Christian, in the only sense he wished any one to be; sincerely attached to his doctrines, in preference to all others; ascribing to himself every <u>human</u> excellence; & believing he never claimed any other...
>
> "I am moreover averse to the communication of my religious tenets to the public; because it would countenance the presumption of those who have endeavored to draw them before that tribunal, and to seduce public opinion to erect itself into that inquisition over the rights of conscience, which the laws have so justly proscribed. It behoves every man who values liberty of conscience for himself, to resist invasions of it in the case of others; or their case may, by change of circumstances, become his own. It behoves him, too, in his own case, to give no example of concession, betraying the common right of independent opinion, by answering questions of faith, which the laws have left between God & himself."[139]

"The artificial structures they have built on the purest of all moral systems, for the purpose of deriving from it pence and power."
- President Thomas Jefferson

Jefferson praised what he called the deism of Jesus.

> Thomas Jefferson letter to John Adams, 1817:
> "I join you therefore in sincere congratulations that this den of the priesthood is at length broken up, and that a protestant popedom is no longer to disgrace the American history and character. if, by

religion, we are to understand Sectarian dogmas, in which no two of them agree, then your exclamation on that hypothesis is just, 'that this would be the best of all possible worlds, if there were no religion in it': but if the moral precepts, innate in man, and made a part of his physical constitution, as necessary for a social being, if the sublime doctrines of philanthropism, and deism taught us by Jesus of Nazareth in which all agree, constitute true religion, then, without it, this would be, as you again say, 'something not fit to be named, even indeed a Hell.'"[140]

Thomas Jefferson letter to Margaret Bayard Smith, Aug. 6, 1816: "For it is in our lives, and not from our words, that our religion must be read. by the same test the world must judge me. but this does not satisfy the priesthood. they must have a positive, a declared assent to all their interested absurdities. my opinion is that there would never have been an infidel, if there had never been a priest. the artificial structures they have built on the purest of all moral systems, for the purpose of deriving from it pence and power, revolts those who think for themselves, and who read in that system only what is really there."[141]

To Jefferson, the deism of Jesus and natural morality accessible by reason represented true Christianity. Presidents Jefferson and Adams left us a wealth of information as to their religious thinking in the many letters written between them. The religious establishment over the previous fifteen centuries was often a target of their contempt, even as the teachings of Jesus was often praised.

Thomas Jefferson writing to John Adams in 1814:
"The Christian priesthood, finding the doctrines of Christ leveled to every understanding, and too plain to need explanation, saw in the mysticisms of Plato materials with which they might build up an artificial system, which might, from its indistinctness, admit everlasting controversy, give employment for their order and introduce it to profit, power and pre-eminence."[142]

Thomas Jefferson, letter to John Adams, Apr. 11, 1823: "The truth is that the greatest enemies to the doctrines of Jesus are those calling themselves the expositors of them, who have perverted them for the structure of a system of fancy absolutely incomprehensible, and without any foundation in his genuine words. and the day will come when the mystical generation of Jesus, by the supreme being as his father in the womb of a virgin will be classed with the fable of the generation of Minerva in the brain of Jupiter. but we may hope that the dawn of reason and freedom of thought in these United States will do away all this artificial scaffolding, and restore to us the primitive and genuine doctrines of this the most venerated reformer of human errors."[143]

"A short time elapsed after the death of the great reformer of the Jewish religion, before his principles were departed from."
- President Thomas Jefferson

Jefferson considered the Bible corrupted.

> Thomas Jefferson, letter to John Adams, January 24, 1814:
> "The whole history of these books [the Gospels] is so defective and doubtful that it seems vain to attempt minute enquiry into it: and such tricks have been played with their text, and with the texts of other books relating to them, that we have a right, from that cause, to entertain much doubt what parts of them are genuine. In the New Testament there is internal evidence that parts of it have proceeded from an extraordinary man; and that other parts are of the fabric of very inferior minds. It is as easy to separate those parts, as to pick out diamonds from dunghills."[144]
>
> Thomas Jefferson to Moses Robinson, March 23, 1801:
> "The Christian religion, when divested of the rags in which they [the clergy] have enveloped it, and brought to the original purity and simplicity of its benevolent institutor, is a religion of all others most friendly to liberty, science, and the freest expansion of the human mind."[145]
>
> Thomas Jefferson, to Samuel Kercheval, Feb. 19, 1810:
> "A short time elapsed after the death of the great reformer of the Jewish religion, before his principles were departed from by those who professed to be his special servants, and perverted into an engine for enslaving mankind, and aggrandising their oppressors in Church and State; that the purest system of morals ever before preached to man, has been adulterated and sophisticated by artificial constructions, into a mere contrivance to filch wealth and

> power to themselves; that rational men not being able to swallow their impious heresies, in order to force them down their throats, they raise the hue and cry of infidelity, while themselves are the greatest obstacles to the advancement of the real doctrines of Jesus, and do in fact constitute the real Anti-Christ."[146]

Jefferson described his belief in a creator God, the existence of which he found every evidence in favor.

> Thomas Jefferson letter to John Adams, 1823:
> "I hold (without appeal to revelation) that when we take a view of the Universe, in it's parts general or particular, it is impossible for the human mind not to percieve and feel a conviction of design, consummate skill, and indefinite power in every atom of it's composition. the movements of the heavenly bodies, so exactly held in their course by the balance of centrifugal and centripetal forces, the structure of our earth itself, with it's distribution of lands, waters and atmosphere, animal and vegetable bodies, examined in all their minutest particles, insects mere atoms of life, yet as perfectly organised as man or mammoth, the mineral substances, their generation and uses,
>
> "it is impossible, I say, for the human mind not to believe that there is, in all this, design, cause and effect, up to an ultimate cause, a fabricator of all things from matter and motion, their preserver and regulator while permitted to exist in their present forms, and their regenerator into new and other forms. we see, too, evident proofs of the necessity of a superintending power to maintain the Universe in it's course and order. stars, well known, have disappeared, new ones have come into view, comets, in their incalculable courses, may run foul of suns and planets and require renovation under other laws; certain races of animals are become extinct; and were there no restoring power, all existences might extinguish successively, one by one, until all should be reduced to a shapeless chaos."

Jefferson predated Darwin and the introduction of evolution, and I can't help but wonder what he would have thought of it. He went to great lengths to separate what he saw as the moral teachings of Jesus from the religion created around him. In his later years, he went so far as to use scissors to cut out only the parts of the Bible that he felt truly originated from Jesus and then compiled them into a revised order. The result was something that has come to be known as the Jefferson Bible, now available online at the Smithsonian Institute web site.[147] Jefferson was considerate of the church he was brought up in, even if he wasn't a follower.[148]

> Thomas Jefferson to Charles Thompson Jan 9, 1816:
> "A more beautiful or precious morsel of ethics I have never seen; it is a document in proof that I am a real Christian, that is to say, a disciple of the doctrines of Jesus, very different from the Platonists, who call me infidel and themselves Christians and preachers of the gospel, while they draw all their characteristic dogmas from what its author never said nor saw. They have compounded from the heathen mysteries a system beyond the comprehension of man, of which the great reformer of the vicious ethics and deism of the Jews, were he to return on earth, would not recognize one feature."[149]

"The greatest of all the reformers of the depraved religion of his own country, was Jesus of Nazareth." - President Thomas Jefferson

---

> Thomas Jefferson to William Short, October 31, 1819: "As you say of yourself, I too am an Epicurian. I consider the genuine (not the imputed) doctrines of Epicurus as containing everything rational in moral philosophy which Greece and Rome have left us... The greatest of all the reformers of the depraved religion of his own country, was Jesus of Nazareth. Abstracting what is really his from the rubbish in which it is buried, easily distinguished by its lustre from the dross of his biographers, and as separable from that as the diamond from the dunghill, we have the outlines of a system of the most sublime morality which has ever fallen from the lips of man; outlines which it is lamentable he did not live to fill up.
>
> "Epictetus and Epicurus give laws for governing ourselves, Jesus a supplement of the duties and charities we owe to others. The establishment of the innocent and genuine character of this benevolent moralist, and the rescuing it from the imputation of imposture, which has resulted from artificial systems, invented by ultra-Christian sects, unauthorized by a single word ever uttered by him, is a most desirable object, and one to which Priestley has successfully devoted his labors and learning. It would in time, it is to be hoped, affect a quiet euthanasia of the heresies of bigotry and

fanaticism which have so long triumphed over human reason, and so generally and deeply afflicted mankind."[150]

The young and brilliant author of much of our nation's financial structure, Alexander Hamilton served as our first Secretary of the Treasury. He was born in the Caribbean but moved to New York to attend college. An aide-de-camp to George Washington in the Revolutionary War, Hamilton would become an author of the Federalist Papers and was credited with establishing the National Mint, the Bank of the United States, the first Coast Guard and promoting industry and trade.[151]

"How clearly is it proved by this that the praise of a civilized world is justly due to Christianity." - Alexander Hamilton

---

He was opposed to both Adams and Jefferson in their runs for President and remained very politically active even after leaving office.[152] Only after Jefferson and Aaron Burr tied in electoral votes in 1800 did Hamilton move to support Jefferson. Burr would kill Hamilton in a duel four years later. Hamilton denounced the atheism in the French Revolution and felt they relapsed into barbarism because they had rejected Christianity.

"War, by the influence of the humane principles of that religion, has been stripped of half its horrors" - Alexander Hamilton

---

Fragment on the French Revolution by Alexander Hamilton:
"Facts, numerous and unequivocal, demonstrate that the present ÆRA is among the most extraordinary which have occurred in the history of human affairs. Opinions, for a long time, have been gradually gaining ground, which threaten the foundations of religion, morality, and society. An attack was first made upon the Christian revelation, for which natural religion was offered as the substitute. The Gospel was to be discarded as a gross imposture, but the being and attributes of god, the obligations of piety, even the doctrine of a future state of rewards and punishments, were to be retained and cherished."[153]

Alexander Hamilton writing 1799 on The War in Europe: "German patriotism is a heinous offence in the eyes of French patriots. How are we to solve this otherwise than by observing that the French are influenced by the same spirit of domination which governed the ancient Romans. They considered themselves as having a right to be the masters of the world, and to treat the rest of mankind as their vassals. How clearly is it proved by this that the praise of a civilized world is justly due to Christianity; war, by the influence of the humane principles of that religion, has been stripped of half its horrors. The French renounce Christianity, and they relapse into barbarism; war resumes the same hideous and savage form which it wore in the ages of Gothic and Roman violence." [154]

"No provision in our Constitution ought to be dearer to man than that which protects the rights of conscience against the enterprises of the civil authority." - President Thomas Jefferson

---

It is perhaps because some of these men were not orthodox Christians that they battled so fervently for universal religious liberty.

Of Church and State

The United States of America is a bastion for religious liberty because its founders chose to separate ecclesiastical and civil matters. This radical departure from the established tradition was evidenced by the fact that our nation's Constitution was a document of civil authority only and completely devoid of theological adulation and reference, not because they lacked belief in a deity or support for religion, but because they thought belief was a matter best left to the individual and not within the jurisdiction of government. One cannot allow religion a role in government without at the same time allowing government a role in religion. The freedom of thought and belief, or liberty of conscience, freed the people out of religious slavery and brought them one step further on the road to equal liberty for all, but it was controversial.

"It is now no more that toleration is spoken of as if it were the indulgence of one class of people that another enjoyed the exercise of their inherent natural rights." - President George Washington

---

> Thomas Jefferson to the Society of the Methodist Episcopal Church, Feb. 4, 1809:
> "No provision in our Constitution ought to be dearer to man than that which protects the rights of conscience against the enterprises of the civil authority. It has not left the religion of its citizens under the power of its public functionaries, were it possible that any of these should consider a conquest over the consciences of men either attainable or applicable to any desirable purpose." [155]
>
> George Washington, letter to the Hebrew congregation at Newport, August 1790:
> "The citizens of the United States of America have a right to applaud themselves for having given to mankind examples of an enlarged and liberal policy; a policy worthy of imitation. All possess alike liberty of conscience and immunities of citizenship. It is now no more that toleration is spoken of as if it were the indulgence of one class of people that another enjoyed the exercise of their inherent natural rights, for, happily, the Government of the United States, which gives to bigotry no sanction, to persecution no assistance, requires only that they who live under its protection should demean themselves as good citizens in giving it on all occasions their effectual support."[156]

"[The Constitution] has not left the religion of its citizens under the power of its public functionaries." - President Thomas Jefferson

---

> George Washington letter to William White, March 3, 1797: "Believing, as I do, that Religion & Morality are the essential pillars of Civic society, I view, with unspeakable pleasure, that harmony & Brotherly love which characterizes the Clergy of different denominations—as well in this, as in other parts of the United States: exhibiting to the world a new & interesting spectacle, at once

> the pride of our Country and the surest basis of universal Harmony."[157]

George Washington clearly defined religious belief as a matter for which only the individual was responsible. He presumed the existence of a God, but belief in God was not made a prerequisite of American citizenship or civil participation.

> Washington letter to the Annual Meeting of the Quakers, 1789:
> "While men perform their social duties faithfully, they do all that society or the state can with propriety demand or expect; and remain responsible only to their Maker for their religion, or modes of faith, which they may prefer or profess."[158]

"Every man... ought to be protected in worshipping the Deity according to the dictates of his own conscience."
- President George Washington

> Washington letter to United Baptist Churches in Virginia, May 10, 1789:
> "If I could have entertained the slightest apprehension that the Constitution framed in the Convention, where I had the honor to preside, might possibly endanger the religious rights of any ecclesiastical society, certainly I would never have placed my signature to it; and if I could now conceive that the general government might ever be so administered as to render the liberty of conscience insecure, I beg you will be persuaded that no one would be more zealous than myself to establish effectual barriers against the horrors of spiritual tyranny, and every species of religious persecution. For you doubtless, remember that I have often expressed my sentiment, that every man, conducting himself as a good citizen, and being accountable to God alone for his religious opinions, ought to be protected in worshipping the Deity according to the dictates of his own conscience. [159]

"When a religion is good, I conceive it will support itself."
- Benjamin Franklin

This nation was not unique because it was Christian. Most of the European countries from which our forefathers migrated, and in many cases fled, were explicitly founded on Christianity. What differentiated this new nation was the separation of religion and government. In a letter written three years after retiring as President, James Madison spoke of the decision to separate these forces.

"I have no doubt that every new example will succeed... in shewing that religion & Govt. will both exist in greater purity, the less they are mixed together." - President James Madison

---

> James Madison to Edward Livingston, July 10, 1822:
> "Notwithstanding the general progress made within the two last centuries in favour of this branch of liberty, & the full establishment of it, in some parts of our Country, there remains in others a strong bias towards the old error, that without some sort of alliance or coalition between Govt. & Religion neither can be duly supported. Such indeed is the tendency to such a coalition, and such its corrupting influence on both the parties, that the danger cannot be too carefully guarded agst. And in a Govt. of opinion, like ours, the only effectual guard must be found in the soundness and stability of the general opinion on the subject. Every new & successful example therefore of a perfect separation between ecclesiastical and civil matters, is of importance. And I have no doubt that every new example will succeed, as every past one has done, in shewing that religion & Govt. will both exist in greater purity, the less they are mixed together.

[In Virginia] it is impossible to deny that Religion prevails with more zeal, and a more exemplary priesthood, than it ever did when established and patronized by Public authority."
- President James Madison

> "It was the belief of all Sects at one time that the establishment of Religion by law was right & necessary; that the true Religion ought to be established in exclusion of all others; and that the only question to be decided was, which was the true Religion. The

example of Holland proved that a toleration of Sects dissenting from the established Sect, was safe and even useful. The example of the Colonies now States, which rejected Religious establishments altogether, proved that all Sects might be safely & advantageously put on a footing of equal & entire freedom. And a continuance of their example since the Declaration of Independence has shewn, that its success in Colonies was not to be ascribed to their connection with the parent Country.

"If a further confirmation of the truth could be wanted, it is to be found in the examples furnished by the States which have abolished their religious Establishments. I can not speak particularly of any of the cases excepting that of Virginia, where it is impossible to deny that Religion prevails with more zeal, and a more exemplary priesthood, than it ever did when established and patronized by Public authority. We are teaching the world the great truth that Govts. do better without Kings & Nobles than with them. The merit will be doubled by the other lesson that Religion flourishes in greater purity, without than with the aid of Govt."[160]

Benjamin Franklin, to Richard Price, October 9, 1780:
"When a religion is good, I conceive it will support itself; and when it does not support itself, and God does not take care to support it so that its professors are obliged to call for help of the civil power, 'tis a sign, I apprehend, of its being a bad one." [161]

Most of the colonies disbanded religious establishment once the Declaration of Independence was signed. Our Constitution's First Amendment stated "Congress shall make no law respecting an establishment of religion, or prohibiting the free exercise thereof". It removed from the province of civil administration those most sacred natural rights of the mind upon which all freedom is based.

Thomas Jefferson to Chesterfield, Virginia Baptist Association, November 21, 1808:
"We have solved, by fair experiment, the great and interesting question whether freedom of religion is compatible with order in government, and obedience to the laws, And we have experienced the quiet as well as the comfort which results from leaving every one to profess freely and openly those principles of religion which are the inductions of his own reason, and the serious convictions of his own inquiries." [162]

Alexander Hamilton echoed the mindset that people can be obedient to a civil government regardless of their religious leanings.

"Whatever speculative notions of religion may be entertained, men will not, on that account, be enemies to a government that affords them protection and security." - Alexander Hamilton

---

> The Works of Alexander Hamilton, Volume 4:
> "There is a bigotry in politics as well as in religions, equally pernicious in both. The zealots, of either description, are ignorant of the advantage of a spirit of toleration. It was a long time before the kingdoms of Europe were convinced of the folly of persecution with respect to those who were schismatics from the established church. The cry was, these men will be equally the disturbers of the Hierarchy and of the State. While some kingdoms were impoverishing and depopulating themselves by their severities to the non-conformists, their wiser neighbors were reaping the fruits of their folly, and augmenting their own numbers, industry, and wealth, by receiving, with open arms, the persecuted fugitives. Time and experience have taught a different lesson: and there is not an enlightened nation which does not now acknowledge the force of this truth, that whatever speculative notions of religion may be entertained, men will not, on that account, be enemies to a government that affords them protection and security." [163]

Whereas establishment combines religion and government, banning establishment separates the two. The only honest question is to what extent civil and religious matters were to be divided and to that there is no simple answer. Thomas Jefferson coined the phrase "wall of separation between church and state" in describing the original intent of the First Amendment's religion clauses. Not mentioning God in the constitution did not take God away from the people, any more than not leading prayers in public school could take God away from students. They trusted the people to reach their own conclusions and did not trust any representative of government to make those choices for them, even for something as widely agreed upon as the belief in God.

"For I have sworn upon the altar of god, eternal hostility against every form of tyranny over the mind of man." - President Thomas Jefferson

---

> Thomas Jefferson letter to Dr. Benjamin Rush, Monticello, Sept. 23, 1800:
> "The clause of the constitution which while it secured the freedom of the press, covered also the freedom of religion, had given to the clergy a very favorite hope of obtaining an establishment of a particular form of Christianity thro' the U. S.; and as every sect believes its own form the true one, every one perhaps hoped for his own, but especially the Episcopalians & Congregationalists.
>
> "The returning good sense of our country threatens abortion to their hopes, & they believe that any portion of power confided to me, will be exerted in opposition to their schemes. And they believe rightly; for I have sworn upon the altar of god, eternal hostility against every form of tyranny over the mind of man. But this is all they have to fear from me: and enough too in their opinion. And this is the cause of their printing lying pamphlets against me, forging conversations for me."[164]

"That act of the whole American people... thus building a wall of separation between Church & State." - President Thomas Jefferson

---

It is true that the words "separation of church and state" does not appear in the Constitution, but they were the words Thomas Jefferson used to describe the original intent of the religion clauses found there in a letter to the Danbury Baptist Association during his Presidency.

> Thomas Jefferson Letter to Danbury Baptist, Jan. 1, 1802:
> "Believing with you that religion is a matter which lies solely between Man & his God, that he owes account to none other for his faith or his worship, that the legitimate powers of government reach actions only, & not opinions, I contemplate with sovereign reverence that act of the whole American people which declared that their legislature should "make no law respecting an establishment of religion, or prohibiting the free exercise thereof," thus building a wall of separation between Church & State. adhering

> to this expression of the supreme will of the nation in behalf of the rights of conscience, I shall see with sincere satisfaction the progress of those sentiments which tend to restore to man all his natural rights, convinced he has no natural right in opposition to his social duties." [165]

Any promotion of religious belief or activity by the government gives it authority over thought and expression, which the founders believed generally beyond its just power. It is understandable that there were people then and now, who disagree with Jefferson and wish to see government adorned in their beliefs, but it is disingenuous to suggest that he didn't mean exactly what he said. Jefferson's first draft of the letter above was even more clear, adding:

> "Congress thus inhibited from acts respecting religion and the Executive authorised only to execute their acts, I have refrained from prescribing even occasional performances of devotion prescribed indeed legally where an Executive is the legal head of a national church, but subject here, as religious exercises only to the voluntary regulations and discipline of each respective sect."[166]

Jefferson explained, "this paragraph was omitted on the suggestion that it might give uneasiness to some of our republican friends in the eastern states where the proclamation of thanksgivings &c by their Executive is an antient habit, & is respected." James Madison and fellow presidents did give such proclamations, though Madison later expressed opposition to the practice.

> James Madison, Presidential Proclamation, 4 March 1815: "And to the same Divine Author of every good and perfect gift, we are indebted for all those privileges and advantages, religious as well as civil, which are so richly enjoyed in this favored land. It is for blessings, such as these, and more especially for the restoration of the blessing of peace, that I now recommend, that the second Thursday in April next be set apart as a day on which the people of every religious denomination, may, in their solemn Assemblies, unite their hearts and their voices, in a free will offering to their Heavenly Benefactor, of their homage of thanksgiving, and of their songs of praise."[167]

"I do not believe it is for the interest of religion to invite the civil magistrate to direct its exercises." - President Thomas Jefferson

---

While some of our most prominent founders allowed tax-payer supported chaplains in Congress and several made religious-toned Thanksgiving Proclamations, Jefferson did not. This was a difference of opinion on where the line of separation was to be drawn. Jefferson, along with Madison, sought the strictest application, but there was pushback.

> Thomas Jefferson to Samuel Miller, January 23, 1808:
> "...but it is only proposed that I should recommend, not prescribe a day of fasting & prayer. that is that I should indirectly assume to the US. an authority over religious exercises which the constitution has directly precluded them from. it must be meant too that this recommendation is to carry some authority, and to be sanctioned by some penalty on those who disregard it: not indeed of fine & imprisonment but of some degree of proscription perhaps in public opinion. and does the change in the nature of the penalty make the recommendation the less a law of conduct for those to whom it is directed?

"Fasting & prayer are religious exercises." - President Thomas Jefferson

---

> "I do not believe it is for the interest of religion to invite the civil magistrate to direct its exercises, its discipline or its doctrines: nor of the religious societies that the General government should be invested with the power of effecting any uniformity of time or matter among them. fasting & prayer are religious exercises. the enjoining them an act of discipline, every religious society has a right to determine for itself the times for these exercises & the objects proper for them according to their own particular tenets. and this right can never be safer than in their own hands, where the constitution has deposited it.

"Every one must act according to the dictates of his own reason, & mine tells me that civil powers alone have been given to the President." - President Thomas Jefferson

---

> "I am aware that the practice of my predecessors may be quoted. but I have ever believed that the example of State executives led to the assumption of that authority by the general government, without due examination, which would have discovered that what might be a right in a state government, was a violation of that right when assumed by another. be this as it may every one must act according to the dictates of his own reason, & mine tells me that civil powers alone have been given to the President of the US. and no authority to direct the religious exercises of his constituents."

"The Constitution of the U.S. forbids every thing like an establishment of a national religion." - President James Madison

---

The precedent of the others and the implications did raise concerns. The opinion James Madison offers in the following document, written sometime around 1817-1823 and not made public until years after his death, resembles Jefferson. The document, that researchers identify as "Madison's Detached Memorandum", outlined his views and addressed what he felt were dangerous encroachments on individual liberty allowed by our early leaders, himself included.

> James Madison, Detached Memorandum, ca. 31 January 1820:
> "Is the appointment of Chaplains to the two Houses of Congress consistent with the Constitution, and with the pure principle of religious freedom? In strictness the answer on both points must be in the negative. The Constitution of the U.S. forbids every thing like an establishment of a national religion. The law appointing Chaplains establishes a religious worship for the national representatives, to be performed by Ministers of religion, elected by a majority of them; and these are to be paid out of the national taxes. Does not this involve the principle of a national establishment, applicable to a provision for a religious worship for the Constituent as well as of the representative Body, approved by

the majority, and conducted by Ministers of religion paid by the entire nation.

"The establishment of the chaplainship to Congs is a palpable violation of equal rights, as well as of Constitutional principles: The tenets of the chaplains elected shut the door of worship agst the members whose creeds & consciences forbid a participation in that of the majority. To say nothing of other sects, this is the case with that of Roman Catholics & Quakers who have always had members in one or both of the Legislative branches. Could a Catholic clergyman ever hope to be appointed a Chaplain? To say that his religious principles are obnoxious or that his sect is small, is to lift the evil at once and exhibit in its naked deformity the doctrine that religious truth is to be tested by numbers or that the major sects have a right to govern the minor.

"The object of this establishment is seducing; the motive to it is laudable."
- President James Madison

"If Religion consist in voluntary acts of individuals, singly, or voluntarily associated, and it be proper that public functionaries, as well as their Constituents shd discharge their religious duties, let them like their Constituents, do so at their own expence. How small a contribution from each member of Congs wd suffice for the purpose? How just wd it be in its principle? How noble in its exemplary sacrifice to the genius of the Constitution; and the divine right of conscience? Better also to disarm in the same way the precedent of Chaplainships for the army and navy, than erect it into a political authority in matters of religion. The object of this establishment is seducing; the motive to it is laudable. But is it not safer to adhere to a right principle, & trust to its consequences, than confide in the reasoning however specious in favor of a wrong one..."

"In their individual capacities... they might unite in recommendations of any sort whatever." - President James Madison

---

> "Religious proclamations by the Executive recommending thanksgivings & fasts are shoots from the same root with the legislative acts reviewed. Altho' recommendations only, they imply a religious agency, making no part of the trust delegated to political rulers... In their individual capacities, as distinct from their official station, they might unite in recommendations of any sort whatever; in the same manner as any other individuals might do. But then their recommendations o⟨ught?⟩ to express the true character from which they emanate..."

Madison said, even if the whole country shared a belief in one nation under God, it should be the subject of its religious institutions, not its political institutions.

> "The idea also of a union of all w⟨ho?⟩ form one nation under one Govt. in acts of devotion to the God of all is an imposing idea. But reason and the principles of the Xn religion require that ⟨if?⟩ all the individuals composing a nation were of the same precise creed & wished to unite in a universal act of religio⟨n⟩ at the same time, the union ought to be effected thro' the intervention of their religious not of their political representatives...
>
> The 1st. Proclamation of Genl. Washington dated Jany. 1. 1795 recommending a day of thanksgiving, embraced all who believed in a supreme ruler of the Universe. That of Mr. Adams called for a Xn wors⟨hip.⟩ Many private letters reproached the Proclamations issued by J.M. for usin⟨g⟩ ⟨the⟩ general terms, used in that of Presidt. W—n; and some of them for not inserting particular⟨s⟩ according with the faith of certain Xn sects. The practice if not strictly guarded, naturally terminates in a conformity to the creed of the major⟨ity⟩ and of a single sect, if amounting to a majority. the last & not the least Objection is the liability of the practice, to subserviency to political views; to the scandal of religion, as well as the increase of party animosities."[168]

"The tendency to a usurpation... will be best guarded against by an entire abstinence of the Government from interference." - President James Madison

---

Madison said he did not feel it proper to refuse to issue such proclamations but that he attempted to word them so as to limit as much as possible the appearance of claiming a political right to direct religious observances. Controversy over this issue is aided and confused by the statements of our founders who were both public men and politicians. They certainly spoke more readily in private correspondence and as the years wore on than publicly while in office. James Madison was 83 when he wrote the following.

> James Madison letter to Jasper Adams, Sept. 1833: "I must admit, moreover, that it may not be easy, in every possible case, to trace the line of separation, between the rights of Religion & the Civil authority, with such distinctness, as to avoid collisions & doubts on unessential points. The tendency to a usurpation on one side, or the other, or to a corrupting coalition or alliance between them, will be best guarded against by an entire abstinence of the Government from interference, in any way whatever, beyond the necessity of preserving public order, & protecting each sect against trespasses on its legal rights by others."[169]

President John Adams described the drafting of our Constitution to serve the practical requirements of governance.

"It will never be pretended that [its authors] were in any degree under the inspiration of Heaven." - President John Adams

---

> John Adams, Defence of the Constitutions of Government of the USA, Vol. I:
> "The United States of America have exhibited, perhaps, the first example of governments erected on the simple principles of nature; and if men are now sufficiently enlightened to disabuse themselves of artifice, imposture, hypocrisy, and superstition, they will consider this event as an era in their history. Although the detail of the formation of the American governments is at present little known or regarded either in Europe or in America, it may hereafter become an object of curiosity. It will never be pretended that any persons employed in that service had interviews with the gods, or were in any degree under the inspiration of Heaven, more than those at work upon ships or houses, or laboring in merchandise or agriculture; it will forever be acknowledged that these governments

> were contrived merely by the use of reason and the senses... Neither the people, nor their conventions, committees, or sub-committees, considered legislation in any other light than as ordinary arts and sciences, only more important...

"Thirteen governments thus founded on the natural authority of the people alone." - President James Adams

---

> "Unembarrassed by attachments to noble families, hereditary lines and successions, or any considerations of royal blood, even the pious mystery of holy oil had no more influence than that other one of holy water. The people were universally too enlightened to be imposed on by artifice; and their leaders, or more properly followers, were men of too much honor to attempt it. Thirteen governments thus founded on the natural authority of the people alone, without a pretence of miracle or mystery, and which are destined to spread over the northern part of that whole quarter of the globe, are a great point gained in favor of the rights of mankind. The experiment is made, and has completely succeeded; it can no longer be called in question, whether authority in magistrates and obedience of citizens can be grounded on reason, morality, and the Christian religion, without the monkery of priests, or the knavery of politicians."[170]

That our nation was grounded as such is not to say that this was founded as a Christian nation, a vital distinction as it relates to law and liberty. A reflection of their intent can be seen in the wording of a Treaty negotiated at the behest of President George Washington and passed during John Adam's Presidency.

"As the government of the United States of America is not in any sense founded on the Christian Religion." - Treaty of Tripoli signed by President John Adams

---

In our nation's early years, ships from the North African States of Tripoli, Tunis, Morocco, and Algiers (known as the Barbary Coast) were a major threat in the Mediterranean, capturing merchant ships and holding their crews for ransom in a conflict between Christian and Muslim nations. This official one-page treaty was submitted to the Senate by President Adams, where it was read aloud, unanimously approved, and then signed into law on June 10, 1797. It was also published in U.S. newspapers at the time.

> Treaty of Tripoli, Article XI:
> "As the government of the United States of America is not in any sense founded on the Christian Religion, as it has in itself no character of enmity against the laws, religion or tranquility of Musselmen [Muslim], and as the said States never have entered into any war or act of hostility against any Mehomitan [Muslim] nation, it is declared by the parties that no pretext arising from religious opinions shall ever produce an interruption of the harmony existing between the two countries." [171]

> John Adams, Presidential signing statement:
> "Now be it known, That I John Adams, President of the United States of America, having seen and considered the said Treaty do, by and with the advice and consent of the Senate, accept, ratify, and confirm the same, and every clause and article thereof."

Here the President, the Congress and the public seemed to agree. While future treaties may have left off that initial statement, they said nothing to retract it. The risks of civil and religious entanglements were clear.

> James Madison letter to William Bradford, January 1774:
> "If the Church of England had been the established and general Religion in all the Northern Colonies as it has been among us here and uninterrupted tranquility had prevailed throughout the Continent, It is clear to me that slavery and Subjection might and would have been gradually insinuated among us. Union of Religious Sentiments begets a surprizing confidence and Ecclesiastical Establishments tend to great ignorance and Corruption all of which facilitate the Execution of mischievous Projects."[172]

It was not an oversight that our Constitution had no reference to God or Jesus. The oath prescribed in the Constitution for a President taking office did not include reference to God, even though the English version from which it took its inspiration did.

> U.S. Constitution, Article II, Section I.:
> "Before he [The President] enter on the Execution of his Office, he shall take the following Oath or Affirmation:--"I do solemnly swear (or affirm) that I will faithfully execute the Office of President of the United States, and will to the best of my Ability, preserve, protect and defend the Constitution of the United States."

They did include the option of affirmation because some faiths, particularly Quakers, precluded followers from swearing oaths, thus expanding its application to all. The phrase "so help me god" did appear in the English version of the oath. The phrase later came to be commonly used as a personal addition to ours as well but is not in the Constitution.

"Religion or the duty which we owe to our Creator... can be directed only by reason and conviction, not by force or violence."
 - President James Madison

James Madison detailed his intent regarding the division of church and state in the following document, written in opposition to a proposed Virginia bill called the General Assessment bill, that would have used public money for teaching the Christian religion. Though written with respect to actions of a state, Virginia's laws followed the same ideal as the Bill of Rights that Madison also authored. No text details more clearly his arguments for separation.

> James Madison, Memorial and Remonstrance, reasons for opposition, 1785:
> "We the subscribers, citizens of the said Commonwealth, having taken into serious consideration, a Bill printed by order of the last Session of General Assembly, entitled "A Bill establishing a provision for Teachers of the Christian Religion," and conceiving that the same if finally armed with the sanctions of a law, will be a dangerous abuse of power, are bound as faithful members of a free State to remonstrate against it, and to declare the reasons by which we are determined. We remonstrate against the said Bill,

"Because if Religion be exempt from the authority of the Society at large, still less can it be subject to that of the Legislative Body."
- President James Madison

1. Because we hold it for a fundamental and undeniable truth, "that Religion or the duty which we owe to our Creator and the manner of discharging it, can be directed only by reason and conviction, not by force or violence." The Religion then of every man must be left to the conviction and conscience of every man; and it is the right of every man to exercise it as these may dictate. This right is in its nature an unalienable right. It is unalienable, because the opinions of men, depending only on the evidence contemplated by their own minds cannot follow the dictates of other men: It is unalienable also, because what is here a right towards men, is a duty towards the Creator. It is the duty of every man to render to the Creator such homage and such only as he believes to be acceptable to him. This duty is precedent, both in order of time and in degree of obligation, to the claims of Civil Society...

2. Because if Religion be exempt from the authority of the Society at large, still less can it be subject to that of the Legislative Body. The latter are but the creatures and vicegerents of the former. Their jurisdiction is both derivative and limited: it is limited with regard to the co-ordinate departments, more necessarily is it limited with regard to the constituents. The preservation of a free Government requires not merely, that the metes and bounds which separate each department of power be invariably maintained; but more especially that neither of them be suffered to overleap the great Barrier which defends the rights of the people...

"Who does not see that the same authority which can establish Christianity... may establish... any particular sect of Christians?"
- President James Madison

3. Because it is proper to take alarm at the first experiment on our liberties. We hold this prudent jealousy to be the first duty of Citizens, and one of the noblest characteristics of the late Revolution. The free men of America did not wait till usurped

power had strengthened itself by exercise, and entangled the question in precedents. They saw all the consequences in the principle, and they avoided the consequences by denying the principle. We revere this lesson too much soon to forget it. Who does not see that the same authority which can establish Christianity, in exclusion of all other Religions, may establish with the same ease any particular sect of Christians, in exclusion of all other Sects...

"Implies either that the Civil Magistrate is a competent Judge of Religious Truth; or that he may employ Religion as an engine of Civil policy." - President James Madison

---

4. Because the Bill violates that equality which ought to be the basis of every law, and which is more indispensible, in proportion as the validity or expediency of any law is more liable to be impeached. If 'all men are by nature equally free and independent,' all men are to be considered as entering into Society on equal conditions; as relinquishing no more, and therefore retaining no less, one than another, of their natural rights. Above all are they to be considered as retaining an 'equal title to the free exercise of Religion according to the dictates of Conscience...'

5. Because the Bill implies either that the Civil Magistrate is a competent Judge of Religious Truth; or that he may employ Religion as an engine of Civil policy. The first is an arrogant pretension falsified by the contradictory opinions of Rulers in all ages, and throughout the world: the second an unhallowed perversion of the means of salvation.

"During almost fifteen centuries has the legal establishment of Christianity been on trial. What have been its fruits? More or less in all places, pride and indolence in the Clergy, ignorance and servility in the laity, in both, superstition, bigotry and persecution." - President James Madison

---

6. Because the establishment proposed by the Bill is not requisite for the support of the Christian Religion. To say that it is, is a contradiction to the Christian Religion itself, for every page of it disavows a dependence on the powers of this world: it is a contradiction to fact; for it is known that this Religion both existed and flourished, not only without the support of human laws, but in spite of every opposition from them, and not only during the period of miraculous aid, but long after it had been left to its own evidence and the ordinary care of Providence. Nay, it is a contradiction in terms; for a Religion not invented by human policy, must have pre-existed and been supported, before it was established by human policy...

7. Because experience witnesseth that ecclesiastical establishments, instead of maintaining the purity and efficacy of Religion, have had a contrary operation. During almost fifteen centuries has the legal establishment of Christianity been on trial. What have been its fruits? More or less in all places, pride and indolence in the Clergy, ignorance and servility in the laity, in both, superstition, bigotry and persecution...

8. Because the establishment in question is not necessary for the support of Civil Government. If it be urged as necessary for the support of Civil Government only as it is a means of supporting Religion, and it be not necessary for the latter purpose, it cannot be necessary for the former. If Religion be not within the cognizance of Civil Government how can its legal establishment be necessary to Civil Government...

"It degrades from the equal rank of Citizens all those whose opinions in Religion do not bend to those of the Legislative authority."
 - President James Madison

---

9. Because the proposed establishment is a departure from that generous policy, which, offering an Asylum to the persecuted and oppressed of every Nation and Religion, promised a lustre to our country, and an accession to the number of its citizens... It degrades from the equal rank of Citizens all those whose opinions in Religion do not bend to those of the Legislative authority...

10. Because it will have a like tendency to banish our Citizens. The allurements presented by other situations are every day thinning their number. To superadd a fresh motive to emigration by revoking the liberty which they now enjoy, would be the same species of folly which has dishonoured and depopulated flourishing kingdoms.

"Torrents of blood have been spilt in the old world, by vain attempts of the secular arm to extinguish Religious discord." - President James Madison

---

11. Because it will destroy that moderation and harmony which the forbearance of our laws to intermeddle with Religion has produced among its several sects. Torrents of blood have been spilt in the old world, by vain attempts of the secular arm, to extinguish Religious discord, by proscribing all difference in Religious opinion. Time has at length revealed the true remedy. Every relaxation of narrow and rigorous policy, wherever it has been tried, has been found to assuage the disease...

"Attempts to enforce by legal sanctions, acts obnoxious to so great a proportion of Citizens, tend to enervate the laws in general, and to slacken the bands of Society." - President James Madison

---

12. Because the policy of the Bill is adverse to the diffusion of the light of Christianity. The first wish of those who enjoy this precious gift ought to be that it may be imparted to the whole race of mankind. Compare the number of those who have as yet received it with the number still remaining under the dominion of false Religions; and how small is the former! Does the policy of the Bill tend to lessen the disproportion? No; it at once discourages those who are strangers to the light of revelation from coming into the Region of it...

13. Because attempts to enforce by legal sanctions, acts obnoxious to so great a proportion of Citizens, tend to enervate the laws in general, and to slacken the bands of Society...

“The equal right of every citizen to the free exercise of his Religion according to the dictates of conscience... is equally the gift of nature.” - President James Madison

---

> 14. Because a measure of such singular magnitude and delicacy ought not to be imposed, without the clearest evidence that it is called for by a majority of citizens, and no satisfactory method is yet proposed by which the voice of the majority in this case may be determined, or its influence secured...
>
> 15. Because finally, “the equal right of every citizen to the free exercise of his Religion according to the dictates of conscience” is held by the same tenure with all our other rights. If we recur to its origin, it is equally the gift of nature; if we weigh its importance, it cannot be less dear to us...” [173]

Now we have national polls. Other than that, every objection to such an entanglement still stands. This proposed bill, which failed to pass, was in contrast to the previously passed bill of religious freedom, authored by Jefferson and strongly supported by Madison.

“That to compel a man to furnish contributions of money for the propagation of opinions which he disbelieves and abhors, is sinful and tyrannical.” - President Thomas Jefferson

---

> Thomas Jefferson, Statute of Religious Freedom, 1779:
> "Well aware that the opinions and belief of men depend not on their own will, but involuntarily the evidence proposed to their minds; that Almighty God hath created the mind free, and the manifested his supreme will that free it shall remain by making it altogether insusceptible of restraint; that all attempts to influence it by temporal punishments, or burthen, or by civil incapacitations, tend only to beget habits of hypocrisy and meanness, and are a departure from the plan of the holy author of our religion, who being lord both of body and mind, yet choose not to propagate it by coercions on either, as was in his Almighty power to do, but to exalt it by its influence on reason alone...

"Our civil rights have no dependance on our religious opinions, any more than our opinions in physics or geometry." - President Thomas Jefferson

---

> "That to compel a man to furnish contributions of money for the propagation of opinions which he disbelieves and abhors, is sinful and tyrannical; that even the forcing him to support this or that teacher of his own religious persuasion, is depriving him of the comfortable liberty of giving his contributions to the particular pastor whose morals he would make his pattern, and whose powers he feels most persuasive to righteousness... that our civil rights have no dependance on our religious opinions, any more than our opinions in physics or geometry...

"That the opinions of men are not the object of civil government, nor under its jurisdiction." - President Thomas Jefferson

---

> "that it tends also to corrupt the principles of that very religion it is meant to encourage, by bribing, with a monopoly of worldly honours and emoluments, those who will externally profess and conform to it; that though indeed these are criminal who do not withstand such temptation, yet neither are those innocent who lay the bait in their way; that the opinions of men are not the object of civil government, nor under its jurisdiction; that to suffer the civil magistrate to intrude his powers into the field of opinion and to restrain the profession or propagation of principles on supposition of their ill tendency is a dangerous falacy, which at once destroys all religious liberty... that truth is great and will prevail if left to herself; that she is the proper and sufficient antagonist to error, and has nothing to fear from the conflict unless by human interposition disarmed of her natural weapons, free argument and debate; errors ceasing to be dangerous when it is permitted freely to contradict them." [174]

Discussing the Virginia bill above, Jefferson relayed attempts to Christianize the terms. The reference to religious belief in the preamble was limited though not entirely eliminated.

> Thomas Jefferson, Autobiography, 1821:
> "A singular proposition proved that it's protection of opinion was meant to be universal. where the preamble declares that coercion is a departure from the plan of the holy author of our religion, an amendment was proposed, by inserting the words 'Jesus Christ' so that it should read 'a departure from the plan of Jesus Christ, the holy author of our religion' the insertion was rejected by a great majority, in proof that they meant to comprehend, within the mantle of it's protection, the Jew and the Gentile, the Christian and Mahometan, the Hindoo and infidel of every denomination."[175]

James Madison also mirrored that description and explained that they felt "better proof of reverence for that holy name wd. Be not to profane it by making it a topic of legisl. Discussion & particularly by making his religion the means of abridging the natural and equal rights of all men in defiance of his own declaration that his Kingdom was not of this World."

"The settled opinion here is that religion is essentially distinct from Civil Govt." - President James Madison

---

Six years after his second term ended, James Madison wrote a letter discussing the establishment of a taxpayer supported university that would not include religious studies. These actions weren't oversights.

> James Madison to Edward Everett, Mar. 19, 1823:
> "Our University has lately received a further loan from the Legislature, which will prepare the buildings for ten professors and about 200 students... The difficulty of reconciling the Xn mind to the absence of a religious tuition from a University established by law and at the common expence, is probably less with us than with you. The settled opinion here is that religion is essentially distinct from Civil Govt. and exempt from its cognizance; that a connexion between them is injurious to both; that there are causes in the human breast, which ensure the perpetuity of religion without the aid of the law; that rival sects, with equal rights, exercise mutual censorships in favor of good morals; that if new sects arise with absurd opinions or overheated maginations, the proper remedies lie in time, forbearance and example;

"Every relaxation of the alliance between Law & religion... has been found as safe in practice as it is sound in theory."
- President James Madison

> "that a legal establishment of religion without a toleration could not be thought of, and with a toleration, is no security for public quiet & harmony, but rather a source itself of discord & animosity; and finally that these opinions are supported by experience, which has shewn that every relaxation of the alliance between Law & religion, from the partial example of Holland, to its consummation in Pennsylvania Delaware N. J., &c, has been found as safe in practice as it is sound in theory."[176]

Religion and freedom have flourished here as in no other country *because* the founders chose to protect religion *and* government from corrupting entanglements between the two. This country always was and is still overwhelmingly Christian and its history and culture are deeply influenced by that religion. Even though I am not an adherent, a great deal of my culture can be traced to Christianity. While my views are most similar to Madison and Jefferson, I realize even they were not always able to strictly walk that line of separation they advocated. It is also clear that other founders did not feel strict division was necessary, particularly for traditionally common practices.

Still, it was clearly their intention to separate civil and religious authorities and it is not a misinterpretation or misquote to reference the intent of the First Amendment as erecting a wall of separation between the two. While adversaries of our nation and culture regularly assault Christianity, the answer is not to undermine our government's secular design but to confine it to the limited role of its founding by removing inappropriate ideologies from its realm.

Revisions

Revisions have since been made which I would argue run counter to their intension, but it remains controversial. The founders did not add reference to God on our nation's money or national motto. The Pledge of Allegiance we recited in school did not even exist in their time. The first publicly available coins, half cent and one cent coins minted in 1793, instead featured the word liberty with the goddess Liberty (long ago discarded as an actual god), along with a chain and wreath, symbolic references. The effort was made, mostly in the 20th Century, to alter the nature of our government and use it to promote theology, brought on by fear that our nation appeared "heathen" and that old fear that religion or belief in God requires the state's endorsement to flourish. It has now gone on long enough that it seems as though these encroachments have always been there, though the record proves otherwise. Whether or not the founders themselves would favor the additions, we can be sure only that they did not add it themselves.

"Would not the antiquaries of succeeding centuries rightly reason from our past that we were a heathen nation?" - M. R. Watkinson

---

While the United States Constitution was adopted on September 17, 1787, by the Constitutional Convention in Philadelphia, Pennsylvania, and later ratified by conventions in each state, 77 years passed before God was first added to our government coinage. The words In God We Trust was first minted in 1864 but appeared only sporadically during the following 74 years. From Treasury Department records, it appears that the first appeal from religious citizens to reference god on U.S. coins came in a letter dated November 13, 1861, written to Secretary Chase by Rev. M. R. Watkinson, a Minister of the Gospel from Ridleyville, Pennsylvania.

> "Dear Sir: You are about to submit your annual report to the Congress respecting the affairs of the national finances. One fact touching our currency has hitherto been seriously overlooked. I mean the recognition of the Almighty God in some form on our coins. You are probably a Christian. What if our Republic were not shattered beyond reconstruction? Would not the antiquaries of succeeding centuries rightly reason from our past that we were a heathen nation? What I propose is that instead of the goddess of liberty we shall have next inside the 13 stars a ring inscribed with the words PERPETUAL UNION; within the ring the all-seeing eye, crowned with a halo; beneath this eye the American flag, bearing in its field stars equal to the number of the States united; in the folds of the bars the words GOD, LIBERTY, LAW.
>
> "This would make a beautiful coin, to which no possible citizen could object. This would relieve us from the ignominy of heathenism. This would place us openly under the Divine

> protection we have personally claimed. From my hearth I have felt our national shame in disowning God as not the least of our present national disasters."[177]

Rather than a historical reference, In God We Trust was a statement of belief and its addition was requested solely for religious reasons. It's hard then, however popular, to say that adding it did not have a purely religious purpose that exceeded the government's authority. That's not to say that historical religious references were not made by our founders, such as in various proposals for the creation of an emblem for the new country, called a great seal. They drew from biblical, Greek and Anglo-Saxon imagery and allegory, representing the history and religions of the people. The Great Seal approved on June 20, 1782, though, featured the American bald eagle, with a shield and holding arrows and an olive leaf in its claws, the unfinished pyramid and Eye of Providence. The mottos "Novus Ordo Seclorum" (new secular/worldly order) and "Annuit Coeptis" (Favored undertakings) were located with the Eye.[178]

James Madison asked, "Who does not see that the same authority which can establish Christianity, in exclusion of all other religions, may establish with the same ease any particular sect of Christians, in exclusion of all other sects?" One might add, who does not see that the same authority which can add In God We Trust to our money, could with the same ease under a different influence, add Allahu Akbar there instead? What if it was a rainbow? Or a hammer and sickle? What if it was Black Lives Matter? Or All Lives Matter? Each conveys very meaningful concepts that are felt by some as exclusionary. Should the atheist have to use money that professes a belief contrary to their own, any more than bakers should be forced to design a cake celebrating a union contrary to their beliefs and conscience? Tolerance and force are two very different things. And the intent of the government was equality of treatment, not just tolerance.

Prayers and the reading of scripture, though long allowed on a state level, caused conflict well before reaching the Supreme Court. Violence broke out in 1844, known as the Philadelphia Bible Riots, between Protestants and Catholics about which biblical text to use in schools. Homes and churches were vandalized and burned, leaving nine dead and dozens wounded. The armed conflict was finally put down by state militia. Similar conflict, though not as extreme, also occurred in other parts of the nation at the time.[179] I would argue that getting the government out of education and placing it instead under the parents' control would eliminate the constitutional issue. In the meantime, every child retains the right and ability to pray in school and parents are free to teach their children how and when to pray, without direction by the State or its representatives, which these days do not often reflect the beliefs of the parents.

The original Pledge of Allegiance, written 105 years after the adoption of the U.S. Constitution and at the verge of the 20th Century, was: "I pledge allegiance to my flag and the republic for which it stands, one nation indivisible, with liberty and justice for all." On September 8, 1892, the "The Youth's Companion" magazine out of Boston published the pledge, written by Christian-Socialist Francis Bellamy, as a text for students to read on Columbus Day that year. The pledge was printed and sent to public schools across the country. Based on a proclamation by President Benjamin Harrison, more than 12 million public school children recited the pledge on that day to celebrate the 400th anniversary of Columbus' arrival.[180] In 1942 Congress officially recognized the Pledge of Allegiance, though one year later the Supreme Court ruled that school children could not be forced to recite it. It was not until 1954 that the words "under God" were added by President Eisenhower after a campaign by religious leaders and a Catholic men's organization who argued that the pledge needed to be distinguished from similar ones used by godless communists. Eisenhower also made In God We Trust our national motto. In adding "under God" Eisenhower said:

> "In this way we are reaffirming the transcendence of religious faith in America's heritage and future; in this way we shall constantly strengthen those spiritual weapons which forever will be our country's most powerful resource in peace and war."[181]

Most Americans would not disagree but, I argue that it was beyond civil authority for a reason. Another area of dispute is the posting of the Ten Commandments in government facilities. Tough the Ten Commandments are part of the foundation of Jewish and Christian theology, it was not a foundation of American law or government. Both the Commandments and the American legal system could be considered as equally descendent from earlier Sumerian law, but the Commandments, in so much as they are unique from the Sumerian law, are entirely religious and not antecedent in any sense to our legal system. Thomas Jefferson denied that Christianity was a matter of common law, on which our legal system does rely to some extent.

"The common law existed while the Anglo-Saxons were yet Pagans, at a time when they had never yet heard the name of Christ pronounced."
- President Thomas Jefferson

> Thomas Jefferson letter to Major John Cartwright, June 5, 1824:
> "I was glad to find in your book a formal contradiction, at length, of the Judiciary usurpation of legislative powers; for such the judges have usurped in their repeated decisions that Christianity is a part of the Common law. The proof of the contrary, which you have adduced, is incontrovertible; to wit, that the common law existed while the Anglo-Saxons were yet Pagans, at a time when they had never yet heard the name of Christ pronounced, or knew that such a character had ever existed." [182]

"Here, then, was a space of two hundred years, during which the common law was in existence, and Christianity no part of it."
- President Thomas Jefferson

> Thomas Jefferson letter to Dr. Thomas Cooper, February 10, 1814:
> "For we know that the common law is that system of law which was introduced by the Saxons on their settlement in England, and altered from time to time by proper legislative authority from that time to the date of Magna Charta, which terminates the period of the common law, or lex non scripta, and commences that of the statute law, or Lex Scripta. This settlement took place about the middle of the fifth century. But Christianity was not introduced till the seventh century ... Here, then, was a space of two hundred years, during which the common law was in existence, and Christianity no part of it ... Finally, in answer to Fortescue Aland's question why the ten commandments should not now be a part of the common law of England? we may say they are not because they never were made so by legislative authority."[183]

What made the Old and New Testament Commandments unique from previous law was the declaration of one true god that should be worshiped over all other gods, to not misuse god's name, that the worship of idols would be punished and that loving of this one god and the keeping of its commandments would be rewarded. None of these things can be claimed as antecedent to the U.S. legal system and, in fact, they conflict with our most cherished American ideals of liberty of conscience and freedom of speech. The founders and the people of the time supported God and religion, but also supported their separation because they understood the lessons of history. The majority may have long represented the threat to minority liberties, but today a minority has gained inordinate sway. The same principles can protect us from both.

> James Madison to Thomas Jefferson, 1788:
> "Wherever the real power in a Government lies, there is the danger of oppression. In our Governments the real power lies in the majority of the Community, and the invasion of private rights is cheifly to be apprehended, not from acts of Government contrary to the sense of its constituents, but from acts in which the Government is the mere instrument of the major number of the constituents."[184]

Limiting the government's power to indoctrinate, however, should not infringe on the individual liberties of students.

Liberty

While the church once condemned the 'unbridled lust for freedom', it was the very thing that most animated our nation's founders and why the Bill of Rights began with the protection of our personal liberties.

"We both value too much the freedom of opinion sanctioned by our constitution, not to cherish it's exercise even where in opposition to ourselves." - President Thomas Jefferson

---

> Thomas Jefferson to John Jay, 1786:
> "It is really to be lamented that after a public servant has passed a life in important and faithful services, after having given the most plenary satisfaction in every station, it should yet be in the power of every individual to disturb his quiet, by arraigning him in a gazette and by obliging him to act as if he needed a defence, an obligation imposed on him by unthinking minds which never give themselves the trouble of seeking a reflection unless it be presented to them.

However it is a part of the price we pay for our liberty, which cannot be guarded but by the freedom of the press, nor that be limited without danger of losing it. To the loss of time, of labour, of money, then, must be added that of quiet, to which those must offer themselves who are capable of serving the public, and all this is better than European bondage."[185]

Thomas Jefferson to Peter H. Wendover, 1815: "Difference of opinion leads to enquiry, and enquiry to truth; and that, I am sure, is the ultimate and sincere object of us both. we both value too much the freedom of opinion sanctioned by our constitution, not to cherish it's exercise even where in opposition to ourselves."[186]

"Whoever would overthrow the Liberty of a Nation, must begin by subduing the Freeness of Speech." - Benjamin Franklin

---

Benjamin Franklin, via pseudonym to the New-England Courant, 1722:
"Without Freedom of Thought, there can be no such Thing as Wisdom; and no such Thing as publick Liberty, without Freedom of Speech; which is the Right of every Man, as far as by it, he does not hurt or controul the Right of another: And this is the only Check it ought to suffer, and the only Bounds it ought to know. This sacred Privilege is so essential to free Governments, that the Security of Property, and the Freedom of Speech always go together; and in those wretched Countries where a Man cannot call his Tongue his own, he can scarce call any Thing else his own. Whoever would overthrow the Liberty of a Nation, must begin by subduing the Freeness of Speech."[187]

"The freedom of Speech may be taken away—and, dumb & silent we may be led, like sheep, to the Slaughter." - President George Washington

---

George Washington to Officers of the Army, 1783: "With respect to the advice given by the Author—to suspect the Man, who shall recommend moderate measures and longer

> forbearance—I spurn it—as every Man, who regards that liberty, & reveres that Justice for which we contend, undoubtedly must—for if Men are to be precluded from offering their sentiments on a matter, which may involve the most serious and alarming consequences, that can invite the consideration of Mankind; reason is of no use to us—the freedom of Speech may be taken away—and, dumb & silent we may be led, like sheep, to the Slaughter."[188]

The ability to think things uncommon, to say things repugnant and to publish boldly the disdained or revolutionary, is the foundation upon which all liberty rests.

Chapter 4

Where Equal Rights Prevail

The leaders of the past no more trusted the common people to make decisions about their own lives economically or civilly than they did their ability to follow their own conscience in religion. Our founders thought otherwise. This nation is unique in history for shearing apart the entanglements of civil and ecclesiastical establishment and enshrining in our Constitutional Republic the personal, religious and civil liberty of its citizens. If we are to be free to choose for ourselves what religious ideology or belief to embrace, we must also accept the political and economic liberty which is its natural counterpart and accept equally the personal responsibility that comes with those freedoms. Thomas Jefferson identified the general principles of our American Republic in his first inaugural address, ideas that promoted the happiness and prosperity of the American people. Despite the restrictions and limitations of the time, nothing in his words or the constitution limited the application of American ideals by race or sex.

"We have yet gained little if we countenance a political intolerance, as despotic, as wicked, and capable of as bitter and bloody persecutions."
- President Thomas Jefferson

> Thomas Jefferson, 1st Inaugural Address, March 4, 1801: "All too will bear in mind this sacred principle, that though the will of the majority is in all cases to prevail, that will, to be rightful, must be reasonable; that the minority possess their equal rights, which

equal laws must protect, and to violate would be oppression. Let us then, fellow citizens, unite with one heart and one mind, let us restore to social intercourse that harmony and affection without which liberty, and even life itself, are but dreary things. And let us reflect that having banished from our land that religious intolerance under which mankind so long bled and suffered, we have yet gained little if we countenance a political intolerance, as despotic, as wicked, and capable of as bitter and bloody persecutions.

"During the throes and convulsions of the ancient world, during the agonising spasms of infuriated man, seeking through blood and slaughter his long lost liberty, it was not wonderful that the agitation of the billows should reach even this distant and peaceful shore; that this should be more felt and feared by some and less by others; and should divide opinions as to measures of safety; but every difference of opinion is not a difference of principle. We have called by different names brethren of the same principle. We are all republicans: we are all federalists. If there be any among us who would wish to dissolve this Union, or to change its republican form, let them stand undisturbed as monuments of the safety with which error of opinion may be tolerated, where reason is left free to combat it...

"A wise and frugal government, which ... shall not take from the mouth of labor the bread it has earned." - President Thomas Jefferson

---

"Let us then, with courage and confidence, pursue our own federal and republican principles; our attachment to union and representative government. Kindly separated by nature and a wide ocean from the exterminating havoc of one quarter of the globe; too high minded to endure the degradations of the others, possessing a chosen country, with room enough for our descendants to the thousandth and thousandth generation, entertaining a due sense of our equal right to the use of our own faculties, to the acquisitions of our own industry, to honor and confidence from our fellow citizens, resulting not from birth, but from our actions and their sense of them,

"enlightened by a benign religion, professed indeed and practised in various forms, yet all of them inculcating honesty, truth, temperance, gratitude and the love of man, acknowledging and adoring an overruling providence, which by all its dispensations proves that it delights in the happiness of man here, and his greater happiness hereafter; with all these blessings, what more is necessary to make us a happy and a prosperous people? Still one thing more, fellow citizens, a wise and frugal government, which shall restrain men from injuring one another, shall leave them otherwise free to regulate their own pursuits of industry and improvement, and shall not take from the mouth of labor the bread it has earned. This is the sum of good government; and this is necessary to close the circle of our felicities.

"Peace, commerce, and honest friendship with all nations, entangling alliances with none." - President Thomas Jefferson

---

"About to enter, fellow citizens, on the exercise of duties which comprehend every thing dear and valuable to you, it is proper you should understand what I deem the essential principles of our government, and consequently those which ought to shape its administration. I will compress them within the narrowest compass they will bear, stating the general principle, but not all its limitations.—Equal and exact justice to all men, of whatever state or persuasion, religious or political:—peace, commerce, and honest friendship with all nations, entangling alliances with none:—the support of the state governments in all their rights, as the most competent administrations for our domestic concerns, and the surest bulwarks against anti-republican tendencies:

"—the preservation of the General government in its whole constitutional vigor, as the sheet anchor of our peace at home, and safety abroad: a jealous care of the right of election by the people, a mild and safe corrective of abuses which are lopped by the sword of revolution where peaceable remedies are unprovided:—absolute acquiescence in the decisions of the majority, the vital principle of republics, from which is no appeal but to force, the vital principle and immediate parent of the despotism:—a well disciplined militia, our best reliance in peace, and for the first moments of war, till regulars may relieve them:—the supremacy of the civil over the military authority:—economy in the public expence, that labor may be lightly burthened:—the honest payment of our debts and sacred preservation of the public faith:

"The wisdom of our sages, and blood of our heroes have been devoted to their attainment." - President Thomas Jefferson

---

> "—encouragement of agriculture, and of commerce as its handmaid: —the diffusion of information, and arraignment of all abuses at the bar of the public reason: —freedom of religion; freedom of the press; and freedom of person, under the protection of the Habeas Corpus[189]:—and trial by juries impartially selected. These principles form the bright constellation, which has gone before us and guided our steps through an age of revolution and reformation. The wisdom of our sages, and blood of our heroes have been devoted to their attainment:—they should be the creed of our political faith; the text of civic instruction, the touchstone by which to try the services of those we trust; and should we wander from them in moments of error or of alarm, let us hasten to retrace our steps, and to regain the road which alone leads to peace, liberty and safety."[190]

While the Constitution was the foundation of our nation, the Declaration was the foundation of the revolution. The truths it described were a radical departure from the oppressive past.

> Declaration of Independence, 1776:
> "When in the Course of human events it becomes necessary for one people to dissolve the political bands which have connected them with another and to assume among the powers of the earth, the separate and equal station to which the Laws of Nature and of Nature's God entitle them, a decent respect to the opinions of mankind requires that they should declare the causes which impel them to the separation. We hold these truths to be self-evident: that all men are created equal; that they are endowed by their Creator with certain inalienable rights; that among these are life, liberty, and the pursuit of happiness."[191]

"We have a right to [liberty], derived from our Maker! But if we had not, our fathers have earned and bought it for us." - President John Adams

The principal idea our founders were trying to convey was that rights are not granted by government or a leader, and therefore cannot be taken away by one. They are instead a part of our nature, intrinsic in our very existence or our creation, that we possess equal rights to life and liberty, limited only by the equal liberty of others.

> John Adams, Dissertation on the Canon and Feudal Law, 1765: "Be it remembered, however, that liberty must at all hazards be supported. We have a right to it, derived from our Maker! But if we had not, our fathers have earned and bought it for us at the expence of their ease, their estates, their pleasure, and their blood."[192]
>
> John Adams letter to Thomas Jefferson, July 16, 1814: "Government has never been much studied by mankind; but their attention has been drawn to it in the latter part of the last century and the beginning of this, more than at any former period, and the vast variety of experiments which have been made of constitutions in America, in France, in Holland, in Geneva, in Switzerland, and even in Spain and South America, can never be forgotten. They will be studied, and their immediate and remote effects and final catastrophes noted. The result in time will be improvements; and I have no doubt that the horrors we have experienced for the last forty years will ultimately terminate in the advancement of civil and religious liberty, and amelioration in the condition of mankind."[193]

Though written in a time when slavery was still practiced, some religious beliefs were still oppressed and women were not equally participating citizens, the language of our Bill of Rights reflected no such prejudices and stand today, as written, to apply to all. It took time for our society to catch up to those ideals, but the structure of our government and its respect for individual liberty laid the foundations for a tremendous leap in civilization, the elimination of slavery and an unparalleled advancement to the human condition. Yes, there used to be terrible abuse and discrimination here and some of this still exists, but these things are not what America is about and are no longer as impactful as we are led to believe.

> New York Governor Andrew Cuomo, CNN, August 16, 2018: "We're not going to make America great again. It was never that great. We have not reached greatness. We will reach greatness when every American is fully engaged. We will reach greatness when discrimination and stereotyping of women, 51% of our population, is gone, and every woman's full potential is realized and unleashed and every woman is making her full contribution."[194]

In reality, we are all privileged to be in America. Even the poor here often own cell phones, games, refrigerators, microwaves, televisions, a variety of clothes and access to all manner of other luxuries, from electricity, air conditioning and running water to fast food, lattes and beer, not to mention medical care. Immigrants see the difference even if we cannot.

"What distinguishes America is that it provides a remarkably high standard of living for the 'common man'." - Dinesh D'Souza

---

> Dinesh D'Souza, Report Political Process, Feb. 23, 2006: "As a 'person of color,' I am competent to address such questions as what it is like to be a nonwhite person in America, what this country owes its minority citizens, and whether immigrants can expect to be granted full membership in this society. While I take seriously the issues raised by the critics of America, I have also developed an understanding of what makes America great, and I have seen the greatness of America reflected in my life. Unlike many of America's homegrown dissidents, I am also acutely conscious of the daily blessings that I enjoy in America... America provides an amazingly good life for the ordinary guy. Rich people live well everywhere, but what distinguishes America is that it provides a remarkably high standard of living for the 'common man'...

"Never in the history of the world, outside of the West, has a group of people eligible to be slave owners mobilized against slavery." - Dinesh D'Souza

---

> "The moral triumph of America is that it has extended the benefits of comfort and affluence, traditionally enjoyed by a very few, to a large segment of society... Never in the history of the world, outside of the West, has a group of people eligible to be slave owners mobilized against slavery... The descendants of African slaves owe their freedom to the exertions of white strangers, not to the people in Africa who betrayed and sold them... America offers more opportunity and social mobility than any other country... American Founders altered the moral hierarchy of the ancient world. They argued that trade based on consent and mutual gain was preferable to plunder. The Founders established a regime in which the self-interest of entrepreneurs and workers would be directed toward serving the wants and needs of others."[195]

A variety of things made this nation different and contributed to its remarkable success, including the acknowledgement of inalienable rights and the elimination of classes and heredity as determiners of station.

> Norman Podhoretz, Hillsdale publication: Imprimis, Oct. 2012: "First of all, unlike all other nations past or present, this one accepted as a self-evident truth that all men are created equal. What this meant was that its Founders aimed to create a society in which, for the first time in the history of the world, the individual's fate would be determined not by who his father was, but by his own freely chosen pursuit of his own ambitions... There remained, of course, the two atavistic contradictions of slavery and the position of women; but so intolerable did these contradictions ultimately prove that they had to be resolved—even if, as in the case of the former, it took the bloodiest war the nation has ever fought.

"We and our forebears have fashioned a country in which more liberty and more prosperity are more widely shared than among any other people in human history." - Norman Podhoretz

---

He explained that citizenship was not about birth or lineage, as America was an idea, and rights were not given by and therefore able to be taken away by a king or other human authority.

> "By remaining faithful in principle—and to a considerable extent in practice—to the ideas by which the Founders hoped to accomplish

> these ends, we and our forebears have fashioned a country in which more liberty and more prosperity are more widely shared than among any other people in human history... The significant upward and downward mobility in the dynamic U.S. labor market. No such mobility can be found in any of the member countries of the European Union, or anywhere else for that matter. Even in the dismal economic state our nation has fallen into today, it is still exceptional where the degree and the distribution of prosperity are concerned."[196]

That was written in 2012. Our condition since has gotten worse.

> The Monument Builders by Ayn Rand, 1962:
> "The most profoundly revolutionary achievement of the United States of America was the subordination of society to moral law. The principle of man's individual rights represented the extension of morality into the social system - as a limitation on the power of the state, as man's protection against the brute force of the collective, as the subordination of might to right. The United States was the first moral society in history. All previous systems had regarded man as a sacrificial means to the ends of others, and society as an end in itself."

Previous peoples saw a person's life as belonging to society, but here, Rand said, "the only moral purpose of a government is the protection of individual rights."[197] Our founding set the course for an incredible leap forward in health, opportunity and technology. It is better to be a minority here than perhaps anywhere else in the world. Yet, even our own citizens have the hardest time seeing America's exceptionalism.

> Brittney Griner, U.S. basketball player, in Russian court July 27, 2022:
> "No, my rights were never read to me. No one explained any of it to me."[198]

It is sadly ironic that an American athlete who was arrested in Russia in February of 2022 for possession of an unlawful drug, should be shocked that the rights enjoyed in America are not offered in other nations. This was after she had protested the American anthem the previous year. She was sentenced to 9 years in Russian prison but the same country she protested made a deal to set her free.

"How little do my countrymen know what precious blessings they are in possession of, and which no other people on earth enjoy."
- President Thomas Jefferson

> Thomas Jefferson from Paris to James Monroe, 1785:
> "I sincerely wish you may find it convenient to come here. The pleasure of the trip will be less than you expect but the utility greater. It will make you adore your own country, it's soil, it's climate, it's equality, liberty, laws, people and manners. My god! How little do my countrymen know what precious blessings they are in possession of, and which no other people on earth enjoy. I confess I had no idea of it myself."[199]

"We're not going to make America great again. It was never that great."
- NY Governor Andrew Cuomo

The greatest luxury we enjoy (or at least expect to enjoy) is the ability to think, write, believe and exist without cancellation, fines, imprisonment or death due simply to the fact that one's ideas do not meet with the approval of those in power, but some of those freedoms are slipping away. Now, being proud of American ideals is automatically considered xenophobic. To achieve greatness, we must restore our country's foundation and intent, and provide equal justice and equal liberty to all under the law regardless of race, sex or things that happened long before your birth.

"The enterprises of individuals... where equal laws and equal rights prevail." - President George Washington

---

> George Washington letter to David Humphreys, March 23, 1793:
> "If we are permitted to improve without interruption the great advantages, which nature and circumstances have placed within our reach, many years will not revolve before we may be ranked, not only among the most respectable, but among the happiest people on this globe. Our advances to these points are more rapid, than the most sanguine among us ever predicted. A spirit of

> improvement displays itself in every quarter, and principally in objects of the greatest public utility, such as opening the inland navigation, which is extensive and various beyond conception, improving the old roads and making new ones, building bridges and houses, and, in short, pursuing those things, which seem eminently calculated to promote the advantage and accommodation of the people at large. Besides these, the enterprises of individuals show at once what are the happy effects of personal exertions in a country, where equal laws and equal rights prevail."[200]

These are the same ideals upon which Martin Luther King relied in the quest for racial equality and were the ideals upon which the civil rights movement was based.

"I have a dream that one day this nation will rise up, live out the true meaning of its creed." - Martin Luther King

---

> Martin Luther King, "I have a dream" speech in D.C., 1963:
> "In a sense we've come to our nation's capital to cash a check. When the architects of our Republic wrote the magnificent words of the Constitution and the Declaration of Independence, they were signing promissory note to which every American was to fall heir. This note was a promise that all men - yes, black men as well as white men - would be guaranteed the unalienable rights of life, liberty the pursuit of happiness. It is obvious today that America has defaulted on the promissory note in so far as her citizens of color are concerned... I say to you today, my friends, though, even though we face the difficulties of today and tomorrow, I still have a dream. It is a dream deeply rooted in the American dream. I have a dream that one day this nation will rise up, live out the true meaning of its creed: 'We hold these truths to be self-evident, that all men are created equal'... I have a dream that my four little children will one day live in a nation where they will not be judged by the color of their skin but by the content of their character."[201]

Along with securing our individual freedoms, our constitution was uniquely designed to restrain the power of the federal government and balance each of its parts; as well as to balance the federal and the state powers, and small states with large states. By limiting and balancing power, the founders hoped to prevent the abuses which characterized preceding nations.

"Power is a Thing of infinite Danger and Delicacy, and was never yet confided to any Man or any Body of Men without turning their Heads."
- President John Adams

James Madison, National Gazette Essay, January 18, 1792:
"In Europe, charters of liberty have been granted by Power. America has set an example of Charters of power, granted by Liberty. This revolution in the practice of the world may, with an honest praise, be pronounced the most triumphant Epoch in its history, and the most consoling presage of its happiness, We look back, already, with astonishment at the daring outrages committed by despotism on the reason and the rights of man; we look forward, with joy, to the period, when it shall be despoiled of all its usurpations, and bound forever in the chains, with which it had loaded its miserable victims."[202]

John Adams, An Essay on Man's Lust for Power, 1807:
"Power is a Thing of infinite Danger and Delicacy, and was never yet confided to any Man or any Body of Men without turning their Heads.—Was there ever, in any Nation or Country, since the fall, a standing Army that was not carefully watched and contrould by the State so as to keep them impotent, that did not, ravish, plunder, Massacre and ruin, and at last inextricably inslave the People,—Was there ever a Clergy, that have gained, by their Natural Ascendancy over private Consciences, any important Power in the State, that did not restlessly aspire by every Art, by Flattery and Intrigues, by Bribery and Corruption, by wresting from the People the Means of Knowledge, and by inspiring misterious and awful apprehensions of themselves by Promises of Heaven and by Threats [of] Damnation, to establish themselves in oppulence, Indolence and Magnificence, at the Expence of the Toil, and Industry, the Limbs, the Liberties and Lives of all the rest of Mankind."[203]

Thomas Jefferson to C. Hammond, 18 August 1821:
"The germ of dissolution of our federal government is in the constitution of the federal judiciary; an irresponsible body, (for

> impeachment is scarcely a scare-crow) working like gravity by night and by day, gaining a little to-day & a little tomorrow, and advancing it's noiseless step like a thief, over the field of jurisdiction, until all shall be usurped from the states, & the government of all be consolidated into one. to this I am opposed; because whenever all government, domestic and foreign, in little as in great things, shall be drawn to Washington as the center of all power, it will render powerless the checks provided of one government on another, and will become as venal and oppressive as the government from which we separated."[204]

The division of powers could be seen in the structure of Congress as the House reflected equal representation of the people while the Senate reflected the equal representation of the states; the first voted on by the people and the latter by state legislatures, though that was later changed by Amendment. Our government was limited to make passing legislation more difficult.

> The Federalist No. 62, James Madison and Alexander Hamilton: "It will be of little avail to the people that the laws are made by men of their own choice, if the laws be so voluminous that they cannot be read, or so incoherent that they cannot be understood; if they be repealed or revised before they are promulged, or undergo such incessant changes that no man who knows what the law is today can guess what it will be to-morrow. Law is defined to be a rule of action; but how can that be a rule, which is little known and less fixed?"[205]

"He who knows how most skilfully to make this 'public opinion' serve his own interests becomes forthwith master in the State." – Adolf Hitler [206]

Democracy alone is not great. We seem today to have lost an awareness of the nature of our government and why a Constitutional Republic is in fact preferable to the mob rule of pure democracy, why liberty is preferable to dependency. Direct democracy would leave minorities of every type at the mercy of the majority and whoever is best able to shape their opinion. The mob is easy to manipulate.

"The ancient democracies... their very character was tyranny."
- Alexander Hamilton

> Alexander Hamilton, Speech at New York Ratifying Convention, 1788:
> "It has been observed by an honorable gentleman, that a pure democracy, if it were practicable, would be the most perfect government. Experience has proved, that no position in politics is more false than this. The ancient democracies, in which the people themselves deliberated, never possessed one feature of good government. Their very character was tyranny; their figure deformity: When they assembled, the field of debate presented an ungovernable mob, not only incapable of deliberation, but prepared for every enormity. In these assemblies, the enemies of the people brought forward their plans of ambition systematically. They were opposed by their enemies of another party; and it became a matter of contingency, whether the people subjected themselves to be led blindly by one tyrant or by another."[207]

"Democracies... have ever been found incompatible with personal security, or the rights of property." - President James Madison

---

> James Madison, Federalist # 10, November 23, 1787
> "Hence it is, that such democracies have ever been spectacles of turbulence and contention; have ever been found incompatible with personal security, or the rights of property; and have in general been as short in their lives, as they have been violent in their deaths. Theoretic politicians, who have patronized this species of government, have erroneously supposed, that by reducing mankind to a perfect equality in their political rights, they would, at the same time, be perfectly equalized, and assimilated in their possessions, their opinions, and their passions. A republic, by which I mean a government in which the scheme of representation takes place, opens a different prospect, and promises the cure for which we are seeking."[208]

"It would be the interest of the majority in every community to despoil & enslave the minority." - President James Madison

---

> James Madison letter to James Monroe, 1786: "There is no maxim in my opinion which is more liable to be misapplied, and which therefore more needs elucidation than the current one that the interest of the majority is the political standard of right and wrong. Taking the word "interest" as synonomous with "Ultimate happiness," in which sense it is qualified with every necessary moral ingredient, the proposition is no doubt true. But taking it in the popular sense, as referring to immediate augmentation of property and wealth, nothing can be more false. In the latter sense it would be the interest of the majority in every community to despoil & enslave the minority of individuals; and in a federal community to make a similar sacrifice of the minority of the component States.[209]

"An elective despotism was not the government we fought for."
- President James Madison

> James Madison, The Federalist Number 48, 1788: "An elective despotism was not the government we fought for; but one which should not only be founded on free principles, but in which the powers of government should be so divided and balanced among several bodies of magistracy, as that no one could transcend their legal limits, without being effectually checked and restrained by the others. For this reason, that convention which passed the ordinance of government laid its foundation on this basis, that the legislative, executive and judiciary departments, should be separate and distinct, so that no person should exercise the powers of more than one of them at the same time."

> James Madison, age 78, Speech in Virginia Convention, 1829: "The essence of Government is power; and power lodged as it must be, in human hands, will ever be liable to abuse. In Monarchies the interests and happiness of all may be sacrificed to the caprice and passion of a despot: In Aristocracies, the rights and welfare of the many may be sacrificed to the pride and cupidity of a few: In

> Republics, the great danger is that the majority may not sufficiently respect the rights of the Minority."[210]

"My ardent desire is... to keep the United States free from political [connections] with every other country." - President George Washington.

Today George Washington would be called an isolationist. Like his fellows, he believed in free trade. It was political alliances that they hoped to avoid.

> George Washington to Patrick Henry, 9 October 1795: "I can most religiously aver, I have no wish that is incompatible with the dignity, happiness and true interest of the people of this country. My ardent desire is, and my aim has been (as far as depended upon the Executive Department) to comply Strictly with all our engagements foreign and domestic; but to keep the United States free from political Connexions with every other country. To See them independent of all, and under the influence of none. In a word, I want an American Character; that the powers of Europe may be convinced we act for ourselves and not for others. This in my Judgement, is the only way to be respected abroad and happy at home—and not, by becomeing the partisans of Great Britain or France, Create dissentions; disturb the public Tranquility; and dissolve, perhaps forever, the Cement which binds the union."[211]

"The principle of spending money to be paid by posterity, under the name of funding, is but swindling futurity on a large scale."
- President Thomas Jefferson

The founders understood that government spending was a great threat to the country and to the liberty of those whose production must be forcibly precured to support it.

> Thomas Jefferson letter to John Taylor, May 28, 1816:
> "I sincerely believe, with you, that banking establishments are more dangerous than standing armies; and that the principle of spending money to be paid by posterity, under the name of funding, is but swindling futurity on a large scale."[212]

"As a very important source of strength and security, cherish public credit... avoiding likewise the accumulation of debt."
- President George Washington

George Washington Farewell Address, Sept. 19, 1796:
"As a very important source of strength and security, cherish public credit. One method of preserving it is to use it as sparingly as possible: avoiding occasions of expence by cultivating peace, but remembering also that timely disbursements to prepare for danger frequently prevent much greater disbursements to repel it; avoiding likewise the accumulation of debt, not only by shunning occasions of expence, but by vigorous exertions in time of Peace to discharge the Debts which unavoidable wars may have occasioned, not ungenerously throwing upon posterity the burthen which we ourselves ought to bear."[213]

"If we can prevent the government from wasting the labors of the people, under the pretence of taking care of them..." - President Thomas Jefferson

Thomas Jefferson Letter to Thomas Cooper, 1802:
"The path we have to pursue is so quiet that we have nothing scarcely to propose to our Legislature. A noiseless course, not meddling with the affairs of others, unattractive of notice, is a mark that society is going on in happiness. If we can prevent the government from wasting the labors of the people, under the pretence of taking care of them, they must become happy."[214]

"To preserve their independence, we must not let our rulers load us with perpetual debt." - President Thomas Jefferson

Thomas Jefferson to "Henry Tompkinson" (Samuel Kercheval), July 12, 1816:
"I am not among those who fear the people. they and not the rich, are our dependance for continued freedom. and, to preserve their independance, we must not let our rulers load us with perpetual

debt. we must make our election between economy & liberty, or profusion and servitude. if we run into such debts as that we must be taxed in our meat and in our drink, in our necessaries & our comforts, in our labors & our amusements, for our callings and our creeds, as the people of England are, our people, like them, must come to labor 16 hours in the 24 give the earnings of 15 of these to the government for their debts and daily expences; and the 16th being insufficient to afford us bread, we must live, as they now do, on oatmeal & potatoes; have no time to think, no means of calling the mismanagers to account; but be glad to obtain subsistence by hiring ourselves to rivet their chains on the necks of our fellow sufferers. our land holders too, like theirs, retaining indeed the title and stewardship of estates called theirs, but held really in trust for the treasury, must wander, like theirs, in foreign countries, and be contented with penury, obscurity, exile, and the glory of the nation. this example reads to us the salutary lesson that private fortunes are destroyed by public, as well as by private extravagance. and this is the tendency of all human governments."[215]

Our Constitution did not authorize the federal government to spend taxpayer funds on many of the things commonly done today, even something as fundamental as infrastructure.

"I am constrained, by the insuperable difficulty I feel in reconciling the Bill with the Constitution." - President James Madison

---

President James Madison veto issued to U.S. House of Representatives, March 1817:
"Having considered the Bill this day presented to me, entitled 'An act to set apart and pledge certain funds for internal improvements', and which sets apart and pledges funds 'for constructing roads and canals, and improving the navigation of water courses, in order to facilitate, promote, and give security to internal commerce among the several States, and to render more easy and less expensive the means and provisions for the common defence'; I am constrained, by the insuperable difficulty I feel in reconciling the Bill with the

> Constitution of the U. States, to return it with that objection, to the House of Representatives in which it originated...

"Seeing that such a power is not expressly given, by the Constitution, and believing that it cannot be deduced from any part of it without an inadmissible latitude of construction." - President James Madison

---

> "'The power to regulate commerce among the several States' cannot include a power to construct roads and Canals and to improve the navigation of water courses, in order to facilitate, promote, and secure such a commerce, without a latitude of construction departing from the ordinary import of the terms... I am not unaware of the great importance of roads & canals, and the improved navigation of Water courses; and that a power in the national Legislature to provide for them might be exercised with signal advantage to the general prosperity. But seeing that such a power is not expressly given, by the Constitution, and believing that it cannot be deduced from any part of it without an inadmissible latitude of construction...I have no option but to withold my signature from it."[216]

The constitution was intended to prevent the injustice of taxing one state to pay for improvements in another, of favoring one citizen or enterprise over another. To claim an authority beyond the powers laid out in the Constitution would require a constitutional amendment. This is something the general public still understood when they passed the 18th Amendment establishing the prohibition of alcohol. As the twentieth century wore on, the government quit asking permission to ban substances and committed other actions beyond their legitimate authority. The wall of separation between government and private commerce is at least as vital as the wall that prevented religious establishment. What we call public-private partnerships today is what used to be called fascism. Yet the distortion of the Constitution started almost from its birth. Alexander Hamilton disagreed with Madison's assessment and was willing to ignore the limits.

"The public purse must supply the deficiency of private resource."
- Alexander Hamilton

> Alexander Hamilton, Secretary of the Treasury, 1791: "It is a truth as important, as it is agreeable, and one to which it is not easy to imagine exceptions, that everything tending to establish substantial and permanent order, in the affairs of a country, to increase the total mass of industry and opulence, is ultimately beneficial to every part of it. On the credit of this great truth, an acquiescence may safely be accorded, from every quarter, to all institutions, and arrangements, which promise a confirmation of public order, and an augmentation of national resource. In countries where there is great private wealth much may be effected by the voluntary contributions of patriotic individuals; but in a community situated like that of the United States, the public purse must supply the deficiency of private resource. In what can it be so useful as in prompting and improving the efforts of industry?"[217]

This exposes a critical philosophical divide between Hamilton, Washington's Secretary of Treasury, and his Secretary of State, Thomas Jefferson. At the Constitutional Convention, both men were federalists, because they both supported the adoption of a constitution creating a limited federal government. From there, they split into two competing versions of federalism. In a letter Jefferson wrote George Washington, urging him to accept a second term as President, Jefferson identified the divide between what he called Monarchical Federalists, who supported the government "merely as a stepping stone to monarchy", and Republican Federalists, like himself, who supported the government for "its intrinsic merits".[218]

"To recover therefore in practice the powers which the nation had refused, and to warp to their own wishes those actually given."
- President Thomas Jefferson

> Thomas Jefferson to William Johnson, 1823:
> "[The federalists] endeavored to draw the cords of power as tight as they could obtain them, to lessen the dependance of the general functionaries on their constituents, to subject to them those of the states, to weaken their means of maintaining the steady equilibrium which the majority of the Convention had deemed salutary for both branches general and local. to recover therefore in practice the powers which the nation had refused, and to warp to their own

> wishes those actually given, was the steady object of the federal party.
>
> "ours, on the contrary, was to maintain the will of the majority of the Convention, and of the people themselves. we believed with them that man was a rational animal, endowed by nature with rights, and with an innate sense of justice, and that he could be restrained from wrong, & protected in right, by moderate powers, confided to persons of his own choice, and held to their duties by dependance on his own will... the cherishment of the people then was our principle, the fear and distrust of them that of the other party. composed, as we were, of the landed and laboring interests of the country, we could not be less anxious for a government of law and order than were the inhabitants of the cities, the strong holds of federalism."[219]

Alexander Hamilton started the Federalist Party, while Jefferson and James Madison created the Republican Party (later called the Democratic-Republican party). Our second president, John Adams, was a Federalist, though he often clashed with Hamilton. An event Jefferson later recounted seems particularly striking.

"Mr. Adams was honest as a politician, as well as a man; Hamilton honest as a man, but, as a politician, believing in the necessity of either force or corruption to govern men." - President Thomas Jefferson

---

> Thomas Jefferson to Dr. Benjamin Rush, Jan. 16, 1811: "I invited them to dine with me, and after dinner, sitting at our wine, having settled our question, other conversation came on, in which a collision of opinion arose between Mr. Adams and Colonel Hamilton, on the merits of the British constitution, Mr. Adams giving it as his opinion, that, if some of its defects and abuses were corrected, it would be the most perfect constitution of government ever devised by man. Hamilton, on the contrary, asserted, that with its existing vices, it was the most perfect model of government that could be formed; and that the correction of its vices would render it an impracticable government. And this you may be assured was the real line of difference between the political principles of these two gentlemen.

> "Another incident took place on the same occasion, which will further delineate Mr. Hamilton's political principles. The room being hung around with a collection of the portraits of remarkable men, among them were those of Bacon, Newton and Locke, Hamilton asked me who they were. I told him they were my trinity of the three greatest men the world had ever produced, naming them. He paused for some time: 'the greatest man,' said he, 'that ever lived, was Julius Cæsar.' Mr. Adams was honest as a politician, as well as a man; Hamilton honest as a man, but, as a politician, believing in the necessity of either force or corruption to govern men... The nation at length passed condemnation on the political principles of the federalists, by refusing to continue Mr. Adams in the Presidency."[220]

I visited Jefferson's Virginia home, called Monticello, where the three pictures he revered still hang. I felt honored to be where those men stood, looking upon those same pictures. Their political battles would forecast our own, even if the names changed over time. Jefferson was Adam's vice president, having received the next highest number of votes for the top office. Adams did not win a second term, with Jefferson elected instead. Jefferson's Republicans, changing its party name to the Democratic-Republicans in 1798, represented a limited government philosophy, referred to as Jeffersonian Democracy, that remained in power for 28 years, through the Presidency of Adam's son, John Quincy Adams. His successor, Andrew Jackson, split off from Jefferson's party, calling his simply the Democratic Party. It was opposed then by the National Republicans and, later, the Whigs, both representing ideas more common to the Federalists.[221] Abraham Lincoln was the first modern Republican. The party system was not built into our founding and the two leading parties have gained an extreme level of control over our election system.

An Armed Nation

Permitting the people to have and carry arms was a great departure from European tradition and intentionally so. No king or other despot would trust their own people with the means of self-defense, self-sufficiency or revolt. Little today draws more heated debate than the ownership and use of firearms. Emotions are manipulating in an effort to disarm the people. It is a right that has been progressively restricted, often by those who do not think the common people competent enough to handle and use them and would rather only trained specialists under their direction have access. Some further contend that the Constitution only allows state militias to keep and use arms, thus individuals would have them only at the discretion and under the supervision of the state, something our founders would never have permitted.

"A well-regulated militia, being necessary to the security of a free state, the right of the people to keep and bear arms, shall not be infringed." - U.S. Constitution, Amendment II [222]

For our nation, arms served as self-defense, but was also our means of escaping tyranny and our security against its return. For that reason alone, arms had to be in the possession of the people and not just the federal government or the states. Without the existence of privately armed citizens, we would not have won the Revolutionary War or the War of 1812. Jefferson also noted that our losses in the Revolutionary War were far less than that of the British, due to the colonists' experience with firearms and ability to aim, having been intimate in the use of arms from childhood.[223] When there was a shortage of arms during the American Revolution, George Washington was forced to retain the private weapons of departing soldiers, which he and his top officer recognized as repugnant.[224]

"Provisions will be continued for making the American people an armed nation." - President James Madison

---

President Madison responded briefly and succinctly to a letter that questioned whether Americans might conceivably be disarmed.

> James Madison to David Rogerson Williams, 1816: "The Magnitude of the object of the Legislature, so well enforced by your Excellencies own remarks, with the disposition heretofore manifested by Congress, justify a confidence that provisions will be continued for making the American people an armed nation, as the true security for their remaining a free and independent one."[225]

Patrick Henry, a legendary advocate for American liberty and five-term Governor of Virginia, spoke most eloquently.

"If our defence be the real object of having those arms, in whose hands can they be trusted?" - Patrick Henry

---

Patrick Henry speech, June 9, 1788:
"Are we at last brought to such a humiliating and debasing degradation, that we cannot be trusted with arms for our own defence? Where is the difference between having our arms in our own possession and under our own direction, and having them under the management of Congress? If our defence be the real object of having those arms, in whose hands can they be trusted with more propriety, or equal safety to us, as in our own hands?"[226]

In an earlier speech calling for rebellion against the king, Henry said:
"They tell us, sir, that we are weak; unable to cope with so formidable an adversary. But when shall we be stronger? Will it be the next week, or the next year? Will it be when we are totally disarmed, and when a British guard shall be stationed in every house? Shall we gather strength by irresolution and inaction? Shall we acquire the means of effectual resistance by lying supinely on our backs and hugging the delusive phantom of hope, until our enemies shall have bound us hand and foot?"[227]

"A free people ought not only to be armed but disciplined."
- President George Washington

George Washington, First Annual Message:
"To be prepared for war is one of the most effectual means of preserving peace. A free people ought not only to be armed but disciplined; to which end a Uniform and well digested plan is requisite: And their safety and interest require that they should promote such manufactories, as tend to render them independent on others, for essential, particularly for military supplies."[228]

"None but an armed nation can dispense with a standing army."
- President Thomas Jefferson

Along with having arms, the founders also saw the need for states to actually train and prepare militias for their own and the nation's defense.

> Thomas Jefferson, Circular to the Governors of the States, 1803: "In compliance with a request of the House of Representatives of the US. as well as with a sense of what is necessary, I take the liberty of urging on you the importance and indispensible necessity of vigorous exertions, on the part of the state governments, to carry into effect the militia system adopted by the national legislature, agreeably to the powers reserved to the states respectively, by the constitution of the US. and in a manner the best calculated to ensure such a degree of military discipline, & knowledge of tactics, as will, under the auspices of a benign providence, render the militia a sure and permanent bulwark of national defence. None but an armed nation can dispense with a standing army. to keep ours armed and disciplined, is therefore at all times important."[229]

"The constitutions of most of our states assert that... it is [the people's] right and duty to be at all times armed." - President Thomas Jefferson

---

> Thomas Jefferson letter to John Cartwright, 1824: "The constitutions of most of our states assert that all power is inherent in the people; that they may exercise it by themselves, in all cases to which they think themselves competent, (as in electing their functionaries executive and legislative, and deciding by a jury of themselves, both fact and law, in all judiciary cases in which any fact is involved) or they may act by representatives, freely and equally chosen; that it is their right and duty to be at all times armed; that they are entitled to freedom of person; freedom of religion; freedom of property; and freedom of the press."[230]

A well-armed citizenry will not be oppressed or invaded easily.

"Let them take arms... The tree of liberty must be refreshed from time to time with the blood of patriots & tyrants."
- President Thomas Jefferson

Thomas Jefferson to William Stephens Smith, 1787, speaking of Shay's Rebellion:
"We have had 13. states independant 11. years. There has been one rebellion. That comes to one rebellion in a century & a half for each state. What country before ever existed a century & half without a rebellion? & what country can preserve its liberties if their rulers are not warned from time to time that their people preserve the spirit of resistance? Let them take arms. The remedy is to set them right as to facts, pardon & pacify them. What signify a few lives lost in a century or two? The tree of liberty must be refreshed from time to time with the blood of patriots & tyrants. It is its natural manure."[231]

"Before a standing army can rule, the people must be disarmed; as they are in almost every kingdom in Europe." - Noah Webster

---

Noah Webster was a founding father and compiler of the first U.S. dictionary, who supported a stronger central government in opposition to Jefferson. Though differing on some issues, on this right they agreed.

"The advantage of being armed, which the Americans possess over the people of almost every other nation." - President James Madison

---

Noah Webster, pamphlet on the Constitution, 1787:
"Before a standing army can rule, the people must be disarmed; as they are in almost every kingdom in Europe. The supreme power in America cannot enforce unjust laws by the sword; because the whole body of the people are armed, and constitute a force superior to any band of regular troops that can be, on any pretence, raised in the United States."[232]

James Madison, The Federalist Papers No. 46:
"Besides the advantage of being armed, which the Americans possess over the people of almost every other nation, the existence of subordinate governments, to which the people are attached, and by which the militia officers are appointed, forms a barrier against the enterprises of ambition, more insurmountable than any which

> a simple government of any form can admit of. Notwithstanding the military establishments in the several kingdoms of Europe, which are carried as far as the public resources will bear, the governments are afraid to trust the people with arms. And it is not certain, that with this aid alone, they would not be able to shake off their yoke."[233]

Disarming the citizens to facilitate their oppression was nothing new, nor is the incremental method of achieving it.

"When the resolution of enslaving America was formed... the British Parliament was advised ... to disarm the people." - George Mason

---

> George Mason, delegate from Virginia to the U.S. Constitutional Convention, 1788:
> "No man has a greater regard for the military gentlemen than I have. I admire their intrepidity, perseverance, and valor. But when once a standing army is established in any country, the people lose their liberty. When, against a regular and disciplined army, yeomanry are the only defence, – yeomanry, unskilful and unarmed, – what chance is there for preserving freedom? Give me leave to recur to the page of history, to warn you of your present danger.
>
> "Recollect the history of most nations of the world. What havoc, desolation, and destruction, have been perpetrated by standing armies! An instance within the memory of some of this house will show us how our militia may be destroyed. Forty years ago, when the resolution of enslaving America was formed in Great Britain, the British Parliament was advised by an artful man, who was governor of Pennsylvania, to disarm the people; that it was the best and most effectual way to enslave them; but that they should not do it openly, but weaken them, and let them sink gradually, by totally disusing and neglecting the militia."[234]

In the American Colonies, the militia was made up of regular citizens who organized and had some training for the defense of their own communities, often with their own weapons. The militias helped protect the colonies from Indian raids and played a role in every U.S. war through the Civil War.[235]

"The Citizens of America... should be borne on the Militia Rolls, provided with uniform Arms, and so far accustomed to the use of them." - President George Washington

---

George Washington's remarks makes clear that it was intended to be made up of average citizens, with everyone in the nation being armed who was capable of bearing and using arms, with few exceptions.[236] However, the impracticality of a plan to train an entire, growing country in arms became clear. In one of the Federalist Papers attributed to Hamilton and Madison, this reality was addressed. The answer was an armed citizenry plus select sets of trained militias.

"[An] army can never be formidable to the liberties of the people, while there is a large body of citizens, little, if at all, inferior to them in discipline and the use of arms." - Alexander Hamilton

---

> Alexander Hamilton/James Madison, Federalist, # 29:
> "The project of disciplining all the militia of the United States, is as futile as it would be injurious, if it were capable of being carried into execution. A tolerable expertness in military movements, is a business that requires time and practice. It is not a day, nor a week, nor even a month, that will suffice for the attainment of it... Little more can reasonably be aimed at, with respect to the people at large, than to have them properly armed and equipped; and in order to see that this be not neglected, it will be necessary to assemble them once or twice in the course of a year. But, though the scheme of disciplining the whole nation must be abandoned as mischievous or impracticable; yet it is a matter of the utmost importance, that a well digested plan should, as soon as possible, be adopted for the proper establishment of the militia."

The founders saw the use of guns as a last resort.[237] However, they made no distinction between the type of arms the people could carry and those an army might possess.

The Acquisitions of Industry

For most of human history, property was held by the very few, while those who didn't own any toiled and survived only at the will of those who did. Under these systems, the people were not free and their lives were often short and miserable. They had little opportunity, nor the time or the means to pursue happiness or ponder any future except one they envisioned beyond this world. Their freedom and autonomy lay, not in the elimination of private property as some imagine, but in the opening to all the ability to possess it and the security that comes with it. Property and the free market are the only things that provide individuals with any measure of control over their own lives. Centralization of control and property at the top takes that away.

Property is a product of work, a store of wealth and independence and available here to anyone. The United States of America changed history by creating opportunity and an economy that allowed a majority of its citizens to own property as we do now. Without the right to property, people have no right to anything they do, not the products of their labor or the creations of their minds, and it is the role of government to protect it.

"A distinction of property results from that very protection which a free Government gives to unequal faculties of acquiring it."
- President James Madison

> James Madison, Speech during the Virginia Convention, December 1829:
> "It is sufficiently obvious, that Persons and Property, are the two great subjects on which Governments are to act: and that the rights of persons, and the rights of property are the objects for the protection of which Government was instituted. These rights cannot well be separated. The personal right to acquire property, which is a natural right, gives to property when acquired a right to protection as a social right. "[238]
>
> James Madison to Thomas Jefferson, Oct. 24, 1787: "In all civilized Societies, distinctions are various and unavoidable. A distinction of property results from that very protection which a free Government gives to unequal faculties of acquiring it."[239]

"The moment the idea is admitted into society, that property is not as sacred as the laws of God, and that there is not a force of law and public justice to protect it, anarchy and tyranny commence."
- President John Adams [240]

In addition to providing independence, private property, as a product of labor and skills, gives its owner 'skin in the game' as to all expense of national credit. The writings of the founders defended and the various state constitutions specifically secured the right to own property, meaning land and its improvements. President James Madison describes property to its full extent in an essay he wrote for the National Gazette.

> James Madison, The National Gazette, Mar. 27, 1792: "Property. This term in its particular application means 'that dominion which one man claims and exercises over the external things of the world, in exclusion of every other individual'. In its larger and juster meaning, it embraces every thing to which a man may attach a value and have a right; and which leaves to every one else the like advantage. In the former sense, a man's land, or merchandize, or money is called his property. In the latter sense, a man has a property in his opinions and the free communication of them. He has a property of peculiar value in his religious opinions, and in the profession and practice dictated by them. He has a property very dear to him in the safety and liberty of his person. He has an equal property in the free use of his faculties and free choice of the objects on which to employ them.
>
> "In a word, as a man is said to have a right to his property, he may be equally said to have a property in his rights. Where an excess of power prevails, property of no sort is duly respected. No man is safe in his opinions, his person, his faculties, or his possessions. Where there is an excess of liberty, the effect is the same, tho' from an opposite cause. Government is instituted to protect property of every sort... That is not a just government, nor is property secure under it, where the property which a man has in his personal safety and personal liberty, is violated by arbitrary seizures of one class of citizens for the service of the rest...

"A just security to property is not afforded by that government, under which unequal taxes oppress one species of property and reward another." - President James Madison

---

> "That is not a just government, nor is property secure under it, where arbitrary restrictions, exemptions, and monopolies deny to part of its citizens that free use of their faculties, and free choice of their occupations... A just security to property is not afforded by that government, under which unequal taxes oppress one species of property and reward another species: where arbitrary taxes invade the domestic sanctuaries of the rich, and excessive taxes grind the faces of the poor; where the keenness and competitions of want are deemed an insufficient spur to labor, and taxes are again applied, by an unfeeling policy, as another spur; in violation of that sacred property, which Heaven, in decreeing man to earn his bread by the sweat of his brow, kindly reserved to him, in the small repose that could be spared from the supply of his necessities."[241]

"Every new regulation... presents a new harvest to those who watch the change and can trace its consequences; a harvest reared not by themselves but by... their fellow citizens." - Federalist No. 62

Without the ability to own property, we are slaves to those who do. If only the state owns property, we are slaves to the state and its managers. Property is so vital as to be held inviolable. Instead, our laws today often reward trespassers and squatters by letting them stay and giving them ownership of the property that they illegally invade, reverting to the rules of conquest. I spent a lot of money and time going to court to prevent my neighbor from doing this very thing. I've no doubt the founders would have argued on my side.

> The Federalist No. 62 by James Madison, Alexander Hamilton, 1788:
> "Another effect of public instability is the unreasonable advantage it gives to the sagacious, the enterprising and the moneyed few, over the industrious and uninformed mass of the people. Every new regulation concerning commerce or revenue; or in any manner affecting the value of the different species of property, presents a

new harvest to those who watch the change and can trace its consequences; a harvest reared not by themselves but by the toils and cares of the great body of their fellow citizens. This is a state of things in which it may be said with some truth that laws are made for the few not for the many."[242]

"The less this exchange is cramped by Government, the greater are the proportions of benefit to each." - President James Madison

---

James Madison, Speech in the First Congress, First Session; on Duties on Imports:

"I am a friend to free commerce, and, at the same time, a friend to such regulations as are calculated to promote our own interest, and this on national principles... I own myself the friend to a very free system of commerce, and hold it as a truth, that commercial shackles are generally unjust, oppressive, and impolitic; it is also a truth, that if industry and labor are left to take their own course, they will generally be directed to those objects which are the most productive, and this in a more certain and direct manner than the wisdom of the most enlightened Legislature could point out... we should find no advantage in saying that every man should be obliged to furnish himself, by his own labor, with those accommodations which depend on the mechanic arts, instead of employing his neighbor, who could do it for him on better terms.

"It would be of no advantage to the shoemaker to make his own clothes to save the expense of the tailor's bill, nor of the tailor to make his own shoes to save the expense of procuring them from the shoemaker. It would be better policy to suffer each of them to employ his talents in his own way. The case is the same between the exercise of the arts and agriculture–between the city and the country–and between city and town; each capable of making particular articles in abundance to supply the other: thus all are benefited by exchange, and the less this exchange is cramped by Government, the greater are the proportions of benefit to each. The same argument holds good between nation and nation, and between parts of the same nation."[243]

They opposed interventionism and the manipulation of the market to favor some over others. Today we have to be able to separate the free market from its corruptions or we will surely lose it.

"That 't is folly in one nation to look for disinterested favors at from another." - President George Washington

---

> George Washington, Farewell Address, Sept. 17, 1796:
> "Harmony, liberal intercourse with all nations, are recommended by policy, humanity, and interest. But even our commercial policy should hold an equal and impartial hand:—neither seeking nor granting exclusive favours or preferences;—consulting the natural course of things;—diffusing and diversifying by gentle means the streams of commerce, but forcing nothing;—establishing with Powers so disposed—in order to give trade a stable course, to define the rights of our Merchants, and to enable the Government to support them—conventional rules of intercourse, the best that present circumstances and mutual opinion will permit; but temporary, and liable to be from time to time abandoned or varied, as experience and circumstances shall dictate; constantly keeping in view that 't is folly in one nation to look for disinterested favors at from another,—that it must pay with a portion of its independence for whatever it may accept under that character."[244]

"I think all the world would gain by setting commerce at perfect liberty." - President Thomas Jefferson

---

> Thomas Jefferson Letter to John Adams:
> "As far as my enquiries enable me to judge France and Holland make no distinction of duties between Aliens and natives. I also rather believe that the other states of Europe make none, England excepted, to whom this policy, as that of her navigation act, seems peculiar. The question then is, Should we disarm ourselves of the power to make this distinction against all nations in order to purchase an exemption from the Alien duties in England only; for if we put her importations on the footing of native, all other nations with whom we treat will have a right to claim the same. I think we

> should, because against other nations who make no distinction in their ports between us and their own subjects, we ought not to make a distinction in ours. And if the English will agree in like manner to make none, we should with equal reason abandon the right as against them. I think all the world would gain by setting commerce at perfect liberty."[245]

We can discuss how to protect individual autonomy or restrain those who engage in unfair practices, but you cannot completely distort and corrupt the market and then blame the outcome on capitalism. Capitalism was why my father's dad could go from being a teenaged indentured servant on his own in a foreign nation to becoming a homeowner and farmer. It is why my mother's parents could go from being migrant pickers to business owners. And it was why my parents, with the foothold in life given to them by their parents, could achieve the American Dream, to provide for their own children and enjoy a comfortable retirement. The market isn't perfect and does necessitate some regulation, but it works far better than an administrative state ruled by academics without real market experience. Even those who choose to work for someone else benefit from the effort of business owners. I am not deifying the free market but giving it instead the just appreciation of a fair, logical and honest system of commerce.

"Both parties undertake the exchange because each expects to gain from it." - Murray Rothbard

---

Murray Rothbard, the founder of the Center for Libertarian Studies and co-founder of the Mises Institute, explained the free market and its value:

> Murray N. Rothbard, American Economist, Mises Institute, Nov. 4, 2019:
> "The Free Market is a summary term for an array of exchanges that take place in society. Each exchange is undertaken as a voluntary agreement between two people or between groups of people represented by agents. These two individuals (or agents) exchange two economic goods, either tangible commodities or nontangible services. Thus, when I buy a newspaper from a news dealer for fifty cents, the news dealer and I exchange two commodities: I give up fifty cents, and the news dealer gives up the newspaper. Or if I work

> for a corporation, I exchange my labor services, in a mutually agreed way, for a monetary salary...
>
> "Both parties undertake the exchange because each expects to gain from it... Trade, or exchange, is engaged in precisely because both parties benefit; if they did not expect to gain, they would not agree to the exchange."

This, he explained, is how free trade differs from the 'mercantilist period' in Europe, where trade was seen as an exchange where only one party benefits.

> "The mercantilists argued that in any trade, one party can benefit only at the expense of the other, that in every transaction there is a winner and a loser, an 'exploiter' and an 'exploited.' We can immediately see the fallacy in this still-popular viewpoint: the willingness and even eagerness to trade means that both parties benefit..."

"The ultimate in government coercion is socialism." - Murray N. Rothbard

---

Some exchanges, though, are coerced. The exchange between a thief and a person being stolen from, for instance. Robbery is the mercantilist model of exploitation, not the free market.

> "Government, in every society, is the only lawful system of coercion. Taxation is a coerced exchange, and the heavier the burden of taxation on production, the more likely it is that economic growth will falter and decline. Other forms of government coercion (e.g., price controls or restrictions that prevent new competitors from entering a market) hamper and cripple market exchanges, while others (prohibitions on deceptive practices, enforcement of contracts) can facilitate voluntary exchanges. The ultimate in government coercion is socialism."

Workers do not share of the profits of a venture because they are not sharing in the risk. Capitalism worked well for Democratic Socialist Bernie Sanders. Speaking during the early days of his campaign for President, he defended the fact that he was a socialist millionaire, "I wrote a best-selling book. If you write a best-selling book, you can be a millionaire, too."[246] That is true, of course, because we have a mostly capitalist economy. There are those who claim that wealth and success are a matter of privilege only; that the only difference between the rich and the poor, the successful and the unsuccessful, is circumstance. Author George Orwell, who called himself a Democratic Socialist, and also envisioned the oppression of Big Brother in the book 1984,[247] expressed this same perspective in a non-fiction memoir.

> George Orwell, "Down and Out in Paris and London", 1933:
> "The mass of the rich and the poor are differentiated by their incomes and nothing else, and the average millionaire is only the average dishwasher dressed in a new suit. Change places, and handy dandy, which is the justice, which is the thief?"[248]

The difference between the business owner and the welfare dependent, between the justice and the thief, is not simply privilege or fortune but because as individuals they made different choices in life and put different efforts forward. No matter where you start economically, you have a choice to make about what you are going to do about it. Getting a head start from the hard work and sacrifices of one's parents does not guarantee success any more than lacking that head start guarantees failure. Life, sadly, is not fair, but it is fairer here than in the old systems where birth determined station.

"Somebody invested in roads and bridges. If you've got a business -- you didn't build that." - President Barack Obama

---

> President Barack Obama, July 13, 2012 Campaign Event in Roanoke, Virginia:
> "If you were successful, somebody along the line gave you some help. There was a great teacher somewhere in your life. Somebody helped to create this unbelievable American system that we have that allowed you to thrive. Somebody invested in roads and bridges. If you've got a business -- you didn't build that. Somebody else made that happen. The Internet didn't get invented on its own. Government research created the Internet so that all the companies could make money off the Internet.
>
> "The point is, is that when we succeed, we succeed because of our individual initiative, but also because we do things together. There

> are some things, just like fighting fires, we don't do on our own. I mean, imagine if everybody had their own fire service. That would be a hard way to organize fighting fires. So, we say to ourselves, ever since the founding of this country, you know what, there are some things we do better together. That's how we funded the GI Bill. That's how we created the middle class. That's how we built the Golden Gate Bridge or the Hoover Dam. That's how we invented the Internet. That's how we sent a man to the moon. We rise or fall together as one nation and as one people, and that's the reason I'm running for President -- because I still believe in that idea. You're not on your own, we're in this together."[249]

Our accomplishments and unity as a people and nation are extraordinary but human value does not lie only in the group. When President Barrack Obama told small business owners that they didn't build the roads and bridges used to facilitate their success, he was patently wrong. Who else paid the taxes to build those things if not business owners and the workers they employ? This is the ideology of another place, distant and yet similar. And no, I am not equating President Obama with Adolf Hitler. There is simply a commonality to the ideologies voiced by both.

> Adolf Hitler, Oct 9, 1934 speech, quoted on Mises.org: "The view that the utilization of a fortune no matter of what size is solely the private affair of the individual requires to be corrected all the more in the National Socialist state, because without the contribution of the community no individual would have been able to enjoy such an advantage."[250]

Modern progressives are closer ideologically to Hitler than to, say, Ron Paul. We *do* help each other but we also hurt each other's efforts. As Americans we have joined together in many ways and have accomplished great things, but that takes nothing away from individual initiative and private production that underlies every joint activity we undertake. Everyone may have used the public roads and enjoyed the protections of police and firefighters, but everyone did not stay late each night doing difficult, sometimes dirty work. Everyone did not work away their weekends and holidays. Everyone did not go without pay when necessary in order to pay their employees. Everyone did not make the necessary sacrifices and commitments it took to build a business, did not stress and struggle and risk every cent they earned for a chance at success and a better life. Everyone did not even pay taxes, and that is where we should be looking for everyone to "pay their fair share".

If the provision of government services were responsible for individual success, then all individuals would be successful. If the roads, national defense, public education and other services which the government or the whole provides are a benefit to those who succeed, they are also provided to those who fail and all those who never even try. Because enterprises succeed, the society maintains its roads, its defenses and its peace, and jobs are created which give others a chance to earn an income and improve their own lives. Government does not have money to spend until it takes it from the people who produce it. If, despite this burden, the entrepreneurs and inventers manage to succeed, it is a tribute to the effort, talent, ingenuity and sometimes luck they brought to the situation. Slavery was the antithesis of a free market and had to be ended for it to truly flourish. The free market economy America embraced spread around the world and, vastly reduced the number of people in poverty to, now, its lowest level ever.[251]

The American dream is not about inheriting great wealth, winning the lottery or discovering priceless art in a yard sale. The American dream, as realized by my parents and their parents before them, and so many others across this nation, is that of earning your way to success and providing a better life for your children than you had yourself. My parents, with hard work and sacrifice, were able to build a successful business that not only paid a significant amount of taxes but also employed thousands of individuals over the years, allowing them and their families to get ahead as well. We produced quality products which others were willing to buy.

Unfortunately, in the many decades since my parents began their business, regulations and taxes have severely restricted the manufacturer's ability to produce anything in America. Meeting these complex, often arbitrary or retributive regulations cost money or require the employment of professionals like lawyers and accountants. You can't build your own building or manage your own office without the sanction of government. Many businesses operate on a very small profit margin. Some regulations are specifically developed to ensure the use of best practices but most are a means of control, creating benefits for some at the expense of others, and do little to actually improve the safety and quality of products and services. The first house my parents built for my grandfather Themistocles still stands. It has been added onto and is still lived in. Perhaps not everyone is capable of doing these things themselves, but people are far more capable than many give them credit for.

The Political Spectrum

The left-right political spectrum originated in the French revolution and was based on which group, conservative or liberal, sat on either side of the government assembly.[252] Today it is defined differently in America than in Europe, but either way, it needs to be refined. There have been many versions of the spectrum but the one I remember being taught was a diamond with libertarianism at the top, authoritarianism on the bottom, liberalism to the left and conservatism on the right, known as the Nolan Chart. Top and bottom follow logic well enough but it tells you absolutely nothing about the other two, aside from suggesting they are opposites and either equal distant to top and bottom or as likely to be closer to one than the other, making it fairly meaningless.

Other charts include terms like reactionary or radical, which really doesn't tell you anything either. I believe the true spectrum of the political theory of government is simple and profound and must in fact be a single left-right scale where systems can be placed in comparison to each other based on common criteria. Where an ideology appears on the scale depends on their degree of freedom or control. The left wing or the farthest one can go, politically, to the left is tyranny and the farthest right is liberty. Saying one is a Republican or Democrat doesn't, on its own, identify a particular place on the scale, as, generally, the leadership of both parties belong well to the left.

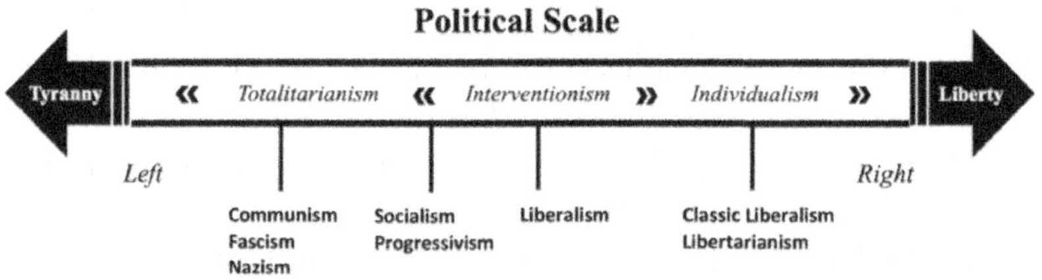

Tyranny and authoritarianism are generally interchangeable, but I use the former in order to avoid any particular political system. The more the people are free, within the bounds of civil society, the closer they move to the right on the scale. The more the people are controlled the closer it moves to the left. Tyranny is the principal characteristic of the left. The true right (not today's establishment right) is consistent with the ideology upon which our nation as founded: equality under the law, free trade and free markets, laws applied to all equally, individual liberty, and personal responsibility, which approaches individualism and in so doing nears a government of liberty. The far right is not an absence of law or anarchy because that would allow any stronger individual to play the tyrant and control and subvert the liberty of another. The more equal individual liberty is protected, the farther right that society becomes. It must be rightful liberty, as Jefferson called it, individual liberty limited only by the equal liberty of others, as we are talking about political systems, not applicable to an individual in isolation.

While it has been politically expedient to throw some systems of centralized, authoritarian control over to the right, it is not accurate. Tyranny or totalitarianism on the left can be seen in heavily controlled regimes such as communism, Nazism, fascism and religious tyranny (whether under the old Roman Catholic Church or extreme Islam). All of these governments approach tyranny through a centralized rule of a party, select group or dictator. While these regimes differ, their similarities are far more significant and none of them have any similarity with the ideals of our republic or the right as our founders saw it. The more socialized or centralized a country gets, the more individuals are sacrificed for a collective goal, the more control its government has over its people and their industry, the closer it comes to totalitarianism and tyranny.

Calling oneself a Republican or Democrat does not necessarily identify a location on that scale because politicians are neither that consistent nor that honest. Being religious or non-religious does not necessitate a particular location either. Those who wish to force a religion or ideology on others, whether in a tyrannical theocracy or nation-building, are not compatible with the beliefs of the founders. The elitists who imagine they are better qualified to run our lives than we are, due to a distorted notion of superiority, are by their very nature leftist. Our government at this point falls deep in the realm of interventionism; that is, a government that intervenes in the lives and industry of its people through progressive restrictions, extensive regulation, heavy and unequal taxation, redistribution and surveillance. Relative to other countries, though, we are still farther right than most, based on similar scales. That, unfortunately, is changing. In fact, it's fair to argue that we have now sunk well into authoritarianism – far closer to tyranny than liberty.

Figure 1 Data source Heritage.org, 2022

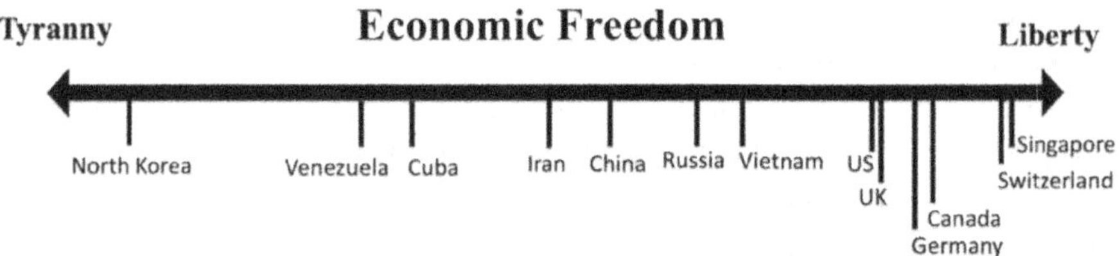

One example is the Heritage Foundation which created a ranking of nations (Figure 1) relating to their records of freedom on various economic grounds, including rule of law, government size, regulatory efficiency and open markets. This is then broken down to property rights, judicial effectiveness, government integrity, tax burden, government spending, fiscal health, and freedom in business freedom, labor, monetary, trade, investment and finances.[253] Another scale of freedom comes from the Cato Institute. These scales are my creations based on their data.

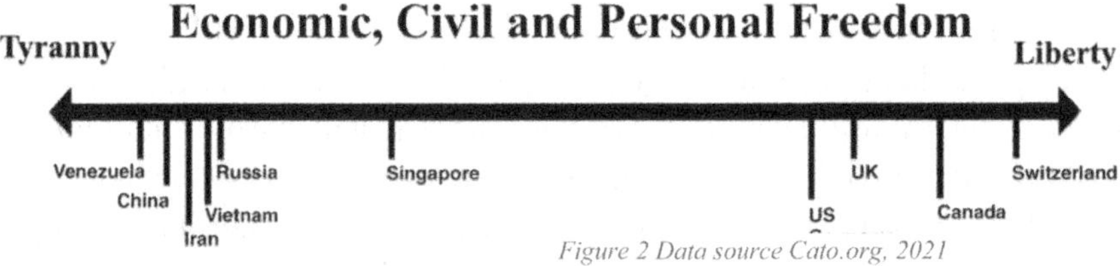

Figure 2 Data source Cato.org, 2021

Nations here (Figure 2) were ranked based on broader terms to also include personal and civil rights.[254] In both cases, I attempted to plot relative locations based on the data and then match a selection of sample nations in the two scales for comparison. While I charted them in relation to each other, locating their proximity to each end of the scale was not attempted. Tyranny and liberty have always been the two sides of governance, with most nations in recorded history falling well into the hands of tyranny, being formed and operated by a few people ambitious for control over others. We are all now a long way from true liberty. There are people who claim to be on the right, or Republican, that I would place, by behavior and advocacy for control, on the left, say, progressive Republicans and warmongers. The same could be said for some on the left, for instance, the free speech and tolerance of 1960s liberals. They were farther to the right than progressive Republicans.

The right seems to be defined in no small part by its opponents. As a consequence, Nazism, Fascism and other authoritarian regimes are falsely provided as examples of the extreme right. If you judge the spectrum by the policies supported, the real division becomes clear. On the left you would find ideas like income redistribution, big government, strong regulation of industry, centralized control and banking, open borders, income equality, social justice, higher taxes on the wealthy, government healthcare, extreme environmentalism, gun control, food stamps, government controlled education, planned or mixed economies and artificially high minimum wages. These might be reduced to "government interventionism and redistributive justice".

On the right, we have limited government, property rights, states' rights, individual liberty, free market, low equal taxes, limited regulation, strong military focused on American defense, secure border, school choice, pro-Second Amendment, right to life, free speech, right to work, rule of law and individualism. These might be boiled down to "freedom and security". How, then, is it that despotic leaders like Hitler and Mussolini end up on the far right, when the people under their rule were, by design, neither secure in their lives nor free? Hitler's Germany was a socialist nation-state defined by its people's race without constitutional protections. America is a free nation-state defined by its ideals, designed to protect everyone equally, though we are far from that now.

Hitler believed the German people were inherently, racially superior to other people and sought authoritarian control for the "common good" of those people. This country as designed allows any people from anywhere and any race are to become American citizens if they follow the process and the law. National dictatorships have nothing to do with the classic liberalism of our founders, the country they created or the right in America based on my experience and study. To conflate America and Nazi Germany and their ideologies is depraved. The similarity between America First nationalism and Hitler's National Socialism amounts to little more than the idea that a nation puts its own interests first, as all must if they intend to remain independent nations. The whole point of having a political association or government is joining together for security.

> Definition by Merriam-Webster Dictionary Nationalism: "A sense of national consciousness exalting one nation above all others and placing primary emphasis on promotion of its culture and interests as opposed to those of other nations or supranational groups."[255]

That definition, however, doesn't specify whether one is promoting culture and interests within their own country or trying to forcefully impose those on others. By falsely connecting America First nationalism and other movements on the right with racist nationalism and authoritarianism, its ideals and proponents are villainized. That perception is advanced by intentionally mistaking patriotism and American exceptionalism for xenophobia and white nationalism, which are all about race. The U.S. is not based on race. Hitler's National Socialism and racial prejudice are the opposite of the American principles of inalienable rights, equal liberty and equal justice under the law that actually characterizes the America First movement.

Ours is a representative government, meaning it's leaders are expected to represent the interests of its citizens, not to serve global masters or non-citizens who are unwilling to follow our laws. American exceptionalism believes that our system of government and the liberties and opportunities it provides is superior to other systems and exceptional in the history of civilization, not that we as human beings are superior. Our Constitutional Republic was designed to secure the equal liberty of its citizens which requires putting their interests first, responsibly managing their money and resources and securing their well-being from any who would do them harm. This is the social contract in the sense that our founders believed in.

Expecting people to follow the law and to immigrate legally is not xenophobic. A nation simply can't absorb an unlimited flow of immigrants. The amount of immigration permitted must be restricted to an amount of people who can be successfully assimilated into American society and not overstress the nations' resources. Shortly after my grandfather immigrated to the United States, further immigrations from Greece were paused to allow those already here time to assimilate. To the right, immigrants are not the problem. Our unenforced laws and terrible border security are the issue.

National origin should logically play a part when considering American security from hostile actors, but it is not racist or unreasonable to want to vet potential immigrants and even reject those intending to do us harm. Also, being against the corruptions of our system of government does not make one anti-government - it all depends on the power of that government. We expect it to have balanced powers as laid out in the Constitution, not giving a single leader or group dictatorial control and not expanding into an oppressive police state. We do share a desire to make our nation ever more successful, strong, secure and able to defend itself, even while seeking trade with the rest of the world. Imposing our culture on other nations and nation-building are not right wing philosophies, and it's why the real right turned on President George W. Bush.

Actual policies and ideology identify where one falls on the political scale. Republicans tend to be closer to the right than Democrats, but both are more alike than they are opposed. Republicans who historically fought to end slavery, extend citizen rights and equal protection under the law, were on the right. Republicans supporting Blue Laws, outlawing consensual adult behavior and fomenting coups in other countries move left. Those censoring and banning adults from access to books are leftist, while making sure books in school libraries are age and subject matter appropriate is a different matter altogether, tied instead to parental controls.

Democrats were almost entirely responsible for the Confederacy, segregation, Jim Crow laws and the Ku Klux Klan. Today, Democrats will argue that all of the racists of their party suddenly switched over and became Republicans after civil rights legislation passed. There was a little crossover,[256257] but, historically, the more Republican the south became, the less racist it became.[258] The first 23 blacks in Congress were Republicans.[259] There was not a sudden, fundamental change in party ideology for either side. I think both top political parties in this country have too much power, both a large part of the machine.

Southern Democrats were called conservative, because they wanted to conserve and maintain the status quo, and were inaccurately conflated with Barry Goldwater and Republican conservatism, which hoped to conserve the Constitution and the ideals of our nation's founding. The former was on the left, the latter on the right. Bigotry and racism were not unique to either party and people have a right to their opinions, even if we find them repulsive. Where they do not have a right is when they act on those opinions in ways that infringe on the equal liberties of others. America sprang from the heart of western civilization and became the leader of the free world because of its unrivaled freedom and opportunity. It became even more so as the freedom of blacks and other previously oppressed peoples increased.

> Senator Tim Scott, South Carolina, 2020 Republican National Convention:
> "My grandfather's 99th birthday would have been tomorrow. Growing up, he had to cross the street if a white person was coming. He suffered the indignity of being forced out of school as a third grader to pick cotton, and never learned to read or write. Yet, he lived to see his grandson become the first African American to be elected to both the United States House and Senate. And that's why I believe the next American century can be better than the last."[260]

I know there is too much wrong in this world, too much suffering and need. I cannot begin to understand what it meant to be a black person under slavery or when the Klan terrorized with impunity, what it meant to flee the World Trade Center as it crumbled to the ground in a poisonous cloud of debris or to be a Greek youth, alone, working in indentured servitude in New York City in the early twentieth century. I can't imagine putting your sixteen year old daughter on a ship with thousands of others to go and work in foreign country you've never seen, like happened to my dad's grandmother. Like so many others, mother and daughter chose that out of need and hope.

America is not a failure simply because it is imperfect. We can argue over language, statistics and percentages, but this is not the 1850s or even the 1950s. Because of the government the founders framed, we went from a place where slavery was legal to a nation where a successful, gay, black man had to pay two guys in Chicago to pretend to attack him so he could pretend to be persecuted.[261] The cult of victimhood aside, we've come a long way.

Chapter 5

Wicked Designs of Misguided Men

American tradition and ideals have found opposition in a variety of different forms since its founding, as liberty always has, all of them fed by the desire of some to exert control over others. One of the most dangerous comes in the form of collectivism, which pursues an envy-fueled narrative of redistribution while increasing centralized government control, entwined with the fascism of corrupt pseudo-capitalism. This pretends to value the group and, in its pure form, to place property and production in the hands of the workers but, in reality, just places control in the hands of a dictator, a privileged few or, at best, mob rule (the so-called "dictatorship of the proletariat" or dictatorship of the industrial working class).

It leads, in every example of history, only to slavery and the devaluing of human beings, while elevating a privileged few. A lot of people have fallen prey to these ideas because, on the surface, they seem compassionate. It permeates our society and the previously free-speech, anti-war ideology of liberalism, replacing critical thinking and historical reality with submission and obedience. Collectivism is the tool they use to convince the people at large to give up their own independence and power.

Dependence and Servitude

The advocates of collectivism have worked toward the incremental conversion of the American system into a corrupt, political ruling class that enriches themselves on the backs of the people they claim to champion. This is both the history and future of collectivism. Whether it's called socialism, communism, Marxism, Leninism, Stalinism, Maoism or some other variation, this ideology advocates common or collective ownership or control of property, resources and industry.[262] In practice, it centralizes management of these things. I understand there are differences between these systems and Nazism or National Socialism (what could be called Collective Nationalism), but I believe their similarities far outweigh those distinctions. Nazism had centralized power, advanced for the common good of a race of German people. All of these systems value people as groups rather than individuals, as possessions of the collective and not of themselves. Regardless of variations in rhetoric, these systems create dictatorships by gaining control over the people, property and production.

> Britannica definition of collectivism:
> "Any of several types of social organization in which the individual is seen as being subordinate to a social collectivity such as a state, a nation, a race, or a social class. Collectivism may be contrasted with individualism (q.v.), in which the rights and interests of the individual are emphasized."[263]

> The American Heritage Dictionary of the English Language:
> "1) The principles or system of ownership and control of the means of production and distribution by the people collectively, usually under the supervision of a government. 2) The socialistic theory or principle of centralization of all directive social and industrial power, especially of control of the means of production, in the people collectively, or the state: the opposite of individualism. 3) The doctrine that land and capital should be owned by society collectively or as a whole; communism."[264]

Lumping various ideologies together as I do is sure to draw the ire of those steeped in their particulars, but intellectual debates of this kind cannot obscure the underlining similarities and inevitable consequences of these systems. They are all authoritarian, all tyrannical.

> Britannica.com definition of Authoritarianism:
> "The principle of blind submission to authority, as opposed to individual freedom of thought and action. In government, authoritarianism denotes any political system that concentrates power in the hands of a leader or a small elite that is not constitutionally responsible to the body of the people."[265]

In communism, this blind submission is theoretically to the will of the collective, but it is inevitably submission to the state or party and its leaders.

It should not be imagined that Lenin or Stalin, or the Communist Party, answered to the will or to the interests of workers just because that was their rhetoric or because their devotion to socialism may have been genuine. All collectivist regimes pretend to create a society where industry is controlled so that laborers are not exploited to feed the greed of others, but in reality, the state owns and controls everything, including the workers, and the administrators and the beneficiaries of that state exploit the workers for their own greed. Even if those administrators were to act at the will of the majority of its people rather than their own self-interest, such nations, without institutional protections for individual human rights, are authoritarian and tyrannical, having traded a single leader for a majority vote.

"Not until the two main tenets of socialism: abolition of private property... and equality of income, have taken hold of the people as religious dogmas... will a stable socialist state be possible." – George Bernard Shaw

---

> George Bernard Shaw, Definition of Socialism, Encyclopedia Britannica, 13th Ed. 1926:
> "Socialism, reduced to its simplest legal and practical expression, means the complete discarding of the institution of private property by transforming it into public property, and the division of the resultant public income equally and indiscriminately among the entire population... Not until the two main tenets of socialism: abolition of private property (which must not be confused with personal property), and equality of income, have taken hold of the people as religious dogmas, as to which no controversy is regarded as sane, will a stable socialist state be possible."[266]

"Whatever portion of the working class had become convinced of the insufficiency of mere political revolutions... that portion, then, called itself Communist." – Friedrich Engels

---

Friedrich Engels, in the preface of a 1906 English translation of the Communist Manifesto, which he co-authored with Karl Marx, described the distinctions between the collectivism of Communism and Socialism and the evolution of terminology since the document's original publication in 1848:

> Friedrich Engels, Preface to the Communist Manifesto, 1906: "The history of the Manifesto reflects, to a great extent, the history of the modern working-class movement; at present it is undoubtedly the most widespread, the most international production of all Socialist Literature, the common platform acknowledged by millions of working men from Siberia to California. Yet, when it was written, we could not have called it a Socialist Manifesto. By Socialists, in 1847, were understood, on the one hand, the adherents of the various Utopian systems: Owenites in England, Fourierists in France, both of them already reduced to the position of mere sects, and gradually dying out; on the other hand, the most multifarious social quacks, who, by all manners of tinkering, professed to redress, without any danger to capital and profit, all sorts of social grievances, in both cases men outside the working class movement and looking rather to the 'educated' classes for support.
>
> "Whatever portion of the working class had become convinced of the insufficiency of mere political revolutions, and had proclaimed the necessity of a total social change, that portion, then, called itself Communist... Thus, Socialism was, in 1847, a middle-class movement, Communism a working class movement. Socialism was, on the Continent at least, 'respectable'; Communism was the very opposite...
>
> "The whole history of mankind (since the dissolution of primitive tribal society, holding land in common ownership) has been a history of class struggles, contests between exploiting and exploited, ruling and oppressed classes; that the history of these class struggles forms a series of evolution in which, now-a-days, a stage has been reached where the exploited and oppressed class - the proletariat - cannot attain its emancipation from the sway of the exploiting and ruling class - the bourgeoisie - without, at the same time, and once and for all, emancipating society at large from all exploitation, oppression, class-distinctions and class-struggles." [267]

"From each according to his ability, to each according to his needs."
- Karl Marx

The real difference between communism and socialism is the speed of adoption. The Encyclopedia Britannica notes: "Marx and Engels maintained that the poverty, disease, and early death that afflicted the proletariat (the industrial working class) were endemic to capitalism: they were systemic and structural problems that could be resolved only by replacing capitalism with communism." The truth was quite the opposite. The reason this ideology failed outright in America was because this nation had already escaped the static class systems of Europe *through* capitalism.

Lenin and his Bolsheviks belonged to the Russian Social-Democratic Workers' Party which later became the Communist Party of the USSR. Lenin, however, put the party, made up of select intellectuals, ahead of the dictatorship of the workers whom he did not trust to rule themselves. Like other versions of collectivism, in practice, select bureaucrats ruled under the leadership of a dictator. Communism arose from more rural, developing countries, not from capitalism of developed countries as Marx imagined.[268] It would appear that the only way to collectivize a capitalist government is through the incremental progression of socialism; that is, it must be done on the sly.

Marx based Communism on the principle: "From each according to his ability, to each according to his needs." The basic tenets, according to Engels, included the abolishment of private property, institution of a heavy, progressive income tax, the equal obligation to work, the elimination of competition and the right of inheritance, centralization of money and credit in a national bank, centralized control by government of communication, transportation and labor, of factories and industries and government-controlled education at taxpayer expense.

Though Russia and China implemented more sudden, forced collectivization, Engels thought these tenets could not all be achieved at once but would need to be pursued over time. The transformation of society would be accomplished through the implementation of progressively extreme attacks on the property and freedoms of the people. Private property would be limited through taxation, including heavy inheritance taxes. Government involvement in economics and industry would be increasingly expanded through taxes and regulation.[269] The similarities of those ambitions to what has happened in this country is startling.

Following along with Marxist ideas, our federal government has worked to increasingly regulate and control communication, transportation, environment, education, labor and all manner of other areas through a variety of federal agencies, departments, commissions and boards until larger and larger segments of private enterprise now act only at the discretion of government, making the economy inefficient and its government corrupt. When Marx and Engels devised Communism, it was not actually a new idea. The founders addressed these same ideas in their time.

"When decided, and the principle settled, it is to be equally and fairly applied to all." - President Thomas Jefferson

---

> Thomas Jefferson's Addition to Destutt de Tracy's Treatise on Political Economy, 1816:
> "Whether property alone, and the whole of what each citizen possesses, shall be subject to contribution, or only it's surplus after satisfying his first wants, or whether the faculties of body and mind shall contribute also from their annual earnings, is a question to be decided. but, when decided, and the principle settled, it is to be equally and fairly applied to all. to take from one, because it is thought that his own industry and that of his father has acquired too much, in order to spare to others, who, or whose fathers have not exercised equal industry and skill, is to violate arbitrarily the first principle of association, 'the guarantee to every one of a free exercise of his industry, & the fruits acquired by it'."[270]

"If all were to be decided by a vote of the majority, the eight or nine millions who have no property, would not think of usurping over the rights of the one or two millions who have?" - President John Adams

---

Collectivism, as a philosophy, is equality of outcomes. Today it's called equity. No notion of justice could allow the products (money) to be taken from those whose labor created them in order to redistribute it to others who did nothing for it, a practice which became the foundation of the modern welfare state.

> John Adams, The Works of John Adams, Vol. 6, Pub. 1851:
> "Suppose a nation, rich and poor, high and low, ten millions in number, all assembled together; not more than one or two millions will have lands, houses, or any personal property; if we take into the account the women and children, or even if we leave them out of the question, a great majority of every nation is wholly destitute of property, except a small quantity of clothes, and a few trifles of other movables. Would Mr. Nedham be responsible that, if all were to be decided by a vote of the majority, the eight or nine millions who have no property, would not think of usurping over the rights of the one or two millions who have? Property is surely a right of mankind as really as liberty.

"Debts would be abolished first; taxes laid heavy on the rich, and not at all on the others; and at last a downright equal division of everything be demanded." - President John Adams

---

> "Perhaps, at first, prejudice, habit, shame or fear, principle or religion, would restrain the poor from attacking the rich, and the idle from usurping on the industrious; but the time would not be long before courage and enterprise would come, and pretexts be invented by degrees, to countenance the majority in dividing all the property among them, or at least, in sharing it equally with its present possessors. Debts would be abolished first; taxes laid heavy on the rich, and not at all on the others; and at last a downright equal division of every thing be demanded, and voted. What would be the consequence of this?

"If 'Thou shalt not covet,' and 'Thou shalt not steal,' were not commandments of Heaven, they must be made inviolable precepts in every society, before it can be civilized or made free." – President John Adams

---

"The idle, the vicious, the intemperate, would rush into the utmost extravagance of debauchery, sell and spend all their share, and then demand a new division of those who purchased from them. The moment the idea is admitted into society, that property is not as sacred as the laws of God, and that there is not a force of law and public justice to protect it, anarchy and tyranny commence. If 'Thou shalt not covet,' and 'Thou shalt not steal,' were not commandments of Heaven, they must be made inviolable precepts in every society, before it can be civilized or made free. If the first part of the proposition, namely, that 'the people never think of usurping over other men's rights,' cannot be admitted, is the second, namely, 'they mind which way to preserve their own,' better founded?

"There is in every nation and people under heaven a large proportion of persons who take no rational and prudent precautions to preserve what they have, much less to acquire more." – President John Adams

---

"There is in every nation and people under heaven a large proportion of persons who take no rational and prudent precautions to preserve what they have, much less to acquire more. Indolence is the natural character of man, to such a degree that nothing but the necessities of hunger, thirst, and other wants equally pressing, can stimulate him to action, until education is introduced in civilized societies, and the strongest motives of ambition to excel in arts, trades, and professions, are established in the minds of all men. Until this emulation is introduced, the lazy savage holds property in too little estimation to give himself trouble for the preservation or acquisition of it. In societies the most cultivated and polished, vanity, fashion, and folly prevail over every thought of ways to preserve their own. They seem rather to study what means of luxury, dissipation, and extravagance they can invent to get rid of it."[271]

"The diversity in the faculties of men... The protection of these faculties is the first object of government." – President James Madison

---

Compare Adams' estimate of land ownership, then roughly 10 to 20 percent, to the 65% of Americans today that own their own homes.[272] Even of those without real estate, most have an impressive amount of personal property, as well as private, rented residences and services. The luxuries we take for granted are immeasurable. Equality of property in a free nation, however, can never be expected.

> James Madison, The Federalist #10, Nov. 22, 1787: "The diversity in the faculties of men from which the rights of property originate, is not less an insuperable obstacle to an uniformity of interests. The protection of these faculties is the first object of government. From the protection of different and unequal faculties of acquiring property, the possession of different degrees and kinds of property immediately results: And from the influence of these on the sentiments and views of the respective proprietors, ensues a division of the society into different interests and parties.

"The most common and durable source of factions, has been the various and unequal distribution of property." - Federalist Papers No. 10

> "The latent causes of faction are thus sown in the nature of man; and we see them every where brought into different degrees of activity, according to the different circumstances of civil society. A zeal for different opinions concerning religion, concerning government, and many other points, as well of speculation as of practice; an attachment to different leaders ambitiously contending for pre-eminence and power; or to persons of other descriptions whose fortunes have been interesting to the human passions, have in turn divided mankind into parties, inflamed them with mutual animosity, and rendered them much more disposed to vex and oppress each other, than to co-operate for their common good. So strong is this propensity of mankind to fall into mutual animosities, that where no substantial occasion presents itself, the most frivolous and fanciful distinctions have been sufficient to kindle their unfriendly passions, and excite their most violent conflicts.

"A rage for paper money, for an abolition of debts, for an equal division of property, or for any other improper or wicked project, will be less apt to pervade the whole body of the union." - Federalist papers No. 10

> "But the most common and durable source of factions, has been the various and unequal distribution of property. Those who hold, and those who are without property, have ever formed distinct interests in society. Those who are creditors, and those who are debtors, fall under a like discrimination. A landed interest, a manufacturing interest, a mercantile interest, a monied interest, with many lesser interests, grow up of necessity in civilized nations, and divide them into different classes, actuated by different sentiments and views. The regulation of these various and interfering interests forms the principal task of modern legislation, and involves the spirit of party and faction in the necessary and ordinary operations of government."[273]

Many people today do not realize the dark road ahead for us all if collectivism takes hold here or the role government dependency plays in that journey.

> Samuel Adams, written on behalf of Massachusetts House of Representatives, 1768:
> "The utopian schemes of leveling a community of goods are as visionary and impracticable, as those which vest all property in the Crown, are arbitrary, despotic, and in our government unconstitutional. Now, what property can the colonists be conceived to have, if their money may be granted away by others, without their consent?" [274]

Like the collectivism of communism and socialism, the Roman Catholic Church consolidated its ownership of land so that it was by far the largest landowner in Europe, and it remains today one of the largest landowners in the world. The fact that private property and individual liberty still exist at all in an increasingly socialized America is not to say they are secure.

"Turbulence, violence and abuse of power, by the majority trampling on the rights of the minority... have more frequently than any other cause, produced despotism." - President James Madison

> James Madison in General Defense of the Constitution, 1788: "Since the general civilization of mankind, I believe there are more instances of the abridgment of the freedom of the people, by gradual and silent encroachments of those in power, than by violent and sudden usurpations: but on a candid examination of history, we shall find that turbulence, violence and abuse of power, by the majority trampling on the rights of the minority, have produced factions and commotions, which, in republics, have more frequently than any other cause, produced despotism."[275]

"Republicans call every Democrat who want people to have healthcare a socialist." - Hillary Clinton

---

After President Biden accused President Donald Trump's supporters of being semi-fascists, Hillary Clinton defended the move, repeating the argument that socialist programs are not literally socialism.

> Hillary Clinton, former Secretary of State, Sept. 7, 2022: "The final thing I would say is, you know, fascism is a very big word. I know that. But so is socialism and the Republicans call every Democrat who want people to have healthcare a socialist."[276]

I would say, only those Democrats who want to forcibly take other people's money to give it to them.

"I am for doing good to the poor, but I differ in opinion about the means."
- Benjamin Franklin

Collectivist policies have now been implemented in some of America's largest liberally governed cities, where homelessness, drug use and crime have exploded, encouraged and condoned under the auspices of compassion. Some of California's largest cities in particular have devolved into failing socialist states.[277] These cities create the greatest income disparity between the high-living upper class and the average person of the lower income. Meanwhile, the middle class are fleeing. The mass homelessness is not a failure of liberal policy but the result of it, and, more importantly, the intended result.

It leaves most people powerless and creates undeniable evidence of the disparity of outcomes, which can be used to rile public sentiment against "greedy" capitalists and the "system". The suffering of individuals is a minor price to pay in their eyes in the pursuit of power, providing just enough government aid to keep people down and dependent. There is a reason why "dependency" is a synonym for "enslavement". Another part that advocates avoid when promoting this socialism is the common obligation to work, which comes later (when the people no longer have any choice).

"The more public provisions were made for the poor, the less they provided for themselves, and of course became poorer." - Benjamin Franklin

---

> Benjamin Franklin, Letter on the Price of Corn; Management of the poor, May 9, 1753:
>
> "I am for doing good to the poor, but I differ in opinion about the means. I think the best way of doing good to the poor, is, not making them easy in poverty, but leading or driving them out of it. In my youth, I travelled much, and I observed in different countries, that the more public provisions were made for the poor, the less they provided for themselves, and of course became poorer. And on the contrary, the less was done for them, the more they did for themselves, and became richer. There is no country in the world where so many provisions are established for them; so many hospitals to receive them when they are sick or lame, founded and maintained by voluntary charities; so many almshouses for the aged of both sexes, together with a solemn general law made by the rich to subject their estates to a heavy tax for the support of the poor.

"You offered a premium for the encouragement of idleness, and you should not now wonder, that it has had its effect in the increase of poverty." - Benjamin Franklin

---

> "Under all these obligations, are our poor modest, humble, and thankful? And do they use their best endeavours to maintain

> themselves, and lighted our shoulders of this burden? On the contrary, I affirm, that there is no country in the world in which the poor are more idle, dissolute, drunken, and insolent. The day you passed that act, you took away from before their eyes the greatest of all inducements to industry, frugality, and sobriety, by giving them a dependence on somewhat else than a careful accumulation during youth and health, for support in age or sickness.

"More will be done for their happiness by inuring them to provide for themselves, than could be done by dividing all your estates among them."
- Benjamin Franklin

> "In short, you offered a premium for the encouragement of idleness, and you should not now wonder, that it has had its effect in the increase of poverty. Repeal the law, and you will soon see a change in their manners. St. Monday and St. Tuesday will soon cease to be holidays. Six days shalt thou labour, though one of the old commandments long treated as out of date, will again be looked upon as a respectable precept; industry will increase, and with it plenty among the lower people; their circumstances will mend, and more will be done for their happiness by inuring them to provide for themselves, than could be done by dividing all your estates among them."[278]

Coerced government aid has a dark purpose, trading liberty for servitude to the state and its masters. Somehow the left convinces many Americans that dependency is what they are *entitled* to, what they deserve. Eventually, they will convince them that they are entitled to slavery. Our liberal welfare system is systemic slavery for all races. As Benjamin Franklin described, making people content in their dependency is an evil that retains them in servitude, and for collectivism, it is merely a step toward something even worse.

In Practice

The idle are drawn to collectivism but it actually leaves no room for them in its utopia. An example of its twisted ideology, when taken to its inevitable conclusion, can be found in a video clip of George Bernard Shaw, an outspoken (and truly frightening) socialist and 1925 Nobel Prize winner:

"Sir or madam, will you be kind enough to justify your existence?"
- George Bernard Shaw

> George Bernard Shaw, discussing capital punishment, 1931: "I never know exactly how to make my opinion clear because I object to all punishment whatsoever. I don't want to punish anybody, but there are an extraordinary number of people who I might want to kill. Not in any unkind or personal spirit, but it must be evident to all of you, you must all know half a dozen people, at least, who are no use in this world, who are more trouble than they are worth.
>
> "I think it would be a good thing to make everybody come before a properly appointed board just as he might come before the income tax commissioner and say every 5 years or every 7 years, just put them there and say, 'Sir or madam, will you be kind enough to justify your existence?' If you can't justify your existence, if you're not pulling your weight in the social boat, if you're not producing as much as you consume, or perhaps a little bit more, then clearly, we cannot use the big organization of our society for the purpose of keeping you alive. Because your life does not benefit us and it can't be of very much use to yourself."[279]

This is not hyperbole, but the dark consequences of collectivist ideals that proponents usually fail to mention when encouraging its implementation. Under communism, a person must work and has no choice in where they work, when they work or the type of work they do. They have no privacy or autonomy. Their leaders will decide what type of education people can pursue or where they live. If being a worker subjects one to the tyranny of the business owner, what do they expect will happen when the worker is subject instead to the tyranny of a dictator, a party or the mob?

"The equality of nature is moral and political only and means that all men are independent." - President John Adams

---

We are not all equal physically, mentally or economically, and equality in these things no society can hope to establish or enforce, short of making the people equally destitute. Our founders intended, instead, an equality of rights and liberty.

> John Adams, Works of John Adams, Vol 1, Chapter XI:
> "By the law of nature, all men are men, and not angels–men, and not lions–men, and not whales–men, and not eagles–that is, they are all of the same species; and this is the most that the equality of nature amounts to. But man differs by nature from man, almost as much as man from beast. The equality of nature is moral and political only and means that all men are independent. But a physical inequality, an intellectual inequality, of the most serious kind, is established unchangeably by the Author of nature; and society has a right to establish any other inequalities it may judge necessary for its good. The precept, however, do as you would be done by, implies an equality which is the real equality of nature and Christianity, and has been known and understood in all ages."[280]

Over the last century, our nation has suffered various fundamental alterations which have brought it closer to the tyranny side of the spectrum and more distant from the free market economy and individual liberty of its founding. There have been many real world examples of these ideologies but history has glossed over the consequences. Collectivism has been implemented numerous times, in various degrees and to horrifying effect from Lenin and Mao to Chávez. Venezuela is a glaring modern example of this ideology's outcome when implemented, where the people scrounged for food from garbage cans while the ruling elite reveled in opulence.[281]

Hugo Chávez, the Venezuelan President and dictator who nationalized most of the nation's means of production, finance and communications, replaced the owners and operators of its oil industry with inexperienced cronies, destroying a prosperous industry and nation. Like all collectivist nations, the leadership failed to comprehend the economic forces and operational needs that make a company, and in turn an economy, function.[282]

"Eating your children is an act of barbarism."- Sign Posted in Stalin's Ukraine

---

Should there be any question about the realities of collectivism, historical investigations such as the Black Book of Communism: Crimes, Terror, Repression[283] open a ghastly window. Where collectivism has been tried, it has never led to utopia but, to the contrary, has created the dystopian horror shows seen under Lenin, Stalin, Pol Pot and Mao, where mass famine was used to quell uprisings and eliminate dissidents. Lenin expanded Marxism to refer to nations instead of just workers, as if Russia was a proletariat nation oppressed by capitalist nations like the United States.

These collectivist dictators starved millions of their own people to death and drove many not only to cannibalism but to eat their own children. Stalin's policies in the Ukraine alone starved millions of peasants to death, leading to cannibalism that was so widespread that authorities posted signs stating: "Eating your children is an act of barbarism." I suspect they probably knew that. Communism is an act of barbarism. Despite its claims of compassion and social justice, collectivism always leads to progressive injustice and inhumanity.

J.A. Fragoules 1988

I did see communism in practice. As a teenager I participated in an exchange program with a high school in Schorndorf, West Germany, which allowed me to live with a German family for nearly a month and to visit other parts of Europe with a group of students from my class. A German student also came to live with me and my family for an equivalent time.

We traveled through the territory of East Germany by bus to Berlin, a city then divided into pieces amongst the allied forces and surrounded by the communist territory. I remember the repetitive and seemingly endless thump, thump, thump of the concrete joints in the road as we passed through the barren East German countryside. The East German soldiers at a check point, all tall with pale faces, walked through the bus while we held up our passports for their inspection, their body odor nauseating.

In their world, I guessed, odor didn't rank among their highest concerns. Once in West Berlin, we enjoyed the busy modern city, but also sneaked out to paint our names on the Berlin Wall, leery of East German guards in towers on the wall with automatic weapons, even though we were safely on the western side of that great barrier. It was a boundary between joy and misery that virtually overnight divided families and destroyed lives.

I had friends there who were separated from family since the night the barriers went up. We also had the opportunity to pass through the concrete monstrosity at Checkpoint Charlie to visit the eastern side of the city, an intimidating process conducted in quiet nervousness. On the American side, there were posters for sale of iconic pictures taken, in one case, of an East German guard jumping over fencing and making a break for freedom. Another showed an East German guard helping a child escape through barbed wire fencing, while looking behind him tensely. Their fear and desperation were palatable.

JFragoules 1988

As we went through security, one of our group had to turn his t-shirt inside out because East German authorities considered the subject matter subversive. I cannot recall the subject, possibly a rock band, but it seemed innocuous enough to us at the time. On the other side, we emerged into the surreal world of 1987 East Berlin. It was the face of communist oppression, stark and dangerous beyond comprehension, a place where the most basic rules of civilization were discarded and life became disposable.

The poverty and hopelessness of the East German people was palatable. There were cameras on the roof corners of every building so that nothing occurred outside the view of the East German government. Such obvious surveillance, especially government surveillance, was as foreign to us as the censorship had been, though both are all too common now. It was chilling.

Everything about the East was depressed. Citizens sold trinkets and meals to tourists.

I ate a small pizza-like meal with meat that was disturbingly unrecognizable (I later stopped eating meat, having never been a big fan and finding it increasingly unappetizing). I imagined the meals eaten by the people we met there would probably make that little pizza seem a luxury. We walked about a city that seemed trapped in an earlier age where there was no freedom, no joy, only fear. A wrong move, unsanctioned attire or intemperate word would not be tolerated. I was in Germany two years before the wall came down.

I thought at the time that having been on the communist side of the wall would date me: I was around before communism fell. I saw it firsthand. Unfortunately, too many Americans seem to have forgotten the evils of this ideology. Collectivism demonizes people's ability to think for themselves or have any control over their own lives. It is attractive, apparently, to those who fear freedom and responsibility. Collectivism creates a government-managed market where workers are indentured servants with nothing of their own but whatever meager personal property they may assemble, no voice except as a member of a protected group and no rights at all if belonging to a targeted group.

The first national implementation of collectivism came from Lenin and his fellow Bolsheviks in Russia, who started by levying huge taxes to impoverish those with wealth, nationalizing all businesses and collectivizing farming and food production as they pursued rapid industrialization. Peasants prosperous enough to own their own farms, called kulaks, were deported to concentration camps, forced labor or to "colonies" in the uninhabitable parts of the nation with little to no food or tools. With the kulaks gone, their possessions and lands were divvied up. Those left were either relocated or were expected to work the farms and meet increasingly untenable requisition requirements.

Since the government owned or controlled every significant business, any minor misstep at work was considered treasonous and punished accordingly. When the economy of Russia and the USSR failed to produce as expected, leadership saw conspiracies and saboteurs everywhere, leading to more violence, more deaths and even less production.

"Here, the genocide of a 'class' may well be tantamount to the genocide of a 'race'." - The Black Book of Communism

---

Starting at the end of the 1920's, the Russia "introduced a quota method - each region and district had to arrest, deport, or shoot a certain percentage of people who were members of several 'enemy' social classes. These quotas were centrally defined under the supervision of the Party." Both communism under Lenin and Stalin and Nazism under Hitler engaged in the mass deportation of peoples to concentration camps, large scale forced labor and mass murder. The Nazi camps were actually patterned after the Russian camps already long in use. More than sharing atrocities, these two systems shared ideologies to a far greater extent than generally acknowledged, which is why they both belong on the left side of the political spectrum.

The introduction to the Black Book of Communism acknowledged: "The ultimate distinguishing characteristic of Nazism, of course, is the Holocaust, considered as the historically unique crime of seeking the extermination of an entire people, a crime for which the term 'genocide' was coined around the time of Nuremberg. And therewith the Jewish people required this solemn obligation to keep the memory of its martyrs alive in the conscience of the world." It takes nothing away from the horror and evil of Hitler's Germany or the Holocaust to realize that his crimes against humanity, on varying scales, have turned out not to be unique in history or isolated in geography or ethnicity.

"The regime aimed to control the total available food supply, and with immense ingenuity to distribute food purely on the basis of 'merits' and 'demerits.'" - The Black Book of Communism

---

> "As for the great famine in Ukraine in 1932-33, which resulted from the rural population's resistance to forced collectivization, 6 million died in a period of several months. Here, the genocide of a 'class' may well be tantamount to the genocide of a 'race' - the deliberate starvation of a child of a Ukrainian kulak as a result of the famine caused by Stalin's regime 'is equal to' the starvation of a Jewish child in the Warsaw ghetto as a result of the famine caused

> by the Nazi regime. Such arguments in no way detract from the unique nature of Auschwitz - the mobilization of leading-edge technological resources and their use in an 'industrial process' involving the construction of an 'extermination factory,' the use of gas, and cremation."

The authors of this massive book point out that communism used famine as a weapon, systematically controlling the food supply, so that only certain people were fed. The crimes of Leninism and Stalinism included those committed under Mao Zedong, Kim Il Sung, and Pol Pot. Some opposition to The Black Book of Communism[284] comes from those who argue Adolf Hitler was guilty of more murders than were accounted for there,as if there is a balance of horror between right and left that makes it all ok, and as if National Socialism and Communism were not seeds of the same authoritarian ideology and very much on the same end of the true political spectrum.

"Communism... like Nazism... deems a part of humanity unworthy of existence." - The Black Book of Communism

---

The Nazi Party was in fact the National Socialist German Workers' Party. Though Hitler focused on race, his crimes against humanity absolutely parallel those of various communist nations. They identified enemies differently, but behaved similarly. Russian Communists eliminated classes and Nazis eliminated races. Their enemies included the bourgeoisie, a social class, comparable to the middle or upper middle class, something of a merchant class. The proletariat was the oppressed working class. For Nazis, the enemies were Jews, Gypsies, and capitalists. In reality, both systems extended the targets of their aggression to many other groups as well.

> The Black Book of Communism by multiple authors, Harvard University Press, 1999:
> "Thus, the techniques of segregation and exclusion employed in a 'class-based totalitarianism' closely resembles the techniques of a 'race-based totalitarianism'. The future Nazi society was to be built upon a 'pure race,' and the future Communist society was to be built upon a proletarian people purified of the dregs of the bourgeoisie. The restructuring of these two societies was envisioned in the same way, even if the crackdowns were different. Therefore,

> it would be foolish to pretend that Communism is a form of universalism. Communism may have a worldwide purpose, but like Nazism it deems a part of humanity unworthy of existence."

It doesn't matter if this was based on race, territory or class. Both governments assumed centralized control of their economies and their people, sacrificing human beings for the common good or public interest as determined by dictatorial leaders and corrupt political parties. Hitler took a very socialist economy and turned it into a completely controlled one, even if not attempting collectivization.[285] Like Communism, Hitler opposed the individual liberty upon which America was founded. He saw the political scale more for what it is, though, the balance between individual liberty one side and collective tyranny on the other. However, he envisioned Nazism as somewhere in the middle, and I hope we are not that far gone.

"The interests of the community became the regulating and, if necessary, the commanding factor." - Adolf Hitler

---

> Adolf Hitler, Speech of January 30, 1941. My New Order: "We chose a course which lay between two extremes. In the first place, we had fallen into one extreme, the liberal and individualistic, which made the individual the center, not only of speculation, but of action. On the other side stood the theory of humanitarianism as a universal doctrine. Between these two extremes lay our ideal, a national community in body and in spirit, designed and founded by providence into the midst of which man is set to achieve the purpose of his life... Out of this arose the ideology of National Socialism.
>
> "In itself it represents the conquest of individualism - not in the sense of curtailing individual faculties or paralyzing individual initiative, but in the sense of setting the interest of the community above the liberty and the initiative of the individual. The interests of the community became the regulating and, if necessary, the commanding factor."[286]

"When the state has the unrestricted right to determine the decisions of the owners of the means of production, then the formal legal institution of private ownership no longer means very much." - Rainer Zitelmann

Communism is referred to as a *universal* doctrine because the word comes from Latin communis, meaning 'common, universal', as in common ownership.[287] It is easy enough to recognize the similarities of these regimes. Hitler promoted both socialism and, to some extent, still allowed private property, but as the Mises institute's Rainer Zitelmann notes:

> "For Hitler the formal maintenance of private ownership was not important. When the state has the unrestricted right to determine the decisions of the owners of the means of production, then the formal legal institution of private ownership no longer means very much."

National Socialism was still socialism. The same article included the quotation below from the institute's founder.[288]

> Ludwig von Mises, June 18, 1942 letter to New York Times: "The German pattern of socialism (Zwangswirtschaft) is characterized by the fact that it maintains, although only nominally, some institutions of capitalism. Labor is, of course, no longer a "commodity"; the labor market has been solemnly abolished; the government fixes wage rates and assigns every worker the place where he must work. Private ownership has been nominally untouched. In fact, however, the former entrepreneurs have been reduced to the status of shop managers... Market exchange and entrepreneurship are thus only a sham... Some of the labels of capitalistic market economy are retained, but they signify something entirely different from what they mean in a genuine market economy."

"It is of no importance if we ourselves live—as long as our Volk lives, as long as Germany lives!" - Adolf Hitler

Hitler also spoke of the German people as a class, much like the proletariat in communism. He subordinated individual human beings to the society, which he called the Volk (meaning the folk or people). He was entirely racist and, I think, consumed by self-hatred, but he was also an ideologue, a believer. In Germany, its people were defined by race, not citizenship.

> Adolf Hitler, Sept. 1, 1939 speech:
> "All of us pledge ourselves to the one ancient principle: it is of no importance if we ourselves live—as long as our Volk lives, as long as Germany lives! This is essential."[289]

> Adolf Hitler, May 10, 1933 speech from his book, "My New Order":
> "I am an independent man, and I have set before myself no other goal than to serve, to the best of my power and ability, the German people, and above all to serve the millions who, thanks to their simple trust and ignorance and thanks to the baseness of their former leaders, have perhaps suffered more than any other class."[290]

> Adolf Hitler, July 15, 1932 Speech:
> "As long as Nationalism and Socialism march as separate ideas, they will be defeated by the united forces of their opponents. On that day when both ideas are molten into one, they will become invincible!"[291]

"People are not born socialists, but must first be taught how to become them." - Adolf Hitler

---

> Adolf Hitler, Oct. 5, 1037 Speech:
> "With the aid of this tremendous society [Winterhilfswerk] countless people are being relieved of the feeling of social abandonment and isolation. Many are thus regaining the firm belief that they are not completely lost and alone in this world, but sheltered in their Volksgemeinschaft [people's community]; that they, too, are being cared for, that they, too, are being thought of and remembered. And beyond that: there is a difference between the theoretical knowledge of socialism and the practical life of socialism. People are not born socialists, but must first be taught how to become them."[292]

> Adolf Hitler, April 17, 1934 speech:
> "The Winterhilfswerk [Winter Relief of the German People[293]] is to alleviate the misery which cannot be alleviated by official

> measures. It shall also contribute to educating the Volk in socialist thinking. In the affluent Germany of the pre-war age, it was not possible to establish such an organization. In months of the most intensive propaganda, pre-war Germany obtained a total of no more than seven million marks in donations for the zeppelin project, although it was a cause involving the entire Volk."[294]

"He who knows how most skilfully to make this 'public opinion' serve his own interests becomes forthwith master in the State."
- Adolf Hitler

> Adolf Hitler, Speech of April 12, 1922. Quoted in My New Order: "The Right does not understand that directly every small question of profit or loss is regularly put before so called 'public opinion,' he who knows how most skillfully to make this 'public opinion' serve his own interests becomes forthwith master in the State. And that can be achieved by the man who can lie most artfully, most infamously; and in the last resort he is not the German, he is, in Schopenhauer's words, 'the great master in the art of lying' - the Jew."[295]

Hitler identified capitalism as a threat to his power just as the left does today in the U.S. Despite the unfathomable atrocities of Hitler's Germany and the Soviet Union, both were surpassed in the sheer number of deaths by Mao Zedong, who was responsible for the murder of 45 million people in a period of just five years as he collectivized China.[296] While these leaders created misery on an unfathomable scale, smaller countries like North Korea, Cambodia, and Venezuela have often mirrored their tactics and outcomes. Beyond the direct human cost, these ideologies undermined their nations' economies by trying to centrally manage production based on a desired outcome rather than a sustainable balance of supply and demand. They consumed their own people, figuratively where not literally.

Fascism is another authoritarian movement to which the right is held responsible but belongs with its fellow tyrannies on the left. Though not having the numbers of atrocities committed by its German ally or its Russia enemy, Italy rose from a comparable ideology. Benito Mussolini, the totalitarian dictator of Italy during World War II, was a longtime revolutionary socialist before creating his own, even more violent ideology. He created the Fascist Party, which used viciousness and chaos to overthrow the socialist government and target his former allies.[297] The same thing is happening today in the U.S. and U.K. The description that follows seems as appropriate to Hitler's Germany as the many faces of communism, but does not resemble in any way the ideology of individual liberty found on the American right. Fascism admits outwardly that a dictator rules and controls everything while collectivists create the same situation with different rhetoric.

> The Merriam-Webster Dictionary defines Fascism:
> "A political philosophy, movement, or regime (such as that of the Fascisti) that exalts nation and often race above the individual and that stands for a centralized autocratic government headed by a dictatorial leader, severe economic and social regimentation, and forcible suppression of opposition." [298]

Nothing in my experience today resembles this more than the leftist establishment in our country.

"Individual interests would be subordinated to the good of the nation." - Encyclopedia Britannica

---

> According to Encyclopedia Britannica, fascism is characterized as:
> "An extreme militaristic nationalism, contempt for electoral democracy and political and cultural liberalism, a belief in natural social hierarchy and the rule of elites, and the desire to create a Volksgemeinschaft (German: "people's community"), in which individual interests would be subordinated to the good of the nation.[299]

Despite some differences, the outcome and practical operation of Fascism, Nazism and Communism are all the same. They are all led by dictators who centrally control everything for what they claim is the common or national good at the expense of the individual human beings they rule. Today the Fascists call themselves the anti-Fascists or Antifa as they use intolerance, viciousness and chaos to tear down our constitutional system and impose their will on everyone else. Communism, Nazism, fascism, and religious tyranny all identified others as enemies that were demonized or eliminated and all justified their actions as a response to victimhood.

They used propaganda and violence to manipulate and control their own people. All suppressed dissent and arrested, imprisoned and killed their opponents. All used a police state to enforce their control, regulating everything and punishing people who did not conform. All propelled leaders into dictatorships. All denied individual human liberty and sacrificed individuals to the state. Across the world, over a hundred million people have been killed under Communism according to the Black Book of Communism (far more when you add Hitler's tallies to the total). The philosophy of collectivism cannot be separated from real world horrors of communism and socialism because the latter is a direct and inescapable consequence of the former.

"Communism... is absolutely contrary to the natural law itself, and if once adopted would utterly destroy the rights, property and possessions of all men, and even society itself." - Pope Pius IX

Despite its initial abhorrence of reason and liberty, the Roman Catholic church came to voice support for these ideals when faced with atheistic communism, in some part because they saw the evil of this new system but probably also because it threatened their power.

> Divini Redemptoris on Atheistic Communism, Pope Pius XI, 1937:
> "This modern revolution, it may be said, has actually broken out or threatens everywhere, and it exceeds in amplitude and violence anything yet experienced in the preceding persecutions launched against the Church. Entire peoples find themselves in danger of falling back into a barbarism worse than that which oppressed the greater part of the world at the coming of the Redeemer. This all too imminent danger, Venerable Brethren, as you have already surmised, is bolshevistic and atheistic Communism, which aims at upsetting the social order and at undermining the very foundations of Christian civilization...
>
> "Ever since the days when groups of 'intellectuals' were formed in an arrogant attempt to free civilization from the bonds of morality and religion, Our Predecessors overtly and explicitly drew the attention of the world to the consequences of the dechristianization of human society. With reference to Communism, Our Venerable Predecessor, Pius IX, of holy memory, as early as 1846 pronounced a solemn condemnation, which he confirmed in the words of the Syllabus directed against 'that infamous doctrine of so-

> called Communism which is absolutely contrary to the natural law itself, and if once adopted would utterly destroy the rights, property and possessions of all men, and even society itself.' Later on, another of Our predecessors, the immortal Leo XIII, in his Encyclical Quod Apostolici Muneris, defined Communism as 'the fatal plague which insinuates itself into the very marrow of human society only to bring about its ruin...'

"The preachers of Communism are also proficient in exploiting racial antagonisms and political divisions and oppositions." - Pope Pius XI

> "How is it possible that such a system, long since rejected scientifically and now proved erroneous by experience, how is it, We ask, that such a system could spread so rapidly in all parts of the world? The explanation lies in the fact that too few have been able to grasp the nature of Communism. The majority instead succumb to its deception, skillfully concealed by the most extravagant promises. By pretending to desire only the betterment of the condition of the working classes, by urging the removal of the very real abuses chargeable to the liberalistic economic order, and by demanding a more equitable distribution of this world's goods (objectives entirely and undoubtedly legitimate), the Communist takes advantage of the present world-wide economic crisis to draw into the sphere of his influence even those sections of the populace which on principle reject all forms of materialism and terrorism.

"A third powerful factor in the diffusion of Communism is the conspiracy of silence on the part of a large section of the... press." – Pope Pius XI

> "And as every error contains its element of truth, the partial truths to which We have referred are astutely presented according to the needs of time and place, to conceal, when convenient, the repulsive crudity and inhumanity of Communistic principles and tactics. Thus the Communist ideal wins over many of the better minded members of the community. These in turn become the apostles of the movement among the younger intelligentsia who are still too

> immature to recognize the intrinsic errors of the system. The preachers of Communism are also proficient in exploiting racial antagonisms and political divisions and oppositions...

The Roman Church was certainly correct about the mainstream press but has itself, since, been drawn into a form of socialism. Pope Pius XI continued:

> "A third powerful factor in the diffusion of Communism is the conspiracy of silence on the part of a large section of the non-Catholic press of the world. We say conspiracy, because it is impossible otherwise to explain how a press usually so eager to exploit even the little daily incidents of life has been able to remain silent for so long about the horrors perpetrated in Russia, in Mexico and even in a great part of Spain; and that it should have relatively so little to say concerning a world organization as vast as Russian Communism."[300]

"We have created a 'throw away' culture which is now spreading.
 - Pope Francis

Under Pope Francis, the first pope to emerge from the Americas, the church echoed collectivism

> Apostolic Exhortation, Evangelii Gaudium, of the Holy Father, Francis, Nov. 24, 2013:
> "We have created a 'throw away' culture which is now spreading. It is no longer simply about exploitation and oppression, but something new. Exclusion ultimately has to do with what it means to be a part of the society in which we live; those excluded are no longer society's underside or its fringes or its disenfranchised - they are no longer even a part of it. The excluded are not the 'exploited' but the outcast, the 'leftovers'. In this context, some people continue to defend trickle-down theories which assume that economic growth, encouraged by a free market, will inevitably succeed in bringing about greater justice and inclusiveness in the world. This opinion, which has never been confirmed by the facts, expresses a crude and naïve trust in the goodness of those wielding economic power and in the sacralized workings of the prevailing economic system. Meanwhile, the excluded are still waiting. To

> sustain a lifestyle which excludes others, or to sustain enthusiasm for that selfish ideal, a globalization of indifference has developed."

"Not to share one's wealth with the poor is to steal from them and to take away their livelihood. It is not our own goods which we hold, but theirs." - Pope Francis[301]

> "While the earnings of a minority are growing exponentially, so too is the gap separating the majority from the prosperity enjoyed by those happy few. This imbalance is the result of ideologies which defend the absolute autonomy of the marketplace and financial speculation. Consequently, they reject the right of states, charged with vigilance for the common good, to exercise any form of control. A new tyranny is thus born, invisible and often virtual, which unilaterally and relentlessly imposes its own laws and rules. Debt and the accumulation of interest also make it difficult for countries to realize the potential of their own economies and keep citizens from enjoying their real purchasing power. To all this we can add widespread corruption and self-serving tax evasion, which have taken on worldwide dimensions. The thirst for power and possessions knows no limits. In this system, which tends to devour everything which stands in the way of increased profits, whatever is fragile, like the environment, is defenseless before the interests of a deified market, which become the only rule."

"Until exclusion and inequality in society and between peoples are reversed, it will be impossible to eliminate violence." - Pope Francis

---

In the vein of the distribution of wealth, the pope quotes a previous leader, "Not to share one's wealth with the poor is to steal from them and to take away their livelihood. It is not our own goods which we hold, but theirs." From an outsider's perspective, I have to say this is absolutely leftist socialism, not Christian generosity. Pope Francis continued:

> "Today in many places we hear a call for greater security. But until exclusion and inequality in society and between peoples are reversed, it will be impossible to eliminate violence. The poor and

> the poorer peoples are accused of violence, yet without equal opportunities the different forms of aggression and conflict will find a fertile terrain for growth and eventually explode. When a society – whether local, national or global – is willing to leave a part of itself on the fringes, no political programmes or resources spent on law enforcement or surveillance systems can indefinitely guarantee tranquility. This is not the case simply because inequality provokes a violent reaction from those excluded from the system, but because the socioeconomic system is unjust at its root.
>
> "Just as goodness tends to spread, the toleration of evil, which is injustice, tends to expand its baneful influence and quietly to undermine any political and social system, no matter how solid it may appear. If every action has its consequences, an evil embedded in the structures of a society has a constant potential for disintegration and death. It is evil crystallized in unjust social structures, which cannot be the basis of hope for a better future. Today's economic mechanisms promote inordinate consumption, yet it is evident that unbridled consumerism combined with inequality proves doubly damaging to the social fabric. Inequality eventually engenders a violence which recourse to arms cannot and never will be able to resolve. It serves only to offer false hopes to those clamouring for heightened security, even though nowadays we know that weapons and violence, rather than providing solutions, create new and more serious conflicts."[302]

Thankfully, the Roman Catholic Church is no longer the purveyor of inquisitions and witch burnings, no longer torturing and killing to terrorize dissenters into conformity. It does, however, bear similarities to socialism when engaging in matters of government.[303]

"Labor continues to assist in the destruction of the only order under which at least some degree of independence and freedom has been secured to every worker." – Friedrich Hayek

---

Collectivism has found its way into American society, but the consequences of the leftward path our nation has undertaken in the last hundred plus years was clearly foreseeable. Friedrich Hayek, an Austrian-Hungarian born economist, warned of the outcome of collectivist thinking and government interventionalism in his influential 1944 book "The Road to Serfdom":

> "It is true that the virtues which are less esteemed and practiced now - independence, self-reliance, and the willingness to bear risks, the readiness to back one's own conviction against a majority, and the willingness to voluntary cooperation with one's neighbors - are essentially those on which the working of an individualist society rests. Collectivism has nothing to put in their place, and in so far as it already has destroyed them it has left a void filled by nothing but the demand for obedience and the compulsion of the individual to do what is collectively decided to be good... So long as labor continues to assist in the destruction of the only order under which at least some degree of independence and freedom has been secured to every worker, there is indeed little hope for the future."[304]

"No justice can be done for one person that requires doing an injustice be done to another."

For decades we seemed to heed Hayek's warning, but the collectivists just became more covert. Collectivism has never in practice equated to a better quality of life for the average person.[305]

"The ordaining of laws in favor of one part of the nation, to the prejudice and oppression of another, is certainly the most erroneous and mistaken policy." - Benjamin Franklin

---

Though cries ring out these days for social justice as an early salvo of collectivism, it is a contradiction of terms. To be just, law must apply to every single person equally. No justice can be done for one person that requires doing an injustice be done to another.

> Memoirs of the Life and Writings of Benjamin Franklin: "The ordaining of laws in favor of one part of the nation, to the prejudice and oppression of another, is certainly the most erroneous and mistaken policy. An equal dispensation of

> protection, rights, privileges, and advantages, is what every part is entitled to, and ought to enjoy." [306]

The collectivism that pervades our universities today stands in stark contrast to the ideals of our nation's founding and reflects the corruption of our entire education system. An example is a book by a professor of Educational Foundations program at Chicago's Northeastern Illinois University, Kenneth N. Addison, about the roots of racism in America:

"Individual freedom flies in the face of collective equality."
- Professor Kenneth N. Addison

> "Property rights continue to trump human rights; oligarchy masquerades as democracy, with the wealthy lobbying to control and buy the government; individual freedom flies in the face of collective equality as the greed of the rich is pitted against the public interest of the majority; compassionless rationalizations are pressed forward as reasoned alternatives to empathy and advocacy for the poor." [307]

The left sees that oligarchy masquerades as democracy but is completely erroneous with respect to the source. Individual rights and property are the greatest defense against oligarchy. It is not greed to want to keep the fruits of your labor, to see your children benefit from your efforts and to expect others to work for the improvement of their own lives. It is greedy to see things other people have and think that you are entitled to some piece of it or all of it. There can be no collective rights without individual rights, no value in society unless every member is valued. The engine of our economy is the ingenuity and effort of free individuals, working alone and together, something crushed under any version of collectivism.

Chapter 6

Seductive of Simple Minds

A parallel arose in my research between the Roman Catholic Church during the height of its tyranny and the elitist of the left today, not just because the left employs the conceptual trappings of religion, as I detail in the next chapter, but because they were both compelled by the same delusions of superiority and tyrannical zeal. The machinations of those who once controlled, or thought they controlled, the gates to heaven echo those today who consider themselves the intellectual and moral superiors of the common people, entitled to tell them what to think and how to behave, certain of the public's ignorance and ineptitude. The bureaucracy of our government serves the same purpose as the bureaucracy of the church, administrators enjoying a small share of power and ego while leaders further their own ambitions. Public schools preach the doctrine and propagate the mentality. Oligarchs at the top - not capitalists but criminals - have the real power, the rest are merely useful tools.

Their differences aside, both the church of the past and the leftist establishment today see people as sheep with simple minds that were easily led astray, ignorant and incapable of acting without the direction of more knowledgeable, morally superior rulers. Both expected conformity of thought and considered dissent an evil or contagion to be eradicated for the good of the whole. As ripe with arrogance as the religious establishments of the past, the left today imagines their opponents are narrow-minded, anti-intellectuals who are, unfathomably, just unwilling to listen when they're being told what to believe and do. The left is far more radical and dangerous than most liberal Americans, though mainstream support does aid their totalitarian ambitions.

A sample of their superiority complex can be seen in their response to the Tea Party and President Donald Trump, both of which represented movements of America's founding principles as identified in this book, as well as the Covid-19 pandemic. Much of this is history now, a vague memory, but it exposes the pattern. Those who do not know history will continue to fall victim to those who do. Though I disagreed with President Barrack Obama on every policy, I did hope, and I think a great many people hoped, that at the very least electing a black President would demonstrate that America had finally moved past the racial divisions of the past.

Instead, anyone who disagreed with the policies of his administration were immediately condemned as racists. Racism is an insult used to indicate someone is simple minded and ignorant. Obama's policies took America a giant leap to the left toward the concentration of power and there was a lot more at stake than race. They could have disagreed with our policy arguments and attempt to justify their own, but instead, they assumed we were too feeble to recognize their obvious superiority. This elitist attitude today come from the establishment in both parties. Whereas the modern right cares little about race, it is the center stone of leftist dogma.

A Mad Dog

Like the church, the elitist left saw dissent as an ideological infection that threatened their power, a rabid dog that needed to be put down. While the left was long known for protests, for the right, taking to the streets was something new. Like many others across the country, my family and I attended political protests for the first time in our lives in the spring of 2009 during the debate over the administration's policies, particularly an acceleration of our already reckless spending and government involvement in the healthcare industry. We coalesced, not around racism or hatred, but around a set of common American principles, the same ones I describe in this book. There were few honest descriptions of the Tea Party movement but the following was one.

> Katie Connolly, BBC News, Sept. 16, 2010:
> "Perhaps the most important thing to understand about the Tea Party is that, in some ways, it defies traditional categorisations. It was founded amid a groundswell of populist anger over government bail-outs of failing banks, insurers and auto companies following the economic meltdown of 2008... This nascent group of conservative activists called itself the Tea Party. 'We realized that

> government spending without the will of the people is a form of taxation without representation,' says Ms Botteri, referencing the motto of the original Tea Party protest in Boston, when early American colonists threw taxed British tea into the harbour... The modern day Tea Party has three central tenets: fiscal responsibility, limited government and free markets... The Tea Partiers are as disillusioned with George W. Bush's big-spending Republicans as they are with Barack Obama's Democrats."[308]

For practical reasons, many Americans base their votes on limited information and proceed in their lives with only the most cursory appreciation of how the current national policy effects their personal liberty, economy and future. This was less perilous when we still trusted the integrity of leading news sources, when we believed the free press competed in a race to expose the truth and held our leaders accountable and that, in some significant measure, our government answered to the people. This became something we could no longer believe and, as a consequence, we got involved.

The Tea Party came as many Americans saw our nation under the influence of liberally educated intellectuals who didn't seem to understand the real world economy or simply weren't acting in the interests of Americans. We started attending town halls and tax protests. Many of these people gained a substantial understanding of our history and politics from schools and universities but also from reading books, from our own experience and interactions with the mechanics of a market economy, and the real-world knowledge passed down from our parents and grandparents. We were met with a visceral hatred and contempt by those on the left who could not fathom that the middle of the country, and other places beyond the upper floors of the high-rises and gated communities, could harbor informed voters with an understanding of the ideals and values on which our nation was founded and that were responsible for its remarkable success.

"Literally dozens of FOX News viewers – sorry – dozens of outraged citizens protest having to pay their fair share of the taxes the rest of us pay." - Keith Olbermann

---

When my family and I attended the Tax Day protest in 2009 in our small North Arkansas town, similar protests were held around the nation. While there were several dozen gathered here, ours was just one small town among many. They were civil events as we gathered to listen to speakers. These protests were described that day with disdain as the left projected their own vitriol and bigotry on the group.

> Keith Olbermann, MSNBE host, April 15, 2009: "From Dixon, Illinois, to Duncan, Arizona; from El Cajon, California, to Sag Harbor, New York – literally dozens of FOX News viewers – sorry – dozens of outraged citizens protest having to pay their fair share of the taxes the rest of us pay..."
>
> Howard Fineman, MSNBC Political Analysist, re: Louisville, Kentucky Tea Party:
> "Well, the point is, Keith, that I didn't interview all the people at the rally about this. But my guess is that most of them thought a tea bag was a tea bag, OK? So, they had no sense whatsoever that there was a whole subtext to this, whatever urban language is involved, they don't know anything about, don't want to know anything about." [309]

"They don't know their history at all. This is about hating a black man in the White House." - Janeane Garofalo

---

He didn't ask, but just assumed these protesters were too ignorant to know about American history or the foundation of the movement of which they were a part. The next day Olbermann declared that the people involved were motivated by simple hatred of our first black president, Barrack Obama, and his guest, actress and activist Janeane Garofalo, joined in.

> Olbermann: "Well, the tea bagging is all over, except for the clean-up. That will be my last intentional double entendre on this one, at least until the end of the segment. The number two story tonight, the sad reality behind the corporate sponsored tea parties, visual proof that this is not about spending deficits or taxes, but about some Americans getting riled up now about these things, riled up by the people who caused these things, and finally about some Americans who just hate the president of the United States... we're

now joined by actor and activist Jeanine Garofalo. Good to see you."

Garofalo: "You know, there's nothing more interesting than seeing a bunch of racists become confused and angry at a speech they're not quite certain what he thinks. It sounds right to them, and then it doesn't make sense. Let's be very honest about what this is about. It's not about bashing Democrats, it's not about taxes, they have no idea what the Boston tea party was about."

Olbermann: "That's right."

"If you have a cerebral electorate, Fox news goes down the toilet, very, very fast." - Janeane Garofalo

---

Garofalo: "They don't know their history at all. This is about hating a black man in the White House. This is racism straight up. That is nothing but a bunch of tea-bagging rednecks. And there is no way around that. And you know, you can tell these type of right-wingers anything and they'll believe it, except the truth. You tell them the truth and they become -- it's like showing Frankenstein's monster fire. They become confused, and angry and highly volatile. That guy caused in them feelings they don't know, because their limbic brain - we've discussed this before, the limbic brain inside a right-winger or Republican or conservative or your average white power activist, the limbic brain is much larger in their head space than in a reasonable person, and it is pushing against the frontal lobe. So their synapses are misfiring...

"Fox News loves to foment this anti-intellectualism because that's their bread and butter. If you have a cerebral electorate, Fox news goes down the toilet, very, very fast. It is sick and sad to see Neil Cavuto doing this. They've been doing it for years. That's why Roger Ailes and Rupert Murdoch started this venture, to disinform and to coarsen and dumb down a certain segment of the electorate. But what is really - I didn't know there were so many racists left. I didn't know that. As I've said, the Republican hype and the conservative movement has now crystallized into the white power movement."[310]

She may have thought her delivery comical, but there's little humor in level of derision and hatred about people she clearly knew nothing about. Attacks on Fox News were common, not because it was right wing but because it was one of the few news outlets at the time that was not entirely left wing.

"The tea party is almost entirely about race, and there's no comparative group on the left that's similarly motivated by bigotry, ignorance and racial hatred." - Bob Cesca

---

The tendency to accuse their opponents of their own behavior became a theme of the left. Our fears were about the state of our economy, the growth of tyranny and the destruction of the rule of law. Many of these commenters continued to blindly accept legislation for what their leaders told them it would do, without any question about their actual content.

> Bob Cesca, The Huffington Post, March 3, 2010: "Because when you strip away all of the rage, all of the nonsensical loud noises and all of the contradictions, all that's left is race. The tea party is almost entirely about race, and there's no comparative group on the left that's similarly motivated by bigotry, ignorance and racial hatred... There's no other way to explain why these people were silent and compliant for so long, and only decided to collectively freak out when this 'foreign' and 'exotic' president came along and, right out of the chute, passed the largest middle class tax cut in American history -- something they would otherwise support, for goodness sake, it was $288 billion in tax cuts! -- we're left to deduce no other motive but the ugly one that lurks just beneath the pale flesh, the tri-corner hats and the dangly tea bag ornamentation."[311]

"The members of this movement have no sense of moral decency."
- David Brooks

The Tea Party can be traced by to Ross Perot and Ron Paul. It was fueled by a reaction to the expansion of government, war and wild spending of the George W. Bush administration. As opposition to the establishment grew, their opinion of the people fell even farther.

"[Republicans] do not accept the legitimacy of scholars and intellectual authorities." - David Brooks, New York Times

---

> In 2011, New York Times, columnist David Brooks: "The Republican Party may no longer be a normal party. Over the past few years, it has been infected by a faction that is more of a psychological protest than a practical, governing alternative. The members of this movement do not accept the logic of compromise, no matter how sweet the terms.... The members of this movement do not accept the legitimacy of scholars and intellectual authorities. A thousand impartial experts may tell them that a default on the debt would have calamitous effects, far worse than raising tax revenues a bit. But the members of this movement refuse to believe it. The members of this movement have no sense of moral decency. A nation makes a sacred pledge to pay the money back when it borrows money... The members of this movement have no economic theory worthy of the name."[312]

"All of a sudden they're looking at a country that - where South Asians run all the mini marts and motels. And there are Mexican Americans all over the place." - Joe Klein, Time Magazine

---

The fact that the right thought we should reduce spending to keep from defaulting on our debts was inconceivable. The left's misconception of economics collided with a pure hatred for Americans in what they called "flyover country" (the part of the nation between the coasts which the elitists only see when flying between them). The following comments about protesters in my home state reveals far more about the author than the subjects of his piece.

> Time Magazine political columnist Joe Klein, New York Historical Society panel, 2012:
> "You know, you go to a Tea Party meeting and you see a forest of people who are scared to death because this country has changed underneath them. You go to a Tea Party meeting in Arkansas, which I did, and all of a sudden they're looking at a country that-where South Asians run all the mini marts and motels. And there

> are Mexican Americans all over the place and their grandchildren are marrying out of their race or becoming gay. The President of the United States doesn't have the good sense to be either black or white and his middle name is Hussein. The economy sucks. The jobs they used to be able to hold without having a high school diploma have disappeared. And as a New Yorker, I have to say that the things they're most afraid of are the things I love the most about the country."[313]

Though ignorant of our motives, pundits were free to lavish insults on us because of our accents or our ancestry, our jobs, where we lived and assumptions about our level of education and intelligence. This person's own use of stereotypes aside, he was right about one thing: there was fear in these gatherings, a low, rumbling, building fear, but not of the things he imagined. We feared that our republic was at risk. We were right.

"The Tea Party... are corporate America's useful idiots." - Bill Maher

---

> Commentator Bill Maher, Late Show with David Letterman, CBS, April 15, 2011:
> "Well, the Tea Party, you know, they are sad, unfortunate people because -- well, they are, because they are, you know, corporate America's useful idiots. They are they -- I would have more respect for them if they knew a thing, if any fact could get in that tin foil helmet. If they would get out of their chat rooms and have their house tested for lead for just a minute... I don't have any respect for the tea-(baggers) [word silenced] and I do call them the tea-(baggers) [word silenced] -- even though they hate it. I will stop calling them Tea-(baggers) [word silenced] when they stop calling it Obamacare, that's my deal.
>
> "But here's the thing. Their whole campaign is based on money. It's all about we have too much debt, the deficit is too high. They are, after all, named after a tax revolt. But you know, there's these things called facts. Where did all this debt come from. Well, the facts will tell us it was mostly ran up under Bush. Two wars that we put on the credit card. Prescription drug program that was unpaid for. Tax cuts for the richest one percent, that was unpaid for. Where were the Tea Party then? Crickets. But suddenly, when President Nosferatu took office -- suddenly debt became

> intolerable. So, there's just something about him that they don't like. I can't put my finger on what it is. (audience laughter) But there's some way that he's just not like them."[314]

In time, Maher would begin to understand our true motivations but still accepted the deluded view of Donald Trump.

On September 12, 2009, while I happened to be working in our nation's capital, I attended the gathering on the National Mall put on by the 9-12 Project[315] and FreedomWorks[316], among other groups, which brought hundreds of thousands of people (at the low end of my best estimate based on comparing photos and other events) from across the nation at their own expense. This gathering hoped to rekindle how Americans came together the day after the 9/11 attacks and to address Tea Party concerns about the direction of our nation. I saw families riding the subway on the way to the National Mall, parents and kids carrying handmade signs. Others came by buses that lined the Mall or walked from nearby hotels. As I walked on my

J Fragoules 9-12 Event

own through the massive crowd of all ages, I found them friendly and determined. The speakers and people attending were focused on American principles and values. I saw nothing violent or vulgar. No windows were broken, no fires set, no police in riot gear needed or arrests made.

After the crowd dispersed, leaving the Mall noticeably cleaner than they found it, I was crossing Pennsylvania Avenue on my way to the Archives Metro Station. I was wearing a t-shirt with the U.S. Constitution printed on it which I had recently purchased (before I had even heard of the event) at the Smithsonian's American History museum just a short walk away. A well-dressed young woman and man were also crossing the street not far from me. I heard her comment about my shirt, which she said, emphatically, that she just couldn't understand.

A family across the street were making their way down the sidewalk toward the metro as well, carrying their signs under arm and pushing a young man in a wheelchair. The woman near me commented again, "What about him? Doesn't he want health care?" She equated opposition to the legislation that would come to be known as Obamacare, with opposition to the availability and affordability of health care, two radically different things. It exposed a tendency on the left to believe what they are told by their leaders.

> Edmund Haislmaier, Abigail Slagle, Heritage Foundation, March 21, 2021:
> "Eleven years after the passage of Obamacare, Americans buying health insurance under the law are still worse off financially than before the health law was enacted. Obamacare more than doubled health insurance costs for workers and families, with the national average premium increasing by 129 percent from 2013 to 2019."[317]

The lady I overheard seemed to accept the nearly 1.2-million-word law without even a suspicion that there may have been more to it than she had been told.[318] It hadn't crossed her mind that she might have been lied to about it or that her perception of it was inaccurate. Even the politicians who vote on bills like this have little idea what they actually contain as they are too long to read and decipher in the time given. The reality of the legislation involved a great expansion of government and regulation, at extraordinary expense, funneling money to insurance companies. It also put us one step closer to rationing of services that occurs in every nation that embraces socialized-style medicine.[319] A similar, startling level of naivety could be found years later coming from one of the many anti-Trump celebrities. The threat to Mr. De Niro referenced below, of course, was reprehensible, but Carrey's gullibility and egotism were breathtaking.

"Almost half of America at this moment believes there is a sinister, deep state diabolically plotting to what? Give them health care?" - Jim Carrey

---

> Actor Jim Carrey, Acceptance Speech at Bafta Britannia Awards in L.A., October 2018:

> "Chaplin criticized 'capitalism without a conscious'... And that's what we have now, capitalism without a conscious. He showed the common man being fed through the gears of a brutal, dehumanizing industrial age... He took on the American right wing of his day, its worst evils - hatred of immigrants, contempt for the truth, greed and the abuse of power. Shamelessness is not, and will never be, a superpower. It is the work of a villain, kidnapping children is not what great nations do. Almost half of America at this moment believes there is a sinister, deep state diabolically plotting to what? Give them health care? What is the sinister plan here?

"How dare they besmirch such people, how dare they!"- Jim Carrey

---

> "We in America are misinformed. Reality shows have warped our idea of what a hero is, or what the truth is. So tonight, I would like to dedicate this award to those who remind us of our virtues, who remind us of the truth. To Sir Charles Chaplin, who battled McCarthyism into exile, to Christopher Steele, who tried to pull a thorn out of the paw of an ungrateful beast, to Christine Blasey Ford, to Colin Kaepernick. He'll stand for the anthem when the anthem stands for him. One of the greatest artists of our time, Robert De Niro whose life was threatened this week, and many other decent people who bring joy to the world and who have been dedicated to it for years, for decades, how dare they besmirch such people, how dare they! We are fighting the same evils today. In America, the United Kingdom and across the globe."[320]

Insults on our intelligence were usually followed by the distortion of our beliefs into irrational misrepresentations.[321] If we opposed the policies of the Obama administration, we must be racists. If we were against the extreme environmentalism, we were against having a clean air and water. If we wanted to reduce government spending, we were against teachers, police and firefighters and wanted to stop paying our debts. If we opposed Obamacare, we were against healthcare for the poor. If we opposed illegal immigration, we hated immigrants and believed they were all murders and rapists. This was the establishment and media being intentionally obtuse. Others just couldn't see past their own bigotry.

A large number of influential stars, including many whose work I once enjoyed, came out impulsively condemning the Tea Party, permanently damaging my opinion of them. Actor Morgan Freeman comes to mind.

"Screw the country...we're going to do whatever we can to get this black man outta here." - Morgan Freeman

---

> Morgan Freeman on British TV, December, 2017: "Their stated policy, publicly stated, is to do whatever it takes to see to it that Obama only serves one term. What's, what does that, what underlines that? 'Screw the country. We're going to whatever we do to get this black man, we can, we're going to do whatever we can to get this black man outta here...' it's a racist thing... Well, it just shows the weak, dark, underside of America. We're supposed to be better than that. We really are. That's, that's why all those people were in tears when Obama was elected president. 'Ah, look at what we are. Look at how, this is America.' You know? And then it just sort of started turning because these people surfaced like stirring up muddy water."[322]

It has always been the stated policy of the losing party in presidential elections to hold the other side to one term, but perhaps this was the first presidential election he had bothered to engage in?

Sources of Depravity

The left did not miss a beat in turning the derision and bigotry they felt for the Tea Party toward a new target. Donald Trump became everything evil in the world and his supporters deplorable. Their elitism went into overdrive. I attended a Trump rally during the last stretch of his 2016 Presidential campaign in North Carolina as I happened to be working in the area. He had already won the nomination but my support was still somewhat reluctant. I had hope, but not a lot of confidence. The event was held in a large field filled with supporters, their vehicles parked up and down the freeway because the extensive parking was insufficient for the crowd on hand. Most were white. Of course, so are most Americans. They were friendly and respectful as we filtered through the metal detectors that had been set up for the occasion. People were excited, much like the Tea Party crowd, except this included new element: optimism for our country and its people.

"They're bringing drugs. They're bringing crime. They're rapists. And some, I assume, are good people." - President Donald Trump

---

In Donald Trump's initial announcement speech, he talked about trade, ISIS and Islamic terrorism, foreign policy failures like the war in Iraq, unemployment, illegal immigration and the unsecured border. The left saw his comments as an opportunity to label him racist from day one and it became the ongoing theme.

"It's coming from more than Mexico. It's coming from all over South and Latin America, and it's coming probably— probably— from the Middle East." - President Donald Trump

---

> Candidate Donald Trump Announcement Speech, June 2015: "The U.S. has become a dumping ground for everybody else's problems... When Mexico sends its people, they're not sending their best. They're not sending you. They're not sending you. They're sending people that have lots of problems, and they're bringing those problems with us. They're bringing drugs. They're bringing crime. They're rapists. And some, I assume, are good people.
>
> "But I speak to border guards and they tell us what we're getting. And it only makes common sense. It only makes common sense. They're sending us not the right people. It's coming from more than Mexico. It's coming from all over South and Latin America, and it's coming probably— probably— from the Middle East. But we don't know. Because we have no protection and we have no competence, we don't know what's happening. And it's got to stop and it's got to stop fast...

"We have people that have no incentive to work."
- President Donald Trump

> "Our country has tremendous potential. We have tremendous people. We have people that aren't working. We have people that

> have no incentive to work. But they're going to have incentive to work, because the greatest social program is a job. And they'll be proud, and they'll love it, and they'll make much more than they would've ever made, and they'll be– they'll be doing so well, and we're going to be thriving as a country, thriving. It can happen."[323]

He was right, at least until Covid-19. Trump was far from the most eloquent speaker when he came on the political scene. Previously the darling of liberals, suddenly his character was ruthlessly attacked. He did not say that everyone coming over the border illegally were rapists, but that became the narrative. I understood the casual observer's reaction to Donald Trump. His boastful manner aggravated his adversaries and left him open to willful mischaracterizations, but his policies were surprisingly on target. Economic optimism exploded when Trump won the election in 2016 with an immediate effect on business because people had hope that his policies were on the horizon. The change that rippled through the supply chain was infectious even before he took office, felt in small businesses around the country, including my family's.

This happened, not simply because Trump was pro-business so much as that he was pro-America. In a country where elections always seem to have candidates who argue about being pro-choice, pro-life, pro-immigrant, pro-this or pro-that, how peculiar was it that a United States Presidential candidate being pro-America was cast as a negative? Instead of listening to his policies and reasoning, his detractors created an elaborate caricature, casting him as all sorts of villainous things. The slogan "Make America Great Again" was condemned as an attempt to reverse civil rights as opposed to the true intent of restoring the rule of law, liberty and our economic health. It also had nothing to do with hate or any phobia. Trump fought back when attacked but he did it irrespective of the race or identity of who he was addressing.

"You do not know anyone as stupid as Donald Trump."
- Fran Lebowitz

> Entertainer and Actress Cher at Private Hillary Clinton Fundraiser, August 2016:
> "He doesn't mean we want to make America great again. He means we want to make America straight and white."[324]

Fran Lebowitz, author, social commentator, public speaker, March 2018:
"Everyone says he is crazy - which maybe he is - but the scarier thing about him is that he is stupid. You do not know anyone as stupid as Donald Trump... He allowed people to express their racism and bigotry in a way that they haven't been able to in quite a while and they really love him for that. It's a shocking thing to realize people love their hatred more than they care about their own actual lives. The hatred - what is that about? It's a fear of your own weakness."[325]

"We need a new America, without pollution, without obscenities, without insults, without revenge." - Barbara Streisand

---

Barbara Streisand column in 'Variety', March 2020:
"He has demolished our standing in the world with his laughable boasts and breathtaking ignorance. He has put the security of this country, and our planet, in a precarious position by abandoning the Paris climate accord and the Iran nuclear deal. He's a one-man weapon of mass destruction ... so reckless that he almost started a war... But Trump thinks the rules don't apply to him. He, and his appointees, have set a whole new level of misconduct. His recent spree of pardons looks like a transparent attempt to normalize his own corruption and pave the way for pardoning his cronies, who have lied for him. (He fires people who obey the law and tell the truth.) That's Trump's world. It's a place of paranoia, hypocrisy and lies, so many lies (16,000 and counting) ... We need a new America, without pollution, without obscenities, without insults, without revenge. We need to restore the nobility of truth... and only then will America be great again."[326]

These types of wild accusations were common but untethered to reality as time would prove. As for an America without insults, perhaps Streisand should have conferred with her fellow liberals. The following was just a taste of the vitriol De Niro would lob at Trump and his supporters as time went on. He was not alone but maybe one of the more unhinged.

Actor Robert De Niro, anti-Trump video for a voter's initiative, October 2016:

"He's so blatantly stupid. He's a punk. He's a dog. He's a pig. He's a con, a bullshit artist, a mutt who doesn't know what he's talking about, doesn't do his homework, doesn't care. Thinks he's gaming society. Doesn't pay his taxes. He's an idiot. Colin Powell said it best, he's a national disaster. He's an embarrassment to this country. It makes me so angry that this country has gotten to this point where this fool, this bozo, has wound up where he has." [327]

"Trump voters who believe... anyone who can be defined as 'other' are responsible for their misfortunes." - Eric Alterman

---

Trumpism and the 'Liberal Elite', Eric Alterman, The Nation, May 2016:
"Now that it's clear the Republican Party will nominate a delusional, dishonest, disinforming, ethnocentric, egomaniacal billionaire with virtually no understanding of foreign or domestic policy to be president of the United States, the obvious question is who to blame... Some key characteristics of the average Trump voter are ignorance, poverty, bigotry, and a desire to turn back the clock on what most Americans consider to be social progress. Both blame games—the pundits and politicians who attack liberals to explain the rise of Trump, as well as the Trump voters who believe that immigrants, Muslims, and anyone who can be defined as "other" are responsible for their misfortunes—share one key similarity: a purposeful blindness to reality...

"An easily manipulated mass movement that is simply unwilling to listen to reason." - Eric Alterman

---

"Most economically and educationally disadvantaged citizens are also likely aware that the people doing the gardening and housekeeping for sub-minimum wage are not the real reason their family's future feels so bleak. Unfortunately, because establishment politicians refuse to admit the economic costs of globalization, and because conservative politicians and intellectuals are unwilling to stand up to the bigotry that has been thriving inside the movement in recent decades, those being left behind have heard no better

> explanations. Now throw in all the scaremongering related to Islamic terrorism – as opposed to, say, handgun violence – and you have a recipe for an easily manipulated mass movement that is simply unwilling to listen to reason. Trump voters want action– what kind hardly matters, so long as there is someone to attack. Consistent with the long tradition of American know-nothingism, they don't care who is genuinely responsible for their misfortune as long as they can find a target for their blind and unquenchable anger."[328]

The fact that elitists like him see immigrants only as servants exposes their bigotry. Most Americans do not have gardeners or housekeepers.

"Trump's essential appeal is based on racism." - Jeet Heer

> Jeet Heer, The New Republic, 2016:
> "Far from being idiots, [Trump's supporters] are people who would normally be considered functioning and successful. Trump's supporters are better educated and wealthier than the American average. Rather than characterizing them as losers who are easily fooled, Trump's supporters—who amount to at least a plurality of the Republican primary electorate—deserve to be looked at in their own terms. Trump's essential appeal is based on racism. He launched his campaign talking about Mexican 'rapists,' and subsequently stirred up xenophobia against many other groups, especially Muslims. His racist pitch succeeded because the Republican Party is overwhelmingly white and has relied heavily on dog-whistle appeals to racism since the early 1960s.
>
> "Trump is appealing to the aggrieved privilege of well-to-do white Republicans who feel threatened by America's changing demographics and challenges to the traditional racial hierarchy in the age of Obama. Racism is evil, but it is not idiotic from the point of view of racists. White racists see themselves as benefitting from Trump's proposal to shore up the old racial status quo. Their value

system deserves to be challenged, but they aren't being fooled by Trump. They know what he's selling and they like it."[329]

"I'm not talking about the neo-Nazis and the white nationalists - because they should be condemned totally." - President Donald Trump

---

The left latched onto the idea that Trump and his supporters were white nationalists for the same reason they called the Tea Party racist: it was a way to demonize their opponents and avoid having to debate them on policy. Neither promoted anything of the sort, but for some reason it was easy for many to believe. It fit with their preconceptions. When protesters came to Charlottesville, North Carolina in 2017 to oppose the removal of a Robert E. Lee statue, others gathered to support its removal. Both sides drew violent and peaceful protesters. Trump said there were fine people on both sides, but he made it clear that he was not talking about the extremists, one of which drove a car into a crowd of counter-protesters, killing one and wounding 19 others. Curiously, the reporter below was arguing a point, not asking questions.

> Trump: The driver of the car is a murderer. And what he did was a horrible, horrible, inexcusable thing...
>
> Reporter: "The neo-Nazis started this. They showed up in Charlottesville to protest --"
>
> Trump: "Excuse me, excuse me. They didn't put themselves -- and you had some very bad people in that group, but you also had people that were very fine people, on both sides. You had people in that group. Excuse me, excuse me. I saw the same pictures as you did. You had people in that group that were there to protest the taking down of, to them, a very, very important statue and the renaming of a park from Robert E. Lee to another name."
>
> Reporter: "George Washington and Robert E. Lee are not the same."
>
> Trump: "George Washington was a slave owner. Was George Washington a slave owner? So, will George Washington now lose his status? Are we going to take down -- excuse me, are we going to take down statues to George Washington? How about Thomas

Jefferson? What do you think of Thomas Jefferson? You like him?"

Reporter: "I do love Thomas Jefferson."

Trump: "Okay, good. Are we going to take down the statue? Because he was a major slave owner. Now, are we going to take down his statue? So you know what, it's fine. You're changing history. You're changing culture. And you had people -- and I'm not talking about the neo-Nazis and the white nationalists -- because they should be condemned totally. But you had many people in that group other than neo-Nazis and white nationalists. Okay? And the press has treated them absolutely unfairly. Now, in the other group also, you had some fine people. But you also had troublemakers, and you see them come with the black outfits and with the helmets, and with the baseball bats. You had a lot of bad people in the other group."

"Sir, I just didn't understand... You were saying the press has treated white nationalists unfairly?" – Unnamed Reporter

---

Reporter: "Sir, I just didn't understand what you were saying. You were saying the press has treated white nationalists unfairly? I just don't understand what you were saying."

Trump: "No, no. There were people in that rally -- and I looked the night before -- if you look, there were people protesting very quietly the taking down of the statue of Robert E. Lee. I'm sure in that group there were some bad ones. The following day it looked like they had some rough, bad people -- neo-Nazis, white nationalists, whatever you want to call them. But you had a lot of people in that group that were there to innocently protest, and very legally protest -- because, I don't know if you know, they had a permit. The other group didn't have a permit. So, I only tell you this: There are two sides to a story. I thought what took place was a horrible moment for our country -- a horrible moment."[330]

This exchange, and the narrative it generated, furthered a political objective. It didn't need to be true. The left divides America into groups by class or race or income or gender or any other way that might create voting blocks, raise animosity and provide political advantage, rather than seeing us all as Americans.

"The President of the United States is a racist." - Rob Reiner

---

> Joy Behar, host of The View, talking about Trump supporters, October 2017:
> "These people on that side are crazy. Don't you understand? They're crazy! You don't deal with white supremacists."[331]
>
> Actor and Filmmaker Rob Reiner, @robreiner, Twitter, July 29, 2019:
> "The President of the United States is a racist. He's made it abundantly clear his re-election is based on white nationalism. If you support him, there can be no distinction between you being a racist and a racist enabler. They are the same."[332]

"[Trump voters] support the notion that... all Mexicans are rapists and all Muslims are bad." - President Joe Biden

---

> Future President Joe Biden, during a virtual fundraiser, April 2020:
> "There are people who support the president because they like the fact that he is engaged in political division. They really support the notion that, you know, all Mexicans are rapists and all Muslims are bad and ... dividing this nation based on ethnicity, race..."[333]

After Trump's election, pundits struggled to understand why it happened. The intellectual inferiority and racism of half of the nation was the only answer they could fathom, exposing their racism, hatred and ignorance.

"My sort of shock to the system was just sort of how gullible a big chunk of the country was to this." - Chuck Todd

---

> Chuck Todd, MSNBC host, Comments printed in the Washington Times, Dec. 2018:
> "Prominent journalists gathered this week to discuss why President Trump sits in the White House and came to the following

conclusion: 'Gullible' voters and 'unfair' coverage – toward Democrat Hillary Clinton – are to blame. The Recode Decode podcast this week featured NBC's Chuck Todd, Andrea Mitchell, and Hallie Jackson talking about the state of American politics. They told host Kara Swisher that Mr. Trump's campaign tricked the former secretary of state into responding to non-issues while stupid voters took care of the rest on Election Day. 'I knew the gaslighting was out there,' Mr. Todd told the panel Dec. 5 in reference to Mr. Trump's psychological prowess. 'I knew it was every day. But I think there was part of me in my head assumed people were discerning it out, knew the BS from the non-BS. So, I think what my sort of shock to the system was just sort of how gullible a big chunk of the country was to this and gullible because maybe they want to be gullible."[334]

Jonathan Chait, New York Magazine, May 11, 2016, regarding Trump's election:
"Here's the factor I think everybody missed: The Republican Party turns out to be filled with idiots. Far more of them than anybody expected."[335]

"Americans... don't understand the issues. They're too stupid."
- Bill Maher

Bill Maher, on Lopez Tonight, TBS, October 26, 2010: "What's the point of having Democrats? We have Democrats for one reason - to drag the ignorant hillbilly-half of this country into the next century, which in their case is the 19th... I'll tell you this about Americans - about the American electorate, the voter. They love a winner. You know, as soon as he [Obama] passed health care, [his approval rating] went up 15 points. They don't understand the issues. They're too stupid. They're like a dog. They can understand inflection. They can understand fear. They can understand dominance. They don't understand issues. But when he won on that issue, he went up."[336]

Ron Reagan, The Daily Beast, March 2018:
"For many of us, mornings have taken on a certain nauseating sameness. We roll out from beneath the blankets and, before the

scent of coffee has reached our nostrils, we are checking the news feeds for the latest semi-literate tweet coughed up by the ranting, traitorous squatter occupying the Oval Office. The rest of the day is spent in a kind of horrified suspension, holding our breath, waiting for whatever outrage will inevitably belch forth from the White House—once a bastion of seriousness and decorum, now ground zero for the demise of western democracy...

"They know very little about the world they inhabit and what they do 'know' is often woefully incorrect." - Ron Reagan

---

"We are understandably reluctant to impugn the intelligence and integrity of our fellow citizens. It is arrogant, uncivil, bad form. Who are we, any of us, to hold ourselves superior? When Hillary Clinton referred to some Trump supporters as 'deplorables', she was roundly castigated on all sides. How dare she? Yet it is an uncomfortable reality that anywhere from a fifth to a third of our electorate can be fairly (if gently) described as low-information voters. If the results of numerous polls and questionnaires are to be trusted, they know very little about the world they inhabit and what they do "know" is often woefully incorrect... It is a mistake to regard concern about such ignorance as effete snobbery or elitist condescension. While misapprehensions about basic astronomy, earth science and biology may have little impact on these folk's daily lives, does anyone actually believe that similarly uninformed views aren't likely to affect their grasp of policies regarding, say, climate change? Income inequality? Gun violence? Immigration? Profound knowledge gaps like the aforementioned reveal an inability to think critically and leave a person vulnerable to all manner of chicanery."[337]

"Trump owes his victory to the uninformed." – Jason Brennon

An FBI employee re: Hillary Clinton email investigation per Breitbart.com:
"Trump's supporters are all poor to middle class, uneducated, lazy POS that think he will magically grant them jobs for doing nothing.

They probably didn't watch the debates, aren't fully educated on his policies, and are stupidly wrapped up in his unmerited enthusiasm... the crazies won finally. This is the tea party on steroids." [338]

Jason Brennan, Foreign Policy.com, Nov. 10, 2016: "Trump owes his victory to the uninformed. But it's not just Trump. Political scientists have been studying what voters know and how they think for well over 65 years. The results are frightening. Voters generally know who the president is but not much else. They don't know which party controls Congress, what Congress has done recently, whether the economy is getting better or worse (or by how much)." [339]

To the contrary, we understand how economies work, how jobs are created and most of us watched debates obsessively. Fueled by Ronald Reagan, Rush Limbaugh and talk radio, these Americans often followed politics with the fervor of sports. Of course, the belief in Americans' ignorance was nothing new.

"Blame the childish, ignorant American public—not politicians—for our political and economic crisis." - Jacob Weisberg

---

Slate.com, Jacob Weisberg, "Blame the childish, ignorant American public" Feb 5, 2010:
"In trying to explain why our political paralysis seems to have gotten so much worse over the past year, analysts have rounded up a plausible collection of reasons including: President Obama's tactical missteps, the obstinacy of congressional Republicans, rising partisanship in Washington, the blustering idiocracy of the cable-news stations, and the Senate filibuster, which has devolved into a super-majority threshold for any important legislation. These are all large factors, to be sure, but that list neglects what may be the biggest culprit in our current predicament: the childishness, ignorance, and growing incoherence of the public at large.

"Anybody who says you can't have it both ways clearly hasn't been spending much time reading opinion polls lately... "[Senator Scott Brown] says we can lower deficits above 10 percent of GDP... simply by cutting government waste. No sensible person who has

> spent five minutes looking at the budget thinks that's remotely possible. The charitable interpretation is that Brown embodies naive optimism, an approach to politics that Ronald Reagan left as one of his more dubious legacies to Republican Party. A better explanation is that Brown is consciously pandering to the public's ignorance and illusions the same way the rest of his Republican colleagues are."[340]

What he didn't understand is that we consider 80 percent of government as waste. He points out illogical contradictions in public opinion poll results, but polls are easily manipulated and seldom actually grasp complex political issues. They are instead often designed poorly or to produce certain results. The dismissive, elitist attitude did increase in the Trump era. Their distortions have twisted our world into absurdities. Former First Lady and Secretary of State Hillary Clinton did this during her campaign against Donald Trump in 2016. Below, she talked about "showing respect and appreciation for one another lifts us up" and then went on to grossly demean many of her opponent's supporters.

"I am all that stands between you and the apocalypse."
 - Hillary Clinton

> Presidential Candidate Hillary Clinton to an LGBTQ fundraiser in NYC on Sept. 9, 2016:
> "You know, I've been saying at events like this lately, I am all that stands between you and the apocalypse... You know, the idea of our country is so rooted in continuing progress that we make together. Our campaign slogan is not just words. We really do believe that we are stronger together. We really do believe that showing respect and appreciation for one another lifts us all up...
>
> "We are living in a volatile political environment. You know, to just be grossly generalistic, you could put half of Trump's supporters into what I call the basket of deplorables. Right? The racist, sexist, homophobic, xenophobic, Islamophobic – you name it. And unfortunately, there are people like that. And he has lifted them up. He has given voice to their websites that used to only have 11,000 people – now how 11 million. He tweets and retweets their

offensive hateful mean-spirited rhetoric. Now, some of those folks – they are irredeemable, but thankfully they are not America.

"You could put half of Trump's supporters into what I call the basket of deplorables." - Hillary Clinton

---

"But the other basket – and I know this because I see friends from all over America here – I see friends from Florida and Georgia and South Carolina and Texas – as well as, you know, New York and California – but that other basket of people are people who feel that the government has let them down, the economy has let them down, nobody cares about them, nobody worries about what happens to their lives and their futures, and they're just desperate for change. It doesn't really even matter where it comes from. They don't buy everything he says, but he seems to hold out some hope that their lives will be different. They won't wake up and see their jobs disappear, lose a kid to heroine, feel like they're in a dead-end. Those are people we have to understand and empathize with as well."[341]

Democratic consultant James Carville, The Hill, Aug. 17, 2022: "The problem the Republican Party has is they got really stupid people that vote in their primaries. And when you have that, you're going to get in - really stupid people demand to have really stupid leaders. And that's where the Republican Party is now... Huge majorities of the Republican Party don't believe in evolution. Alright. Huge majorities of the Republican Party followed Donald Trump... People that believe that the election was stolen and have a right to storm the Capitol, which is a substantial number of people in the Republican Party, are evil... It's not you know, not all of it. There's obviously some very high quality, you know, smart, patriotic Republicans. But they're not in the majority. And they will tell you that themselves."[342]

Twitter via The Washington Examiner Former, August 17, 2022: Edward Luce, U.S. national editor and columnist at Financial Times:
"I've covered extremism and violent ideologies around the world over my career. Have never come across a political force more

nihilistic, dangerous & contemptible than today's Republicans. Nothing close."

CIA Director Michael Hayden:
"I agree. And I was the CIA Director."[343]

Slaughtering men, women and children, burning babies alive and beheading them, is deplorable (see Hamas, October 2023). Half of the country supporting American principles is not. writer for the New York Times finally realized that he grossly mischaracterized Trump's supporters long after the president left office.

Bret Stephens, New York Times, July 21, 2022: "The worst line I ever wrote as a pundit – yes, I know, it's a crowded field – was the first line I ever wrote about the man who would become the 45th president: 'If by now you don't find Donald Trump appalling, you're appalling.' This opening salvo, from August 2015, was the first in what would become dozens of columns denouncing Trump as a unique threat to American life, democratic ideals and the world itself. I regret almost nothing to what I said about the man and his close minions. But the broad swipe at his voters caricatured them and blinkered me. It also probably did more to help than hinder Trump's candidacy. Telling voters they are moral ignoramuses is a bad way of getting them to change their minds.

"What were they seeing I wasn't? That ought to have been the first question to ask myself. When I looked at Trump, I saw a bigoted blowhard making one ignorant argument after another. What Trump supporters saw was a candidate whose entire being was a profoundly raised middle finger at the self-satisfied elite that had produced a failing status quo. I was blind to this... I belonged to a social class that my friend Peggy Noonan called 'the protected.' My family lived in a safe and pleasant neighborhood. Our kids went to an excellent public school. I was well paid, fully insured, insulated against life's hard edges. Trump's appeal, according to Noonan, was largely to people she called 'the unprotected.' Their neighborhoods weren't so safe and pleasant. Their schools weren't so excellent. Their livelihoods weren't so secure. Their experience of America was often one of cultural and economic decline, sometimes felt in the most personal of ways. It was an experience confounded by the insult being treated as losers and racists."[344]

Mr. Stephens realized that he lived in an isolated bubble and had no idea what it was like in the real world where Americans have to live with the consequences of the liberal policies he promoted. Yet, he remained isolated from the reality of Trump's Presidency and the competence of the man himself. He could not see past the propaganda of which he is a part. It was more than a protest vote. He missed Trump's policy speeches while campaigning and his successes in office. Trump kept inflation down, unemployment at record lows, kept us out of war, beat down ISIS, fostered peace agreements in the Middle East, made us energy independent and created a roaring economy before Covid-19. It was even recovering after that, despite everything others did to destroy it.

Trump definitely spent too much of our money, as each president sadly does, but still had the most successful presidency in my lifetime. The left's "Trump Derangement Syndrome" was so unhinged that it could be entertaining. Unfortunately, even Mr. Stephens' minor realization was rare. People like those quoted here also failed to see that Trump was often being facetious in order to mock his distracters who were absent a sense of humor. Rush Limbaugh used to do the same thing, though more eloquently.

"I know nothing about it. It's one of the most farfetched I've ever heard." - President Donald Trump

---

> Donald Trump, Campaign News Conference, C-SPAN, Doral, Florida, July 27, 2016:
> "It's just a total deflection, this whole thing with Russia. In fact, I saw her campaign manager, I don't know his title, Mook. I saw him on television and they asked him about Russia and the hacking. By the way, they hacked -- they probably have her 33,000 e-mails. I hope they do. They probably have her 33,000 e-mails that she lost and deleted because you'd see some beauties there. So, let's see. But I watched this guy Mook and he talked about we think it was Russia that hacked. Now, first of all was what was said on those that's so bad but he said I watched it. I think he was live. But he said we think it was Russia that hacked.
>
> "And then he said -- and this is in person sitting and watching television as I've been doing -- and then he said could be Trump,

> yeah, yeah. Trump, Trump, oh yeah, Trump. He reminded me of John Lovitz for 'Saturday Night Live' in 'the liar' where he'd go yes, yes, I went to Harvard, Harvard, yes, yes. This is the guy, you have to see it. Yes, it could be Trump, yes, yes. So, it is so farfetched. It's so ridiculous. Honestly, I wish I had that power. I'd love to have that power but Russia has no respect for our country. And that's why -- if it is Russia, nobody even knows this, it's probably China, or it could be somebody sitting in his bed. But it shows how weak we are, it shows how disrespected we are... So, I know nothing about it. It's one of the most farfetched I've ever heard...
>
> "Why do I have to get involved with Putin? I have nothing to do with Putin. I've never spoken to him. I don't know anything about him other than he will respect me. He doesn't respect our president. And if it is Russia -- which it's probably not, nobody knows who it is -- but if it is Russia, it's really bad for a different reason, because it shows how little respect they have for our country, when they would hack into a major party and get everything. But it would be interesting to see -- I will tell you this -- Russia, if you're listening, I hope you're able to find the 30,000 e-mails that are missing. I think you will probably be rewarded mightily by our press. Let's see if that happens. That'll be next."[345]

This was the closest thing his adversaries every came up with to tie Donald Trump to Russian activity: a snide joke that I laughed at out loud when he said it. But it distracted from the content of the Democratic Party emails that were exposing their own corruption at the time.

Questioning Authority

They also called us anti-intellectual and anti-science, which is another way to suggest not just incompetence but naivety. A United States Congressman can say something absolutely idiotic without reproach from the left (for instance, when Representative Hank Johnson said he was worried extra troops stationed on the island of Guam would cause the island to become so over populated that it would "tip over and capsize"[346]), but express skepticism of the advice coming from one of their conceited technocrats and you will be treated as an inferior species. One reason the right has long been accused of being anti-science is because of the religious reluctance to accept evolution. While evolution is today one of the most well evidenced areas of science, the same cannot be said about many modern claims of the left.

"Millions of people who follow [Trump] as a savior of sorts and consider anti-intellectualism a sign of liberty and free speech."
- Emanuel Perarella

Nevertheless, liberals flocked to Twitter (aka X), becoming the unasked-for moral compass of the woke world and spokespeople for the leftist narrative, undeterred by their own hypocrisy and naivety. They seemed to believe intellectuals and government scientists were infallible and "reputable" organizations and institutions above question. The snobby elitists were so convinced of their own superiority that they assumed it was why the masses didn't trust them, but they were demonstrably untrustworthy.

Our founders did not imagine our nation should be ruled by experts any more than it should be run by popes and bishops. They trusted that the people were inherently less likely to be corrupt than the leaders who manage their tax dollars and freedoms. Many today, though, see themselves as elites, not based on skill or knowledge, but on attitude. They saw Americans as anti-intellectual who were unwilling to blindly defer to people pursuing a clear political agenda. Highly educated people can still be wrong and are very often biased by the indoctrination of the very institutions that were designed to educate them.

"How did we descend this low? The short answer is this: by the dumbing-down of the general population." - Emanuel L. Pararella

> Emanuel L. Pararella, Ph.D., Ovi Magazine, May 2016:
> "The apotheosis of this strange anti-intellectualism which denies even the empirical evidence of science, which Asimov believes has always been integral part of American culture, arrived lately with the bizarre phenomenon of Donald Trump, who in many ways has become an icon for the millions of people who follow him as a savior of sorts and consider anti-intellectualism a sign of liberty and free speech. The question arises: How did we descend this low? The short answer is this: by the dumbing-down of the general population. Trump is nothing less than the proverbial canary in the

> coal mine: a sign that the oxygen of liberty and democracy is diminishing precipitously."[347]

"[The] credulous boomer rube demo that back Donald Trump."
- Rick Wilson

In a CNN Tonight panel hosted by Don Lemon in January of 2020, New York Times columnist and CNN contributor Wajahat Ali and former Republican strategist Rick Wilson, exposed this attitude while discussing comments by Trump's Secretary of State Mike Pompeo. The subject quickly turned to belittling Trump and what they believed to be his uneducated supporters.

> Wilson: "[Pompeo] also knows deep in his heart that Donald Trump couldn't find Ukraine on a map if you had the letter U and a picture of an actual physical crane next to it. He knows that this is, you know, an administration defined by ignorance of the world, and so that's partly him playing to their base and playing to their audience, you know, credulous boomer rube demo that back Donald Trump." Adding a thick southern accent in an attempt to mimic a Trump supporter, he added "Donald Trump's smart one, and y'all -- y'all elitists are dumb."
>
> Ali: "You elitists with your geography and your maps and your spelling even though-"
>
> Wilson: "Your math, your reading."
>
> Ali: "Yes, your reading, you know. Your geography knowing other countries. Sipping your latte."
>
> Wilson: "All those lines on the map".
>
> Ali: "Only them elitists know where Ukraine is."[348]

The CNN host laughed throughout their exchange. They were so confident in their superiority, which made them look like complete idiots. We were told to listen to our intellectual superiors because they knew better. They were smarter. They were the experts. When we questioned their impartiality, we were sheep, too dumb to survive without their guidance.

"The Republican Party, already rife with science-deniers and economic reality-deniers, has thrown itself into the embrace of a man who fabricates realities that ignorant people like to inhabit." - James Traub

---

> James Traub, Foreign Policy.com; June 28, 2016: "It's Time for the Elites to Rise Up Against the Ignorant Masses: If Donald Trump loses, and loses badly (forgive me my reckless optimism, but I believe he will) the Republican Party may endure a historic split between its know-nothing base and its K Street/Chamber of Commerce leadership class... Donald Trump has, of course, set a new standard for disingenuousness and catering to voters' fears, whether over immigration or foreign trade or anything else he can think of. The Republican Party, already rife with science-deniers and economic reality-deniers, has thrown itself into the embrace of a man who fabricates realities that ignorant people like to inhabit. Did I say "ignorant"? Yes, I did. It is necessary to say that people are deluded and that the task of leadership is to un-delude them. Is that 'elitist'? Maybe it is; maybe we have become so inclined to celebrate the authenticity of all personal conviction that it is now elitist to believe in reason, expertise, and the lessons of history. If so, the party of accepting reality must be prepared to take on the party of denying reality, and its enablers among those who know better. If that is the coming realignment, we should embrace it."[349]

As the economy and industry began to thrive under the Trump presidency, the "economic reality-deniers" were to be found on the left. Those who imagine themselves elite cannot help but look down on everyone unlike them - true xenophobia. That is the irony. They are everything they accuse us of being.

> Text from FBI agent and deep state actor, Peter Strzok, to former FBI lawyer Lisa Page:
> "Just went to a Southern Virginia Walmart. I could SMELL the Trump support."[350]

"They're fine people, except they're ignorant about these things."
 - Sam Donaldson

> Former CBS News correspondent Sam Donaldson to Don Lemon on CNN re: President's impeachment, Oct. 2019: "We'll see whether there's enough time for Americans out there who are busy with their lives doing other things, not even watching your show to get interested in it. To think it's not just a bunch of politicians squabbling in Washington. I'm tired of that. But there's something going on here. If enough Americans -- remember, Trump has 30%, 31% of hardcore. They'll follow him to hell or wherever he is going. They don't care about the facts. They don't know about the facts. Okay. They're fine people, except they're ignorant about these things that we're talking about and they will not budge on that."[351]

Like the others, Donaldson was utterly dismissive of our level of political engagement and comprehension of the issues at hand. He should have spent some time listening to conservative talk radio. Journalists' awareness of current events did not preclude ideological blinders and certainly did not make them elite or correct. Brzezinski later took back that last part of the following statement, but the Freudian slip was priceless.

"[Trump] can actually control exactly what people think... and that is our job." - Mika Brzezinski

---

> Mika Brzezinski on 'Morning Joe', MSNBC, Feb 22, 2017: "Well, I think that the dangerous, you know, edges here are that [Trump] is trying to undermine the media and trying to make up his own facts. And it could be that while unemployment and the economy worsens, he could have undermined the messaging so much that he can actually control exactly what people think. And that, that is our job."[352]

Most Americans have great respect for college degrees and many have worked hard to achieve that for themselves or their children. It is because so many worked so hard for it, and paid so much, that they got so angry when news came out about just how liberal, biased and even absurd many college classes and professors had become, resulting in a substandard education. The video function on cell phones and then the virtual learning forced on Americans during the Covid-19 shutdowns exposed a lot of questionable information being preached by educators.

There is a lot of ignorance out there in our nation about history, economics and politics, but it is at least as prevalent, and perhaps more so, on elitist college campuses and the streets of liberal cities than in small schools and Middle America. We begrudge no one an education, but we very much resent people who talk down to us and delude themselves into thinking they are superior based on their zip code, which college they attended or how much virtue signaling they do, when a lot of them are, in fact, often conspicuously ignorant about the things on which they pontificate.

"Lack of transparency is a huge political advantage." - Jonathan Gruber

---

Their history of bias, conceit and a willingness to lie in order to manipulate their audience also had a lot to do with the public's hesitancy to believe what their various experts were selling.

> Obamacare 'architect' and MIT professor Jonathan Gruber, Nov. 10, 2014:
> "In terms of risk rated subsidies, if you had a law which said that healthy people are going to pay in, you made explicit healthy people pay in and sick people get money, it would not have passed. Lack of transparency is a huge political advantage. And basically, call it the stupidity of the American voter or whatever, but basically that was really really critical to get for the thing to pass. Look, I wish Mark was right that we could make it all transparent, but I'd rather have this law than not."[353]

"It's not surprising then that they get bitter, they cling to guns or religion." - President Barack Obama

---

> Presidential Candidate Barack Obama, San Francisco Fund-Raiser, April 6, 2008:
> "You go into some of these small towns in Pennsylvania, and like a lot of small towns in the Midwest, the jobs have been gone now for

> 25 years and nothing's replaced them. And they fell through the Clinton administration, and the Bush administration, and each successive administration has said that somehow these communities are gonna regenerate and they have not. So it's not surprising then that they get bitter, they cling to guns or religion or antipathy to people who aren't like them or anti-immigrant sentiment or anti-trade sentiment as a way to explain their frustrations."[354]

President Trump proved that the right policies could reverse those conditions.

"Let competent experts take over." - Rob Reiner

Hard work, talent and the ability to expand one's knowledge are the bedrock of American enterprise and innovation. We want the best and the brightest to lead in our military, our classrooms, trauma centers and our favorite football teams. Accusations of anti-intellectualism was actually a response by a liberal clique, a vocal and influential minority who considered themselves and their 'experts' superior and belittled anyone who disagreed with them.

> Actor and Filmmaker Rob Reiner, @robreiner, Twitter, re: COVID-19, March 16, 2020:
> "We will get through this. But unfortunately not with the help of this President. First, he must be removed from the public square to let competent experts take over, then he must be removed from office to allow US to heal."[355]

Leaders regularly avail themselves of the foremost minds in whatever the subject is at hand, consider their recommendations and then act in whatever way those leaders feel is best for their constituents and their nation. That's what Americans hired Trump to do. Besides, their experts did a real bang up job.

"Now he is our president... disappointment and despair will darken the lives of the poorly educated." - David Masciotra

---

> David Masciotra, Salon magazine, Nov. 20, 2016: "During the Republican presidential primary, Donald Trump declared, 'I love the poorly educated.' They love him back, and now he is our president. It seems inevitable that disappointment and despair will darken the lives of the poorly educated when the jobs never return, as college graduates, maybe even those within their families, continue to earn salaries. Will 'elitism' still look so undesirable then?"[356]

"...putting an irresponsible, ignorant man who takes his advice from all the wrong people in charge of the nation..." - Paul Krugman

---

> Economist Paul Krugman column, New York Times, election night 2016:
> "It really does now look like President Donald J. Trump, and markets are plunging. When might we expect them to recover? Frankly, I find it hard to care much, even though this is my specialty. The disaster for America and the world has so many aspects that the economic ramifications are way down my list of things to fear. Still, I guess people want an answer: If the question is when markets will recover, a first-pass answer is never. Under any circumstances, putting an irresponsible, ignorant man who takes his advice from all the wrong people in charge of the nation with the world's most important economy would be very bad news. What makes it especially bad right now, however, is the fundamentally fragile state much of the world is still in, eight years after the great financial crisis...
>
> "Now comes the mother of all adverse effects – and what it brings with it is a regime that will be ignorant of economic policy and hostile to any effort to make it work. Effective fiscal support for the Fed? Not a chance. In fact, you can bet that the Fed will lose its independence, and be bullied by cranks. So, we are very probably looking at a global recession, with no end in sight. I suppose we could get lucky somehow. But on economics, as on everything else, a terrible thing has just happened."[357]

This "Nobel Peace Prize winning" economist was not alone in claiming the markets would never recover from Trump's victory. After Trump's first three years in office, with all of the metrics of the economy breaking records, did these elitists rejoice at the lack of disappointment and despair? Did they cheer the manufacturing jobs that came back or the thriving stock market, the record low unemployment, energy independence, the better pay and expanded opportunities created by Trump's policies? Did they cheer the new trade deals with Mexico and China, NATO nations "paying their fair share" or the peace deals being brokered? Were they happy that we began gaining control over our southern border with common sense policies and 450 miles of new and replacement border wall, or that he defeated ISIS?[358] He wasn't a savior, per se, but his policies made a clear and measurably positive impact that regular people could see and feel.

"I think one way you get rid of Trump is a crashing economy."
- Bill Maher

Bill Maher may have been the only one to put it so bluntly, a couple years earlier, but he was representative of the left's desire to see Trump lose.

> Bill Maher, Real Time, HBO, June 2018:
> "Can I ask about the economy because this economy is going pretty well? I feel like the bottom has to fall out at some point. And by the way, I'm hoping for it. Because I think one way you get rid of Trump is a crashing economy. So, please, bring on the recession. Sorry if that hurts people, but it's either root for a recession or you lose your democracy."[359]

Did they cheer the American economy when it exploded upward instead? Or did they just cheer when the pandemic tore it down? The virus would have been manageable with far fewer deaths and detriment had we focused efforts on those most at risk, but the response had other goals. The release of Covid-19 on the world from an American-backed Chinese lab engaged in bioweapons research was undeniably fortunate for opponents of the President. Years later, after President Biden took over and engaged in wild spending, the stock market did crash and that same Paul Krugman was surprised at the entirely predictable outcome of Biden's policies.

> Economist Paul Krugman, New York Times, November 2021:
> "Some warned that the package would be dangerously inflationary; others were fairly relaxed. I was Team Relaxed. As it turned out, of

> course, that was a very bad call... the debate and the way things have played out were more complicated than I suspect more people realize."[360]

Nonetheless, Krugman did not hesitate to support the next ridiculous spending bill, never learning the lesson that a government cannot tax and spend its way out of inflation and debt.[361] Overall, my stocks continued to do better under Biden despite massive crashes but inflation meant the value of that money was worth much less. It was an artificial high. These economists and pundits were entirely oblivious to their absence of impartiality. Any scientist who does not toe the line is discounted as ludicrous hacks. By the end of Trump's Presidency, despite the damage of lockdowns, the economy was recovering, but the left, in the form of the central bank chair, again exposed their erroneous thinking.

> CNN Business, Sept. 16, 2020:
> "Federal Reserve Chairman Jerome Powell, ever the careful wordsmith, called on lawmakers to get with the program and spend more money to stimulate the US economy... If Congress and the Trump administration fail to act, Powell essentially predicted the stock market would crash."[362]

Instead, Biden's spending caused the crash, recession and crippling inflation, instead of preventing it. They hid it for a time by redefining "recession" and Fed manipulation. This period in American history exposed the liberal expert dynamic as well as any could. According to the left, President Trump should have just turned decision-making over to a career technocrat like Dr. Anthony Fauci, Director of the National Institute of Allergy and Infectious Diseases (NIAID). In fact, Trump gave him too much influence as it was, falsely assuming he was an unbiased professional just doing his job.

"President Donald Trump, dislikes and distrusts the expert bureaucrats who make the government actually function." - Professor Noah Feldman

---

> Noah Feldman, Bloomberg Opinion, professor at Harvard Law, March 23, 2020:
> "With every passing day, it becomes more and more apparent that the U.S. federal government's response to Covid-19 has been appallingly slow and inadequate. A major reason is that the person

at the apex of that institution, President Donald Trump, dislikes and distrusts the expert bureaucrats who make the government actually function. The laws that govern emergencies like the coronavirus pandemic give enormous power to the executive branch to direct and coordinate disaster response. These laws are not designed to empower the president personally. To the contrary, the whole point of the emergency laws is to empower government experts who know what must be done in a crisis – that is, career technocrats who work at agencies like the Centers for Disease Control and Prevention (CDC) and the federal emergency management agency (FEMA). Congress doesn't trust the president in an emergency. It trusts the experts.

"Emergency laws vest executive decision-making authority in expert-run agencies, not the White House." - Professor Noah Feldman

---

"But Trump has spent his three-plus years in office attacking exactly these kinds of non-partisan career experts as a "swamp" that needs to be drained... The Tea Party worldview that Trump took on is profoundly anti-elitist. And experts are card carrying members of the American elite... The people whom Trump disparages as the "deep state" are precisely and exactly the people on whom the system is designed to rely in an emergency... emergency laws vest executive decision-making authority in expert-run agencies, not the White House...

"... the experts who are supposed to be in charge."
- Professor Noah Feldman

"Those agency decisions have to be based on rational decision making and have to be explained publicly, even if after the fact. These laws are supposed to avoid a situation where a president relies on his own instincts or advice from non-experts in his circle... If Kushner can re-empower the experts who are supposed to be in charge, that would be a big win for the way government is supposed to work. And it would almost certainly save lives."[363]

If expert bureaucrats actually made the government function, we wouldn't be in this mess. The reality is that many career bureaucrats, even scientists, are absolutely partisan and the American people did not elect them to run their country. Experts from various agencies or disciplines are expected to contribute their knowledge and advice, but a leader must put that information into perspective with the circumstances and consequences in mind in order to make informed decisions. Just because someone makes their way to the top of a government agency does not mean that they have a comprehensive understanding of the situation.

"We are very worried about the president's incompetence and lack of focus on fighting the spread of coronavirus." - Senator Chuck Schumer

---

The right obviously embraces science. Our modern world depends on it. But science evolves and, where it intersects with government and politics, is susceptible to extraordinary corruption. Scientific authorities provided conflicting and sometimes dubious guidance and then rued the American public for their skepticism. The pandemic was clearly politicized as the media and politicians engaged in scaremongering, based either their desire to see Trump fail or their certainty that he was incapable of doing anything else. It is easy to forget the level of graft being wielded at the time.

> Senate Minority Leader Chuck Schumer, D-NY, March 10, 2020: "We are very worried about the president's incompetence and lack of focus on fighting the spread of coronavirus. We believe that his lack of focus, his hamstringing efforts to address this public crisis, and inflicting pain on the stock market. One word could describe thus far the administration's response, incompetence... Let me tell President Trump what does stop the spread of coronavirus, steady smart scientific and competent leadership from the government."[364]

President Trump, though sometimes expressing disagreement, followed the advice of these experts as the virus began to spread in our country. Sadly, much of that advice turned out to be, not only wrong, but fraudulent and the treatment was far more damaging than the disease.

"The President went with the health recommendations."
- Dr. Anthony Fauci

Dr. Anthony Fauci, Coronavirus Task Force briefing, April 13, 2020:
"The first and only time that Dr. Birx and I went in and formally made a recommendation to the President to actually have a quote, shut down in the sense of -- not really shut down -- but to really have strong mitigation. We discussed it. Obviously, they would be concerned by some that, in fact, that might have some negative consequences. Nonetheless, the President listened to the recommendation and went to the mitigation. The next second time that I went with Dr. Birx into the President and said 15 days are not enough. We need to go 30 days. Obviously, there were people who had a problem with that because of the potential secondary effects. Nonetheless, at that time, the President went with the health recommendations, and we extended it another 30 days... I can just tell you the first and only time that I went in and said we should do mitigation strongly. The response was, yes, we'll do it."[365]

Dr. Fauci re: President Trump, Fox News, Sept. 9,2020: "I didn't get any sense that he was distorting anything. I mean in my discussions with him, they were always straightforward about the concerns that we had. We related that to him. And when he would go out, I'd hear him discussing the same sort of things... when we would get up in front of the press conferences, which were very, very common after our discussions with the president, he really didn't say anything different than we discussed when we were with him. I may not be tuned in to the right thing that they're talking about. But, I didn't see any discrepancies between what he told us and what we told him, and what he came out publicly and said."[366]

"For reasons that sometimes are... inconceivable and not understandable - they just don't believe science and they don't believe authority." - Dr. Anthony Fauci

---

Saying the lockdowns might have negative consequences was a considerable understatement, revealing either an incredible lack of awareness or an unfathomable callousness. But much of the public just wasn't willing to blindly follow orders, especially when authorities were contradicting themselves or other equally credentialed experts.

> Dr. Anthony Fauci on U.S. DHHS podcast "Learning Curve", June 18, 2020:
> "One of the problems we face in the United States is that unfortunately, there is a combination of an anti-science bias that people are – for reasons that sometimes are, you know, inconceivable and not understandable – they just don't believe science and they don't believe authority. So, when they see someone up in the White House, which has an air of authority to it, who's talking about science, that there are some people who just don't believe that – and that's unfortunate because, you know, science is truth."[367]

Dr. Fauci was a prominent member of Trump's White House Coronavirus Task Force. Early on, Trump was accused of trying to downplay the risk of the virus, but he was simply passing on the advice of these experts. He soon realized their unreliability.

"This is not a major threat for the people of the United States." - Dr. Anthony Fauci

---

> Dr. Fauci on the Coronavirus, Newsmax, January 21, 2020: "Well, you know, obviously, you need to take it seriously and do the kinds of things that the CDC and the Department of Homeland Security are doing. But this is not a major threat for the people of the United States, and this is not something that the citizens of the United States right now should be worried about."[368]
>
> Dr. Robert Redfield, CDC Director, Feb. 27, 2020: "We're still committed to get aggressive containment, and I want the American public to know at this point that the risk is low."[369]

"STOP BUYING MASKS! They are NOT effective." - Surgeon General Jerome Adams

---

It appeared that our scientific leadership vacillated in their guidance, not just in response to changing conditions and data but to encourage different behaviors and achieve different ends.

U.S. Surgeon General Jerome Adams, Twitter, Feb. 29, 2020: "Seriously people, STOP BUYING MASKS! They are NOT effective in preventing general public from catching #Coronavirus, but if healthcare providers can't get them to care for sick patients, it puts them and our communities at risk!"[370]

"There's no reason to be walking around with a mask." - Dr. Anthony Fauci

---

Dr. Anthony Fauci, 60 Minutes, March 8, 2020:
"The masks are important for someone who's infected to prevent them from infecting someone else... Right now, people should not be worried. There's no reason to be walking around with a mask. When you're in the middle of an outbreak, wearing a mask might make people feel a little bit better and it might even block a droplet but it's not providing the perfect protection that people think that it is. And often there are unintended consequences. People keep fiddling with the mask and they keep touching their face... When you think mask, you should think of health care providers needing them and people who are ill. The people who when you look at the films of foreign countries and you see 85% of the people wearing masks that's fine, that's fine. I'm not against it if you want to do it that's fine... It could lead to a shortage of masks for the people who really need it."[371]

"There is no specific evidence to suggest that the wearing of masks by the mass population has any potential benefit."
- Dr. Mike Ryan, World Health Organization (WHO)

Jacqueline Howard, CNN, March 31, 2020: "World Health Organization officials Monday said they still recommend people not wear face masks unless they are sick with Covid-19 or caring for someone who is sick. 'There is no specific evidence to suggest that the wearing of masks by the mass population has any potential benefit. In fact, there's some evidence to suggest the opposite in the misuse of wearing a mask properly or fitting it properly,' Dr. Mike Ryan, executive director of the WHO

> health emergencies program, said at a media briefing in Geneva, Switzerland, on Monday. 'There also is the issue that we have a massive global shortage,' Ryan said about masks and other medical supplies. 'Right now the people most at risk from this virus are frontline health workers who are exposed to the virus every second of every day. The thought of them not having masks is horrific.'"[372]

"Wearing a mask outside health care facilities offers little, if any, protection from infection." - New England Journal of Medicine

---

In April of that year the Centers for Disease Control changed their guidance, advising everyone over 2 years old to wear a face masks in public. Later, around the country, their use became mandated, and Fauci even supported the use of double masks.[373] But some scientists seemed to expose different motives for the recommendations. All of this was clear and available at the time.

"Masks are visible reminders of an otherwise invisible yet widely prevalent pathogen." – New England Journal of Medicine

---

> New England Journal of Medicine, April 1, 2020: "We know that wearing a mask outside health care facilities offers little, if any, protection from infection. Public health authorities define a significant exposure to Covid-19 as face-to-face contact within 6 feet with a patient with symptomatic Covid-19 that is sustained for at least a few minutes (and some say more than 10 minutes or even 30 minutes). The chance of catching Covid-19 from a passing interaction in a public space is therefore minimal. In many cases, the desire for widespread masking is a reflexive reaction to anxiety over the pandemic...

"It is also clear that masks serve symbolic roles." – New England Journal of Medicine

---

> "There may be additional benefits to broad masking policies that extend beyond their technical contribution to reducing pathogen transmission. Masks are visible reminders of an otherwise invisible yet widely prevalent pathogen and may remind people of the importance of social distancing and other infection-control measures. It is also clear that masks serve symbolic roles. Masks are not only tools, they are also talismans that may help increase health care workers' perceived sense of safety, well-being, and trust in their hospitals."[374]

"[Studies] suggest that masks are either useless... or actually counterproductive." - Kaylee McGhee White

---

> Kaylee McGhee White, Aug. 12,2021, Washington Examiner: "How effective are masks really?... In sum, of the 14 [randomized controlled trials] that have tested the effectiveness of masks in preventing the transmission of respiratory viruses, three suggest, but do not provide any statistically significant evidence in intention-to-treat analysis, that masks might be useful. The other eleven suggest that masks are either useless – whether compared with no masks or because they appear not to add to good hand hygiene alone – or actually counterproductive."[375]

"Everyone should wear a mask." - Dean Blumberg, Chief of Pediatric Infectious Diseases

---

We were told the previous advice was wrong, but they had it right this time, experts said. Trust them. *Science is truth. I am science!*

> Dean Blumberg, Chief of Pediatric Infectious Diseases, U.C. Davis Children's Hospital, July 9, 2020: "We've learned more due to research and additional scientific evidence and now we know [that] not only wearing a mask prevents the person wearing the mask to transmit to others, but wearing the mask protects the person who's wearing it... Everyone should wear a mask. People who say, 'I don't believe masks work,' are ignoring

> scientific evidence. It's not a belief system. It's like saying, 'I don't believe in gravity.'"[376]

Not all science is equal in evidence and not all scientists agreed. When the Covid-19 virus came to the U.S., the thriving American economy was shut down and most of its people locked down, quarantined for months on end, because Trump and other authorities *did* listen to the government's experts. The Brownstone Institute for Social and Economic Research reviewed and presented 167 comparative effectiveness research studies and articles on masking, concluding "To date, the evidence has been stable and clear that masks do not work to control the virus and they can be harmful and especially to children."[377]

Masking was only a small part of the detrimental guidance. With jobless claims hitting 10 million in just two weeks during the pandemic, Dr. Fauci dismissed the consequences of the continued lockdown, as if American jobs were an extracurricular activity, rather than a necessity for paying the bills and putting food on the table, as if the entire economy were not at stake.[378] The point was control.

"We find no evidence that lockdowns, school closures, border closures, and limiting gatherings have had a noticeable effect on Covid-19 mortality." - John Hopkins Institute Covid-19 study

---

Instead of a two-week shutdown, these scientists insisted on an almost indefinite one, instituted on a state level, even though all admitted that the best they could hope for was to temporarily slow the spread, not stop the virus. The following study reviewed and compared hundreds of independent studies.

"Lockdowns ... have had devasting effects." - John Hopkins Institute doctors

---

> Jonas Herby, Lars Jonung, Steve Hanke, John Hopkins Institute, Jan 2022:
> "We find no evidence that lockdowns, school closures, border closures, and limiting gatherings have had a noticeable effect on COVID-19 mortality. There is some evidence that business

closures reduce COVID-19 mortality, but the variation in estimates is large and the effect seems related to closing bars... The use of lockdowns is a unique feature of the COVID-19 Pandemic. Lockdowns have not been used to such a large extent during any of the pandemics of the past century. However, lockdowns during the initial phase of the COVID-19 pandemic have had devasting effects. They have contributed to reducing economic activity, raising unemployment, reducing schooling, causing political unrest, contributing to domestic violence, and undermining liberal democracy."[379]

These scientists concluded that lockdowns as a policy for pandemic response should be rejected. Some others were undeterred.

Seth Flaxman, professor, Dept. of Computer Science, University of Oxford, Feb. 2022:
"Smoking causes cancer, the earth is round, and ordering people to stay at home (the correct definition of lockdown) decreases disease transmission. None of this is controversial among scientists. A study purporting to prove the opposite is almost certain to be fundamentally flawed."[380]

The apparent back and forth on guidance, in addition to the way experts tried to manipulate rather than simply inform the public, certainly undermined many Americans' faith in their credibility. Regardless of the efficacy of lockdowns or masks, conflicting data did exist and people had cause to doubt the infallibility of government experts on the subjects, especially when the consequences were so severe. Widespread lockdowns and financial devastation had a debilitating effect on public health by preventing people from getting regular vaccines, mental health and medical treatments. Lives were destroyed and many people died in forced isolation, sometimes confined together in nursing homes with sick patients.

"The policy itself is killing people." - Dr. Scott Atlas

Dr. Scott Atlas, Hoover Institution senior fellow, May 24, 2020:
"I think one thing that's not somehow receiving attention is the CDC just came out with their fatality rates. And lo and behold, they verify what people have been saying for over a month now... that is that the infection fatality rate is less than one-tenth of the original

estimate that prompted the isolation. And more so, if you look at France, the Netherlands, Spain and the U.S. the infection fatality rate for people under 60 is less than or equal to seasonal flu... The policy itself is killing people. I mean, I think everyone's heard about 650,000 people on cancer, chemo, half of whom didn't come in. Two thirds of cancer screenings didn't come in. 40 percent of stroke patients urgently needing care didn't come in. And now we have over half the people, children in the United States not getting vaccinations...This is a tragic, misguided public policy to extend this lockdown, whether or not it was justifiable in the beginning.

"The other critical evidence that hasn't been emphasized is about children here. There's no science whatsoever to keep K-through 12 schools closed nor to have masks or social distancing on children, nor to keep summer programs closed. What we know now is that the risk of death and the risk of even a serious illness is nearly zero in people under 18... And this is validated in the studies of journal JAMA Pediatrics 46 North American hospitals, you look at their conclusion, their bottom line conclusion, is [for people under 60] that the risk of having a critical illness from seasonal influenza is quote 'far greater' than from COVID-19."[381]

Even after it became clear that the mortality rate projections were greatly exaggerated,[382] scientists and politicians heading the response still pushed to continue lockdowns, refusing to release the grip on power the virus afforded them.

"Suggestions to reopen are emerging that are not informed by thoughtful analysis or public-health expertise." - CDC Director Tom Frieden

---

This virus was not unprecedented, but the widespread shutdowns in response to it were. When the public protested, we were roundly condemned. They weren't using the best available data - they were sacrificing some businesses in favor of others. It was a targeted shutdown of small businesses.

Former CDC Director Tom Frieden, Washington Post, 3/25/2020:
"There is increasing pressure to resume social and economic activity soon to limit the economic damage from the coronavirus.

> Suggestions to reopen are emerging that are not informed by thoughtful analysis or public-health expertise. It's critical that decisions about how, when and what to reopen are based on the best data available, with transparency about how choices are made. The choice is not between health and economics but about optimizing the public health response to save lives while minimizing economic harm."[383]

"[Physicians and officials] privately mourned the widening rift between leaders in science and a subset of the communities that they serve." - Open letter

---

Many public health officials reversed course again when protesters gathered after the death of George Floyd, a black man who died at the hands of Minnesota police. An example of the contradictions can be seen in an open letter signed by "1,288 public health and infectious diseases professionals and community stakeholders" supporting the protests in spite of COVID-19. The double standard destroyed any credibility these people might have had.

"This message must be wholly different from the response to white protesters resisting stay-home orders." - Open Letter

---

> Open letter advocating for an anti-racist public health response to demonstrations against systemic injustice occurring during the COVID-19 pandemic:
>
> "On April 30, heavily armed and predominantly white protesters entered the State Capitol building in Lansing, Michigan, protesting stay-home orders and calls for widespread public masking to prevent the spread of COVID-19. Infectious disease physicians and public health officials publicly condemned these actions and privately mourned the widening rift between leaders in science and a subset of the communities that they serve.
>
> "As of May 30, we are witnessing continuing demonstrations in response to ongoing, pervasive, and lethal institutional racism set off by the killings of George Floyd and Breonna Taylor, among

many other Black lives taken by police. A public health response to these demonstrations is also warranted, but this message must be wholly different from the response to white protesters resisting stay-home orders. Infectious disease and public health narratives adjacent to demonstrations against racism must be consciously anti-racist, and infectious disease experts must be clear and consistent in prioritizing an anti-racist message.

"COVID-19 among black patients is yet another lethal manifestation of white supremacy." – Open letter

---

"White supremacy is a lethal public health issue that predates and contributes to COVID-19. Black people are twice as likely to be killed by police compared to white people, but the effects of racism are far more pervasive. Black people suffer from dramatic health disparities in life expectancy, maternal and infant mortality, chronic medical conditions, and outcomes from acute illnesses like myocardial infarction and sepsis. Biological determinants are insufficient to explain these disparities.

"They result from long-standing systems of oppression and bias which have subjected people of color to discrimination in the healthcare setting, decreased access to medical care and healthy food, unsafe working conditions, mass incarceration, exposure to pollution and noise, and the toxic effects of stress. Black people are also more likely to develop COVID-19. Black people with COVID-19 are diagnosed later in the disease course and have a higher rate of hospitalization, mechanical ventilation, and death. COVID-19 among Black patients is yet another lethal manifestation of white supremacy. In addressing demonstrations against white supremacy, our first statement must be one of unwavering support for those who would dismantle, uproot, or reform racist institutions.

"[Protests against stay-home orders] not only oppose public health interventions, but are also rooted in white nationalism." – Open letter

---

> "Staying at home, social distancing, and public masking are effective at minimizing the spread of COVID-19. To the extent possible, we support the application of these public health best practices during demonstrations that call attention to the pervasive lethal force of white supremacy. However, as public health advocates, we do not condemn these gatherings as risky for COVID-19 transmission. We support them as vital to the national public health and to the threatened health specifically of Black people in the United States. We can show that support by facilitating safest protesting practices without detracting from demonstrators' ability to gather and demand change. This should not be confused with a permissive stance on all gatherings, particularly protests against stay-home orders. Those actions not only oppose public health interventions, but are also rooted in white nationalism and run contrary to respect for Black lives. Protests against systemic racism, which fosters the disproportionate burden of COVID-19 on Black communities and also perpetuates police violence, must be supported."[384]

They went on to set guidelines for supporting the protests that included police keeping their distance and wearing masks to protect the rioters, as well as advocating that protesters not be arrested.

> New York City Mayor Bill de Blasio, June 2, 2020: "When you see a nation, an entire nation, simultaneously grappling with an extraordinary crisis seeded in 400 years of American racism, I'm sorry, that is not the same question as the understandably aggrieved store owner or the devout religious person who wants to go back to services."[385]

This double standard for protestors exposed the prejudice that clearly colored their recommendations. Even if racism and injustice were involved, it could not change the science. Not to mention, humanity's history of slavery goes back a heck of a lot farther than that.

"This panic was occasioned by epidemiological models predicting wildly unlikely fatalities." - Heather McDonald

---

> Heather MacDonald, Manhattan Institute, Hillsdale College Symposium, June 18, 2020:

"Over the last four months, Americans have lived through what is arguably the most consequential period of government malfeasance in U.S. history. Public officials' overreaction to the novel coronavirus put American cities into a coma; those same officials' passivity in the face of widespread rioting threatens to deliver the coup de grâce. Together, these back-to-back governmental failures will transform the American polity and cripple urban life for decades... Americans huddled in their homes for months on end, believing that if they went outside, death awaited them. This panic was occasioned by epidemiological models predicting wildly unlikely fatalities from the coronavirus."[386]

"The cure was worse than the disease." - Professor Mark Woolhouse

---

Professor of Infectious Disease Epidemiology Mark Woolhouse, University of Edinburgh, Aug. 26, 2020:
"Lockdown was a panic measure and I believe history will say trying to control Covid-19 through lockdown was a monumental mistake on a global scale, the cure was worse than the disease. I never want to see national lockdown again. It was always a temporary measure that simply delayed the stage of the epidemic we see now... I believe the harm lockdown is doing to our education, health care access, and broader aspects of our economy and society will turn out to be at least as great as the harm done by Covid-19."[387]

"Other than slavery... this is the greatest intrusion on civil liberties in American history." - Attorney General William Barr

---

Attorney General William Barr, speaking at Hillsdale College, Sept. 2020:
"You know, putting a national lockdown, stay-at-home orders, is like house arrest. It's — you know, other than slavery, which was a different kind of restraint, this is the greatest intrusion on civil liberties in American history."[388]

New Jersey congressman Bill Pascrell, Jr. said in a tweet: "Bill Barr is drunk with power, an out-of-control fanatic, a frothing

> enemy of democracy. Barr should be impeached then stripped of his law licenses for life."[389]

Covid-19 science was just one example where the left claims intellectual superiority over anyone who disagrees. Popular liberal movements deny the realities of biological sex, the development of babies in the womb and any opposing data or conclusions on the global climate. They have actually gotten the world to believe that the air we breathe out, that all plants require to live, is a toxin; that the natural energy our civilization depends on and is fed through is evil. Throughout the pandemic, the guidance from their experts was consistently and thoroughly wrong. Setting evolution aside, the leftist establishment no longer has a leg to stand on when it comes to the embrace of science. Their intellectualism is equally suspect, resembling nothing more than indoctrination.

Chapter 7

Religious Fervor

Aside from the object of their worship, today's radical left elitists are in many ways the modern equivalent of the Roman Catholic Church, feudal lords and royal cohorts who once dominated and subjugated Europe. Even if a deity is not central to their mission, the left has beliefs and methodologies for propagation and control that echo the historic Roman Church, religious concepts and tactics. The similarities include more than their leaders' devotion to ideological certainty and superiority, and its mission to save the simple, general public from error. Both also hold certain things sacred, claim to have the only correct view of the world and embrace articles of faith or unquestionable truths, resulting in moral principles that guide behavior and determine salvation or damnation.

What separates a philosophy or ideology from religion revolves around the elements of worship and faith: worship of and complete submission to something "higher" and total belief in things that have not or even cannot be proven. For most religions, that submission is to a god or creator. Sometimes, they deify other things, like nature or the earth. The left's version of religion today is a progressive globalism that employs cultish deviance and worldwide collectivism to enslave the masses and empower an elitist tyranny. Parts of it may have evolved naturally in society but it has been wound together by design for a particular purpose, world subjugation and domination. It is virtually indistinguishable from religion, being structurally, emotionally or symbolically similar to religious systems and ethics normally associated with them.

This includes ideas about proper thinking, rules to follow, prophesies, damnation, proselytizing, "godly" doctrinal elites and authorities, sacrifices, prophets and prophecies, charity, evils, sins, revelation, conversion, communal gatherings and rituals. Being "woke" is like being saved or born again, a revelation. Instead of saving souls, they are saving the planet or the future of humanity. Climate change is their prophesied apocalypse, destined to occur if humanity fails to follow right thinking, to submit and make the sacrifices called for by its masters. In place of heaven, the left has promised a socialist utopia. Offences are sins and dissent is evil. They worship diversity and group identities to which individuals must be sacrificed.

Fidelity to these beliefs are enforced through censorship and oppression, mirroring concepts common to western religious belief like heresy and blasphemy. Heresy is any science or history that contradicts or questions their assertions, doctrine or ideas. To the left, the ideology of our founders, including equal liberty, individualism and free markets, or conflicting evidence on climate change are heresies. While they claim to be the defenders of science, that cannot be farther from the truth. The scientific process itself is heresy because it dares to address cardinal truths that are not to be questioned or debated.

Blasphemy is contemptuous or profane speech or actions that lack the reverence of something considered sacrosanct. For the left, that includes anything that can be branded as xenophobic, racist, Islamophobic, homophobic, misogynistic or hate speech. It is microaggressions, triggers and misused pronouns. These all expose wrong thinking and must be condemned, just as heresy represents wrong doctrine that must be rooted out. Instead of being excommunicated, heretics are cancelled. Instead of burning books, they may be scrubbed from the internet or not allowed to be published in the first place, a far cry from the right's attempts to limit sexually explicit content available to children in school libraries. Their opponents are not wrong, they are evil. They accuse opponents of everything they themselves are doing.

Some describe support of Donald Trump as a cult. He certainly attracted devoted followers. Many saw him as a hero for his defense of American principles and standing strong after the first assassination attempt, pumping a fist in the air with blood streaming down his face, calling for supporters to "fight, fight, fight". His supporters, though, were never in lock-step. Cults of personality have historically been developed around authoritarian leaders through propaganda and government manipulation to justify the. legitimacy.[390] Here, the government and the mass media overwhelmingly worked against Donald Trump. If it is a cult, it is one of American principles, which is fundamentally anti-authoritarian.

Some claim atheism is a religion, but that term says one thing a person does not believe and virtually nothing about what they do believe. Progressive globalism, on the other hand, has a whole suite of doctrinal beliefs and rules, including collectivism (that group identity and the 'common good' are more valuable than human beings or individual rights, and that we are all either oppressors or oppressed), the belief that carbon dioxide from human activity causes apocalyptic global climate change, demonization private gun ownership and promotion of transsexualism. These may seem unconnected, but they are entirely and purposely interwoven.

The progressive globalists have stories and propaganda that take the place of biblical texts, stories about an impending cataclysm, inherited guilt and oppression that justifies extreme acts of faith and sacrifices. They identify whites and the west as oppressors who are condemned as racist and privileged, regardless of circumstances or individual behavior. Capitalism is evil and Donald Trump is Hitler or Satan as a matter of faith that no amount of evidence can dissuade. Since they believe human beings are the problem, abortion is venerated and followers are encouraged not to procreate. Fear is an important motivator.

Where the church saw evil behind every turn, the left sees racism and hatred. Their beliefs about oppression create a reverence for victimhood, justify retributive discrimination and a borderless world of universal migration as a means of justice. They target individuals and certain groups they consider oppressors, believing their rights and needs should be forfeited for others or the collective. Their 'higher power' is the greater good. With this view, even late-term abortion and forced euthanasia of the elderly can be embraced. They seek massive depopulation. Their drive for diversity and inclusion supplant cultural norms, in some cases even to the point of embracing pedophiles and predators. But the centralization of power is the real goal. Migration, pandemics and their doctrines are just the means.

Where science or history disagrees, whether in the biology of sex or immunology, they choose faith. Virtually everything they told us about Covid-19 was wrong, from the vaccine being safe and effective, to the benefits of masks on everyone, to the necessity of standing six feet away [illegible] efit of a targeted economic shutdown. Still, believers were [illegible] Some religions advocate circumcision or celibacy, while the [illegible] s fluid sexuality, surgery and hormone treatments, eup[illegible]ally referred to as "gender-affirming care." They believe in sexual transformation - that a male can become a female and vice versa - so devotedly that they will sacrifice their children's mental and physical health for it, embracing chemical castration and ritualized genital mutilation. There have always been women who identify as men and vice versa. It was a small minority of people and it didn't impact society. Progressive globalism, though, appropriates gender dysphoria as elements of their ritualized behaviors and symbolism.

They train children to venerate alternative behaviors using texts and performances in schools, lude pride parades and drag queen shows with kids. Protests, parades, festivals, and occupations are part of their ritualized communal activities. They dress up as characters from *The Handmaids Tale,* the abortion pill and other bizarre outfits and face paint. Rainbows take the place of crosses and language is changed in an attempt to alter how we see reality. They promote trans ideology, because it undermines the family, disrupts societies and weakens nation-states, while also serving a sacramental role.

For progressive globalists, their temples are schools and universities, where 'end of the world' fears, worship of the government and other tenets are incubated. They are decorated with imagery and terminology of their faith. They venerate perversion, violence and alternative lifestyles as expressions of diversity. Training students in the faith is more important than educated them, because they want followers, not independently reasoning individuals. When those on the left say that facts are not the best judge of truth, as I reference later, it is because most of our colleges have forsaken facts and truth in these issues in favor of belief. They seek conversion, not education. Their experts become high priests or higher authorities, guardians of the truth. Followers are taught to bow to these doctrinal elites for their superiority and wisdom.

They demonize guns rather than those who use them to commit crimes because the goal is to disarm the people. Private ownership of guns is tied to anti-immigrant xenophobia, racism and fear. If you want to be safe, they suggest, you can't have guns. A lot of people fall for this propaganda. Prioritizing one's family is selfish. Meanwhile, globalists fund mass migration in order to overwhelm first world nations, cultures and laws rather than helping them thrive on their homelands.[391]

> Christine Emba, The Washington Post, May 15, 2023:
> "Yet over and over again, people told me they needed their guns to keep themselves safe. Safe from what? Most couldn't answer; they simply had a feeling that the world had become a more dangerous place...Perhaps the most troubling aspect of gun ownership for 'protection' is the sharp-edged individualism it implies: an every-man-for-himself mind-set. Institutions can't be trusted, police will be unresponsive and the government might one day turn on you. Your only obligations are to yourself and your family. Individual fear becomes a greater priority than collective safety. Increasing the number of guns in the system will almost certainly spell death for others, but at least *your* gun will keep *you* safe."[392]

They have councils, gatherings and meetings of leadership and followers, like the World Economic Forum (WEF) at Davos, oligarchical globalists who consider themselves godlike, as if justified in and capable of correcting the course of the human race and the fate of the entire planet. It is their own version of the Council of Nicaea. They condemn fossil fuels as an incomparable evil that must be destroyed at all costs and embrace alternative fuels so that solar panels, windmills and electric cars become symbols or icons of their belief and signifiers of virtue. Their adherents have faith, even though these alternatives so far are often destructive, inefficient and impracticable. Any trees, birds or whales that die in the process are part of the price that must be paid.

An imminent global apocalypse blamed on the sin of oppression, greed, fossil fuels and carbon dioxide, forgiven only through subjugation and reparations, is based on religious faith, not science. For a while the only "evidence" on the issue that got published was funded by the international organizations behind the deception. Climate ideology was taught from childhood and dissent was censored. Things have changed today and many scientists and studies are coming out against their claims, but no science will dissuade adherents.[393] Climate deniers need not be indulged.

The impending end of the world is a tactic utilized by religious and secular ideologies alike to motivate adherents and degrade opponents. They call climate change "the end of human civilization and modern society as we have known it,"[394] "an existential crisis,"[395] or simply the "end of the world."[396] Any extremism is justified in the face of such a thing. These leaders profit through corruption and manipulation. One of progressive globalism's leading prophets, who used this religion to make billions of dollars, is former Vice President Al Gore. In this case, prophet is synonyms with profit. The following statement from Gore, speaking at the WEF in 2023, exposes both the madness of the faith and their ultimate goal: the end of self-rule.

> Al Gore, WEC Annual Meeting at Davos, January 18, 2023:
> "We're still putting 162 million tons [greenhouse gas pollution] into [the troposphere] every single day. And the accumulated amount is now trapping as much extra heat as would be released by 600,000 Hiroshima-class atomic bombs exploding every single day on the earth. That's what's boiling the oceans, creating these atmospheric rivers and the rain bombs and sucking the moisture out of the land and creating the droughts, and melting the ice, and raising the sea level, and causing these waves of climate refugees, predicted to reach one billion in this century. Look at the xenophobia and political authoritarian trends that have come from just a few million refugees. What about a billion? We would lose our capacity for self-governance on this world. We have to act!"[397]

In reality, that is their goal. Gore also noted that he trains young activists around the world, where he is no doubt preaching this apocalyptic prophesy. Beyond the nonsense of the oceans boiling and the rest, the legislation and accords they say are designed to address the climate would have no practical effect on the planet, even by their own science,[398] while damaging if not destroying western economies and the interests of their people, leaving the real polluters to continue unencumbered.[399] Solar and wind are intermittent and require pollution to produce and dispose of, and destruction to implement. In the end, electric vehicles are actually dirtier than gas or diesel.[400] Though we all want a safe, clean environment, modern environmentalism is dishonest and cultish, advanced by people who profit from it and use it to further elitist goals of world domination. Electric engines may prove superior but we must have the energy sources to feed it and battery technology to make it practical for wide spread use. Just making electric vehicles a legal requirement only hastens our demise.

They are not deterred by the fact that *none* of their past apocalyptic climate predictions have come true or that their biggest advocates are hypocritical, traveling the world in high carbon emitting private jets and buying seaside mansions with no fear of rising oceans. Nonetheless, they have led a great many people to believe that the air we breathe out, upon which all plant life depends, is going to catastrophically harm the planet, when instead it is their bioengineering and geoengineering we need to worry about. Bill Gates and his foundation leads the way on a lot of this activity. We have a beautiful, thriving planet that we should protect, but blocking the sun, replacing meat with bugs and genetically manipulating cattle so that they don't fart is not a rational solution.[401]

Their propaganda has been hugely successful. The following comes from one of many of the organizations created to push progressive globalism.

> 'What's at Stake', according to Global citizen.org:
> "Vulnerable communities in the Global South – and the ones who have contributed the least to the climate crisis – are disproportionately suffering the effects of climate change with their lives and livelihoods threatened."[402]

This also highlights why the globalists fund mass migration. It compliments their manufactured climate emergency propaganda, while at the same time feeding the oppressor/oppressed narrative, increasing disorder and destabilization. It's all tied together. Some religions forbid the eating of pork while the left would have us give up ranching and agriculture. They must be rejected, being dependent on fossil fuels and producers of carbon. Civilization literally depends on fossil fuels today, but to meet an ideological objective, they believe any pain on the part of the people is justified. But saving the planet isn't their real goal. They seek equity in the powerlessness of the masses. Meanwhile, these leaders will continue to enjoy their indulgences and the luxuries of civilization. They just don't want *you* to have them.

Another sin for the left is "cultural appropriation", the evil of adopting elements of a culture you were not born into, considered disrespectful and stereotypical. According to the Encyclopedia Britannica, "cultural appropriation, adoption of certain language, behavior, clothing, or tradition belonging to a minority culture or social group by a dominant culture or group in a way that is exploitative, disrespectful, or stereotypical. An imbalance of power between the appropriator and the appropriated is a critical condition of the concept."[403] This goes back again to oppressor and oppressed.

But what happens when people who are born male appropriate female dress, behavior and identity? Are they not guilty of sexual appropriation?

If you say appropriation is wrong, how is that then not an offense against women or womanhood?[404] How about a male competing in female sports? That is pushing women out of competition. How about black women wearing blond hair? I'm a redhead, definitely a minority. Should I be offended every time someone dyes their hair red and rally the crowd to make them lose their job? The right has also been accused of intolerance,[405] but it is a controlling, leftist move. Tolerance has gone out of fashion. Liberty, though, is always on the side of free speech and all speech, even progressive speech, should be protected.

"Censorship and propaganda are the tools the left uses to wield moral outrage for political advantage, condemning and suppressing nonconforming thought, speech and behavior."

When Galileo was convicted of heresy by the Inquisition, he was forced to denounce the science he believed, profess his belief and submission to the church and their claims, and report any heretics he might encounter to the church. The full 1984 treatment. This wasn't about Jesus or religion. Christianity flourished in the U.S. when given freedom and it helped build our nation. This was about control and submission, and a fear of dissidents infecting the simple-minded public with their wicked ideas. People who run afoul of leftist doctrine have faced similar punishments, met with the wrath of liberal pundits and social pressure, often fired, forced to recant and face political and financial ruin.

Censorship and propaganda are the tools the left uses to wield moral outrage for political advantage, condemning and suppressing nonconforming thought, speech and behavior. The fact that the left here may not yet engage in torture or murder that were associated with the darkest days of the Roman Church does not mean they are incapable, as their cohorts in communist, socialist and fascist countries demonstrate. While the church looked to take the opportunity of sinning away from the wicked, it was about keeping people in line and making choices for them, ostensibly for their own good. To the church in earlier times, religion was too often a justification, a means to an end. Again, not universally but notably. When the church began to lose their dominion over the Christian world, its leaders blamed freedom of speech, press and thought, just as we are seeing the left do today.

> Pope Gregory XVI, August 15, 1832:
> "Experience shows, even from earliest times, that cities renowned for wealth, dominion, and glory perished as a result of this single evil, namely immoderate freedom of opinion, license of free speech, and desire for novelty.[406]

> Pope Leo XIII, Nov. 1, 1885:
> "From this the following consequences logically flow: that the judgment of each one's conscience is independent of all law; that the most unrestrained opinions may be openly expressed as to the practice or omission of divine worship; and that every one has unbounded license to think whatever he chooses and to publish abroad whatever he thinks... the unrestrained freedom of thinking and of openly making known one's thoughts is not inherent in the rights of citizens."[407]

As historian David Gibbon put it, "The chain of authority was broken, which restrains the bigot from thinking as he pleases, and the slave from speaking as he thinks."[408] A parallel would be when the left lost their monopoly on social media when Elon Musk bought X, formerly Twitter, and restored free speech. Toleration and liberty were enemies of the church then as much as they are now enemies of the left. Where the church denounced ideas that it considered "heretical, scandalous, false, offensive to pious ears or seductive of simple minds," the left identifies unacceptable ideas as morally repugnant hate speech and racism, equally alluring to the simple minds of the American electorate. Like religion, those who question the left's sacred truths or moral framework have to be censored and destroyed.

"Perhaps the single greatest evil was the perversion of language. As if by magic, the concentration-camp system was turned into a 'reeducation system' and the tyrants became 'educators'." – The Black Book of Communism

---

The manipulation of language is central. The progressive globalists of the left use Orwellian "newspeak" in the place of forbidden words to change how we speak and how we think. It is little different than the Communist Party of Russia and the Soviet Union or the National Socialists of Nazi Germany. It started here with somewhat innocuous political correctness but became increasingly pervasive and more heavily penalized. A disabled person became a person with a disability, blacks became African Americans, illegal aliens became undocumented immigrants or newcomers, prisoners became incarcerated persons, mothers became birthing persons, a raid became a search, an investigation became a matter (i.e. Hillary Clinton's server) and so on. These are but a few examples of the widespread manipulation of language that can be traced back to communism and is used to promote progressive globalism.

"The Communists, thanks to their incomparable propaganda strength grounded in the subversion of language, successfully turn the tables on the criticism leveled against their terrorist tactics." - Black Book of Communism

---

> The Black Book of Communism, Harvard University Press, 1997: "Perhaps the single greatest evil was the perversion of language. As if by magic, the concentration-camp system was turned into a 'reeducation system,' and the tyrants became 'educators' who transformed the people from the old society into 'new people'... Soviet concentration-camp prisoners were forcibly 'invited' to place their trust in a system that enslaved them.
>
> "In China, the concentration-camp prisoner is called a 'student' and he is required to study the correct thoughts of the Party and to reform his own faulty thinking... The Communists, thanks to their incomparable propaganda strength grounded in the subversion of language, successfully turn the tables on the criticism leveled against their terrorist tactics, continually uniting the ranks of their militants and sympathizers by renewing the Communist act of faith."[409]

"What should be banned from campuses - and in fact anywhere - is white supremacist violence and denial of the genocides that this country was founded with." - Professor Katrin Wehrheim

---

Today speech is violence but violence is speech, depending on whether or not the content is sanctioned. In Orwell's 1984 their slogans were War is Peace, Freedom is Slavery and Ignorance is Strength. For the left, Joy is Hate, Liberty is Tyranny, Theft is Charity, and Diversity is Conformity.

There are two principle, interrelated ideas that underlie the progressive globalist's attack on opponents in this country in particular, the one power that stands in the way of their ambitions. The first is conflating a white majority with white supremacy.

The Doctrine of Privilege

A key to the elitist, leftist power grab, and a central tenet in its doctrine, rests on conflating a white majority with white supremacy or white nationalism. This is the only way to explain the left's rabid belief in the widespread existence of an ideology that has long been in the American rear view: racism against black or brown people. There will always be jerks and racists, but one of the things that made our nation unique was that citizenship did not depend on lineage. It should not be surprising that the U.S. has a majority of people with European descent since they founded and first settled the country, but that doesn't make it racist. It was not designed on race.

The left is gleeful of a diminishing white majority here but the change, at least prior to the mass illegal immigration of the Biden years, was actually exaggerated. They intentionally confused the issue by introducing the term Hispanic, which means that one speaks Spanish and is not a signifier of skin color or race. The Spanish and their descendants are just as white as the Italians or Greeks or various other European ethnicities. Non-Spanish whites are certainly the minority in the Americas and in the world.

The United States did not achieve its vast and rapid advancement of civilization because it was mostly white or mostly European, but because it was mostly free. Some of our greatest advances were the work of legal immigrants and minorities. This is why this nation is such a threat to the progressive globalist ambitions. The great replacement theory, the idea that the left is trying to replace native born Americans and particularly whites with non-white immigrants, was created by the left because that was indeed their intention. They accused the right of this, even before most of us knew the level of mass immigration that was occurring.

If speaking the majority language is privilege, then Hispanics are privileged in Puerto Rico. One can certainly get around better there if you know Spanish. While much signage in the U.S. uses English and Spanish, I found most signs in P.R. were only in Spanish. But why shouldn't they speak Spanish, if that's what they want to do? No, it isn't the native language of the island and, yes, the Spanish have a dark history there, but it has been the common language long before the United States had any involvement with the island. In the states, English has long been the common and dominate language. And why shouldn't it be? The English founded the country and made up most of its early settlers. It's not a native language, but English speakers are no more responsible for the actions of some of their predecessors than Spanish speakers or descendants are for theirs.

"Free speech has become a rhetorical tool to elide... the state's support and protection of white supremacists." – P.E. Moskowitz

---

Racism, at least how most dictionaries define it, is the belief that race accounts for differences in human character or ability and that a particular race is superior to others. This is not what most American believe, therefore a new version of racism had to be invented.

> P.E. Moskowitz, The Nation, Aug. 20, 2019:
> "By bolstering the narrative that speech should be protected at all costs, the police, perhaps unwittingly, help smuggle white supremacist thought, policy, and action into the American mainstream... What I've found through my research and reporting is that free speech has become a rhetorical tool to elide something much more sinister: the state's support and protection of white supremacists, and this country's unwillingness to grapple with its racism and vast inequality."[410]

Most Americans were over race by the start of the twenty-first century. Instead of no longer being an issue after the election of a black president, race was suddenly, virtually, the *only* issue so far as the left was concerned. Race became the primary tool they used to attack their political opponents. For the dichotomy of non-racist "racists" to work and to keep racism alive as an issue, some kind of broader definition was needed. It was like dark matter, where scientists imagined something that couldn't be seen or measured directly that had to be there to make their math work out right.

Here, *racism* had to be something utterly pervasive yet unconscious and perceivable only through the manipulation of vague statistics, microaggressions and propagandized media reports. And thus, white privilege was born, and with it an overwhelming bias in media against white people for no other reason than the color of our skin. I understand the irony, but two wrongs still do not make a right. A lot of people start life with more privileges than others, but we have no legal caste system. Opportunity and upward mobility are still more possible here than around the world.

"Most white Americans... have the unconscious, implicit, racial biases." - Professor John Dovidio

---

> John Dovidio, PhD, Pro. of Psychology and Public Health, Yale University:
> "...there's research that shows that only a small proportion of Americans today have old-fashioned kind of racism, explicit kind of racism. But the majority of white Americans, because they've grown up in a culture that has been historically racist in many ways, because they're exposed to the media that associates violence, drugs and poverty with certain groups. Most white Americans, the majority of white Americans, about two-thirds to three-quarters, have the unconscious, implicit, racial biases."[411]
>
> Danyelle Solomon, American Progress, June 16, 2017: "Defined as 'the conscious intentional exclusion from consciousness of a thought or feeling,' suppression has allowed white supremacy to become the baseline for all American structures, institutions, and policies."[412]

"White supremacy and white nationalism are central to the Trump phenomenon." - Chauncey Devega

---

> Chauncey Devega, Salon.com, April 15, 2020:
> "White supremacy cannot be understood as an ideology and set of behaviors only practiced by small groups of white people in America and around the world. It is a far more complicated thing than that. As repeatedly shown by political scientists, social psychologists, historians and other social scientists, white supremacy and white nationalism are central to the Trump phenomenon, which has effectively conquered the Republican Party, the right-wing news media and their collective public."[413]

No race has a monopoly on bias, but as shown earlier, among political parties, the Democrats have always represented the bulk of it. Another attempt to redefine racism came from across our northern border.

> Alberta Civil Liberties Research Centre, "Reverse Racism is a Myth":
> "Assumptions and stereotypes about white people are examples of racial prejudice, not racism. Racial prejudice refers to a set of discriminatory or derogatory attitudes based on assumptions deriving from perceptions about race and/or skin colour. Thus, racial prejudice can indeed be directed at white people (e.g., white people can't dance) but is not considered racism because of the systemic relationship of power. When backed with power, prejudice results in acts of discrimination and oppression against groups or individuals. In Canada, white people hold this cultural power due to Eurocentric modes of thinking, rooted in colonialism, that continue to reproduce and privilege whiteness."[414]

The left redefined racism so that every white person is guilty of it because they defined it as our very culture: that's our holidays, social behavior, institutions, norms, beliefs, arts, laws, customs, capabilities and habits. This is how all manner of things like Mount Rushmore, the 4th of July, Abraham Lincoln, Christmas, conservatism, the Founding Fathers, the Electoral College, private property, Jesus and the law can be called white supremacy. We are told that every culture around the world must be respected, including those who convict women of a crime for being gang raped or where gays are thrown off buildings, but American culture is entirely irredeemable. Equal justice under the law and protections of life, liberty and happiness are racist because racism and slavery existed when they were conceived. Even if we hold no prejudices ourselves, every white person tied to slavery, the Nazis and the Ku Klux Klan. Reality doesn't matter.

To the contrary, our diversity of opinions and ability to express and debate ideas, Christian morality and our founding principles form the core of the culture that rejected traditional racism. We can embrace old world and new world traditions and celebrations, even though we might not all celebrate every holiday or celebrate the one's we do in the same way, but it is our belief in equal freedoms and equal value that are at the heart of the American ethos. There are more diverse places in the world but they do not melt together as much as they have traditionally done here. I have no doubt that racism against non-white people continues in America today but by calling everything racist, we give true racism camouflage and ensure its survival. How long were the Irish and the Polish looked down on here? Both were most certainly white. Race has always been an effective tool used to divide people.

> National Museum of African American History and Culture, Smithsonian:
> "White nationalists in the United States advocate for a country that is only for the white race due to feelings of entitlement and racial superiority. They also believe that the diversity of people in the United States will lead to the destruction of whiteness and white culture - hence, the correlation to white supremacist ideology."[415]

Despite the overwhelming narrative to the contrary, that definitely doesn't describe this nation or its culture today and it doesn't describe the vast majority of the Tea Party or Donald Trump supporters. America is in no sense white nationalist, being built on ideals rather than a people or ethnicity. It is a falsehood that has been extrapolated from the few leftovers of a darker time and intentionally incubated in our schools to shape collective opinion. It is also a main part of the propaganda that turned normal liberals into sufferers of Trump Derangement Syndrome; that is, that changed Donald Trump from being a political rival with different policy positions into an unbearable evil, thoughts of which lead to a visible breakdown.

> Theopia Jackson, PhD, president of the Association of Black Psychologists:
> "Every institution in America is born from the blood of white supremacist ideology and capitalism–and that's the disease."[416]

Our racism and privilege may be nothing we did personally, nothing we chose, but we bear it from birth as an Original Sin, identified upon us by the color of skin like our own Scarlet Letter. If somehow a white person is convincingly non-racist, the whole system of government is blamed instead, not the systems that separated Americans by race but the systems that today protect the legal equality of all through statute. White supremacy used to mean believing the "white race is inherently superior to other races and that white people should have control over people of other races."[417] That is simply to the majority view. The left today claims white people, on the basis of their skin color, are everything undesirable and responsible for every evil. This anti-white hatred is by definition racism. White supremacy has become indistinguishable from just representing a racial majority or having cultural traditions that trace back to historically white countries. Where there is unequal justice, we won't correct it by demonizing the foundations of equality under the law, but by enforcing those ideals!

> Sarah Jaffe, Nation Institute fellow and journalist, Twitter post, Sept. 11, 2017:
> "The carceral state exists to protect private property and is inseparable from white supremacy."[418]

White people do have the most power in this country statistically, given our greater numbers, *if* we voted or acted in unison, but we do not. Our votes are split along different ideological lines, primarily due to a handful of polarizing subjects. The left claimed Donald Trump's 2016 election was due to white racism, because they were unwilling to seriously consider the vital policy differences he championed (in between and sometimes with his trademark bluster), policies that ended up benefiting everyone and minorities in particular.[419] But it's a reality they can't see. The left uses racism as a political weapon. Diversity is gospel. Where the church had holy places and pious ears, the left has safe spaces[420] and snowflakes, that is, places where a diversity of opinion is not tolerated and people who are afraid of ideas. It's ironic that the people who push diversity and inclusion and avidly police speech are often the same people demanding these spaces of exclusion.

"When you're black around white people, you have to explain every little thing." - Sabrina Stevens

---

> Sabrina Stevens, activist and progressive strategist, about safe spaces, Aug. 25, 2020:
> "For me as a black woman, it's really nice to just go out with other black women sometimes. I have to do so much less translation. When you're black around white people, you have to explain every little thing, even with people who are perfectly nice and well-meaning... Everybody has a need to just be able to be themselves somewhere, without having to do that translation and without having to always be on guard to justify yourself."[421]

Though perhaps an understandable observation, I shudder to imagine what would happen if a white person said the same thing. It's not enough to *not* be a white supremacist, you have to be anti-white. White privilege started as a concept introduced by a feminist in the late 1980's who saw it as something akin to male privilege.

"The historic election of President Barack Obama was followed by a resurgence of violent white nationalism... which was key to the election of Donald Trump." - Aastha Uprety & Danyelle Solomon

---

> Aastha Uprety and Danyelle Solomon, Center for American Progress, Aug. 8, 2018:
> "Historically, racial progress in the United States has almost inevitably been followed by racist pushback. The Civil War, emancipation, and Reconstruction were followed by more than 80 years of state-sanctioned violence against African American communities. The gains coming out of the Civil Rights era of the 1960s were immediately met with white backlash and resentment that seeped into the nation's politics. Policies targeted communities of color with draconian actions, not the least being the weaponization of the criminal justice system. More recently, the historic election of President Barack Obama was followed by a resurgence of violent white nationalism—the alt-right movement—which was key to the election of Donald Trump.
>
> "This perplexing pendulum of racial progress followed by a rise in racism helps explain the recent resurgence of white nationalism in the United States. This maddening cycle owes itself to Americans' addiction to collective denial and selective ignorance when it comes to the nation's history."[422]

There was racist pushback to the results of the Civil War, but it wasn't from the right. Racism had nothing to do with why Americans supported Donald Trump. His policies and statements, though often intentionally misconstrued by dishonest actors, had no connection to ideas of white entitlement or superiority, but rather for the betterment of all the American people, including all legal immigrants. It didn't matter which border they crossed or what nation they came from, so long as they followed the law. It is the left that believes in minority entitlement and superiority.

The leftist doctrine of institutional or systemic racism and universal white guilt presumes all any of us are is our skin color or ancestry, ignoring the infinite shades of skin here and wide variety of nationalities. I know white liberals embrace a great deal of self-hatred, but do other ethnicities do the same? A great many blacks in this country are more white than black and Spanish are just as white as vast swaths of other European descendants, like my grandfather. Is our guilt for our predecessors proportional to our degree of whiteness or are there not many other things at play here that are far greater determiners of behavior? It's elitists who imagine themselves better than everybody else, regardless of race, and they are leftists.

> Sophia A. Nelson, The Daily Beast, May 28, 2020: "Central Park, New York City in 2020 and Amy Cooper, the white woman who called the police to threaten a black man out bird-watching who asked her to leash her dog, as park rules require. The worst part is, she knew what she was doing because America has taught her how to do it."[423]
>
> Van Jones, CNN Political Commentator, May 30, 2020: "It's not the racist white person who is in the Ku Klux Klan that we have to worry about. It's the white liberal Hillary Clinton supporter walking her dog in Central Park who would tell you right now, you know, people like that - 'oh, I don't see race, race is no big deal to me, I see us all as the same, I give to charities.' But the minute she sees a black man who she does not respect or who she has a slight thought against, she weaponized race like she had been trained by the Aryan Nation.
>
> "A Klan member could not have been better trained to pick up the phone and tell the police, 'It's a black man, African-American man, come get him.' So even the most liberal, well-intentioned white person has a virus in his or her brain that can be activated at an instant... James Baldwin said it best: White people in these situations are always innocent. [mocking] 'Oh my God, I can't believe this, teach me, educate me, help me understand, how did this happen, talk to me, tell me something, tell me what to do.' White people are always innocent — and their innocence constitutes their crime. It is too late to be innocent."[424]
>
> Jeh Johnson, Obama's Homeland Security Secretary, CNN, June 11, 2020:
> "Defined broadly enough, one could say that there's systemic racism across every institution in America."[425]

Of course, that is part of the problem, as it is made to apply anywhere they look. Most white people do not put race at the center of every decision, but many leftists do. While U.S. liberals concern themselves with microaggressions, polls and statistics, minorities across the world face overt harassment, intimidation, violence, slavery and even genocide right now. These are clearly far worse than statistical inequities and imagined slights. Oprah Winfrey, a multi-billionaire and vastly influential black woman, during a show she hosted on Apple's streaming service, asked questions of a white person named Seth and former NFL linebacker and successful Fox Sports analyst, Emmanuel Acho. Her condescension was overwhelming.

> The Oprah Conversation, AppleTV+, August 7: Oprah: "There are white people who are not as powerful as the system of white people – the caste system that's been put in place – but they still, no matter where they are on the rung, or the ladder of success, they still have their whiteness... You've become 'woke' during this period, and realized in that awakening that you are racist, right? I just want to know how that happened."
> Seth: "I was born in the 70s. I was born and raised in Manhattan. I've always considered myself to be liberal. Now I'm not only a friend of people of color but also an advocate for [them], but this, this movement over the last month has been powerful. I realized that I couldn't be not racist. I realized that I either was a racist or an anti-racist, and I wasn't – I'm not – an anti-racist."
>
> Emmanuel Acho: "Here's what I told my friends with their white children. I said, Y'all live in a white cul-de-sac, in a white neighborhood, in a white city, in a white state. If you were not careful, your children will live their whole life white, and at 26, 27, they'll end up being a part of the problem, because you just let them and allowed them to live a completely white, sheltered, and culture-less life... White privilege isn't saying your life hasn't been hard. White privilege is just saying it hasn't attributed to the difficulty of your life."[426]

Apparently, culture only exists for non-whites and all "white" people have the same ancestry. The woke white population are the self-righteous, the born again, having awoken to the fact that they are subconsciously and yet deeply racist. Winfrey and Acho both lectured white people, however poor or desperate, for a prejudice they may not feel and an advantage they may not experience, simply because the color of their skin. She claims that a caste system separates Americans by color as she prejudges and generalizes all whites for the purpose of accessing blame and assigning privilege.

Sometimes, they convert Christian rituals into expressions of their own by infecting churches with their ideology. Pope Francis continues to do this. A Catholic pastor in New York City had his parishioners affirm various statements acknowledging the unfairness, injustice and suffering caused by white privilege and white supremacy and committing to change church culture to seek racial justice. When white people say they have worked for everything they have and haven't enslaved anyone, the Parish Council there said they are seeking to "sidestep personal complicity in perpetuating the systems and institutions that support racial inequity."[427]

We are born sinful. Where have I heard that before? Migrant Muslims are often culturally incompatible with Western states and those conflicts are the reason globalists fund their relocation.

Former NBA player and psychologist John Amaechi, speaking on a British school education program put on by the British Broadcasting Corporation (BBC), explained white privilege, which he imagines somehow makes white people immune from common impediments.

> John Amaechi, appearing on BBC Bitesize, Aug 5, 2020: "Privilege is a hard concept for some people to understand, because normally when we talk of privilege, we imagine immediate unearned riches and tangible benefits for anyone who has it... But white privilege, and indeed all privilege, is actually more about the absence of inconvenience, the absence of an impediment or challenge, and as such, when you have it, you really don't notice it."[428]

A 19-year-old Canadian writer, Rav Arora, who immigrated there with his family when he was 4, described the difficulties they encountered coming into a mostly white nation, but also the opportunities. Though not in the U.S., he expressed common experiences and values.

> Rav Arora, The fallacy of white privilege, New York Post, July 11, 2020:
> "Fundamentally, privileges of all kinds exist: able-bodiedness, wealth, education, moral values, facial symmetry, tallness (or in other contexts, shortness), health, stamina, safety, economic mobility, and importantly, living in a free, diverse society. Rather than 'whiteness,' an exponentially more predictive privilege in life is growing up with two parents... When surveying the tremendous complexity of racial disparities, it's simply wrong to presuppose all whites are 'privileged,' let alone racist. This is why 41 percent of

> children born to single mothers grow up in poverty whereas only 8 percent of children living in married-couple families are impoverished."[429]

The left ignores these realities in order to assign race as the sole or at least dominate factor in the inequities of life. When women couldn't vote, males had privilege. When blacks couldn't vote, whites had privilege. These were legal privileges. The lingering social advantages were something our society had to work past and largely we have.

> Peggy McIntosh, Wellesley College Center for Research on Women, 1988:
> "I have come to see white privilege as an invisible package of unearned assets that I can count on cashing in each day, but about which I was 'meant' to remain oblivious."[430]

She provided a list of privileges that mostly do not exist for people of any color. They also included some items that were simply a product of having a mostly white nation, like seeing your race represented everywhere. It is easy to find lists online of all of the racist things white people do on a daily basis, but the reality is that it's often common human behavior and not about race at all. We can't expect our neighbors to like us or to avoid mean people, attitudes or harassment or to not be judged on our appearance.

When people do not move aside on a sidewalk or store aisle as you come by, ignoring and excluding you, or don't treat you the way you think you deserve, these things happen, regularly, to everyone. People are mean, insensitive, jerks for a whole spectrum of reasons. Sometimes, it may be that they don't like you because of your race or your accent or your attitude or your success or your height or where you're from or dozens other things you may not have any control over. Being white does not exempt us from these negative experiences nor prevent the microaggressions by people who just assume we are bigots. In its circular logic, if you deny this privilege, that is itself evidence of privilege.

> National Museum of African American History and Culture, Smithsonian:
> "This white-dominant culture also operates as a social mechanism that grants advantages to white people, since they can navigate society both by feeling normal and being viewed as normal. Persons who identify as white rarely have to think about their racial identity because they live within a culture where whiteness has been

> normalized. Thinking about race is very different for nonwhite persons living in America. People of color must always consider their racial identity, whatever the situation, due to the systemic and interpersonal racism that still exists. Whiteness (and its accepted normality) also exist as everyday microaggressions toward people of color. Acts of microaggressions include verbal, nonverbal, and environmental slights, snubs or insults toward nonwhites. Whether intentional or not, these attitudes communicate hostile, derogatory, or harmful messages."[431]

White people do, in fact, have to be always aware of their racial identity because everything we say and do is distorted, seen through a lens that presumes racism, bigotry and oppression behind every thought and action. If something I say or do is misconstrued, my guilt is automatically assumed and my job is on the line. You can't go to Germany and then complain that there are too many Germans there, go to a mostly white country and complain that there are too many whites there or go to Nigeria and complain that there are too many black people there. Unlike most countries, ours allows anyone to become a citizen if they follow the legal process. Where else is that true? The U.S. is a vast and diverse nation, so what is normal in one place can be very different from what is normal in another. As a southerner, little in the north feels normal.

Those little slights that others experience, those microaggressions, are indecipherable landmines for white people, especially when working with people from different parts of the country (even more so than different races). We're expected to know what ethnicity everybody is and walk on eggshells around anything that might be misinterpreted as a reference to it. If I deploy to a new location and ask a coworker if they know where any good Mexican restaurants are, it's not because I have any idea what nationality their forefathers were. It's because they've been working there longer and know the area better and I feel like eating Mexican food.

I've read many lists of so-called white microaggressions that are just examples of some people doing stupid or mean things,[432] not examples of things most white people would say or do. They are stereotypes. There are people, including white liberals, who are always there, waiting to pounce at every misstep or cultural difference. Someone I worked with once referenced an event connected to a Native American reservation that included the words "pow wow". The coworker was immediately incensed, saying the use of those words were bigoted and insensitive. In reality, it was the name that the people on the reservation chose for the event. It wasn't a slight on our part to call it what they named it.

Just because I am white, I can be seen as a racist, my motives corrupt and everything I say or do may be met with prejudice and mistrust from a racial perspective. At best, I am treated as naïve to believe decisions made by other white people are not racially motivated. In the history of this nation, being white or non-white long had extraordinary significance. The laws and the application of the laws were grossly unfair and some of that continues today. However, prejudice or misuse of authority, whether through prosecutorial discretion, police action, or any other abuse, must be countered using the law applied equally, no matter the race of the person wronged. That is racial justice - justice regardless of race. Otherwise, we are just perpetuating racial division.

The United States of America was populated mostly by Europeans, who are all now generally considered white. We went from a multicultural nation, settled by large numbers of people from dozens of different countries, each with a rich cultural heritage (and yes, different shades of skin), to a place where all of those people were consolidated down into a singular group of "cultureless" (and now deplorable) white people who inherently oppress blacks, Native Americans and any others who can be identified as a protected minority group. I see all shades of people. I don't understand why some can only see black and white.

The descendants of Europeans are condemned for all of the evil perpetrated in our history, but no one should be so mistaken as to think the rest of the world was not often equally and even much more violent and evil, or that the ancestors of some did not inevitably commit crimes against the ancestors of others. Virtually every nation on earth was founded in an era of slavery, but the left says America is worse than any other because, here, slavery and later discrimination was fueled and justified with racism. That too was common throughout the previous centuries across the world. With the Enlightenment, the old religious justifications for slavery no longer seemed sufficient. Many of those continuing the institution clung to the idea that Africans or American natives were somehow inferior. They lied to themselves to protect their own conscience and justify their actions to others.

Even though our founders didn't feel this way, the nation they created included slaveholding states with people who did. As a consequence, we are told that no matter where we are from or what we do or say, all white people are guilty and every system of our nation is irrevocably stained by that guilt. It doesn't matter that our free society is a result of the ideals our founders embraced. No, everything is tainted by the worst of our past, not elevated by the best of it.

Many of the same people who condemn European colonialism also celebrate Spanish American history month. I cannot follow the logic. Spain, the very same culture and people who committed widespread genocide (both by the accident of disease and by brutal conquest), who imported African slaves and enslaved the natives en masse to mine the gold and tend the fields stolen in their invasion. The Spanish and Portuguese invaded, conquered and enslaved more of the Americas than did the Northern Europeans, but any culture passed down from them, at least in the U.S., seems somehow untouched by that stain. Meanwhile, descendants of non-Spanish "whites" are responsible for their forefather's sins. Columbus, an Italian, is denounced by many Hispanics today but he was acting on the dime and direction of the Spanish monarchy.

The English were imperialists who did great wrongs to others around the world, but their control in the Americas was less than others. But the left does not blame the Spanish culture, language or people for the acts of some of their ancestors. They speak Spanish and celebrate Spanish culture and history and most are, genetically, much more Spanish than native. To be clear, they *shouldn't* be blamed. The Spanish are *not* responsible for their ancestors any more than the English are for theirs. There's nothing wrong about the Spanish language or culture. They have every right to embrace it and the many great things in their ancestry and culture as others do. If the descendants of the conquistadors are looked down on by any for the actions of their forefathers, that is just as irrational and unfounded. We have a right to be proud of our lineage. The whole goal of this nation was for people to be judged as individuals for their own actions, not those of others.

This is a complicated and often ugly world and many cultures historically identified some people as "others", based on such things as class, ancestry or appearance, as lesser members of society or even as lesser humans. Despite the common narrative, this occurs today far less in the U.S. than in many others. India, for instance, is still strictly ordered by caste and the individual has no control over the caste in which they are born. Africans in the Americas have had an unconscionably tortured history, as have the indigenous people. Neither should be denied or ignored. Africans were abducted and sold into slavery, not just to the Americas, but across much of the East as well, not just by the Spanish or English but by Arabs and others in the East.

It was all horrifying and inexcusable. African culture was destroyed and lost in the process. I also have great sympathy and respect for native American peoples throughout the Western hemisphere and mourn the destruction of their religion, history and culture at the hands of invaders who often justified their assault on religious grounds, but Europeans did not invent war or conquest. The Spanish or English were no more violent and reprehensible than other conquerors across human history or across the world. Most Europeans and most Christians, opposed the brutality of invaders in the early Americas when stories of their actions began to spread. It was no longer widely condoned. Attitudes were changing.

If I treat someone poorly because of the color of their skin, it's my behavior that is reprehensible, not my skin color. When you treat everyone with a specific skin color or ethnicity negatively for the behavior of some, that's racism. It's stereotyping to imagine all white people think the same way or bear the same prejudices or even embrace the same cultural elements in the same way. You can't fairly blame an entire race or a whole country for the behavior or prejudices of some of its people. To do so only encourages division and discourages progress. Whether it was an injustice 200 or 4000 years ago, the evils of the past cannot be justly visited upon the present. It is another instance where a concept from religion is utilized by the left.

> Holy Bible, Old Testament, Exodus 20:5, King James Version: "I the LORD thy God am a jealous God, visiting the iniquity of the fathers upon the children unto the third and fourth generation of them that hate me."

"Guilt was never a rational thing; it distorts all the faculties of the human mind." - Edmund Burke

---

Even though their arguments fail to follow sound reason, this Original Sin of white racism and the guilt it engenders, has value politically. Like the belief in Chicken Little climate hysteria, it shapes policy and blinds rationality. The advantage of the doctrine is that it facilitates control, manipulating Americans by using their guilt and compassion against themselves. It's the same reason organizations on TV solicit donations with images of abused dogs, damaged children and starving Holocaust survivors. Even without having any connection to any of these things, we can scarcely avoid feeling guilty for their existence and want to do something to help. Americans do a great deal to help others.

> Edmund Burke, philosopher and politician, 18th century: "Guilt was never a rational thing; it distorts all the faculties of the human mind, it perverts them, it leaves a man no longer in the free use of his reason, it puts him into confusion."

"Merely learning about the past and apologizing for it is not enough."
- Seth Cohen

The left imagines racism as some kind of half-conscious conspiracy of white supremacy, combining dog whistles and coded language to communicate a message amongst a small-minded multitude who are fighting to return discrimination and segregation to America. This is itself racist and unjust, but the left is not opposed to racism: they just think it's justified when directed at the right people. Any mistreatment white people experience is surely justified retribution given our history and majority privilege. Can any mechanism redeem white people in the eyes of the left for that Original Sin of white racism? Perhaps by sacrificing our majority or giving up our culture and country? Perhaps something else?

> June Tangney, "White Shame," researcher at George Mason University:
> "Guilt can push people towards forward-oriented actions, like apologies and reparations."[433]

> Seth Cohen, Forbes.com, "An Overdue Debt", June 21, 2020: "... merely learning about the past and apologizing for it is not enough. America must finally settle the debts that it has long owed to Black Americans, and do so with the full faith and credit of the nation that enslaved their ancestors."[434]

It is not enough to treat people with civility or avoid causing another harm. You have to profess the correct beliefs, to be actively anti-racist, which in practice translates to anti-white. Just like it wasn't enough for the church for people to be moral, they had to follow the Vatican's every direction in order to be saved.

> Jonathan Greenblatt, President of the Anti-Defamation League (ADL), Vox, July 7, 2020:
> "This is not an issue with two sides. There is nothing partisan or political in pushing back on prejudice."[435]

> Katrin Wehrheim, mathematics professor, University of California-Berkeley:
> "None of this is about free speech. What should be banned from campuses - and in fact anywhere - is white supremacist violence and denial of the genocides that this country was founded with."[436]

When the church was faced with a movement toward tolerance and choice, it changed the meaning of words in an attempt to defeat the ideas they represented. It responded to calls for religious tolerance by recasting the conversation. Tolerance was not a matter of accepting or peacefully allowing other religious beliefs, it meant indifference to the efficacy of different religions and indifference to the fate of those seeking other paths to salvation. The Roman Catholic Church believed it was the sole path to that end and therefore would not tolerate what they saw as falsehoods being peddled by those who disagreed. All opposition was not only wrong but evil because it led people away from their control.

Likewise, the left redefines and recharacterizes terms to change their usefulness. The left changed the meaning of racism and liberalism. There are many examples of this wordplay: independence is heartlessness, freedom is lawlessness, capitalism is greed and free speech is hate-speech. Like the church, the left has redefined and vilified freedom, cast as racism, the license to demean and oppress others. But the oppression of some by others is no part of liberty. By demonizing liberty, the free market and opportunity, the left hopes to prevent the spread of these heresies, because they might lead to the general public having power and not them.

Eradicating Dissent

The second key methodology used by Progressive Globalists is identifying all opposing ideas as hate, one of their words for heresy, proscribing all difference of opinion and silencing dissent. The reason the left has always seen religion as a threat is because of its power and they do not want to share power. There are too many concepts shared by the church of old and elitist today not to reflect similar thought processes and ambitions. Our moral and intellectual superiors have determined the truth. Both heresy and blasphemy represent the oppression of differing ideas, tools for the advancement of the some over others.

Like religion, the left expects to get inside our heads and judge our thoughts and desires. If you harbor dissent in your heart, leftists will know and judge or punish you for it, whether you realize your guilt or not. Criminalizing thoughts is the height of tyranny, a tyranny of the mind, even if those thoughts are repugnant to others. To their articles of faith no opposition is considered sane and against which any level of censorship and retribution are justified. They control and manipulate language and punish, socially and economically, any expression of opposition. By deeming their opponents hateful, racist or otherwise intolerable in a civil society, the left relieves themselves of the obligation to defend their own positions.

This is speech that, in and of itself, is considered an act of violence, in response to which government tyranny and actual violence are justified. Black Lives Matter[437] and the anarchists and Communists of Antifa are examples. Sometimes the left contorts itself in all manner of twisted logic to say that "hate" speech causes physical injury, even though hate against whites is ok.[438]

"Antifa activists have argued that certain types of speech are themselves violent or bound to cause violence." - Katy Steinmetz

---

> Katy Steinmetz, Time Magazine, Aug. 14, 2017: "Groups on the right have used events like the protest in Berkeley to paint Antifa protestors as being out of control and acting as enemies of free speech, because they have mobilized in order to "shut down" speech that they disagree with. Politicians on the right and left have both criticized such tactics. In turn, Antifa activists have argued that certain types of speech are themselves violent or bound to cause violence if they are uttered in the public sphere. They have also said that alt-right groups are using the words "free speech" as cover for spreading racist and bigoted ideologies."[439]

Words do matter, but you can't legislate courtesy without sacrificing human liberty. The emotional or psychological harm that comes with life cannot be eliminated by controlling language and the moral elevation of human beings is not to be achieved by force, as history well demonstrates. Too often, we spend more time worrying about someone else being offended by some inadvertent slight than we do about more significant issues, like actual violence, theft and oppression.

"For Communism, antifascism became a brilliantly effective label that could be used to silence one's opponents quickly." – The Black Book of Communism

---

Fascism to the left means intolerance and oppression but the group Antifa, the so-called "anti-fascists", are prime examples of both. They riot in order to stop opposing views and to oppress and terrify those around them. Any time liberals are out to protest, Antifa and other radicals appear to lead the movement in what certainly seems to involve a lot of hatred. Later, anti-Israel and pro-Palestine activists added to the mayhem. The left intentionally conflates violent acts like lynching or police brutality with differences of opinion about political and moral questions. Anti-fascism grew out of communism as a way to attack their opponents after World War II and continues to serve this purpose.

> The Black Book of Communism:
> "The Communists' participation in the war and in the victory over Nazism institutionalized the whole notion of antifascism as an article of faith for the left. The Communists, of course, portrayed themselves as the best representatives and defenders of this antifascism. For Communism, antifascism became a brilliantly effective label that could be used to silence one's opponents quickly."

Speech is violence. Meanwhile, the left's violence is peaceful protest. Hate is defined as "to dislike intensely or passionately; feel extreme aversion for or extreme hostility toward; detest."[440] In the United States, we have the right to dislike or hate anyone or anything. If that were not so, most of the liberals I quote in this book would be guilty, having freely displayed their extreme aversion and hostility toward American principles, the Tea Party, Donald Trump and his supporters. The left sees the movement against hate speech as a way to punish opponents and cultivate approved feelings and thoughts. Hate speech is how the left disposes of dissent.

The problem with hate speech is that hate is a matter of opinion and some hate is condoned. With hate crimes, the hate is implied by the choice of victim, making crimes against some people subject to more severe punishment than others. By definition, hate speech is "speech that attacks, threatens, or insults a person or group on the basis of national origin, ethnicity, color, religion, gender, gender identity, sexual orientation, or disability."[441] That isn't entirely true, though, because it isn't hate if one is attacking, threatening or insulting people because they are of white, American, of northern European descent, heterosexual or Christian.

Hate and intolerance are ok so long as they are directed toward appropriate targets. There is a reason that countries today who have blasphemy laws are on the tyranny side of the political scale. We cannot pretend to control human beings to such an extent that they will not insult the sensibilities of each other. When I was young, children were taught to separate speech from actions: sticks and stones may break my bones but words will never hurt me. Now, many adults seem incapable of discerning the difference.

In the modern era the control started small, from how much sugar we are permitted to consume to the type of bags we can bring our groceries home in, but the advance of totalitarianism shows no sign of subsiding, short of an American resurgence. The left progressed from the semantics of political correctness to something even more dangerous as they backed up their moral outrage with intimidation and oppression.[442] Like the early church, the left took up the mantle of the censorship crusade, equally convinced that people should not be allowed to have such appalling freedoms.

Instead of literally burning books, these on the left censor publications, search engine results and social media postings.[443] They ban, demonetize and shut down social media accounts. Sometimes, it is defended as necessary to protect the gullible public from manipulation by foreign adversaries, bad science or morals, but surveillance and censorship of something as subjective as "disinformation" opens up widely the opportunity for political oppression. Every totalitarian regime censors information with which they disagree, unsanctioned science and dissent.

"The trend toward greater surveillance and speech control here, and toward the growing involvement of government, is undeniable and likely inexorable." - Professor Jack Goldsmith

---

> Jack Goldsmith, Harvard Law School, April 25, 2020:
> "As surprising as it may sound, digital surveillance and speech control in the United States already show many similarities to what one finds in authoritarian states such as China. Constitutional and cultural differences mean that the private sector, rather than the federal and state governments, currently takes the lead in these practices, which further values and address threats different from those in China. But the trend toward greater surveillance and speech control here, and toward the growing involvement of government, is undeniable and likely inexorable.

"Significant monitoring and speech control are inevitable components of a mature and flourishing internet." - Professor Jack goldsmith

---

> "In the great debate of the past two decades about freedom versus control of the network, China was largely right and the United States was largely wrong. Significant monitoring and speech control are inevitable components of a mature and flourishing internet, and governments must play a large role in these practices to ensure that the internet is compatible with a society's norms and values... The surveillance and speech-control responses to COVID-19, and the private sector's collaboration with the government in these efforts, are a historic and very public experiment about how our constitutional culture will adjust to our digital future."[444]

During the pandemic, the big technology and mainstream media companies, under leftist leadership, took it upon themselves to censor information it considered wrong or hurtful. Any comment expressing concern or hesitancy about taking the vaccine and discussion of treatments was blocked. Debate was stopped, news disappeared and facts were obscured. The media and government, as pawns of the Progressive Globalists, presumed the role of gatekeeper of all truth and information. Social media, search, publication and distribution companies manage the flow of all information on the internet, which should serve instead as a great repository of world knowledge. They simply erased or blocked information they didn't want the public to see, labeled works as false simply because they contradicted the narrative, using the guise of fact-checking to remove content from the public square or discredit it without justification.

"This is what totalitarianism looks like in our century." - Sohrab Ahmari

During Trump's Presidency, leading social media behemoths became increasingly aggressive in their censorship of the right, including censoring the President himself. Videos were blocked from public view. Speakers were banned or de-platformed. Google blocked search results for Breitbart News and other conservative sites. Big tech blocked opinions and reports that questioned the accepted facts about Covid-19, facts that turned out to be wrong, like the ability of the vaccine to prevent the spread of the virus and the efficacy of masks, lockdowns, treatments and antibodies.

Facebook blocked any mention of a possible lab origin of the virus on its platform until summer of 2021.[445] Anyone who dared question their accepted explanation, that it came naturally from a wet market and not the Wuhan lab down the road, were called racists and conspiracy theorists. The truth finally emerged despite the best efforts of the establishment. They even made an election-changing news story from the New York Post, the oldest newspaper in the nation, virtually go away, because it was politically disadvantageous to their ambitions.

> New York Post, Sohrab Ahmari, Oct. 14, 2020: "This is what totalitarianism looks like in our century: not men in darkened cells driving screws under the fingernails of dissidents, but Silicon Valley dweebs removing from vast swaths of the Internet a damaging exposé on their preferred presidential candidate. That's what Facebook and Twitter did to the New York Post's bombshell report on Hunter Biden, revealing why the illustrious vice-presidential son was hired by a shady Ukrainian energy firm in exchange for at least $50,000 a month."[446]

Facebook called it reducing the story's distribution to prevent the spread of misinformation. Twitter called the story "potentially unsafe," not false.[447] Misinformation and oppression are the altar on which the left decided to hang its power-hungry ambitions, complimented by social justice and diversity. The NY Post story in this case was factual, the materials were acquired legally and backed up by other sources.[448] Truth and science were expendable. All that mattered was getting the public to have a particular response. Trust in sanctioned science and government was to replace trust in God or reason. They refused to publish or distribute books through booksellers, the ability to advertise on major platforms has been denied, accounts locked and offending works removed from streaming services.[449] Reporters were fired.

Today book banning is being conflated with restricting sexually explicit books and programs in public school. Parents, along with the community represented by the school board, are obligated to ensure that only age and setting appropriate books or behaviors are promoted at schools. It is the same reason schools do not give kids unfettered access to the internet. Pushing alternative lifestyles is no different from promoting religion. Both are the purview of parents, not schools and certainly not government. While books discussing these subjects may reasonably be available in school libraries, they must be age appropriate. Most agree that sexually explicit materials should not be available to minors. Calling that book banning is simply dishonest. Book banning is removing adult access. These are conflated as a way to heighten animosity and turn Americans against each other, while aggressively pushing leftist ideologies.[450]

"No nation has done more to advance the human condition than the United States of America." - President Donald Trump

---

Where the church excommunicated people, which meant cutting them off to the gates of heaven and the benefits of civil society, the left cancels, unfriends, doxes, censors, boycotts, blacklists, ostracizes and bankrupts those who fail to toe the line.[451] They publicly post people's personal contact and location information (doxing) so that those they disagree with might be harassed or harmed. They forced businesses to censor content and others were run out of business entirely. Government and big business are partners in crime. This is American totalitarianism, a way of thinking that fuels the suppression of ideas and seeks censorship and information control and it is part of a bigger plan. Dialogue has been demonized and freedom of thought suffocated as history was rewritten. Donald Trump saw this clearly.

> President Donald Trump, Mount Rushmore Speech, July 3, 2020: "Our founders launched not only a revolution in government, but a revolution in the pursuit of justice, equality, liberty, and prosperity. No nation has done more to advance the human condition than the United States of America and no people have done more to promote human progress than the citizens of our

great nation. It was all made possible by the courage of 56 patriots who gathered in Philadelphia 244 years ago and signed the Declaration of Independence. They enshrined a divine truth that changed the world forever when they said, 'All men are created equal.' These immortal words set in motion the unstoppable march of freedom...

"Our nation is witnessing a merciless campaign to wipe out our history, defame our heroes, erase our values, and indoctrinate our children. Angry mobs are trying to tear down statues of our Founders, deface our most sacred memorials, and unleash a wave of violent crime in our cities... One of their political weapons is 'Cancel Culture' – driving people from their jobs, shaming dissenters, and demanding total submission from anyone who disagrees. This is the very definition of totalitarianism, and it is completely alien to our culture and our values, and it has absolutely no place in the United States of America...

"The radical view of American history is a web of lies – all perspective is removed, every virtue is obscured, every motive is twisted, every fact is distorted, and every flaw is magnified." - President Donald Trump

---

"In our schools, our newsrooms, even our corporate boardrooms, there is a new far-left fascism that demands absolute allegiance. If you do not speak its language, perform its rituals, recite its mantras, and follow its commandments, then you will be censored, banished, blacklisted, persecuted, and punished. It's not going to happen to us. Make no mistake. This left-wing cultural revolution is designed to overthrow the American Revolution. In so doing they would destroy the very civilization that rescued billions from poverty, disease, violence, and hunger, and that lifted humanity to new heights of achievement, discovery, and progress...

"The violent mayhem we have seen in the streets of cities that are run by liberal Democrats, in every case, is the predictable result of years of extreme indoctrination and bias in education, journalism, and other cultural institutions. Against every law of society and nature, our children are taught in school to hate their own country, and to believe that the men and women who built it were not heroes, but that were villains. The radical view of American history

> is a web of lies — all perspective is removed, every virtue is obscured, every motive is twisted, every fact is distorted, and every flaw is magnified until the history is purged and the record is disfigured beyond all recognition...The radical ideology attacking our country advances under the banner of social justice, but in truth, it would demolish both justice and society. It would transform justice into an instrument of division and vengeance and it would turn our free and inclusive society into a place of a repression, domination, and exclusion."[452]

Politicians or speakers who didn't conform to the dictates of the left were run out of restaurants while dining with their families or mobs surrounded their homes.[453] Numerous (mostly nonconforming) news anchors were removed from their jobs for the mere *accusation* of wrongdoing during these years. If you complemented President Trump, your business would be boycotted. An ill-timed or dumb comment or unpopular joke - no matter how inconsequential - could cost you your job and ruin your career.[454] Sometimes it was permanent. Sometimes people recovered. Humor was no longer permitted. It didn't matter if an offending comment was made many years prior like Paula Dean[455] and Kevin Hart.[456]

When the left marshalled its horde against a person, it was not a minor thing. When liberals attacked, not only did that subdue or silence the speech in question but it effectively chilled peaceful debate everywhere. Even left leaning writers and academics raised the alarm on this trend.

"The result has been to steadily narrow the boundaries of what can be said without the threat of reprisal." - Harper's Magazine

---

> A Letter on Justice and Open Debate, Harper's Magazine, July 7, 2020:
> "The free exchange of information and ideas, the lifeblood of a liberal society, is daily becoming more constricted. While we have come to expect this on the radical right, censoriousness is also spreading more widely in our culture: an intolerance of opposing views, a vogue for public shaming and ostracism, and the tendency to dissolve complex policy issues in a blinding moral certainty. We uphold the value of robust and even caustic counter-speech from all quarters. But it is now all too common to hear calls for swift and

severe retribution in response to perceived transgressions of speech and thought.

"... writers, artists, and journalists who fear for their livelihoods if they depart from the consensus." - Harper's Magazine

---

> "More troubling still, institutional leaders, in a spirit of panicked damage control, are delivering hasty and disproportionate punishments instead of considered reforms. Editors are fired for running controversial pieces; books are withdrawn for alleged inauthenticity; journalists are barred from writing on certain topics; professors are investigated for quoting works of literature in class; a researcher is fired for circulating a peer-reviewed academic study; and the heads of organizations are ousted for what are sometimes just clumsy mistakes. Whatever the arguments around each particular incident, the result has been to steadily narrow the boundaries of what can be said without the threat of reprisal."[457]

"These incidents have drawn worldwide ridicule and damage the credibility of university scientists and scholars." - Professor Steven Pinker

---

> Steven Pinker, liberal Harvard University Professor of Psychology, 2018:
> "Universities are becoming laughing stocks of intolerance, with non-leftist speakers drowned out by jeering mobs, professors subjected to Stalinesque investigations for unorthodox opinions, risible guidelines on 'microaggressions' (such as saying 'I believe the most qualified person should get the job'), students mobbing and cursing a professor who invited them to discuss Halloween costumes, and much else. These incidents have drawn worldwide ridicule, and damage the credibility of university scientists and scholars when they weigh on critical matters, such as climate change."[458]

Unfortunately, he failed to see that censorship and climate change are both part of the same agenda.

The church of the past and the left today also use the same violent tactics of tyranny. The Roman Catholic Church instigated the inquisition, massacres, invasions, crusades and wars to defend and promote its ideology. Likewise, violence was a central feature of leftist regimes from Lenin and Hitler to Pol Pot and Castro. The left in America condoned and encouraged violent rioting and looting, even when people died in the process. Opposition was suppressed through fear and intimidation. Violence destabilizes society and opens it up for a new, authoritarian controls.

The increase in violence also resulted from policies deferential to criminals and can be traced back at least to the spring of 2020, when the policies of leftist D.A.s and the stoking of racial tensions led to numerous large American cities erupting into ongoing riots. Each volley of rioting and looting originated as legal and often peaceful protests against a precipitating event. Sometimes a clear injustice served as the catalyst, but in most cases, the appearance of injustice would suffice. Rather than seeking equal justice under the law, these violent crusades destroyed innocent lives, often minorities, and left devastated cities in their wake. Residents paid the price as authorities often stood by and watched. The death of George Floyd in police custody in 2020, even though it resulted in swift criminal charges against the officers involved, still led many to the streets where they were excused, obscured and justified by the media and politicians.

"This is mostly a protest. It is not generally speaking unruly." - Ali Velshi

---

Legal, peaceful protests were quickly eclipsed by riots and looting, especially at night, that went on for months and months on end. In olden times, that was called pillaging and such violence was condoned by leaders so long as the cause was "just". Even long after the rioting, the pillaging of stores continued. In the heightened emotions of 2020, complicated by a peculiar pandemic and the coming Presidential election, the mainstream media defended violent rioters by falsely and repeatedly insisting they were peaceful.[459]

"They seem to have forgotten, however, that the cameras are rolling." - Guy Birchall

---

MSNBC reporter Ali Velshi, in front of burning building and rioters, May 28, 2020:
"I want to be clear on how I characterize this. This is mostly a protest. It is not generally speaking unruly. But fires have been started and this crowd is relishing that."[460]

Guy Birchall, RT.com, June 12, 2020:
"Virtually every news outlet, from CNN to MSNBC to the BBC and Sky News, even the Daily Mail, have insisted that all the demonstrations in his name have been mainly placid, well-mannered affairs. They seem to have forgotten, however, that the cameras are rolling."[461]

Omar Jimenez, a CNN national correspondent, stood in front of numerous burning vehicles in one report on the rioting in Kenosha, Wisconsin, while the text on the screen read: Fiery but mostly peaceful protests after police shooting.[462] Another reporter praised the "entirely peaceful" protesters even as they hurled a bottle and verbal attacks at him in the middle of his live report.

"It's now just sort of a merry caravan... entirely peaceful."
- Miguel Marquez

CNN national correspondent Miguel Marquez, during riots in MN, May 30, 2020:
"They have not only, not only protesters walking now but they have several cars that have sort of joined the protest as well. And it's now just sort of a merry caravan. It is worth pointing out that it has been entirely peaceful, sometimes angry, but entirely peaceful. A few people doing some graffiti, when others saw them doing the graffiti, they would shut them down, make them stop doing it. [a bottle is hurled at him] A bottle thrown, which is not uncommon. So, there is some of that but for the most part they have been very, very peaceful. They haven't been destroying anything. They like to take it out on the media as everybody does, but rather than yell at us and throw things at us, not in a mean way, and we'll be fine."[463]

Equally oblivious to the world around them, numerous other reporters also talked down the severity of the violence as structures burned behind them. Others even justified the acts of looters.

"To fully eliminate looting, you'd have to eliminate the conditions that make people upset enough to protest." - Olga Khazan

---

> Olga Khazan, The Atlantic, June 2, 2020: "Others, meanwhile, see looting as a form of empowerment–a way to reclaim dignity after decades of abuse at the hands of police and other authorities. 'When you have the ability to gain some of that power back, people take the opportunity to do so,' Rashawn Ray, a sociologist at the University of Maryland, told me. 'The actions of police and protesters tend to mirror each other... To have a very large police presence with riot gear during the day is antithetical to what you want.
>
> "That's when you want the police on bicycles and on foot with the protesters'... Most of the experts I spoke with agreed that looting is a side effect of protests, which are a side effect of the conditions causing the protests. In this case, the root cause is yet another killing of a black man by a white police officer. To fully eliminate looting, you'd have to eliminate the conditions that make people upset enough to protest.'"[464]

"I don't care if someone decides to loot... that is reparations." - Ariel Atkins

---

> Ariel Atkins, a Black Live Matter organizer, Chicago NBC network affiliate WMAQ:
> "I don't care if someone decides to loot a Gucci or a Macy's or a Nike store, because that makes sure that person eats. That makes sure that person has clothes. That is reparations. Anything they wanted to take, they can take it, because these businesses have insurance."[465]

In this case, destroying and stealing was alright to the left because they were attacking capitalism and businesses, so even when destroying lives, the rioters claim the badge of righteousness. Never mind that people were killed in the process. Violence in service to a greater cause is justified. If the cause is just, morality means little.

> Scott Bauer and Todd Richmond, Associated Press, Wisconsin, June 25, 2020:
> "Protesters also attacked a state senator, threw a Molotov cocktail into a government building and attempted to break into the Capitol Tuesday night, only to be repelled by pepper spray from police stationed inside. The violence broke out as a group of 200 to 300 people protested the arrest of a Black man who shouted at restaurant customers through a megaphone while carrying a baseball bat."[466]

"Tonight, I watched Seattle burn." - Kirby Wilbur, Seattle KVI Radio

---

Under pressure from the left, police allowed the ebb and flow of protesting and rioting to continue largely unencumbered. In cities across the country, police were ordered to retreat and stand down while businesses were looted and burned, sacrificing private and public property and leaving local citizens to defend themselves. Minorities and the poor often took the brunt of this destruction. In some cities police vacated large areas that were barricaded off and left to the rule of anarchists.[467] At the same time, laws against homelessness and drug use were widely ignored in cities, creating massive vagrancy and decay.

> Seattle KVI, radio talk-show host Kirby Wilbur, June 3, 2020:
> "Tonight, I watched Seattle burn. Seattle is dying, by fire, looting, weakness of the political leadership. We watched on TV as our law enforcement stood by while vandalism, looting, assaults, pure chaos reigned in the streets of our downtown business district."[468]

"Arrests did not come until after the businesses were destroyed."
- Danielle Wallace

> Danielle Wallace, Fox News June 2, 2020:
> "What began as a peaceful protest in Santa Monica on Sunday over the death of George Floyd descended into violence and some people began looting businesses, including banks, chain stores and smaller mom-and-pop shops and restaurants. Live broadcasts showed officers watching as people ransacked stores and emptied shelves. Though more than 400 people have been taken into

custody on charges like looting, violating curfew, burglary and assault, those arrests did not come until after the businesses were destroyed."[469]

Minneapolis Mayor Jacob Frey address after riots and fires spread to a police building:

"...after having numerous phone calls with [his police chief] about the evolving situation at the third precinct, it became clear that there were imminent threats to both officers and public... and I made the decision to evacuate the third precinct. The symbolism of a building cannot outweigh the importance of life, of our officers or the public, we could not risk serious injury to anyone and we will continue to patrol the third precinct entirely and we will continue to do our jobs in that area and, you know, brick and mortar are not as important as life."[470]

"In the first few days after George Floyd was killed... rioters [caused] millions in property damage to more than 1,500 locations." - Star Tribune

---

Lives matter more than property but there is no justice in destroying what others have built or depriving local residents of access to goods and services. People who tried to protect their businesses and homes were killed in some cases[471] and criminally charged in others.[472] The mayhem spread, destroying lives and livelihoods from Washington to Atlanta and California to New York.

Star Tribune, riots in Minneapolis, St. Paul, July 13, 2020: "In the first few days after George Floyd was killed by Minneapolis police, rioters tore through dense stretches of Minneapolis, St. Paul and other metro communities in retaliation, causing millions in property damage to more than 1,500 locations. In their wake, vandals left a trail of smashed doors and windows, covered hundreds of boarded-up businesses with graffiti and set fire to nearly 150 buildings, with dozens burned to the ground. Pharmacies, groceries, liquor stores, tobacco shops and cell phone stores were ransacked, losing thousands of dollars in stolen merchandise.

> "Many were looted repeatedly over consecutive nights. Other property – like gas stations, restaurants and even parked cars – was set on fire, with much of it completely destroyed. The full extent of damage to Twin Cities buildings – including residences, churches, non-profits and minority-owned businesses – could take weeks or months to calculate. Already on the ropes from months of lost revenue during a global pandemic, some businesses may never reopen as others are still temporarily or indefinitely closed."[473]

"Cops... need to be defunded. They are the armed wing of the American capitalist state." - Solidarity Street

---

Certainly, there are a small number of bad cops in the nation who use excessive force to hurt and kill when nonviolent solutions are available, but blaming and demonizing all law enforcement only fuels the disorder and division.

> Nick Selby, National Review, July 17, 2017:
> "'In 74 percent of all fatal police shootings, the individuals had already fired shots, brandished a gun or attacked a person with a weapon or their bare hands,' the [Washington Post] reported in 2015. 'Another 16 percent of the shootings came after incidents that did not involve firearms or active attacks but featured other potentially dangerous threats.' Those figures are consistent with other data. In 2015, two-thirds of unarmed people of any race killed by police had been in the process of committing violent crime or property destruction. Fourteen percent were engaged in domestic violence. Ten percent were committing a robbery, 20 percent a burglary or vandalism, and 21 percent an assault on another civilian."[474]

"Policing in our country is inherently & intentionally racist." - U.S. Representative Rashida Tlaib

---

Being pulled over by police makes everyone nervous. Black parents are not the only ones who have to teach their kids to be careful when stopped by police, to say "yes sir" and "no sir", or "ma'am", to get your ID out and keep your hands where the officer can see them. Police are in a risky position when they approach a stopped vehicle, and anything they perceive as a threat will be met with force. The difference in what most Americans tell their kids is that many black children are taught that police are racist and looking for an excuse to kill them. How could that not make them resentful and fearful as a consequence, which only increases the likelihood of confrontation? The left gins up this fear quite intentionally and do not care about black people or police hurt as a result. In earlier decades, the police were known to regularly do terrible things to blacks, but that is not generally where we are today.

Another powerful method of control used by the church of old and this new Progressive Globalism is propaganda. It was skillfully employed by both to further their "faith" and dominion. Adolph Hitler did not invent propaganda, though he used it skillfully and to vile intent. Per the Encyclopedia Britannica:

> "Propaganda is the more or less systematic effort to manipulate other people's beliefs, attitudes, or actions by means of symbols (words, gestures, banners, monuments, music, clothing, insignia, hairstyles, designs on coins and postage stamps, and so forth). Deliberateness and a relatively heavy emphasis on manipulation distinguish propaganda from casual conversation or the free and easy exchange of ideas."[475]

The word dates back to the Roman Catholic Church which created a department called "Congregatio de Propaganda Fide" (Congregation for Propagation of the Faith), in 1622[476] (another source puts it at 1718[477]) to promote their faith in missions and against the rising reformation, marking what appears to be the first use of the term. To further their narrative and power, the left pushed a propaganda campaign of, not just racism and oppression, but also of questionable scientific claims about masks, Covid-19 and the vaccine. This was how they fended off dissenting opinions about the vaccine and their mandates. They were completely and absolution wrong.

> U.N. Secretary-General Antonio Guterres, News.UN.org, April 14, 2020:
> "Harmful health advice and snake-oil solutions are proliferating. Falsehoods are filling the airwaves. Wild conspiracy theories are infecting the Internet. Hatred is going viral, stigmatizing and vilifying people and groups."[478]

The propaganda in response to the rise of Donald Trump was intense and often effective. When Trump first started calling stories "fake news," I thought it was a peculiar way to refer to bias, but it turned out to be exceptionally prescient. The "news" increasingly ignored some stories and literally manufactured others.[479] Propaganda established Trump's evilness, stupidity, instability and criminality as an article of faith about which no dissent was considered rational, long before they decided what he was guilty of. It was repeated ad nauseum since he entered the political ring by people who imagined themselves intellectuals and experts, with rabid devotion and such unquestionable certainty, day after day, from virtually every media and political platform since he first announced his intent to seek office. In time, they would manufacture crimes to match the narrative. Meanwhile, the Biden family criminal activity was long ignored and denied.

> Vivek Ramaswamy, 2024 Presidential candidate, Twitter, Aug. 7, 2023:
> "It's not crazy to think a Ukrainian company's multimillion dollar bribe to the Biden family is one reason why Biden is now showering Ukraine with billions of U.S. taxpayer dollars. It's crazier to think it's totally unrelated, and craziest of all is that the GOP is playing along as if they're in on the act."[480]

We were told, by right and left, in the immediate aftermath of the 2020 election that Trump had a failed presidency. In fact, he led an economic boom with record low unemployment before being devastated by Covid-19 and state actors. It was even beginning to recover after Covid. Trump kept us out of new wars and diffused foreign conflicts. He brokered historic peace accords between Israel and Muslim countries and eliminated ISIS as a threat. He led us to energy independence, built hundreds of miles of border wall and repaired or enhanced hundreds more. He put policies in place that secured the border and substantially reduced drug and human trafficking, negotiated advantageous trade deals and made a peace deal in Afghanistan to end the war (and Trump would not have given up a key airbase, left all of our weapons and hardware behind or gotten Americans killed in the withdrawal). Upon taking office, Joe Biden threw out all of the executive orders responsible for many of Trump's accomplishments and opened the border wide, which furthered the plan and theology of the left, just as he promised to do when running.

> Karl Salzmann, The Free Beacon, May 10, 2023:
> "'What I would do as president is several more things,' Biden said at the first Democratic primary debate for the 2020 election. 'I would in fact make sure that there is... We immediately surge to the border, all those people who are seeking asylum.' As president, Biden followed through on reversing the immigration policies of former president Donald Trump, which he called 'cruel' and 'inhumane.'"[481]

Americans could be forgiven in the aftermath of the 2020 election for believing that Donald Trump was a crooked failure because that is what they were told, relentlessly, to the point that no disagreement or contrary evidence was either acceptable or sane. The election itself was obscured. As time went on, propaganda drowned out even the hard realities of Biden's massive spending, inflation, crime and wars, and obscured the dark forces working in the background against America's true common interests. In retrospect, it is clear that the propaganda entered a new stage after the 2020 election, but the manipulation of the American mind started long before that.

"The Freedom of Speech may be taken away – and, dumb & silent we may be led, like sheep, to the slaughter."

– President George Washington, 1783

Chapter 8

Totalitarians at the Gate

Not every rich person or big corporation is bad, just as not every educated person is an elitist, but there are some people, corporations and organizations that corrupt and warp our systems to their own advantage. Their attacks on our founders and capitalism in general is just misdirection. The true totalitarians threatening our peace and liberty may have access to great wealth, but it is their criminality that is the problem. These crooked oligarchs and their accomplices are neither Republican nor Democrat, necessarily or exclusively. They fund both as that serves their needs and willingly sacrifice others to further their own ambitions.

That is the true political divide in America today, between the powerful few who, convinced of their own superiority, think they have a right to rule and the majority of the American people of every ethnicity and party, who believe in the common sense ideals of our nation. These totalitarians have been at work throughout our history and they founded modern Progressive Globalism, though they didn't use that phrase. Tax-free charitable foundations were created in time to avoid income taxes that rose to 70 percent to pay for the First World War and wealth taxes that came with the Revenue Act of 1935. Some of these powerful elitists used foundations and other organizations to exert undue influence over our government and the world to advance their own dominion.

The Rockefeller family made their fortune from Standard Oil and banking. The Trilateral Commission was founded by David Rockefeller, chairman and CEO of Chase Manhattan Corporation, "to incubate ideas and form relationships across sectors and geographies... countries sharing common values and a commitment to the rule of law, open economies and societies, and democratic principles."[482] Described this way, this sound like a legitimate group trying to solve real problems on a global scale, a gathering of the best and the brightest for the betterment of humanity. Unfortunately, their leaders have admitted to more nefarious motivations and goals. They are imperialists masquerading as democratic globalists.

"It would have been impossible for us to develop our plan for the world if we had been subjected to the lights of publicity during those years."
- David Rockefeller

> David Rockefeller, Memoirs, October 2002:
> "For more than a century, ideological extremists, at either end of the political spectrum, have seized upon well-publicized incidents, such as my encounter with Castro, to attack the Rockefeller family for the inordinate influence they claim we wield over American political and economic institutions. Some even believe we are part of a secret cabal, working against the best interests of the United States, characterizing my family and me as 'internationalists,' and of conspiring with others around the world to build a more integrated global political and economic structure - one world, if you will. If that's the charge, I stand guilty, and I am proud of it."

"The super-national sovereignty of an intellectual elite and world bankers is surely preferable to the national auto-determination practiced in past centuries." - David Rockefeller

---

> "We are grateful to the Washington Post, the New York Times, Time Magazine and other great publications whose directors have attended our meetings and respected their promises of discretion for almost 40 years... It would have been impossible for us to develop our plan for the world if we had been subjected to the lights of publicity during those years. But, the world is more sophisticated and prepared to march towards a world government. The supernational sovereignty of an intellectual elite and world bankers

> is surely preferable to the national autodetermination practiced in past centuries."[483]

Clearly, auto-determination, or self-determination, is a threat if your ambitions are power and control. Little is scarier than an independently sovereign group of elitists with virtually unlimited wealth and control, bent on world domination, certain of their superiority and authority to rule. This would make people like him, like the foundations and organizations spawned by the Carnegies, Rothschilds and Guggenheims, just to name a few, the ones all those conspiracies were about. Some of these, like Henry Ford's foundation, were turned against our nation after their founders were gone. Others were designed as vehicles for dominion from the start. I'm not an expert on this, just a citizen researching and sharing what I discover. There have been a handful of writers who exposed these things before but it is just now beginning to leak out to a general audience. Americans have been systematically lied to for a century and it turns out a lot of the conspiracies we condescendingly discounted were real.

"This policy also included the suppression of everything in opposition to the wishes of the interests served." - Oscar Callaway

---

The national media has been part of this collaboration all along. According to the 1917 Congressional record, the powerful have been manipulating the media for more than a century and the intervening history certainly supports this. A three-term Democratic U.S. Representative of Texas, Oscar Callaway read the following into the Congressional record during discussion about false media reports about the war in Europe.

> Rep. Oscar Callaway, United States Congress, February 9, 1917: "In March, 1915, the J. P. Morgan interests, the steel, shipbuilding, and powder interests, and their subsidiary organizations, got together 12 men high up in the newspaper world and employed them to select the most influential newspapers in the United States and sufficient number of them to control generally the policy of the daily press of the United States. These 12 men worked the problem out by selecting 179 newspapers, and then began, by an elimination process, to retain only those necessary for the purpose of controlling the general policy of the daily press throughout the country.

> "They found it was only necessary to purchase the control of 25 of the greatest papers. The 25 papers were agreed upon; emissaries were sent· to. purchase the policy, national and international, of these papers; an agreement was reached; the policy of the papers was bought, to be paid for by the month; an editor was furnished for each paper to properly supervise and edit information regarding the questions of preparedness, militarism, financial policies, and other things of national and international nature considered vital to the interests of the purchasers. This contract is in existence at the present time, and it accounts for the news columns of the daily press of the country being filled with all sorts of preparedness arguments and misrepresentations as to the present condition of the United States Army and Navy, and the possibility and probability of the United States being attacked by foreign foes.
>
> "This policy also included the suppression of everything in opposition to the wishes of the interests served. The effectiveness of this scheme has been conclusively demonstrated by the character of stuff carried in the daily press throughout the country since March, 1915. They have resorted to anything necessary to commercialize public sentiment and sandbag the National Congress into making extravagant and wasteful appropriations for the Army and Navy under the false pretense that it was necessary. Their stock argument is that it is ' patriotism.' They are playing on every prejudice and passion of the American people."

"We are gradually turning over the business of Congress... to a lot of editors, theorists, and college professors who are not capable of conducting our affairs." - Joseph Moore

---

The various congressmen went on to discuss false reports of Americans being killed in the European conflict that were published across the country in an attempt to inflame Americans and push Congress into declaring war on Germany. Representative Joseph Hampton Moore of Pennsylvania, a Republican, agreed with Callaway's assessment, though he also supported building up the military. He dismissed another's suggestion of censorship.

> "I simply urge that the true facts and only the true facts be reported at this time when we are at the verge of an outbreak with a foreign country. I think it would be better for some of the editors to 'shut

> up' when they do not know what they are talking about. I think it would be better for some of these professional patriots who have determined our international relations in advance, and who insist upon adjusting our diplomatic affairs in this crisis, to not only 'shut up,' but go tie a rope around their necks, attach an anchor to it, and jump into the sea.
>
> "We could better afford to dispense with their meddlesome services than to plunge the people of this country into a foreign war. I think it would be far better for this country. Mr. Chairman, I regret to say it, but we are gradually turning over the business of Congress, turning over all our constitutional right, turning over our powers delegated by the people, to a lot of editors, theorists, and college professors who are not capable of conducting our affairs and to whom we should not abdicate."

After some back and forth, Representative James Willard Ragsdale, a Democrat from South Carolina said, "Now, the gentleman from Pennsylvania is undertaking to lecture me," to which Mr. Moore replied, to applause, "Oh, no. I have been lecturing the great editors and the political college professors. I did not have the gentleman in mind at all."[484]

"Financing experiments designed to determine the most effective means by which education could be pressed into service of a political nature."
- Dodd Report

These tycoons, mostly starting around the beginning of the 20th century, were part of the engine of America and very admirable. But some of them created foundations with devious intent, now multiplied into hundreds, which operate tax free and hold property and investments, much like the Roman Catholic Church, on a multi-generational time frame. This created unimaginable wealth and power for their leaders as they used government and manipulated its actions. Their purpose was often described as the "common interest," though, like Benjamin Franklin, I disagree with their idea of what that means.

A U.S. House Special Committee was established in 1953 to investigate tax exempt foundations. The information they uncovered begged for further investigation but that didn't happen. America had had enough of Senator Joseph McCarthy's attempts to root out communist agents and sympathizers, so that the investigator's report didn't get much notice and there was no follow-up. What came out of the investigation, though, sounds eerily predictive of what has happened in this country, giving credibility to its results and potential explanation for why this country has become the way it is today.

According to the report, a network of well-funded, powerful, integrated foundations began operating in this country with the goal of negatively altering American society to bring about a one world government. Norman Dodd was the Director of Research for the investigation. In a lengthy video interview Dodd gave, he seemed to me both reasonable and believable, but his findings were extraordinary. At this writing, it is still on YouTube.

"Changing both school and college curricula to the point where they sometimes denied the principles underlying the American way of life."
- Dodd Report

> Norman Dodd, the Dodd Report to the Reece Committee, 1954: "I directed the staff to explore Foundation practices, educational procedures, and the operations of the Executive branch of the Federal Government since 1903 for reasonable evidence of a purposeful relationship between them. Its ensuing studies disclosed such a relationship and that it had existed continuously since the beginning of this 50-year period. In addition, these studies seem to give evidence of a response to our involvement in international affairs. Likewise, they seemed to reveal that grants had been made by Foundations (chiefly by Carnegie and Rockefeller) which were used to further this purpose by:

"For this freedom [of the individual], it seems to substitute the group, the will of the majority, and a centralized power to enforce this will, presumably in the interest of all." - The Dodd Report

---

> "Directing education in the United States toward an international view-point and discrediting the traditions to which, it [formerly] had been dedicated; Training individuals and servicing agencies to render advice to the Executive branch of the Federal Government, decreasing the dependency of education upon the resources of the

local community and freeing it from many of the natural safeguards inherent in this American tradition; Changing both school and college curricula to the point where they sometimes denied the principles underlying the American way of life; Financing experiments designed to determine the most effective means by which education could be pressed into service of a political nature...

"It is difficult to avoid the feeling that their common interest has led them to cooperate closely with one another and that this common interest lies in the planning and control of certain aspects of American life through a combination of the Federal Government and education. This may explain why the Foundations have played such an active role in the promotion of the social sciences, why they have favored so strongly the employment of social scientists by the Federal Government and why they seem to have used their influence to transform education into an instrument for social change...

"It's product is... an educational curriculum designed to indoctrinate the American student from matriculation to the consummation of his education." – Dodd Report

---

"In summary, our study of these entities and their relationship to each other seems to warrant the inference that they constitute a highly efficient, functioning whole. Its product is apparently an educational curriculum designed to indoctrinate the American student from matriculation to the consummation of his education. It contrasts sharply with the freedom of the individual as the cornerstone of our social structure. For this freedom, it seems to substitute the group, the will of the majority, and a centralized power to enforce this will, presumably in the interest of all...

"The result of the development and operation of the network in which Foundations have played such a significant role seems to have provided this country with what is tantamount to a national system of education under the tight control of organizations and persons, little known to the American public... To summarize, both the general and the specific studies pursued by the staff during the past six months lead me to the tentative conclusion that, within the social science division of education, the Foundations have neglected "the public interest" to a severe degree...

"The growing power of the Executive branch of the Federal government and the seeming indispensability of control over human behavior." - The Dodd Report

---

> "[The Ford Foundation] is without precedent as to size, and it is the first Foundation to dedicate itself openly to "problem solving" on a world scale. In a sense, Ford appears to be capitalizing on developments which took place long before it was founded, and which have enabled it to take advantage of the wholesale dedication of education to a social purpose, the need to defend this dedication against criticism, the need to indoctrinate adults along these lines, the acceptance by the Executive branch of the Federal Government of responsibility for planning on a national and international scale and diminishing importance of the Congress and the states and the growing power of the Executive branch of the Federal government and the seeming indispensability of control over human behavior... It seems incredible that the trustees of typically American fortune-created foundations should have permitted them to be used to finance ideas and practices incompatible with the fundamental concepts of our Constitution. Yet there seems evidence that this may have occurred."[485]

Given six months, Dodd barely scratched the surface but found enough evidence to expose something startling and justify further investigation. There's no doubt that volunteers and the most people involved in these activities are dedicated and may do good work, but their masters' subversive goals and their impact on society remain alarming. In the video interview, Dodd described an interaction he had with the head of the Ford Foundation, which apparently came under control of people outside of the Ford family and acting outside of their ideals.

> Norman Dodd, 1982 television interview with G. Edward Griffin, YouTube:
> "Rowan Gaither was, at that time, President of the Ford Foundation. And Mr. Gaither had sent for me when I found it convenient to be in New York, asked me to call upon him at his office, which I did. On arrival, after a few amenities, Mr. Gaither

said, "Mr. Dodd, we have asked you to come up here this, today, because we thought that, possibly, off the record, you would tell us why the Congress is interested in the activities of foundations such as ourselves."

"We shall use our grant-making power so to alter life in the United States, that it can be comfortably merged with the Soviet Union."
- Rowan Gaither per Norman Dodd

"And, Before I could think of how I would reply to that statement, Mr. Gaither then went on, voluntarily, and stated, said, 'Mr. Dodd, all of us who have a hand in the making of policies here, have had experience either with the OSS during the war, or with European economic administration after the war. We have had experience operating under directives. The directives emanate, and did emanate, from the White House. Now, we still operate under just such directives. Would you like to know what the substance of these directives is?"

"I don't think you're entitled to withhold that information from the people of this country, to whom you're indebted for your tax exemption." - Norman Dodd

---

"I said, 'Yes, Mr. Gaither, I would like very much to know.' Whereupon, he made this statement to me, namely, 'Mr. Dodd, we are here to operate in response to similar directives, the substance of which is that we shall use our grant-making power so to alter life in the United States, that it can be comfortably merged with the Soviet Union.' Well, parenthetically, um, Mr. Griffin, I nearly fell off the chair. I, of course, didn't, but my response to Mr. Gaither then was, 'Oh, Mr. Gaither, I can now answer your first question. You've forced the Congress of the United States to spend a hundred and fifty thousand dollars to find out what you have just told me.' I said, 'Of course, legally, you're entitled to make grants for this purpose. But, I don't think you're entitled to withhold that information from the people of this country, to whom you're indebted for your tax exemption. So why don't you tell the people

> of the country just what you told me?" And his answer was, "We would not think of doing any such thing.'"

During this time Mr. Dodd also sent a letter to the Carnegie Endowment for International Peace with a variety of questions. In response, he was invited to visit and met with Carnegie's President, a Dr. Johnson, who offered an opportunity in lieu of the time and trouble it would cause them to answer all of those questions.

"Well, my first reaction was they had lost their minds." - Norman Dodd

---

> "Our counter-suggestion is that, if you can spare a member of your staff for two weeks, and send that member up to New York, we will give to that member a room in the library, and the minute books of this Foundation since its inception. And we think that, whatever you want to find out or that the Congress wants to find out, will be obvious from those minutes. Well, my first reaction was they had lost their minds. I had a pretty good idea of what those minutes would contain, but I realized that Dr. Johnson had only been in office two years, and the other, the vice-presidents were relatively young men, and counsel also seemed to be a young man and I guessed that, probably, they had never read the minutes themselves."

Dodd selected Kathryn Casey, an attorney from Washington who was put on his staff to make sure he didn't break any Congressional procedures or rules in the process of their investigation.

"Is there any means known more effective than war, assuming you wish to alter the life of an entire people?" - Norman Dodd

---

> "She was a level-headed and very reasonably brilliant, capable lady, and her attitude toward the investigation was: 'What could possibly be wrong with foundations? They do so much good.' Well, in the face of that sincere conviction of Kathryn's, I went out of my way not to prejudice her in any way, but I did explain to her that she couldn't possibly cover fifty years of handwritten minutes in two weeks. So, she would have to do what we call 'spot reading.' And I

blocked out certain periods of time to concentrate on. Off she went to New York. She came back at the end of two weeks, with the following in the way of, on Dictaphone belts. We are now at the year nineteen hundred and eight, which was the year that the Carnegie Foundation began operations.

"How do we involve the United States in a war?... We must control the State Department." - Carnegie Endowment, per Norman Dodd

---

"And, in that year, the trustees meeting, for the first time, raised a specific question, which they discussed throughout the balance of the year, in a very learned fashion. And the question is, is there any means known more effective than war, assuming you wish to alter the life of an entire people? And they conclude that, no more effective means, than war, to that end is known to humanity. So then, in 1909, they raise the second question, and discuss it, namely, how do we involve the United States in a war? ... And finally, they answer that question as follows: we must control the State Department. And then, that very naturally raises the question of how do we do that? And um, they answer it by saying, we must take over and control the diplomatic machinery of this country and, finally, they resolve to aim at that as an objective.

"The key to the success... lay in the alteration of the teaching of American History." - Norman Dodd

---

"And finally, of course, we are, the war is over. At that time, their interest shifts over to preventing what they call a reversion of life in the United States to what it was prior to 1914, when World War I broke out. And at that point, they come to the conclusion that, to prevent a reversion, we must control education in the United States. And they realize that is a pretty big task. So, to them it is too big for them alone. So, they approach the Rockefeller Foundation with a suggestion that, that portion of education which could be considered domestic should be handled by the Rockefeller Foundation, and that portion which is international should be handled by the Endowment. And they then decide that the key to the success of these two operations lay in the alteration of the teaching of American History. So, they approach four of the then most prominent teachers of American History in the country -- people like Charles and Mary Byrd. And Their suggestion to them is, 'Will they alter the manner in which they present their subject.' And they get turned down, flat.

"So, they then decide that it is necessary for them to do as they say, i.e. 'build our own stable of historians.' And then, they approach the Guggenheim Foundation, which specializes in fellowships, and say, 'When we find young men in the process of studying for doctorates in the field of American History, and we feel that they are the right caliber, will you grant them fellowships on our say so?' And the answer is, 'Yes.' So, under that condition, eventually they assemble twenty, and they take these twenty potential teachers of American History to London. There, they're briefed in what is expected of them... That group of twenty historians ultimately becomes the nucleus of the American Historical Association. And then, toward the end of the 1920's, the Endowment grants to the American Historical Association four hundred thousand dollars for a study of our history in a manner which points to what this country looks forward to, in the future.

"The future of this country belongs to collectivism, administered with characteristic American efficiency." - American Historical Association, per Norman Dodd

---

"And uh, that culminates in a seven-volume book study, the last volume of which is, of course, in essence, a summary of the contents of the other six. The essence of the last volume is: the future of this country belongs to collectivism, administered with characteristic American efficiency. That's the story that ultimately grew out of and of course was what could have been presented by the members of this congressional committee to the congress as a whole ... but it never got to that point... I might tell you this experience, as far as its impact on Kathryn Casey is concerned. Well, she never was able to return to her law practice. If it hadn't been for Carroll Reece's ability to tuck her away in a job with the Federal Trade Commission, I don't know what would have

> happened to Kathryn. But ultimately, she lost her mind as a result of it... a terrible shock. It's a very rough experience for her to encounter proof of these kinds."[486]

The American Historical Association, incorporated in 1889, pursued this mission across the United States. They taught professors who taught other professors, teachers and eventually students this twisted historical view. Even so, it took many decades to build, manipulate and infiltrate our educational system so as to intentionally indoctrinate this anti-Americanism, or what could be called Ameriphobia in today's terminology. Dodd was accused of anti-Semitism, an awfully familiar tactic, and the opposition to the investigation managed to get the committee's hearings shut down.

"To create a world system of financial control in private hands able to dominate the political system of each country and the economy of the world as a whole." - Dr. Carroll Quigley

---

The liberal population today are not immoral or simple minded. They have just been thoroughly and professionally proselytized so that they dismiss learned experience, belittle the wisdom of our predecessors and despise our founding ideology. Most of their leaders call themselves progressives, some Democrats and others Republicans, but they are not working toward the interests of the American people, who are often oblivious to these deceptions. It's hard to blame the common people: they have been lied to for more than a century by people who were supposed to mentor them to think for themselves, and by a grossly dishonest media. The multifaceted conspiracy was also exposed in the 1960s by a Georgetown University professor and historian named Carroll Quigley, who, by the way, saw no harm in it.

> Dr. Carroll Quigley, "Tragedy and Hope," The Macmillion Company, 1960:
> "In addition to these pragmatic goals, the powers of financial capitalism had another far-reaching aim, nothing less than to create a world system of financial control in private hands able to dominate the political system of each country and the economy of the world as a whole. This system was to be controlled in a feudalist

> fashion by the central banks of the world acting in concert, by secret agreements arrived at in frequent private meetings and conferences.
>
> "The apex of the system was to be the Bank for International Settlements in Basle, Switzerland, a private bank owned and controlled by the world's central banks which were themselves private corporations. Each central bank... sought to dominate its government by its ability to control Treasury loans, to manipulate foreign exchanges, to influence the level of economic activity in the country, and to influence cooperative politicians by subsequent economic rewards in the business world."

Quigley also discounted what he called the right wing "myth" of a well-organized plot by extreme left-wing elements, Anti-American elitists, manipulating our country to benefit foreign ideologies of socialism and internationalism. However, he admitted there was a "modicum" of truth to it and then went on to describe exactly the conspiracy feared.

> "There does exist, and has existed for a generation, an international Anglophile [England loving] network which operates, to some extent, in the way the ... Right believes the Communists act. In fact, this network, which we may identify as the Round Table Groups, has no aversion to cooperating with the Communists, or any other groups, and frequently does so. I know of the operations of this network because I have studied it for twenty years and was permitted for two years, in the early 1960's, to examine its papers and secret records. I have no aversion to it or to most of its aims... my chief difference of opinion is that it wishes to remain unknown, and I believe its role in history is significant enough to be known."[487]

His desire for recognition for these machinations exposed them to the public eye. The powerful and the connected still conspire to reshape society, control the world and advance their own power. They have public web sites and use terms like public-private cooperation, interconnected world issues and geopolitical realignments. The World Economic Forum (WEF) calls their young leaders "global shapers" and one year noted their meeting's "special emphasis is on gender and geographical diversity." Their global shapers have become political leaders across the world. I am just beginning to understand what Thomas Jefferson was talking about when he said that banks were more dangerous than armies. Central banks are certainly a terrible thing for the general population.

There are also the Bilderberg meetings, which are reportedly "held under the Chatham House Rule, which states that participants are free to use the information received, but neither the identity nor the affiliation of the speaker(s) nor of any other participant may be revealed... so that participants take part as individuals rather than in any official capacity, and hence are not bound by the conventions of their office or by pre-agreed positions."[488] This, I think, any reasoned outsider would call potentially treasonous. Their 2022 meeting was concerned about disinformation, disruption of the global financial system, de-globalization and the fragmentation of Democratic societies.[489] They seek a world where the masses attain an equilibrium, with no power or possessions.

> "Welcome to 2030" by World Economic Forum, Forbes, 2016: "In our city we don't pay any rent, because someone else is using our free space whenever we do not need it. My living room is used for business meetings when I am not there."[490]

The world media successfully undermined opposition by casting it as conspiracy theories.[491] These oligarchs, bankers, organizations, institutions and companies have tremendous power and see independent nation-states as obstacles to their dominion. George Soros is perhaps the most well-known titan of this sort. Initially funded by the Rothschild family,[492] Soros admitted to having a god complex, messianic delusions and a family history of madness.[493] He is certainly a very intelligent and dangerous man. His "Open Society Foundation" is a whole network of major foundations, partnerships and groups across the world that promote a borderless society.

His open, borderless society is more specifically a society of moral relativism. It is contrasted with notions of objective morality, law and religion, that right and wrong exists. Because our knowledge is imperfect, Soros says nothing we comprehend or conclude has any real value or is any more "right" than any other idea, the opposite of natural law.

"Exploiting an event to further an agenda is not in itself reprehensible." - George Soros

---

Despite extraordinary efforts, Soros failed to stop George W. Bush's re-election. Soros did not see Bush's methods as wrong, only as working counter to his own. The Bush family were very much a part of the

American establishment. His father had been CIA director before becoming president.

> George Soros, The Atlantic, December 2003: "Exploiting an event to further an agenda is not in itself reprehensible. It is the task of the President to provide leadership, and it is only natural for politicians to exploit or manipulate events so as to promote their policies. The cause for concern lies in the policies that Bush is promoting... The supremacist ideology of the Bush Administration stands in opposition to the principles of an open society, which recognize that people have different views and that nobody is in possession of the ultimate truth. The supremacist ideology postulates that just because we are stronger than others, we know better and have right on our side."[494]

That's rich, coming from him. George W. Bush was nation-building and fighting "evil" abroad, all very much outside of the founding American philosophy. Soros' organizations claim to be "working for justice, democratic governance, and human rights,"[495] but actually manipulate and undermine democratic systems.

"Facts do not necessarily constitute reliable criteria for judging the truth of statements." - George Soros

---

> George Soros, "The Capitalist Threat", the Atlantic, 1997: "There is a need for institutions that allow them to live together in peace. These institutions protect the rights of citizens and ensure freedom of choice and freedom of speech... In social and political affairs the participants' perceptions help to determine reality. In these situations, facts do not necessarily constitute reliable criteria for judging the truth of statements...

"In an open society each citizen is not only allowed but required to think for himself." - George Soros

---

> "After the collapse of communism, the mission of the foundation network changed. Recognizing that an open society is a more advanced, more sophisticated form of social organization than a

> closed society (because in a closed society there is only one blueprint, which is imposed on society, whereas in an open society each citizen is not only allowed but required to think for himself), the foundations shifted from a subversive task to a constructive one... The open societies of the West did not feel a strong urge to promote open societies in the former Soviet empire. On the contrary, the prevailing view was that people ought to be left to look after their own affairs."[496]

After the fall of Communism, Soros said his new "enemy" was "excessive individualism". "Too much competition and too little cooperation can cause intolerable inequities and instability." The great inequity, however, is between him and us. His new enemy, of course, was the United States, and laissez-faire capitalism. George Soros and others like him are exactly what the left rallies the people against: the corrupt one percent. While he claims to promote democracy, his foundations support pro-criminal policies, mass migration, war and disruptive social movements.

"They know that there is a power somewhere so organized, so subtle, so watchful, so interlocked, so complete, so pervasive."
- President Woodrow Wilson

Soros is just one of an international cache of corrupt oligarchs determined to reshape human civilization that we were warned about. Even progressive President Wilson knew it.

> President Woodrow Wilson, The New Freedom, 1913: "Since I entered politics, I have chiefly had men's views confided to me privately. Some of the biggest men in the United States, in the field of commerce and manufacture, are afraid of something. They know that there is a power somewhere so organized, so subtle, so watchful, so interlocked, so complete, so pervasive, that they had better not speak above their breath when they speak in condemnation of it."[497]

"For we are opposed around the world by a monolithic and ruthless conspiracy." – President John F. Kennedy

---

> John F. Kennedy, American Newspaper Pub Assoc., April 27, 1961:
> "For we are opposed around the world by a monolithic and ruthless conspiracy that relies primarily on covert means for expanding its sphere of influence-on infiltration instead of invasion, on subversion instead of elections, on intimidation instead of free choice, on guerrillas by night instead of armies by day. It is a system which has conscripted vast human and material resources into the building of a tightly knit, highly efficient machine that combines military, diplomatic, intelligence, economic, scientific and political operations. Its preparations are concealed, not published. Its mistakes are buried, not headlined. Its dissenters are silenced, not praised. No expenditure is questioned, no rumor is printed, no secret is revealed."[498]

Kennedy wasn't talking about Republicans or Democrats but people who use these parties and the ideals of their supporters to further their own, devious ambitions. He resisted and very soon was no longer around. The U.S. has its flaws, but it has still done more for the advancement of human beings than any other system in the known history of the world, despite all of the efforts to destroy it. What many Americans have yet to reconcile is that our nation has very often acted in very unamerican ways under the influence of its enemies.

Most capitalists have nothing to do with this corruption and it has nothing to do with capitalism. This is tyranny, advanced by people who are clearly working against our nation and pursuing the destruction of its culture. Cultures vary in ways that may not be objectively right or wrong but are just different based on the people and their history, traditions that connect us to our past and remind us of our roots and the lessons learned. In other ways, as in morality, culture can have objective value, accessible by reason, that justifies its defense. America has and cherishes both. All of this is being attacked and much of it can be traced back to these corrupt, leftist foundations.

"The only unnatural sex act is that which you cannot perform."
- Dr. Alfred Kinsey[499]

Counter Cultural

Our cultural norms, like gender norms, traditional family composition and marriage, ideas of modesty, clothing, manners, and many other aspects of our nation's culture are being overwhelmed with pornographic displays of alternative lifestyles pushed in schools and throughout our entertainment. Traditional ideas and values are belittled and treated as hateful or intolerant. The drive for conformity of thought and belief is what set the western world in flames for millennia. The drive of forced conformity to these new misnamed doctrines of inclusion and diversity may prove equally destructive. Their goal is to undermine the traditions and beliefs of our people in order to undermine our identity and national stability. This is another key part of the Progressive Globalist faith.

Part of this can be tracked back directly to a non-profit initially funded by the Rockefeller Foundation and connected to Indiana University called the Kinsey Institute for Research in Sex, Gender, and Reproduction, and the faulty research of its founder. Started in 1947, the institute was later merged with Indiana University and its ideals have spread throughout the field of study. Drag queen story hour and sexually explicit information promoted in schools to younger and younger kids did not come out of thin air or by accident. The sexualization of children is a direct and intended consequence of books written by a zoologist named Alfred Kinsey about male and female sexuality in 1948 and 1953, the "research" they were founded on and the institute he established to promote the normalization of their conclusions.

> The LibreText libraries, the UC Davis, University of California: "Data was gathered primarily by means of subjective interviews, conducted according to a structured questionnaire memorized by the experimenters. Significantly, the Kinsey research team went out and conducted the interviews themselves, rather than relying upon pre-collected data. What resulted was the largest collection of statistical information about adult sexuality in the United States."[500]

"The positive record on these boys who did have the opportunity [to test their capacities] makes it certain that many infant males and younger boys are capable of orgasm." - Alfred Kinsey

---

He focused his research on criminals and included children. The critics of his work came not just from religious puritans upset with the open discussion or study of human sexuality or a prejudice against homosexuality, but rather the use of pedophiles to collect information about their ongoing abuse and the promotion of other behaviors still illegal today. The pedophilia, incest and bestiality that Kinsey promoted were a far cry from the old taboos of having sex before marriage or homosexual behavior between willing adults. The Kinsey Institute, its disciples and students have conflated the two in order to discredit criticism.

His organization has had a profound effect on how human sexuality is taught, as well as our entire education system, down through the promotion of his ideas to kids under the guise of sex education and HIV awareness programs. The goal was the normalization of sexual deviance, sexual violence, pedophilia, child pornography, incest, rape, bestiality and even child bestiality. According to his books, he recruited pedophiles and trained them to detail their continuing abuse of children using stopwatches and the completion of detailed forms. Subjective information was gathered from these pedophiles as well as a variety of other criminals and sex workers, focusing on those engaged in aberrant behaviors rather than common human sexuality. He used the sexual abuse of children as young as two months old.

Kinsey believed all types of sex at all times and ages were good. He charted how hundreds of these children responded to even "prolonged and varied and repeated stimulation," according to Kinsey's book "Sexual Behavior in the Human Male". His next book, "Sexual Behavior in the Human Female" was equally appalling from a legal respect, not to mention a moral one. Kinsey directed active child molesters and fathers engaged in incest on how to document their activities, then used these results to extrapolate conclusions about the whole of humanity.

"It is difficult to understand why a child... should be disturbed at having its genitalia touched." - Alfred Kinsey

---

> Alfred Kinsey, Founder of the Kinsey Institute, 1948: "In the population as a whole, a much smaller percentage of the boys experience orgasm at any early age, because few of them find themselves in circumstances that test their capacities; but the positive record on these boys who did have the opportunity makes

> it certain that many infant males and younger boys are capable of orgasm, and it is probable that half or more of the boys in an uninhibited society could reach climax by the time they were three or four years of age, and that nearly all of them could experience such a climax three to five years before the onset of adolescence."[501]

In "The Children of Table 34", hosted by Efrem Zimbalist, Jr., Kinsey said, "It is difficult to understand why a child, except for its cultural conditioning, should be disturbed at having its genitalia touched."[502] Instead of looking honestly at his methods, victims and goals, followers of Kinsey blankly denied any wrongdoing on his behalf and treated critics as religious zealots. Talk show host Phil Donahoe is an example.[503] What is startling, if you watch that episode of his show, is that back when it aired in December of 1990, opposing views or advocates were still given airtime and treated professionally on network TV, something that doesn't happen today. Religious groups were certainly the most vocal in their disapproval, but they were not the only critics.

In his book, the child molesters involved in these experiments described their pre-adolescent victims' reactions in horrifying detail.[504] These children's responses to being raped, he called having an orgasm. Babies were said to be having orgasms because of how they cried. This was pleasurable, Kinsey assured. He trusted and directed criminals, including a known Nazi pedophile, to provide information, and suggested the result was objective and valid, constituting normal human behavior. This is what passed for scientific research in his view and upon which an entire field of study has largely been based,[505] effecting an organized and intentional change to American cultural norms and laws.

Many academics and activists revere this man for liberating people from restrictive sexual norms without realizing just how far he went beyond consensual adult behavior. Counter-cultural ideas and behaviors, along with the religious-like devotion to radical ideologies, continue to be funded by these foundations and other globalists.

The main thing that I think the globalists, the feudal lords of the world's leftists, hope to emulate in religion is submission. When submission to civil leaders was considered synonymous with submission to God, they ruled by proxy. To achieve global domination, they needed a way to get people to submit to them like they would to a god. So, they cobbled together a cult of death (abortion and depopulation) and cult of transsexualism with a manufactured world climate crisis and the social justice myth of collectivism into what I call progressive globalism. The goal is not global cooperation but global rule. They have been frighteningly successful.

By Design

There is racism, abuse and corruption in America but is not built into the system and constitution our founders created. It is instead built into the enlarged bureaucratic establishment we have today. Agencies became autonomous fiefdoms. Most lawmakers get rich by misusing insider information, while selling legislation and setting policy that claims to address problems but instead funnels money and power to a particular few. It's not in the interest of the corrupt to actually fix anything and they control both major parties. Our tax code, justice system and foreign policies serve the people and entities that buy it, not the working Americans on the hook for its expenses. The policies that we watch go so terribly wrong across the country are not failures. You could call it Political Chaos Theory. And it is intentional.

They support policies that encourage crime, disorder and terrorism, obscure and distort our perceptions, destabilize family and culture, restrict our freedoms, and destroy our economy as free thought and belief cower under establishment tyranny. It is so pervasive and has been so effective that it must be the intended plan of its instigators. Perhaps the most destructive design at work on the world today involves the war on natural fossil fuels. Our own natural resources and industries are being oppressed and banned in favor of those of our adversaries or undependable and insufficient alternatives, causing shortages, extreme prices and eventually economic collapse that will leave us too weak to stand in the way of their global ambitions.

"Advised by the Rockefeller Foundation, Sri Lankan President Gotabaya Rajapaksa promised to transition the nation's agriculture industry to organic farming." - Helen Raleigh, The Federalist

---

The attack on natural fuels uses the same general theory of Lenin's communism, seeing developed countries as oppressors and the less developed as the oppressed. Like the workers in Communism, though, the outcome is not advantageous to the "oppressed". This is how they convince followers. Instead, it takes everything from them and leaves them at the mercy of masters. It's easy to imagine that the left expects America and the west to do without so that the rest of the world can have the fuels and cash as some kind of worldwide social justice, as if the world has not benefited tremendously from American production and invention.

The situation for the world is even worse if those behind this attack truly expect all countries to give up natural fuels and their products. Without them, modern civilization would collapse, losing centuries of progress and leading to death on an unimaginable scale. Sri Lanka is a start.

"Sri Lanka's adoption of green policies brought nothing but disasters." - Helen Raleigh, The Federalist

---

> Helen Raleigh, The Federalist.com, July 15, 2022: "Advised by the Rockefeller Foundation, Sri Lankan President Gotabaya Rajapaksa promised to transition the nation's agriculture industry to organic farming within ten years. In April 2021, he banned 'the importation and use of synthetic fertilizers and pesticides and order[ed] the country's 2 million farmers to go organic,' according to Foreign Policy magazine... But Sri Lanka's adoption of green policies brought nothing but disasters. Its rice production has dropped more than 50 percent, while domestic rice prices have increased more than 80 percent. Once sufficient in rice production, the nation has been 'forced to import $450 million worth of rice.' In the words of Sen. Rand Paul, R-Ky., Sri Lanka is experiencing 'a government-created famine reminiscent of Mao.'"[506]

As I quoted George Bernard Shaw earlier, "Not until the two main tenets of socialism... have taken hold of the people as religious dogmas, as to which no controversy is regarded as sane, will a stable socialist state be possible." The Progressive Globalist ideologies of the left have definitely attained that status. Like communism, proponents pursue it full throttle even in the face of its manifest failure to, in communism's case, improve the lives of workers or, in the current case, improve the planet. The inevitable consequences instead are horrifying. Virtually every product used in our daily lives, from refrigerators and detergents to fertilizers, antiseptics, electric cars and air conditioning, comes from oil.[507] The vast majority have no practical replacements.

The point, of course, is not to force us to all buy electric vehicles. In truth, these totalitarians despise the independence and power provided by individual ownership, especially of vehicles and homes. In their vision, only the important people like them will have cars but the masses will have to rely on public transportation and limited to what they can access on foot or bicycle. This is already being implemented.[508] They say this is conspiracy theory, but the consequence of the design is to limit the people's mobility. The masses will be totally dependent on the services provided by the government, giving its leaders complete control and unchallengeable power. You will, as they say, own nothing. A dystopian outcome is the inevitable consequence of eliminating natural fuels and their products without having an equivalent power source and alternative products to replace it.

Rest assured that the people behind this have no intention of giving up their own use of natural fuels and the luxuries and technology they make possible. They won't share their homes even as they ask you to share yours; or give up their armed security even as they disarm others who just want to secure their own safety; just as they didn't wear masks during the pandemic while requiring that everyone else, especially servants, to do so. The world cannot give up these natural fuels now nor in the foreseeable future without destroying our civilization. They just think they can manage a controlled demolition. The radical left, in the form of Progressive Globalism, is the apocalypse they threaten us with.

Just as the Inquisition wasn't about Christianity, all of this is not about an existential risk, compassion for the underprivileged, the environment or justice. It's about tyranny, about people who will use anything to manipulate the nation and the world to advance their own power, ideas and interests, certain of their superiority and justification to do so. Like most people, I used to hear "conspiracy theories" and dismiss them with derision. I have come to realize that some of them are frighteningly well-founded. Our country and its ruling class have a history of doing things behind our backs, especially conspiring to get us into wars. Over the years, the manipulation of America has only gotten worse. Finally, one person stood up to it and they rallied everything they had against him.

Chapter 9

Revive or Expire

Donald Trump came on the scene as a populist candidate, meaning he appealed to and claimed to represent the common people acting against the establishment or ruling class. A wealthy businessman and celebrity, he was very unlikely in that role and few took him seriously in the beginning, myself included. Just in case, though, the establishment went to extraordinary lengths to discredit him and, later, to remove him from power. America would be told Trump was a threat to democracy. In truth, he was a threat to the state. It started with the Russian collusion story, later completely discredited, used a manufactured conspiracy of rather bizarre claims by a disgraced foreign asset and losing political campaign against a political opponent and then sitting president.

This was the beginning of an almost unfathomable, contorted web of falsehoods and establishment corruption aimed at Donald Trump and the people around him. Eventually, even the liberal media admitted Russian collusion was a complete lie,[509] but new lies quickly took its place. The contorted, irrational view of Trump and the fanaticism with which they opposed him, described originally in some jest as Trump Derangement Syndrome, cast him first as corrupt, uncouth and ignorant, but then turned much darker. To the totalitarian elitists, he became Hitler. Reality was turned upside down. They told us everything Trump said was a lie. Instead, they sold us the greatest misinformation campaign in U.S. history.

The story of Donald Trump's presidency will be one of America's most significant and controversial in our history. It will either be the story of when America woke up to the long simmering totalitarian threat or when our republic lost its final battle. I'm not speaking of a physical confrontation but a moral one. Some will always cling to the propaganda about him but the facts of this period are available if you look hard enough. Like I have shown in this book, trust what they say in their own words, in context. Watch the full videos.

Spectacle of Turbulence

When Trump announced for President, most Americans had reason to doubt the seriousness of his candidacy. Few on the right pictured him as a bastion for morals or civil liberties. As we learned more and the Trump movement rose, regular Americans began climbing onboard. When he was denounced as a Russian puppet without evidence, the media and most big tech chose a side. It shouldn't be surprising, then, that many casual observers bought the narrative. Yet, after years of investigation and harassment, Special Prosecutor Robert Mueller found no evidence that President Trump colluded with Russia, though vaguely leaving open the idea that he might have obstructed justice by covering up collusion that *never happened.*[510] Likewise, Special Prosecutor John Durham concluded no collusion existed to justify that government investigation into Trump and his campaign, finding investigators did not even try to substantiate the claims against him while conducting a consistently biased investigation.[511]

And yet, Durham failed to hold anyone accountable, allowing the uninformed to falsely assume the instigators did not break the law. This was the common outcome of investigations of the left, be it the FBI's investigation of Hillary Clinton or Special Counsel Robert Hur's investigation of Joe Biden for their misuse of classified materials. In both cases, their reports indicated clear evidence of intentional illegal activity and guilt while still declining to prosecute. The corrupt establishment was only getting started.

"Precious few anti-Trumpers have been honest with themselves about the elaborate hoax." – Bret Stephens, New York Times

---

The liberal writer for the New York Times I quoted as finally realizing that Trump's supporters were not just losers and racists, also finally admitted, as others eventually would, that the collusion campaign against the president was a lie. It was "the big lie" that consumed the 45th Presidency, but it wasn't the only lie. Still, many could not give up that misconception.

Bret Stephens, New York Times, July 21, 2022:

> "To this day, precious few anti-Trumpers have been honest with themselves about the elaborate hoax - there's just no other word for it - that was the Steele dossier and all of the bogus allegations credulously parroted in the mainstream media that flowed from it."[512]

One candidate's manufactured dirt and collection of ill-conceived and absurd claims from disreputable foreign sources was used by an outgoing administration and career bureaucrats as an excuse to deploy the nation's intelligence and investigative agencies to spy on, persecute and attempt to eliminate an incoming and then sitting President. Government leaders repeatedly lied, not just to the public, but to a Foreign Intelligence Surveillance court, which formed the justification for a special prosecutor's investigation. It amounted to significant election interference on Hillary Clinton's behalf during the 2016 election and things only got worse.

"The FBI and the DOJ deliberately and intentionally advanced unverified opposition research paid for by one political party... designed to harm the opposing party." - Harry G. Hutchison

---

> Harry G. Hutchison, American Center for Law and Justice, Feb. 2, 2018:
>
> "With the release of the House Intelligence Committee Memo, it is manifestly clear that the Department of Justice (DOJ) and the FBI participated in a fraud on the Foreign Intelligence Surveillance Court (FISC) in order to surveil Carter Page, a U.S. citizen. The FBI and the DOJ deliberately and intentionally advanced unverified opposition research paid for by one political party (the Democratic National Committee) designed to harm the opposing party by creating a fictional Russian collusion story as reliable fact...
>
> "... the adducible evidence shows that members of the FBI and the DOJ interfered in the 2016 presidential campaign much more than any Russian operative."[513]

"We need an insurance policy against the unthinkable: Donald Trump's actually winning the Presidency." - Benjamin Wittes

---

The hoax was referred to by multiple people as an insurance policy against Trump getting elected.

> Sharyl Attkisson, The Hill, Aug. 9, 2018:
> "On Aug. 15, 2016, after FBI counterespionage chief Peter Strzok and his FBI girlfriend Lisa Page met with Deputy FBI Director Andrew McCabe, Strzok texted Page that they couldn't take the risk of Trump getting elected without having 'an insurance policy' in place. Another figure, Benjamin Wittes, chose the same phrase. In October 2016, in his Lawfare blog, Wittes wrote: 'What if Trump wins? We need an insurance policy against the unthinkable: Donald Trump's actually winning the Presidency.'

"His vision of an 'insurance policy' against Trump would rely on a 'Coalition of All Democratic Forces' to challenge and obstruct Trump." - Sharyl Attkisson

---

> "As it happens, Wittes has acknowledged being a good friend of fired FBI Director James Comey. It's not hard to imagine that the two men share some beliefs, and even discussed some of the issues involved. In fact, Wittes spoke to a New York Times reporter about Comey's interactions with President Trump, right after Robert Mueller's appointment as special counsel. So, in his 2016 blog post, Wittes wrote that his vision of an 'insurance policy' against Trump would rely on a 'Coalition of All Democratic Forces' to challenge and obstruct Trump, using the courts as a 'tool' and Congress as 'a partner or tool.' He even mentioned impeachment – two weeks before Trump was elected."[514]

In office, Trump was impeached at the first opportunity for a phone call where he asked the Ukrainian President to investigate legitimate evidence of Biden corruption as Vice President. Biden is on video bragging that he withheld billions in aid to Ukraine until they fired this prosecutor, which they did.[515] At the time Biden's son, Hunter, was on the board of a Ukrainian natural gas company called Burisma Holdings that the prosecutor was investigating. They said the prosecutor was corrupt or ineffective, but he had successfully seized assets belonging to one of the Burisma executives. After the prosecutor was fired, that investigation into Burisma went away.[516] To prevent that investigation into Joe Biden's corruption, the first impeachment was concocted. Biden faced no consequences for his actions but President Trump was impeached for asking Ukraine to look into it.

The leftist establishment and its supporters - containing both Democrats and Republicans - were surprised when Trump was first elected. It was not an error they were willing to make again. More than ever, the general population was not to be trusted with the choice of leadership. Even though his policies proved successful and the nation under his leadership flourished, an alternative narrative was propagated and a pandemic lockdown was manufactured to destroy it. This time, leaders, elitists, influencers, partisan agency heads and establishment politicians from both parties decided they would do anything necessary to ensure that Donald Trump could not win re-election in 2020. This resulted in a coalition of forces to manipulate Americans and illegally change how voting was conducted to undermine voter integrity and ensure the outcome they considered proper. George Soros funded a lot of these efforts.

"Every attempt to interfere with the proper outcome of the election was defeated." - Molly Ball

---

An article entitled "The Secret History of the Shadow Campaign That Saved the 2020 Election" by Molly Ball, the national political correspondence for Time Magazine, exposed what can only be described as a vast, corrupt conspiracy to prevent President Trump's re-election, most of which played out in the public eye as media and politician lied to our faces. This election interference alone was more than enough to make one reasonably question the legitimacy of the outcome. Many involved may have even believed they were doing the right thing, that they were protecting the election, but their actions accomplished the opposite goal.

"They fended off voter-suppression lawsuits, recruited armies of poll workers and got millions of people to vote by mail for the first time." - Molly Ball

---

> Molly Ball, Time Magazine, Feb. 4, 2021:
> "The handshake between business and labor was just one component of a vast, cross-partisan campaign to protect the

> election–an extraordinary shadow effort dedicated not to winning the vote but to ensuring it would be free and fair, credible and uncorrupted. For more than a year, a loosely organized coalition of operatives scrambled to shore up America's institutions as they came under simultaneous attack from a remorseless pandemic and an autocratically inclined President...

"A well-funded cabal of powerful people... working together behind the scenes to influence perceptions, change rules and laws, steer media coverage and control the flow of information." – Molly Ball

---

> "Their work touched every aspect of the election. They got states to change voting systems and laws and helped secure hundreds of millions in public and private funding. They fended off voter-suppression lawsuits, recruited armies of poll workers and got millions of people to vote by mail for the first time. They successfully pressured social media companies to take a harder line against disinformation and used data-driven strategies to fight viral smears. They executed national public-awareness campaigns...
>
> "Every attempt to interfere with the proper outcome of the election was defeated... Democracy is not self-executing. That's why the participants want the secret history of the 2020 election told, even though it sounds like a paranoid fever dream–a well-funded cabal of powerful people, ranging across industries and ideologies, working together behind the scenes to influence perceptions, change rules and laws, steer media coverage and control the flow of information. They were not rigging the election; they were fortifying it."[517]

Influencing perceptions, extra-legislatively changing laws and rules, controlling media coverage and the flow of information to ensure an outcome was the definition of election fraud. This was done to weaken our systems and subvert their opponent's campaign. Ball's desire for recognition of their activities exposed the conspiracy, much like Carroll Quigley did so many decades earlier. The FBI states that intentionally deceiving qualified voters to prevent them from voting is illegal voter suppression. These conspirators concealed evidence, manipulated information and perceptions so that voters would not be exposed to news that might benefit Trump or expose the left's corruption.

They subverted voter integrity laws and loosened rules about what ballots would be accepted, when and how. This was attempted by legislative action but, when that failed, they used the court system or administrative dictates. Other voter interference included the left's coordinated media propaganda, and government directed censorship in social media and other online platforms. This is without even touching on election day mischief. There were a lot of reasons for the American people to be suspicious.

"Our focus was to get Trump out of office." - Charlie Chester

---

> Video of Charlie Chester, CNN technical Director, New York Post, April 13, 2021:
> "Look what we did, we [CNN] got Trump out. I am 100 percent going to say it, and I 100 percent believe that if it wasn't for CNN, I don't know that Trump would have got voted out... Our focus was to get Trump out of office, right? Without saying it, that's what it was... [Trump's] hand was shaking or whatever, I think. We brought in so many medical people to all tell a story that was all speculation - that he was neurologically damaged, and he was losing it. He's unfit to - you know - whatever. We were creating a story there that we didn't know anything about. I think that's propaganda."[518]

These comments came in a hidden video by Project Veritas (a technique that used to be well-respected when 60 Minutes did it). The attitude was common. Mainstream outfits finally admitted long after the election that the Hunter Biden laptop was real, though largely ignored the evidence of Joe Biden's corruption it contained, dismissing it instead as evidence of Hunter's lude, drug induced criminal behavior. They ignored the evidence of far worse crimes until Joe Biden was nearly out of office.

"50 members of the Intelligence Community released a public statement... that attempted to cast doubt on the laptop story as a 'Russian information operation." - Ashe Schow, DailyWire

---

> Ashe Schow, DailyWire.com, March 19, 2022: "The New York Times on Wednesday finally admitted that the 2020 New York Post story regarding information found on Hunter Biden's laptop was legitimate. The Times confirmed the existence of Biden's laptop... The information contained on the laptop, first published by the Post in the month before the 2020 election, was undermined by numerous news outlets and social media companies, who tried to suggest it wasn't real...
>
> "50 members of the Intelligence Community released a public statement – published by Politico – that attempted to cast doubt on the laptop story as a 'Russian information operation...' Signers of the letter include numerous Obama appointees who went on to become mainstream media commentators, including former Director of National Intelligence James Clapper and former CIA director John Brennan. Other signers included former Director of National Intelligence Michael Hayden and former CIA director Leon Panetta."[519]

When the truth about the laptop was finally admitted, none of these people expressed the slightest bit of regret for their part in the coverup. Whistleblowers revealed that the IRS slow-walked the investigation into Hunter's tax violations until the statute of limitations ran out on the most serious charges.[520] Though the FBI had Hunter Biden's laptop for almost a year before the 2020 election, FBI management told agents not investigate it because it would have benefited the re-election of President Trump.[521] This was clear early on. A Senate investigation into Justice Department and FBI misconduct revealed evidence of the FBI's involvement in efforts to falsely label the laptop evidence as disinformation.[522]

When Elon Musk bought the social media giant Twitter (renamed X), he began releasing internal documents exposing censorship and suppression of political content in coordination with and at the behest of government agents. Musk noted, "Twitter acting by itself to suppress free speech is not a 1st amendment violation, but acting under orders from the government to suppress free speech, with no judicial review, is."[523] The Supreme Court later failed to pull back on that government overreach. We learned that the FBI went to social media just before the news of Hunter's laptop came out, suggesting some disinformation was about to drop. The Twitter files (aka. the X files) reveal this activity in detail, but the same type of activity was also confirmed by the CEO of Meta (formerly Facebook), Mark Zuckerberg. He admitted Meta censored the story, but said Twitter blocked it entirely.[524]

"That's a left-wing conspiracy to deny the presidency to Donald Trump - absolutely it was, absolutely. But I think it was warranted." – Sam Harris

---

They just thought it was justified. Many people developed a full case of Trump Derangement Syndrome, completely unable to see the truth. A best-selling author, Sam Harris, defended the censorship of the story, serving as an example of the common mentality.

> Author Sam Harris, "TRIGGERnometry" podcast, Aug. 18, 2022: "At that point, Hunter Biden could have literally had the corpses of children in his basement, I would not have cared... Whatever scope of Joe Biden's corruption is, if we can just go down that rabbit hole endlessly and understand that he's getting kickbacks from Hunter Biden's deals in Ukraine, or wherever else, or China, it is infinitesimal compared to the corruption we know Trump is involved in... It doesn't even stack up against Trump University, right? Trump University as a story is worse than anything that can be in Hunter Biden's laptop. Now, that doesn't answer the people who say it's still completely unfair to not have looked at the laptop in a timely way and to have shut down the New York Post's Twitter account, that's a left-wing conspiracy to deny the presidency to Donald Trump - absolutely it was, absolutely. But I think it was warranted."[525]

Harris later somewhat walked back his statement, but it was an honest reflection of the level of contempt felt for Trump. Biden selling access to the White House, American policy, and conspiring with our adversaries for power and profit at the expense of American interests and security was somehow less corrupt than an online training program Trump's company was once involved with. In what universe does that kind of moral equivocation appear rational? His statement and others like it exposed a distorted reality that only got worse as the years went on.

"Election security experts have noted for years that our nation's election systems and infrastructure are under serious threat." - Elizabeth Warren, et al.

They condemned Trump for questioning the security of our voting machines, but these questions did not start with him. Democrat Senators Elizabeth Warren, Ron Wyden and Amy Klobuchar and Congressman Mark Pocan sent a letter on December 6, 2019 - less than a year before the 2020 Presidential election - to each of the three main voting machine vendors respecting the vulnerabilities of their systems, including vote switching:

> "Over the last two decades, the election technology industry has become highly concentrated, with a handful of consolidated vendors controlling the vast majority of the market. In the early 2000s, almost twenty vendors competed in the election technology market. Today, three large vendors - Election Systems & Software, Dominion, and Hart InterCivic - collectively provide voting machines and software that facilitate voting for over 90% of all eligible voters in the United States. Private equity firms reportedly own or control each of these vendors, with very limited information available in the public domain about their operations and financial performance... Election security experts have noted for years that our nation's election systems and infrastructure are under serious threat...
>
> "In 2018 alone 'voters in South Carolina [were] reporting machines that switched their votes after they'd inputted them, scanners [were] rejecting paper ballots in Missouri, and busted machines [were] causing long lines in Indiana.' In addition, researchers recently uncovered previously undisclosed vulnerabilities in 'nearly three dozen backend election systems in 10 states.' And, just this year, after the Democratic candidate's electronic tally showed he received an improbable 164 votes out of 55,000 cast in a Pennsylvania state judicial election in 2019, the county's Republican Chairwoman said, '[n]othing went right on Election Day. Everything went wrong. That's a problem.' These problems threaten the integrity of our elections and demonstrate the

> importance of election systems that are strong, durable, and not vulnerable to attack."[526]

Incompetence or criminality existed on both sides. Before 2020, liberal journalists repeated questioned the security of our elections. The New York Times, as referenced in a USA Today article, pointed out connections between voting machines and the internet in an article titled "Exclusive: Critical U.S. Election Systems Have Been Left Exposed Online Despite Official Denials," putting into doubt their security from hackers.[527] They were not alone.

> Frank Bajak, Associated Press, October 29, 2018: "Many voting systems in use today across the more than 10,000 U.S. election jurisdictions are prone to security problems. Academic computer scientists began hacking them with ease more than a decade ago, and not much has changed. Hackers could theoretically wreak havoc at multiple stages of the election process. They could alter or erase lists of registered voters to sow confusion, secretly introduce software to flip votes, scramble tabulation systems or knock results-reporting sites offline. There's no evidence any of this has happened, at least not yet."[528]

"There is bipartisan consensus that mail-in ballots are the form of voting most vulnerable to fraud." - Jessica Huseman, ProPublica

---

The transition to large scale voting by mail was supposedly to reduce Covid-19 transmission but it created other risks, according to the left-leaning ProPublica. To make matters worse in 2020, they added ballot harvesting and drop boxes, which completely undermined chain of custody for ballots.

> Jessica Huseman, ProPublica, March 24, 2020: "Among the possible downsides of a quick transition are increased voter fraud, logistical snafus and reduced turnout among voters who move frequently or lack a mailing address. There is bipartisan consensus that mail-in ballots are the form of voting most vulnerable to fraud. A 2005 commission led by President Jimmy Carter and James A. Baker III – George W. Bush's secretary of state – concluded that these ballots 'remain the largest source of potential voter fraud.'"[529]

> The Carter-Baker Commission Report, September 2005:
> "Oregon appears to have avoided significant fraud in its vote-by-mail elections by introducing safeguards to protect ballot integrity, including signature verification. Vote by mail is, however, likely to increase the risks of fraud and of contested elections in other states, where the population is more mobile, where there is some history of troubled elections, or where the safeguards for ballot integrity are weaker... The electoral system cannot inspire public confidence if no safeguards exist to deter or detect fraud or to confirm the identity of voters. Photo IDs currently are needed to board a plane, enter federal buildings, and cash a check. Voting is equally important...

"In close or disputed elections... a small amount of fraud could make the margin of difference." - 2005 Commission on Federal Election Reform

---

> "While the Commission is divided on the magnitude of voter fraud – with some believing the problem is widespread and others believing that it is minor – there is no doubt that it occurs. The problem, however, is not the magnitude of the fraud. In close or disputed elections, and there are many, a small amount of fraud could make the margin of difference. And second, the perception of possible fraud contributes to low confidence in the system."[530]

When Trump came along, voter ID requirements were denounced as racist, though, the media had previously, widely acknowledged the risks. A 2012 New York Times story titled "Error and Fraud at Issue as Absentee Voting Rises" by Adam Liptak, said that mail-in voting fraud is "vastly more prevalent than the in-person voting fraud." Though questioning its reliability then, the Times changed its tune heading into the 2020 election with a news story that claimed Trump was "Pushing a False Argument on Vote-by-Mail Fraud," by claiming that "voting by mail is a recipe for fraud."[531] Mailing out ballots to everyone on the voter rolls is also far less secure than only mailing out individual absentee ballots to those who request them and complete the required process, as I have done in the past when working out of state.

For decades, various Democrats have denied the outcome of elections won by Republicans, voted against certifying Presidential elections and tried every legal argument imaginable to support their positions, including each one made by President Trump after the conclusion of the 2020 election. Democrat leaders from Hillary Clinton to Jimmy Carter denied that Trump was legitimately elected in 2016.[532] Democrats said the 2000 presidential election was stolen. Stacy Abrams claimed for years to have actually won the 2018 Georgia governor's race. Nonetheless, the media and experts roundly condemned Trump for questioning the outcome and wanting to see suspicions of election fraud properly investigated. Because it was Trump, any question about the vote made one an "election denier," a threat to democracy and, ultimately, a criminal. The 2020 election became a thing of unquestionable faith.

> Ali Swenson and Amanda Seitz, Associated Press, Nov. 12, 2020: "President Donald Trump falsely claimed on Twitter that an election technology firm 'deleted' large numbers of his votes or 'switched' them to count for Joe Biden — the latest in a series of baseless theories suggesting vote counting problems that the president has been promoting. His tweet Thursday amplified a 'report' built on empty claims that originated in anonymous comments on a pro-Trump blog. Trump and his supporters have launched groundless attacks on one of the most widely used technology firms in the U.S., Dominion Voting Systems, seeking to sow doubt in the results of the 2020 election, despite no evidence of any serious irregularities."[533]

"We found that the Dominion Voting Systems is designed intentionally to create inherent and systemic voting errors." - Matthew DePerno

---

There was evidence, but the same people who later hid Hunter's laptop and Joe Biden's mental deterioration ignored it. There were vote changes admitted to that exposed the potential for error if not fraud. In Antrim County, Michigan during the 2020 election, Dominion software gave 6,000 Trump votes to Joe Biden, which was blamed on user error. Officials said it was not a glitch, as initially reported, but a mistake.[534] If mistakes could change the vote there, it could happen again or elsewhere. This created an opening for a deeper look into the Dominion systems to assess integrity of the election equipment, but the investigation was eventually turned on the investigators. In December 2020, Allied Security Operations Group (ASOG) inspected Dominion's software in connection to a lawsuit and claimed to find evidence of serious, designed problems.[535]

The questions raised did not lead to further investigation and Dominion denied the allegations. The Michigan Attorney General and Secretary of State dismissed this report as lies "designed to erode public confidence in the November presidential election."[536] By the summer of 2022, the left had turned the tables. Matthew DePerno, the attorney representing the plaintiff, then the Republican nominee for Michigan attorney general, was being investigated himself by the current Michigan attorney general for "unauthorized access to voting equipment".[537] DePerno lost his election in 2022 as did numerous others that had been condemned as election deniers.

"Statistical anomaly? Fraud? Look at the evidence and decide for yourself."- Rand Paul

---

There were also abnormal vote shifts on election night in the pivotal counties of swing states that ultimately turned the election. This I saw in the numbers being reported that night and as more details came out, it seemed all the more suspicious.

> Senator Rand Paul, KY, Twitter, Nov. 29, 2020: "Interesting . . . Trump margin of "defeat" in 4 states occurred in 4 data dumps between 1:34-6:31 AM. Statistical anomaly? Fraud? Look at the evidence and decide for yourself. (That is, if Big Tech allows u to read this)"[538]

These were not denied, but excused by officials who said the jump represented the counting of densely populated, highly Democrat counties. Data analysis also called out the vote jumps, the findings of which "suggest that four vote count updates – which collectively were decisive in Michigan, Wisconsin, and Georgia, and thus decisive of a critical forty-two electoral votes – are especially anomalous and merit further investigation."[539] We didn't just echo claims made by the Trump team. Like millions of other Americans, I watched as Trump won Florida and Ohio and he was leading in several remaining key states before the count was stopped late into the night, with bizarre explanations given, and then Biden's numbers jumped precipitously. Later, I also watched videos of bizarre activities that night by poll workers.[540]

On election night, it was unclear if any of the odd occurrences were signs of fraudulent activity, but it was certainly suspicious. Instead of being investigated, it was denied and then just disappeared from the news. The following declaration came from Twitter, titled "No evidence of widespread voter fraud in the 2020 US presidential election government officials and election experts confirm." This absurd hyperbole quickly became the indisputable truth, gospel in fact.

"The November 3rd election was the most secure in American history." - Election officials at the Department of Homeland Security

---

> Twitter, Nov. 30, 2021:
> "According to former attorney general William Barr, the Department of Justice found no evidence of 'fraud on a scale that could have effected a different outcome in the election.' Election officials at the Department of Homeland Security said 'the November 3rd election was the most secure in American history.' Voter fraud of any type is incredibly rare, reported The Associated Press and Reuters. Officials and experts warned ahead of Election Day that most interference in US elections comes in the form of misinformation campaigns, many of which are intended to create distrust in America's electoral process."[541]

"It was as if a switch flipped and everyone in the media and government decided an undisputed election was more important than an honest one."

These overly broad statements alone stretched credulity. How could an election where laws were suspended and mail-in ballots allowed on a greater scale and fashion than ever before be the most secure? The 2020 election was curious for another reason. Quickly and uniformly, I found every news person started saying "unfounded" or "baseless" before any mention of election fraud, even though the Trump side already had hundreds of depositions of witnesses and other evidence. Newscasters didn't say "alleged" or "disputed", which a professional journalist would. Follow-up stories on the abnormalities disappeared. Coverage of court cases disappeared and most were not considered on the merits. It was as if a switch flipped and everyone in the media and government decided an undisputed election was more important than an honest one.

> Trump v. Biden, Wisconsin Supreme Court, Rebecca Grassly Bradley, J., 7/8/22:
> "The right to vote presupposes the rule of law governs elections. If elections are conducted outside of the law, the people have not conferred their consent on the government. Such elections are unlawful and their results are illegitimate... The illegality of these drop boxes weakens the people's faith that the election produced an outcome reflective of their will... Unlawfully conducted elections threaten to diminish or even eliminate some voices, destabilizing the very foundation of free government."

In a separate opinion, Bradley added, "When the state's highest court refuses to uphold the law, and stands by while an unelected body of six commissioners rewrites it, our system of representative government is subverted."[542] Though finding that drop boxes were illegal, the court offered no remedy and let the results stand, saying the Trump team should have sued earlier. They were right about that. Lawsuits should have been filed before the election against those illegally changing election laws, deadlines and standards, but it was still illegal.

> Trump Summary of Election Fraud in the 2020 Presidential Election:
> "In the Michigan, Georgia, Arizona, and Wisconsin Petitions, and in the underlying proceedings, Petitioners laid out extensive evidence of massive election fraud and other illegal conduct. In each case, fact and expert witnesses presented sworn and unrebutted testimony establishing that tens of thousands of illegal ballots were counted in favor of candidate Biden. In each case, petitioners established that correcting the multiple acts of illegality and fraud, as established by sworn testimony, would erase candidate Biden's purported margins of victory and flip the relevant state to President Trump. But in each instance, the District Courts failed to grapple with, or even to examine with care, these showings...
>
> "The nation was watching on Election Night when President Trump led by hundreds of thousands of votes in five key swing states–Georgia, as well as Arizona, Michigan, Pennsylvania, Wisconsin–until, nearly simultaneously, the tabulation of votes shut down for several hours in Democrat-run cities in each of those States. When counting resumed, candidate Biden had somehow

> made up the difference and taken a narrow lead in Wisconsin and Michigan, while dramatically closing the gap in other states. (Petitioners' experts have shown that this remarkable turnaround is a statistical impossibility.)"

The Trump team released this report of election fraud in early 2024 called "Summary of Election Fraud in the 2020 Presidential Election in the Swing States," which included the Wisconsin case referenced above.[543] It was mostly ignored but occasionally a couple of claims were pulled out of it and denied. After reading it and reading or watching the linked documentation and video, I have some questions on a couple of points. The overall conclusion I cannot escape is that widespread, illegal election interference and election fraud were committed. Quietly, below the national news radar, there have been investigations and cases exposing the corruption of our elections.[544]

By their own admission, a coalition on the left used the pandemic to justify loosening election laws and policies that had been designed to ensure the identity of voters and the legitimacy of their ballots. They expanded mail-in voting, added drop boxes, loosened restrictions, changed laws and extended voting deadlines illegally. They put in place a drove of additional poll workers to control the process and kept watchers away. Add to that the unusual behavior on election night and the vulnerability of voting machines that the left long complained about, government-led censorship of dissenting voices and negative news about the Biden family and it all looked like election interference to me and many other common Americans.

Yes, by all appearances, this multifaceted election interference was still not enough to tip the election to their candidate, so, as that became obvious on election night, they stopped counting, determined how many additional votes Biden needed to overcome Trump's lead and manufactured them. Americans were unwilling to "listen to reason" so the choice for President needed to be made for them. That conviction among the American people was never disproven, but other things did happen that made it seem all the more likely.

"Everyone here will soon be marching over to the Capitol building to peacefully and patriotically make your voices heard."
 - President Donald Trump

Then, to our shock and horror, we were told that the Trump rally in D.C., held to draw attention to election issues, turned into a violent riot at the Capitol. The right quickly condemned anyone breaking the law or participating in violence. As with most Trump supporters, I was suspicious about who really perpetrated these acts. Violence and illegality by supporters had never happened at previous Trump events. At the same time, we were anxious to see what Congress was going to do as issues with the election would finally be debated that day, making it impossible for the media to ignore. Unfortunately, the breaching of the capitol prevented that from happening.

"States want to revote. The states got defrauded."
- President Donald Trump

Hundreds of thousands attended the Trump rally on January 6th on the Ellipse, a 52-acre park south of the White House fence that day. In his speech, Trump said he wanted his Vice President Mike Pence to send it back to the states. Whether or not this could be done, I couldn't say, but it was a clearly a legal and political fight, not a call to insurrection:

"If they don't fight, we have to primary the hell out of [them]."
- President Donald Trump

> "Because if Mike Pence does the right thing, we win the election. All he has to do, all this is, this is from the number one, or certainly one of the top, Constitutional lawyers in our country. He has the absolute right to do it. We're supposed to protect our country, support our country, support our Constitution, and protect our constitution. States want to revote. The states got defrauded. They were given false information. They voted on it. Now they want to recertify. They want it back. All Vice President Pence has to do is send it back to the states to recertify... And you have to get your people to fight. And if they don't fight, we have to primary the hell out of the ones that don't fight. You primary them...
>
> "Now, it is up to Congress to confront this egregious assault on our democracy. And after this, we're going to walk down, and I'll be there with you, we're going to walk down, we're going to walk down.

> Anyone you want, but I think right here, we're going to walk down to the Capitol, and we're going to cheer on our brave senators and congressmen and women, and we're probably not going to be cheering so much for some of them. Because you'll never take back our country with weakness. You have to show strength and you have to be strong. We have come to demand that Congress do the right thing and only count the electors who have been lawfully slated, lawfully slated. I know that everyone here will soon be marching over to the Capitol building to peacefully and patriotically make your voices heard...
>
> "Our brightest days are before us. Our greatest achievements, still away. I think one of our great achievements will be election security. Because nobody until I came along had any idea how corrupt our elections were. And again, most people would stand there at 9 o'clock in the evening and say I want to thank you very much, and they go off to some other life. But I said something's wrong here, something is really wrong, can have happened. And we fight. We fight like hell. And if you don't fight like hell, you're not going to have a country anymore."[545]

He wasn't talking about a physical fight, but as usual, his words were taken out of context with malicious intent. Afterwards, part of that massive crowd walked to the capitol building to protest the disputed election and cheer on their representatives in Congress who were set to expose it. Others dispersed and enjoyed the city or returned to their hotels. Our representatives in Congress, Rep. Jim Jordan in the lead, were contesting the legitimacy of the election, beginning the argument against certifying the electors based on facts and evidence they were prepared to lay out. That all stopped when the capitol was breached. This coincided with the discovery of two fake pipe bombs, a case no one in power seemed interested in solving. They were no longer needed. Congress was already being evacuated. Other sources say they were potentially planted by law enforcement and intended to draw resources away to leave the capitol understaffed.[546] Crazy as it may sound, the level of government corruption in these years appears extraordinary.

"There were no Americans running, or screaming, or turning over statues, or vandalizing or tearing down anything." - Jennie White

---

> Jennie White, the Federalist.com, January 11, 2021: "There were hundreds of thousands of people all standing together peacefully in one spot for more than five hours. A small percentage of this group entered the capitol and perpetrated mayhem while hundreds of thousands were peacefully milling around outside... As we sat in the hotel room in various states of shock, glued to TV news, we were consistently surprised at how what the reporters were reporting simply didn't even match the footage they were showing. If there was so much chaos, disorder, and confusion, why were people milling around and not running for their lives?
>
> "All we could see from our 10th-floor window were all kinds of Americans walking slowly away from the capitol as though they'd had a leisurely day sightseeing... We decided to walk outside for a better look... Upon arriving at the capitol, we saw masses of people in the street, along the reflecting pool, strewn across the grounds and along the balconies. We saw international media, but no legacy media... We stopped at the stone wall surrounding the capitol grounds and observed for some time. At one point we saw what looked like DC police throw flash-bangs and pepper spray to try and disperse the crowd from around the Capitol building."[547]

Upon returning to their hotel, White and her group were shocked when 16 vans of DC police in full riot gear and other cops blocked all of the hotel entrances as hotels in DC were completely locked down. This was an omen of things to come as Biden would erect tall fences topped with barbed wire around the capitol building. I watched similarly incongruent coverage that day from home. Reporters described a riot as families and other tourists walked by casually behind them. Why did all of the American media set up out of sight of what was going on at the capitol, I wondered? The press never missed any other riot or protest. You would think they would jump at the opportunity to film Trump supporters attacking police, but coverage was sparse. At the very least, there had to be reams of surveillance video, we thought.

Finally, a few cuts of video started coming out that showed protestors swarming the outside of the building and some confronting police. That was ugly and illegal, no matter who committed the act or who they supported. There was tear gas in the air. Later I saw video of protesters inside the Capitol, one dressed ridiculously. Another took a photo sitting at Pelosi's desk, clearly trespassing and breaking the law. Windows were broken. There is no doubt that violence occurred and that the Capitol was entered, criminal acts that needed to be investigated and prosecuted. There was some damage done and a large number of people trespassed. Beyond that, the details were fuzzy and camera footage was not forthcoming. Reporters, though, described terrible violence.

> Anti-Defamation League, adl.org, Jan. 11, 2021: "On Wednesday, January 6, 2021, Congress met in the U.S. Capitol to count electoral votes and certify the results of the 2020 Presidential election. This is a formality that takes place every four years under our country's system for choosing its President and Vice President. While this took place, a violent mob of right-wing extremists and others, who came to Washington, D.C. (and several state capitals) to disrupt and overturn the results of the Presidential election, stormed the Capitol. Their goal was to disrupt the count of electoral college ballots that would formally certify Joe Biden's victory. As House and Senate lawmakers held their floor debates, angry rioters—many wearing and carrying white supremacist symbolism—invaded the Capitol building, spewing rage and hate. To date, five people have died, including one Capitol Police officer. One factor that led to these events is the viral spread of disinformation across the internet, including on major social media platforms."

Apparently, I missed all the white supremacists. Later, I saw a picture of mock gallows with a noose hanging from a 2 by 4 construction. I never heard who built it. Were it a Donald Trump supporter, I'm sure the person behind it would have been all over the news. Instead, like with the bombs, the media didn't want to look too closely. Vice President elect Kamala Harris was still a senator but was not doing her job in Congress that day. Instead, she was at the DNC headquarters where one of the bombs was found.

The article above, still posted two years later with no correction, decried disinformation one sentence after spreading it. In fact, the entire paragraph is littered with false claims and bias. Were the protestors left wing, it would have been called a deadly police crackdown that left four peaceful protestors dead. Instead, the media and government said five died in a violent attack, including a murdered capitol police officer. Eventually, we learned this wasn't true. No officers died at the Capitol that day. The event resulted in the death of four unarmed protestors, though they were barely mentioned if at all.

"Police Officer That Rioters Hit with Fire Extinguisher Dies, Making Capitol Siege a Murder Scene." Slate Magazine

---

In comparison, George Floyd protestors in Seattle were paid millions of dollars because police used flash-bangs and other anti-riot tools on them.[548] The real story about the death of officer Sicknick would finally emerge, though the lie continued to be used by politicians to condemn Trump and his supporters.[549]

> Phil Shiver, The Blaze, Feb. 23, 2021:
> "In the initial report of Brian Sicknick's death, Capitol Police said only that Sicknick was 'injured while physically engaging with protesters' during the riot. 'He returned to his division office and collapsed,' the memo added, noting that he was 'taken to a local hospital where he succumbed to his injuries.' But the following day, the New York Times published an explosive story, based on the flimsy account of two anonymous law enforcement officials, claiming that Sicknick, 42, died after being struck in the head with a fire extinguisher.
>
> "That story set off a firestorm of anger and grandstanding, as anti-Trump lawmakers and mainstream media members alike branded the riot a murderous insurrection. Without verifying facts about the case, Democratic House Speaker Nancy Pelosi (Calif.) called for the 'perpetrators' of Sicknick's death to be 'brought to justice,' and emphatically labeled the riot as a 'violent and deadly act of insurrection.'"[550]

Eventually, the officer's autopsy came out, indicating no evidence of internal or external injuries or reaction to chemical irritants. Some articles were quietly updated but most of the media ignored the truth. Officer Brian Sicknick had two strokes the day *after* the event, dying of natural causes.[551] [552] Of the four protestors who died that day, one woman, Ashli Babbitt, age 35, was shot and killed by Capitol police while apparently trying to climb through a window near the House chamber. There's video of that which eventually emerged, but it's hard to tell what happened between the time when she could be seen confronting the people who were actually doing the damage and when she was shot. There's no explanation as to why police officers who were videoed standing guard there decided to walk away only a few minutes earlier.

Another woman, Roseanne Boyland, age 34, appeared from the video to have been crushed between protesters and police, perhaps even struck by police. Again, it's hard to tell from the video. Officially, she died of amphetamine overdose (from a legal prescription for Adderall[553]). Her death was listed as an accident and virtually never spoken of again. The Trump supporters who tried to save her were arrested and jailed without trial for the three and a half+ years that followed.[554] Two others in the crowd outside died from pre-existing medical conditions.[555] Little was said of them either, but, were the political leanings reversed, their families would have certainly blamed it on the anti-riot grenades. Four unarmed protestors died that day. Police were hurt. These deaths and many injuries among the overwhelmed police led the crackdown afterwards.

There was a lot of strange things about that day. No culprit has been identified in connection to the pipe bombs that were found at the two major party headquarters. Three years later surveillance video of one bomb's discovery showed police with a complete lack of urgency or concern after being made aware of its existence. There were reportedly dozens of federal agents in the crowd at the capitol that day, unbeknownst to Capital police.[556] Many people reported the involvement of instigators.[557] One man, Ray Epps, was on video calling for protestors to break the law, but seemed to have avoided serious charges. In a video from January 5, 2021, he can be seen repeating, "Tomorrow, we need to go <u>into</u> the Capitol!" The people standing around him in the video began chanting "fed, fed, fed."[558] He was found in other videos the next day encouraging others to push through the barriers. Hundreds were jailed for far less, some for many years.

"It is as if the officers there were sacrificed for the 'greater good' of making Donald Trump unelectable in 2024."

We're told the FBI had evidence leading up to that day indicating people were planning violence, but the capitol wasn't properly secured. Reports said many police were injured while doing their jobs that day, certainly a terrible thing that should never have been allowed to happened.[559] Police were shorthanded and unprepared. They were put in a terrible position that left everyone involved at greater risk. The Trump Administration's offer to provide thousands of National Guard troops for security for the day was rejected by the House and Senate Sergeant at Arms, who reported to Nancy Pelosi.[560] Despite the evidence, the left continued to deny the offer was ever made. It is as if the officers there were sacrificed for the "greater good" of making Donald Trump unelectable in 2024.

That might sound ridiculously conspiratorial were it not for the Russia collusion hoax and the conspiracy to subvert the 2020 election. Everything that happened after that day was what convinced me that the election was in fact a coup on the part of Joe Biden and the establishment. The "insurrection" was designed to cover it up. This subterfuge was also used to justify bringing in 26,000 National Guard troops to guard the Capitol afterwards and for Joe Biden's inauguration. Fencing with razor wire was erected around the Capitol for many months, even though there was "no specific, credible threat".[561]

It looked to me like they feared the American people knew what they did and would rise up. But we were silent. This became a pivotal moment in American history, not because anyone on Trump's side thought they were going to overthrow the government but because it laid the groundwork of an appalling new propaganda campaign and judicial witch hunt against President Trump and everyone who supported him. January 6th effectively ended any discussion about the legitimacy of the election.

The left presented their heavily distorted version of that day in Congressional hearings without any rebuttal testimony or evidence, and having denied the minority party the inclusion of their chosen members (illegitimating the entire process). It's one-sided nature (and the two "Republicans" they did put on it were anything but right wing), made it nothing but a show trial (actually produced by Hollywood[562]).

"I will do whatever it takes to ensure Donald Trump is never again anywhere near the Oval Office." - Liz Chaney

---

If the tables were turned, and the inquisition equally one-sided, with the Democrat party denied the ability to choose their appointees, we probably wouldn't get a very clear picture of the truth either. It wasn't Democrats verses Republicans. It was the establishment against Donald Trump and the American people. Without missing a beat, the "January 6th

Insurrection" took the place of the failed Russia collusion hoax and overwhelmed any questions about the election. The people who were responsible for what happened that day need to be held accountable. The January 6th Committee was never intended to accomplish that end.

It was a premeditated, orchestrated attack on President Trump, our republic and the American people. In fact, it was brilliant, if you don't worry about things like the constitution or justice. Republican House Representative Liz Cheney of Wyoming played a lead public role in the hearings.

> Former U.S. Republican Rep-Wyoming Liz Cheney, Yahoo! News, Aug. 16, 2022:
> "Freedom must not, cannot and will not die here. We must be very clear eyed about the threat we face, and about what is required to defeat it. I have said since January 6th, that I will do whatever it takes to ensure Donald Trump is never again anywhere near the Oval Office, and I mean it."[563]

Cheney was not alone and not exaggerating. If the media pronouncement that there was no election fraud wasn't sufficient to convince the populous, they hoped the "insurrection" would serve to finally and forever keep Trump from returning to office and discredit anyone who continued to support him. It had to be an insurrection, because nothing else could conceivably allow them to remove Trump from the ballot in 2024, which they certainly attempted.

Riots occurred in D.C. during Trump's inauguration four years earlier where vehicles and trash bins were burned. Rioters bashed windows and storefronts as they wreaked havoc with crowbars, hammers and baseball bats. In fact, the U.S. Capitol has been invaded by rioters from the left several times before.[564] But this was different. It became clear, in time, that something very unusual was going on. The surveillance video was finally released that showed people walking peacefully through the capitol as police looked on. Others were casually escorted by police. In one video, a uniformed police officer can be seen waving a flood of people through a barrier outside the capitol. Doors were opened for them. Tucker Carlson and The Epoch Times were among the first to publish the footage.

Another video shows fences and signs being torn away so that the coming crowd did not even know they were entering a restricted area. That it was tore down so easily is suspect and it happened before Trump even finished speaking. In most cases officers make no attempt to deter entrance. There was the ridiculously dressed fellow who was shown being walked through the capitol by police who opened or attempted to open doors for him. It was enough to get his conviction thrown out, but many others still faced years in prison or were still being held without trial years later. This event was orchestrated, but not by Donald Trump.

"Why have a political debate when you can just arrest people who disagree with you?" - Tucker Carlson

---

Claims of insurrection were used to remove the then sitting U.S. President from Facebook and Twitter (aka X), the nation's two biggest social media platforms. In some cases, interviews he gave were pulled from these sites and their affiliates. All evidence of the election coup was suppressed. Trump was impeached, again. Again, the Senate acquitted.

By the time Joe Biden gave his inauguration speech condemning violent domestic terrorism, it was clear that he was not talking about the many-months-long siege of numerous U.S. cities by rioters who looted and burned businesses, federal and local facilities, and killed and terrorized citizens during the previous year or the widespread crime epidemic. He wasn't even just talking about the handful of people who committed criminal offenses at the capitol that day. No, he was talking about us: the average American who dared to support Donald Trump despite everything they had done to discredit him.

After President Biden took power, the government used January 6th to begin a full-fledged crackdown, a totalitarian campaign to identify and persecute their adversaries and imprison dissenters. The politically motivated, heavy-handed searches and seizures, arrests and prosecutions were shocking but most of the media hid and misrepresented them. Some who questioned fraud in the 2020 election, were associated with President Trump or dared to represent him legally, were targeted with the full force of the United States government or threatened with financial ruin by specious civil lawsuits. Attorneys, former Trump officials and allies were targeted. Political candidates were targeted. Average, every day supporters were targeted. This was only a piece of an ongoing campaign.

> Tucker Carlson, Tucker Carlson Tonight, Fox News, June 30, 2022:
> "Why have a political debate when you can just arrest people who disagree with you? And that has happened. Far below the media radar since the day Joe Biden was elected. And tonight, to show it, we want to go through a litany, a list of Americans who have been arrested, detained by federal law enforcement on the orders of the Biden administration, not because they committed recognizable crimes, but because they disagreed with the political aims of the Biden administration."

This was the beginning of Carlson's awakening. He went on to list a series of cases, including Peter Navarro, a trade aide to Donald Trump who was "arrested at Washington National Airport and put in leg irons and put in jail. Why? Well, days earlier, he sued the January 6 Committee, he claimed executive privilege in his communications with the president." The 70-year-old Navarro, like several Trump officials during other investigations, posed no physical threat and would have no cause to resist arrest, yet were treated like violent criminals. He was imprisoned for defying a subpoena of the January 6 Committee, thus being in contempt of Congress. Steve Bannon was also jailed for contempt for refusing to participate in the corrupt witch hunt.

"They have only one mission, to concoct a fake hoax around January 6... to prevent [Trump] from... taking back the White House."
 - Peter Navarro

Another man was arrested because he made fun of Hillary Clinton in an internet meme. That man was convicted and sentenced to a decade in jail for "suppressing the vote" of her supporters in 2016.[565] Now memes could get you put away. This was just the start of an organized campaign of lawfare against Donald Trump, his associates and the American people as minor crimes or non-crimes were manipulated into felony charges. It revealed the two-tiered justice system had advanced to unimaginable scale.

> Peter Navarro, former Trump trade aid, Tucker Carlson Tonight, June 30, 2022:
> "The mission of that partisan witch hunt kangaroo committee, which is unduly authorized and not properly constituted and has no subpoena power, they have only one mission, to concoct a fake hoax around January 6 based on criminal charges against Trump to prevent him from running for reelection and taking back the White House in 2025 January."

Having already discovered many classified documents in Joe Biden's possession but keeping it under wraps, his agencies raided Donald Trump's Mar-a-Lago property. As president, Trump had the full authority to declassify and take whatever he wanted, unlike Hillary Clinton, who had vast amounts classified, even top secret information on an unsecured private server, or Joe Biden who, as a Senator and Vice President, removed classified information later found at his residence and various other unsecured locations. Yet they went free and he was prosecuted.

The prosecution of Trump on his non-crimes covered up their real crimes. If you point this out, however, they claim "what-about-ism," as if their guilt is irrelevant. Then came the series of spurious indictments and prosecutions against President Trump from a variety of prosecutors and locations, based on laws that had been changed just to apply to Trump or twisted out of shape in an attempt to justify charges.

They coordinated Trumps prosecutions to hit as the election neared in an attempt to put the administration's leading political opponent in jail, remove him from the ballot or, at the very least, keep him off of the campaign trail. Had he not run for President a third time, none of it would have been pursued. His conviction was a forgone conclusion. It didn't matter that it would be thrown out on appeal. When it mattered, during the election, they could call Trump a convicted felon.

This effort to turn the accusations and abuses on the innocent people trying to expose them was very successful. The January 6th propaganda was also quite successful for a while, but the heavy-handed prosecutions finally turned the American people against the manufactured narrative. There have been and certainly will continue to be many books written about it and I cannot hope to cover it here. My point here is to illustrate why the

American people still supported Trump and that the people in charge were willing to do anything to stop him.

The modus operandi was clear: accuse your opponents of exactly what you are doing, but more than that, criminally prosecute and civilly sue them for trying to expose your actions. The fact that many people under this pressure pled guilty in order to escape years of prison time or financial ruin can hardly be surprising. It happened again and again. Trump tried to look into Biden's corruption in Ukraine while the former Vice President was tasked with Ukraine policy, a quid pro quo, so they falsely impeached Trump of very same thing. Investigation over. Again, and again, whether it was media outlets, politicians, attorneys or regular Americans, the left used the court system to aggressively target opponents, bankrupting and jailing, or threatening long prison terms. It is no coincidence that George Soros funded D.A.s and Secretaries of State were in position to make all of this happen. I know how that sounds. I also know that it is true.

Rather than answer legitimate questions about their own behavior, these political actors used the justice system to shut down their accusers and investigations. When Trump tried to look into interference and fraud in the election, they charged him with doing that very thing. Defamation lawsuits were used to preempt investigations and silence questions. Nearly four years later, if you searched for 2020 election interference online, the only thing that came up was the manufactured case against Trump, his lawyers and other associates. Some were jailed, others bankrupted. Whistleblowers were targeted.[566] Debate was shut down.

Not only were Americans systematically lied to about the election, they were lied to about every vile thing the left accused Donald Trump of doing or saying. He never called for violence or retribution, never seriously desired dictatorship, threatened a bloodbath or said white nationalists were fine people. "Fight like hell" referred to the legal process, "bloodbath" referred to the economic consequences of liberal politics, being a "dictator on day one" was being facetious. Each lie was blatant and easily uncovered, but the media just repeated them instead, feeding Americans a terribly distorted and contorted view of reality. Throughout his presidency, Joe Biden repeated these lies, even after he was forced out of the 2024 race by leaders on his own side in what is widely seen as a silent coup. And then there was the attempted assassination of President Donald Trump, that appears to be more coverup than investigation.

It was only as I neared the end of researching and writing this book that I accidentally became a conspiracy believer. Certainly, some conspiracies in this country are fabricated, but far more of them than I would have ever imagined are exactly what we've been told they were. Americans have been lied to and manipulated at least as far back as the early 1900s by people who think they deserve to lead the "ignorant masses". They've indoctrinated our educators, journalists and government administrators against American principles and to promote distortions and propaganda. Our own government has participated in coups and assassinations. Meanwhile, Americans are turned on each other so that we will be too busy playing politics to see the truth and take back control of our country.

I embrace and will defend America and people of all races, genders and background. We all deserve what the founder's envisioned: individual liberty limited only by the equal individual liberty of others and the opportunity to pursue happiness. It is sad that our founders escaped the oppression of despotic leaders and the tyranny of thought and expression which came from the collusion of religious and civil authorities only to turn our nation over to a new religious establishment under the control of wealthy oligarchs and elitists. They think we are incompetent fools as they conspire to enslave the world.

Some will say the words and intent of America's founders are irrelevant in the modern would. Nothing could be further from the truth. What they fought for is what we fight for.

"What other principles from that era should we discard?" Ron Paul

---

> U.S. Representative Ron Paul, April 16, 2002, Antiwar.com: "When I mentioned Washington the other guest on the show quickly repeated the tired cliché that 'We don't live in George Washington's times.' Yet if we accept this argument, what other principles from that era should we discard? Should we give up the First amendment because times have changed? How about the rest of the Bill of Rights? It's hypocritical and childish to dismiss certain founding principles simply because a convenient rationale is needed to justify foolish policies today. The principles enshrined in the Constitution do not change."[567]

"From the conclusion of [the revolution] we shall be going down hill." - President Thomas Jefferson

---

Our best hope is a revival of the principles of our nation's founding. Free speech has been partially restored thanks in large part to Elon Musk and his operation of X. We too must stand up for the ideals of our nation.

> The Works of Thomas Jefferson, Chapter XVII, published 1904: "From the conclusion of [the revolution] we shall be going down hill. It will not then be necessary to resort every moment to the people for support. They will be forgotten therefore, and their rights disregarded. They will forget themselves, but in the sole faculty of making money, and will never think of uniting to effect a due respect for their rights. The shackles, therefore, which shall not be knocked off at the conclusion of this war, will remain on us long, will be made heavier and heavier, till our rights shall revive or expire in a convulsion." [568]

The shackles of slavery remained for many years until Civil War finally corrected that failing. Now, the left's policies, an expression of Progressive Globalism, are accomplishing the degradation of the United States of America, culturally, financially and militarily. With it goes the world's best hope at a future of self-rule instead of subjugation to masters, freedom instead of slavery, prosperity instead of poverty and starvation, civilization instead of dystopia, opportunity instead of hopelessness, and equal rights instead of corruption and injustice. Those are our choices. Our planet is not at stake but our entire civilization is balancing on the edge of collapse.

The American experiment in self-rule was a tremendous success before moneyed elitists got their claws into it. I think this country does have a possibility for revival, if only because "the powers that be" could be so terrified of one flawed but generally honorable man who was not part of their schemes.

> Former Vice President Dick Cheney, X, Sept. 8, 2023: "In our nation's 246 year history, there has never been an individual who is a greater threat to our republic than Donald Trump. He tried to steal the last election using lies and violence to keep himself in power after the voters had rejected him. He was a coward. A real man wouldn't lie to his supporters. He lost his election and he lost

> big. I know it. He knows it. And deep down, I think most Republicans know it."[569]

In contrast to everything we were told, Donald Trump gave up power when he had every reason to believe it was still justifiably his. Trump threatened the corrupt establishment to an extent never before imagined. That was his real crime. He was not a perfect president. He spent too much money in this first term and failed to purge the deep-rooted corruption and bloat from our civil establishment. Nonetheless, his policies did a tremendous amount of good and can do so again. We don't have to let backroom tyrants throw the world into constant war, pillage the resources of struggling, third world nations and force mass migrations for social and political effect. We can use energy independence to as leverage to stop aggression by our adversaries and join nations together in a teeming economy. We can return the power to the people, but Americans have to see through the distortions first, the façade of divisive tribalism and utter dishonesty of the mainstream media and establishment politicians.

When I chose to use the word "uprising" in the subtitle of this book, it was not because there existed or that I anticipated or meant to call for a physical or violent response from the American people. An armed response to the pervasive corruption of our system is the last resort and least palatable option to common, patriotic Americans. The system our founders devised provides the people with great power if we stand up, politically, and that continues to be my hope. If we can overcome the corruption in our elections and institutions, we have a chance to eradicate this malignancy from our system. This is also my hope because I am not sure as Americans we have it in us anymore to win our freedom the way our founders did.

A strong United States, with leadership that is representative of and responsive to all of its citizens, has the ability to provide affordable food and fuels to the world, far cleaner than what our adversaries use and sell now. Globalists are using countries as pawns and using the threat of a climate apocalypse to keep more of the world poor and powerless as they continue plundering their resources and dictating their futures. We can lift the Third World up rather than bring the United States of America and the Western World down. But it's going to take a radical realignment of our government to bring our nation back to the limited design of the Constitution. The question before us is whether we will submit to the rule of others determined to oppress us or stand up and take responsibility for our own lives and future. And time is running out.

"I would rather be exposed to the inconveniences attending too much liberty than those attending too small a degree of it."

– President Thomas Jefferson

About the Author

Julie A. Fragoules is not an academic, Washington insider or typical political pundit, though she is college educated and has decades of experience in the federal government. Julie is a common American, the product of the American Dream. She grew up in the small custom shop her parents started out of an old school bus in the Ozark Mountains of North Arkansas, which grew into an industry leader. While still based in Arkansas, Julie became a Hazard Mitigation Community Education and Outreach Task Force Leader for the Federal Emergency Management Agency (FEMA), spending the last twenty years living and working for weeks to months at a time in communities across our nation devastated by disaster, promoting methods to reduce future losses by becoming more self-reliant and disaster resistant.

Prior to that, she was an Associated Press and the Society of Professional Journalism award winning reporter and weekend news host at KTLO radio stations in Mountain Home, Arkansas. She holds a B.A. in Political Science from the University of Central Arkansas. Julie is also the author of a dystopian novel, "The Serpent Underneath" which was the bronze winner of the 2023 FAPA President's Book Awards for Adult Sci-Fi and a Finalist for the Best Thriller Book Awards. Julie enjoys sailing, kayaking, and woodworking.

Endnotes

[1] Madison, James. "Virginia Resolutions, 21 December 1798," Founders Online, National Archives, https://founders.archives.gov/documents/Madison/01-17-02-0128. [Original source: The Papers of James Madison, vol. 17, 31 March 1797–3 March 1801 and supplement 22 January 1778–9 August 1795, ed. David B. Mattern, J. C. A. Stagg, Jeanne K. Cross, and Susan Holbrook Perdue. Charlottesville: University Press of Virginia, 1991, pp. 185–191.] https://founders.archives.gov/documents/Madison/01-17-02-0128

[2] Norway-Heritage. Accessed November 13, 2023. http://norwayheritage.com/steerage.htm

[3] Keeling, Drew. "Oceanic Travel Conditions and American Immigration, 1890-1914." June 26, 2013. https://mpra.ub.uni-muenchen.de/47850/1/MPRA_paper_47850.pdf.

[4] "Strawberry Industry." CALS Encyclopedia of Arkansas. Accessed November 17, 2023. https://encyclopediaofarkansas.net/entries/strawberry-industry-5732/.

[5] Pope Leo XIII. *Immortale Dei: On the Christian Constitution of States.* 1885.

[6] "Trial by Ordeal: A Life or Death Method of Judgement." Ancient-origins.net. October 30, 2018. https://www.ancient-origins.net/history/trial-ordeal-life-or-death-method-judgement-004160.

[7] Hancock, Graham. *Fingerprints of the Gods.* Three Rivers Press, 1996.

[8] Hooker, Richard. *World Cultures Glossary.* Washington State University, 1996. http://www.wsu.edu:8080/~dee/MESO/SUMER.HTM. Accessed February 2, 2011.

[9] The British Museum. "The Flood Tablet, relating part of the Epic of Gilgamesh from Nineveh, northern Iraq, Neo-Assyrian, 7th century BC." http://www.britishmuseum.org/explore/highlights/highlight_objects/me/t/the_flood_tablet.aspx. Accessed February 2, 2011.

[10] Bauer, S. Wise. *The History of the Ancient World: From the Earliest Accounts to the Fall of Rome.* W.W. Norton & Company, March 26, 2007.

[11] Kramer, Samuel Noah. *From the Tablets of Sumer: Twenty-Five Firsts in Man's Recorded History.* The Falcon's Wing Press, 1956.

[12] Harper, Robert Francis. *Law Code of Hammurabi, King of Babylon, about 2250 BC.* Chicago: University Press, 1904.

[13] Yale Law School, Lillian Goldman Law Library. The Avalon Project. http://avalon.law.yale.edu/ancient/athe1.asp. Accessed February 2, 2011.

[14] Plato. *The Apology of Socrates.* F.E. Robinson & Company, 1901.

[15] Yale Law School, Lillian Goldman Law Library. The Avalon Project. http://avalon.law.yale.edu/ancient/twelve_tables.asp. Accessed February 2, 2011.

[16] Encyclopædia Britannica. "Ten Commandments." Encyclopædia Britannica, January 31, 2011.

[17] McDowell, Michael. World Religions at Your Fingertips. Nathan Robert Brown, 2009.

[18] "Edict of Thessalonica by Emperors Gratianus, Valentinianus and Theodosius, 380 C.E."

[19] Thatcher, Oliver J., ed. *The Library of Original Sources.* Milwaukee: University Research Extension Co., 1907. Vol. IV: The Early Medieval World, pp. 69-71.

[20] Adams, John. *The Works of John Adams.* Vol. 4. Novanglus, Thoughts on Government, Defence of the Constitution, 1851.

[21] Cosman, Madeleine Pelner. *Handbook to Life in the Medieval World.* Vol. 1, 2008.

[22] "Meeting of Council Fathers at the Third Council of Constantinople, 680-681 C.E."

[23] "Second Council of Nicaea, Council Fathers - 787 A.D., Decrees of the Ecumenical Councils."
[24] Cormenin, Louis-Marie de Lahaye. *A Complete History of the Popes of Rome.* J. & J. L. Gihon, 1851: 244.
[25] Bongars, Gesta. *Dei per Francos,* 1, pp. 382 f. Translated in Oliver J. Thatcher and Edgar Holmes McNeal, eds. *A Source Book for Medieval History.* New York: Scribners, 1905, 513-17.
[26] "Unam Sanctam, Bull of Pope Boniface VIII promulgated November 18, 1302."
[27] "Fourth Lateran Council, 1215 C.E., Constitutions: On Heretics."
[28] Peters, Edward. *Torture.* New York: B. Blackwell, 1985.
[29] Homza, Lu Ann. *The Spanish Inquisition, 1478-1614: An Anthology of Sources.* Hackett Pub Co, 2006.
[30] *Directorium Inquisitorum, edition of 1578, Book 3, page 137, column 1. Online in the Cornell University Collection. Accessed May 16, 2008.*
[31] Diehl, Daniel, and Mark P. Donnelly. *The Big Book of Pain: Torture & Punishment through History.* 2009.
[32] Galileo Galilei. University of Missouri-Kansas City. http://law2.umkc.edu/faculty/projects/ftrials/galileo/recantation.html.
[33] Pope Alexander VI. Frances Gardiner Davenport, ed. *European Treaties Bearing on the History of the United States and Its Dependencies to 1648.* Washington, D.C.: Carnegie Institution of Washington, 1917, 61-63.
[34] Delumeau, Jean. *Catholicism Between Luther and Voltaire: A New View of the Counter-Reformation.* Burns & Oates, Westminster Press in London, Philadelphia, 1977.
[35] "Sublimus Dei, On the Enslavement and Evangelization of Indians, by Pope Paul III, 1537." Papal Encyclicals Online.
[36] "Inter Praecipuas, On Biblical Societies, Papal Encyclical of Pope Gregory XVI, 1844."
[37] *"Magna Carta." Featured document, U.S. Archives & Records Administration, 1297.*
[38] Diehl, Daniel, and Mark P. Donnelly. *The Big Book of Pain: Torture & Punishment through History.* 2009.
[39] "Bulla Innocentii Papae III. pro rege Johanne, contra barones. (In membr.) 1216. 151. Created: 24 August 1215, Anagni, Italy." British Library. Shelfmark: Cotton MS Cleopatra E I, ff. 155–156. https://www.bl.uk/collection-items/the-papal-bull-annulling-magna-carta.
[40] Erasmus, Desiderius. *Roteradamus: A Dutch Humanist and Moderate Catholic Priest of the Renaissance Period.*
[41] Gibbon, Edward. The History of the Decline and Fall of the Roman Empire. Vol. 6, Methuen, 1898.
[42] "Decet Romanum Pontificem, Papal Bull of Excommunication of Martin Luther and His Followers, Pope Leo X, 1521."
[43] Luther, Martin, and Alexander Chalmers. *The Table Talk of Martin Luther.* Oxford University, 1857, 164.
[44] *"Second Sunday in Epiphany, 17 January 1546. Martin Luther's Werke: Kritische Gesamtausgabe". Weimar: Herman Boehlaus Nachfolger, 1914, Band 51:126, Line 7ff.*
[45] Luther, Martin. *Martin Luther's Last Sermon in Wittenberg: Second Sunday in Epiphany, Jan. 17, 1545.* Vol. 51, p. 374.
[46] *The Popular Science Monthly.* Vol. 8, 1876, 394.
[47] Luther, Martin. *Against the Heavenly Prophets,* 1525.
[48] Robinson, James Harvey. *Readings in European History.* 2 vols. Boston: Ginn & Company, 1906. 2:106-108.
[49] *"Exsurge Domine: Condemning the Errors of Martin Luther by Pope Leo X, 1520."*

[50] Calvin, John. *Commentary on Matthew, Mark, Luke - Volume 3.* 1509-1564. https://www.ccel.org/ccel/calvin/calcom33.txt.
[51] Calvin, John. *Institutes of the Christian Religion.* Vol. 1 of 2. Translated by John Allen. Sixth American Edition. Philadelphia: Presbyterian Board of Publication, 1813.
[52] Luther, Martin. *On Secular Authority,* 1523. In *Martin Luther: Selections from His Writings,* edited by John Dillenberger. Anchor Books, 1961.
[52] "The Cathars Christian Sect in France, for Example. Also the Waldenses, Arianism and Dozens of Other Sects Were Also Opposed and Oppressed by the Catholic Church in the Many Centuries Before the Reformation."
[54] Arman, Steve, Simon Bird, and Malcolm Wilkinson. *Reformation and Rebellion 1485-1750.* Heinemann, July 29, 2002.
[55] Brown, Gilbert Patten. "Some Rare Colonial History." In *The Christian Work and the Evangelist.* Vol. 79, New York Public Library, 1905, 310.
[56] Encyclopedia Britannica. "Inquisition." Last modified 2024. Accessed July 12, 2024. https://www.britannica.com/topic/inquisition.
[57] Adams, John, and Charles Francis Adams. *The Works of John Adams, Second President of the United States: With a Life of the Author, Notes and Illustrations.* Vol. 10. Boston: Little, Brown and Co., 1856. Chapter: "To F. A. Vanderkemp."
[58] Adams, John. *A Dissertation on the Canon and Feudal Law.* In *The Works of John Adams, Vol. 3: Autobiography, Diary, Notes of a Debate in the Senate, Essays.* Boston: Little, Brown and Co., 1851.
[59] Winsor, Justin, and Clarence F. Jewett. *The Memorial History of Boston: Including Suffolk County, Massachusetts, 1630-1880.* Vol. 1. Boston: Ticknor and Company, 1881. Chapter IV, p. 131.
[60] Winsor, Justin, and Clarence F. Jewett. The Memorial History of Boston: Including Suffolk County, Massachusetts, 1630-1880. Boston: Ticknor and Company, 1881.
[61] Locke, John. Second Treatise on Government. 1690. Chapter VIII, "Of the Beginning of Political Societies," Sect. 57. Published by The Internet Encyclopedia of Philosophy. Accessed July 12, 2024.
[62] Locke, John. Second Treatise on Government. 1690. Chapter VI, "Of Paternal Power," #57. Published by The Internet Encyclopedia of Philosophy. Accessed July 12, 2024.
[63] Locke, John. *A Letter Concerning Toleration.* 1689. Translated by William Popple. Published by The Internet Encyclopedia of Philosophy. Accessed July 12, 2024.
[64] Rousseau, Jean-Jacques. *The Social Contract.* 1762. Chapter 3, "Of the Right of the Strongest," "The Civil State." Published by The Internet Encyclopedia of Philosophy. Accessed July 12, 2024.
[65] Pope Pius VI. *Inscrutabile: On the Problems of the Pontificate.* Encyclical, December 25, 1775. In *The Papal Encyclicals Volume 2,* edited by Claudia Carlen. Catholic Church: Pierian Press, 1990. Published by Papal Encyclicals Online. Accessed July 12, 2024.
[66] Pope Gregory XVI. The Encyclical Letter of Pope Gregory XVI: Issued August 15, 1832. Published by the Vatican. Accessed July 12, 2024.
[67] Pope Leo XIII. *Immortale Dei: Encyclical on the Christian Constitution of States.* November 1, 1885. Published by the Vatican, Libreria Editrice Vaticana. Accessed July 12, 2024.
[68] Voltaire, Francois-Marie Arouet. *A Philosophical Dictionary.* 1764. Published by The Internet Encyclopedia of Philosophy. Accessed July 12, 2024.
[69] Edward Gibbon. *The History of the Decline and Fall of the Roman Empire.* Chapter 3c.
[70] "Who are the Uyghurs and why is China being accused of genocide?" *BBC.com.* May 24, 2022. https://www.bbc.com/news/world-asia-china-22278037.

[71] "The Uighurs and the Chinese state: A long history of discord." *BBC News.* July 20, 2020. Accessed September 4, 2020. https://www.bbc.com/news/world-asia-china-22278037.
[72] Gary Jennings, Junius Podrug, and Robert Gleason. *Aztec Series.* McMillan Publishers. https://us.macmillan.com/series/Aztec.
[73] Jean Delumeau. *Catholicism between Luther and Voltaire: A New View of the Counter-Reformation.* London: Burns & Oates, Westminster Press, 1977.
[74] Pope Leo XIII. "ENCYCLICAL OF POPE LEO XIII ON the Columbus Quadricentennial, July 16, 1892." *Vatican.va.* Accessed September 3, 2020. http://www.vatican.va/content/leo-xiii/en/encyclicals/documents/hf_l-xiii_enc_16071892_quarto-abeunte-saeculo.html.
[75] Wilson, Ruth Danenhower. "Justifications of Slavery, Past and Present." *The Phylon Quarterly,* Vol. 18, No. 4 (4th Qtr., 1957), pp. 407-412. Clark Atlanta University. Accessed July 13, 2020. https://www.jstor.org/stable/273281?read-now=1&seq=6#page_scan_tab_contents.
[76] "Empire in the Americas, Portuguese." *Encyclopedia.com.* Accessed July 8, 2020. https://www.encyclopedia.com/history/encyclopedias-almanacs-transcripts-and-maps/empire-americas-portuguese.
[77] MacKechnie, Johan. "Justifying Slavery: The changing shape of the slave trade in the medieval Mediterranean." *History Today.* April 20, 2017. Accessed July 8, 2020. https://www.historytoday.com/justifying-slavery.
[78] Gates Jr., Henry Louis. "Slavery, by the Numbers." *The Root.* February 10, 2014. Accessed July 12, 2020. https://www.theroot.com/slavery-by-the-numbers-1790874492.
[79] History.com Editors. "Congress abolishes the African slave trade." *History.com.* A&E Television Networks. Last updated February 28, 2020. Originally published February 9, 2010. Accessed July 12, 2020. https://www.history.com/this-day-in-history/congress-abolishes-the-african-slave-trade.
[80] Adams, John. "From John Adams to William Tudor, Jr., 20 November 1819."
[81] "Popular Election of the First Branch of the Legislature, [6 June] 1787." *Founders Online,* National Archives. Accessed April 11, 2019. https://founders.archives.gov/documents/Madison/01-10-02-0021. [Original source: *The Papers of James Madison,* vol. 10, 27 May 1787–3 March 1788, ed. Robert A. Rutland, Charles F. Hobson, William M. E. Rachal, and Frederika J. Teute. Chicago: The University of Chicago Press, 1977, pp. 32–34.]
[82] History.com Editors. "John Jay." *History.com.* Updated March 22, 2022. Originally published January 28, 2010. https://www.history.com/topics/us-government/john-jay.
[83] "Roger Sherman was a lawyer in Connecticut who was a delegate to the Constitutional Convention and later a member of the U.S. House."
[84] "Robert Livingston was a lawyer who became the first chancellor of New York."
[85] Carl Lotus Becker. *The Declaration of Independence: A Study on the History of Political Ideas.* New York: Harcourt, Brace and Co., 1922. Chapter: "THE ROUGH DRAFT as it probably read when Jefferson made the 'fair copy' which was presented to Congress as the report of the Committee of Five."
[86] Adams, John. *The Works of John Adams, Second President of the United States: With a Life of the Author, Notes and Illustrations.* Vol. 2. Edited by Charles Francis Adams. Boston: Little, Brown and Co., 1856. Chapter: "AUTOBIOGRAPHY."
[87] Franklin, Benjamin. "Address to the Public." *Benjamin Franklin, President of the Pennsylvania Society in Philadelphia, 9th of November, 1789.* http://www.pbs.org/benfranklin/pop_address.html.

[88] Washington, George. *The Writings of George Washington.* Collected and edited by Worthington Chauncey Ford. Vol. XI (1785-1790). New York and London: G. P. Putnam's Sons, 1890. Chapter: "TO THE MARQUIS DE LAFAYETTE."
[89] Washington, George. "From George Washington to Lawrence Lewis, 4 August 1797." *Founders Online*, National Archives. Accessed April 11, 2019. https://founders.archives.gov/documents/Washington/06-01-02-0245. [Original source: *The Papers of George Washington, Retirement Series*, vol. 1, 4 March 1797 – 30 December 1797, ed. W. W. Abbot. Charlottesville: University Press of Virginia, 1998, pp. 288–289.]
[90] Washington, George. *The Writings of George Washington: Being His Correspondence, Addresses, Messages, and Other Papers, Official and Private.* Vol. IX. Boston: American Stationer's Company, John B. Russell, 1835. Private letters.
[91] Adams, John. "From John Adams to Joseph Ward, 8 January 1810." Founders Online, National Archives, accessed April 11, 2019, https://founders.archives.gov/documents/Adams/99-02-02-5495.
[92] Adams, John. "From John Adams to Robert J. Evans, 8 June 1819." Founders Online, National Archives, https://founders.archives.gov/documents/Adams/99-02-02-7148. [This is an Early Access document from The Adams Papers. It is not an authoritative final version.]
[93] "Epicurus was a Greek philosopher."
[94] Adams, John. "From John Adams to George Churchman, 24 January 1801." Founders Online, National Archives, accessed April 11, 2019, https://founders.archives.gov/documents/Adams/99-02-02-4766.
[95] Jefferson, Thomas. *The Works of Thomas Jefferson, Federal Edition.* New York and London: G.P. Putnam's Sons, 1904-5. Vol. 1. Chapter: "Autobiography 1743–1790."
[96] "Speech in Virginia Convention, 2 December 1829." Founders Online, National Archives, accessed April 11, 2019, https://founders.archives.gov/documents/Madison/99-02-02-1924. [This is an Early Access document from The Papers of James Madison. It is not an authoritative final version.]
[97] "A Full Vindication of the Measures of the Congress, &c., [15 December] 1774." Founders Online, National Archives, accessed April 11, 2019, https://founders.archives.gov/documents/Hamilton/01-01-02-0054. [Original source: The Papers of Alexander Hamilton, vol. 1, 1768–1778, ed. Harold C. Syrett. New York: Columbia University Press, 1961, pp. 45–78.]
[98] "Memorial to Abolish the Slave Trade, 13 March 1786." Founders Online, National Archives, accessed April 11, 2019, https://founders.archives.gov/documents/Hamilton/01-03-02-0503. [Original source: The Papers of Alexander Hamilton, vol. 3, 1782–1786, ed. Harold C. Syrett. New York: Columbia University Press, 1962, pp. 654–655.]
[99] Madison, James. *The Debates on the Adoption of the Federal Constitution in the Convention Held at Philadelphia in 1787, with a Diary of the Debates of the Congress of the Confederation as Reported by James Madison, Revised and Newly Arranged by Jonathan Elliot. Complete in One Volume.* Vol. V. Supplement to Elliot's Debates. Philadelphia, 1836. Chapter: "Debates in the Federal Convention of 1787."
[100] "The Federalist Number 54, [12 February] 1788," Founders Online, National Archives, https://founders.archives.gov/documents/Madison/01-10-02-0291. [Original source: The Papers of James Madison, vol. 10, 27 May 1787–3 March 1788, ed. Robert A. Rutland, Charles F. Hobson, William M. E. Rachal, and Frederika J. Teute. Chicago: The University of Chicago Press, 1977, pp. 499–503.]
[101] "Constitution What the Constitution Really Says About Race and Slavery", The Heritage Foundation, December 28, 2015, accessed July 12, 2022, https://www.heritage.org/the-constitution/commentary/what-the-constitution-really-says-about-race-and-slavery.

[102] "Edward Coles to Thomas Jefferson, 31 July 1814," Founders Online, National Archives, accessed April 11, 2019, https://founders.archives.gov/documents/Jefferson/03-07-02-0374. [Original source: The Papers of Thomas Jefferson, Retirement Series, vol. 7, 28 November 1813 to 30 September 1814, ed. J. Jefferson Looney. Princeton: Princeton University Press, 2010, pp. 503–504.]
[103] "Thomas Jefferson to Edward Coles, 25 August 1814," Founders Online, National Archives, accessed April 11, 2019, https://founders.archives.gov/documents/Jefferson/03-07-02-0439. [Original source: The Papers of Thomas Jefferson, Retirement Series, vol. 7, 28 November 1813 to 30 September 1814, ed. J. Jefferson Looney. Princeton: Princeton University Press, 2010, pp. 603–605.]
[104] Gladstone, Rick. "Modern Slavery Estimated to Trap 45 Million People Worldwide." *The New York Times*, May 31, 2016. https://www.nytimes.com/2016/06/01/world/asia/global-slavery-index.html.
[105] Jefferson, Thomas. *The Works of Thomas Jefferson, Federal Edition.* New York and London: G.P. Putnam's Sons, 1904-5. Vol. 4. Chapter: "Query XVII The Different Religions Received into That State?"
[106] Madison, James. *The Writings of James Madison, Comprising His Public Papers and His Private Correspondence, Including His Numerous Letters and Documents Now for the First Time Printed,* ed. Gaillard Hunt. New York: G.P. Putnam's Sons, 1900. Vol. 1. Chapter: "1774 - To William Bradford, Jr."
[107] Adams, John. *The Works of John Adams, Second President of the United States: With a Life of the Author, Notes and Illustrations, by His Grandson Charles Francis Adams.* Boston: Little, Brown and Co., 1856. 10 vols. Vol. 1. Chapter: "Education of Mr. Adams—School at Worcester—Choice of a Profession."
[108] Adams, John. "John Adams to H. Niles, February 13, 1818." In *The Works of John Adams,* Vol. 10, Letters 1811-1825, Indexes. Boston: Little, Brown and Co., 1856.
[109] *United States Constitution,* 14th Amendment. Accessed February 2, 2011. http://www.archives.gov/exhibits/charters/constitution_amendments_11-27.html.
[110] Adams, John. *The Works of John Adams, Second President of the United States: With a Life of the Author, Notes and Illustrations, by His Grandson Charles Francis Adams.* Boston: Little, Brown and Co., 1856. 10 vols. Vol. 10. Chapter: "To Thomas Jefferson."
[111] Adams, John. *The Works of John Adams, Second President of the United States: With a Life of the Author, Notes and Illustrations, by His Grandson Charles Francis Adams.* Boston: Little, Brown and Co., 1856. 10 vols. Vol. 10. Chapter: "To Thomas Jefferson."
[112] Washington, George. *The Writings of George Washington: Volume 3.* New York: G.P. Putnam's Sons, 1889. Pg. 126.
[113] Wirt, William. *Sketches of the Life and Character of Patrick Henry.* Ithaca, NY: Andrus, Gauntlett, & Co., 1850.
[114] Jefferson, Thomas. *The Works of Thomas Jefferson, Federal Edition.* New York and London: G.P. Putnam's Sons, 1904-5. Vol. 6. Chapter: "To Archibald Stuart."
[115] Paine, Thomas. *The Writings of Thomas Paine, Vol. 3.* New York: G.P. Putnam's Sons, 1895. Pg. 277. Dissertation on First Principles of Government.
[116] Monticello.org. "Research and Collections. The Thomas Jefferson Papers Series 1. General Correspondence. 1651-1827, Thomas Jefferson to Isaac H. Tiffany, April 4, 1819." Accessed April 11, 2019. http://hdl.loc.gov/loc.mss/mtj.mtjbib023463. Original located on the Library of Congress American Memory digital archive.
[117] Washington, George. "From George Washington to John Armstrong, 11 March 1792." *Founders Online*, National Archives. Accessed April 11, 2019. https://founders.archives.gov/documents/Washington/05-10-02-0044. [Original source: *The Papers of George Washington, Presidential Series,* vol. 10, 1 March 1792–15

August 1792, ed. Robert F. Haggard and Mark A. Mastromarino. Charlottesville: University of Virginia Press, 2002, pp. 85–87.]

[118] Washington, George. "From George Washington to the Grand Lodge of Pennsylvania, 3 January 1792." *Founders Online*, National Archives. Accessed April 11, 2019. https://founders.archives.gov/documents/Washington/05-09-02-0230. [Original source: *The Papers of George Washington, Presidential Series*, vol. 9, 23 September 1791–29 February 1792, ed. Mark A. Mastromarino. Charlottesville: University Press of Virginia, 2000, p. 371.]

[119] Washington, George. "From George Washington to the Savannah, Ga., Hebrew Congregation, 14 June 1790." *Founders Online*, National Archives. Accessed April 11, 2019. https://founders.archives.gov/documents/Washington/05-05-02-0279. [Original source: *The Papers of George Washington, Presidential Series*, vol. 5, 16 January 1790–30 June 1790, ed. Dorothy Twohig, Mark A. Mastromarino, and Jack D. Warren. Charlottesville: University Press of Virginia, 1996, pp. 448–450.]

[120] Freemasonry. "Porchway Lodge No 7027." Viewed June 13, 2022. https://porchwaylodge7027.co.uk/masonic-glossary-of-terms/.

[121] Britannica. "Freemasonry." Accessed June 13, 2022. https://www.britannica.com/topic/Freemasonry.

[122] *Washington, George. The Writings of George Washington. Washington, D.C., 1932. Vol. XV, p. 55.*

[123] Washington, George. "From George Washington to Lafayette, 15 August 1787." *Founders Online*, National Archives. Accessed April 11, 2019. https://founders.archives.gov/documents/Washington/04-05-02-0270. [Original source: *The Papers of George Washington, Confederation Series*, vol. 5, 1 February 1787–31 December 1787, ed. W. W. Abbot. Charlottesville: University Press of Virginia, 1997, pp. 294–297.]

[124] Jefferson, Thomas. "Notes on a Conversation with Benjamin Rush, 1 February 1800." *Founders Online*, National Archives. Accessed April 11, 2019. https://founders.archives.gov/documents/Jefferson/01-31-02-0299. [Original source: *The Papers of Thomas Jefferson*, vol. 31, 1 February 1799–31 May 1800, ed. Barbara B. Oberg. Princeton: Princeton University Press, 2004, pp. 352–353.]

[125] Franklin, Benjamin. *Autobiography of Benjamin Franklin.* Harvard University, 1895. Pg. 108.

[126] Franklin, Benjamin. "From Benjamin Franklin to Jane Mecom, 28 July 1743." *Founders Online*, National Archives. Accessed April 11, 2019. https://founders.archives.gov/documents/Franklin/01-02-02-0095. [Original source: *The Papers of Benjamin Franklin*, vol. 2, January 1, 1735, through December 31, 1744, ed. Leonard W. Labaree. New Haven: Yale University Press, 1961, pp. 384–385.]

[127] Franklin, Benjamin. *Memoirs of the Life and Writings of Benjamin Franklin.* Vol. 6. Published by T.S. Manning, 1817.

[128]Adams, John. "John Adams to Samuel Miller." In *The Works of John Adams*, vol. 10, Letters 1811-1825. Boston: Little, Brown and Co., 1854.

[129] Adams, John. "From John Adams to Hannah Adams, 16 March 1804." *Founders Online*, National Archives. Accessed April 11, 2019. https://founders.archives.gov/documents/Adams/99-03-02-1248. [This is an Early Access document from The Adams Papers. It is not an authoritative final version.]

[130] Adams, John. The Works of John Adams, Second President of the United States: with a Life of the Author, Notes and Illustrations, by his Grandson Charles Francis Adams (Boston: Little, Brown and Co., 1856). 10 volumes. Vol. 10. Chapter: To Thomas Jefferson

[131] Adams, John. *The Works of John Adams, Second President of the United States: with a Life of the Author, Notes and Illustrations, by his Grandson Charles Francis Adams* (Boston: Little, Brown and Co., 1856). 10 volumes. Vol. 10. Chapter: To Thomas Jefferson.
[132] Adams, John. *The Works of John Adams, Second President of the United States: with a Life of the Author, Notes and Illustrations, by his Grandson Charles Francis Adams* (Boston: Little, Brown and Co., 1856). 10 volumes. Vol. 10. Chapter: To Thomas Jefferson.
[133] Adams, John. *The Works of John Adams, Second President of the United States: with a Life of the Author, Notes and Illustrations, by his Grandson Charles Francis Adams* (Boston: Little, Brown and Co., 1856). 10 volumes. Vol. 6. Chapter: Letters to John Taylor, of Caroline, Virginia, in Reply to His Strictures on some parts of the defence of the American Constitutions.
[134] Adams, John. "From John Adams to Thomas Jefferson, 16 July 1814." *Founders Online*, National Archives. Accessed April 11, 2019. https://founders.archives.gov/documents/Adams/99-02-02-6321. [This is an Early Access document from The Adams Papers. It is not an authoritative final version.]
[135]

https://founders.archives.gov/?q=universe%20Author%3A%22Madison%2C%20James%22&s=1111311113&r=4&sr=
[136] Irelan, John Robert. *History of the Life, Administration and Times of James Madison, Fourth President of the United States: Struggle for Constitutional Government and Second War with England.* Fairbanks & Palmer, 1886. Pg. 529.
[137] Madison, James. "From James Madison to William Bradford, 25 September 1773." *Founders Online*, National Archives. Accessed April 11, 2019. https://founders.archives.gov/documents/Madison/01-01-02-0025. [Original source: *The Papers of James Madison*, vol. 1, 16 March 1751–16 December 1779, ed. William T. Hutchinson and William M. E. Rachal. Chicago: The University of Chicago Press, 1962, pp. 95–97.]
[138] Adams, John. "From John Adams to Benjamin Rush, 4 September 1812." *Founders Online*, National Archives. Accessed April 11, 2019. https://founders.archives.gov/documents/Adams/99-02-02-5863. [This is an Early Access document from The Adams Papers. It is not an authoritative final version.]
[139] Jefferson, Thomas. *The Works of Thomas Jefferson, Federal Edition.* New York and London: G.P. Putnam's Sons, 1904-5. Vol. 9. Chapter: "Syllabus of an Estimate of the Merit of the Doctrines of Jesus, Compared with Those of Others."
[140] Jefferson, Thomas. "Thomas Jefferson to John Adams, 5 May 1817." *Founders Online*, National Archives. Accessed April 11, 2019. https://founders.archives.gov/documents/Jefferson/03-11-02-0271. [Original source: *The Papers of Thomas Jefferson, Retirement Series*, vol. 11, 19 January to 31 August 1817, ed. J. Jefferson Looney. Princeton: Princeton University Press, 2014, pp. 311–313.]
[141] Jefferson, Thomas. "Thomas Jefferson to Margaret Bayard Smith, 6 August 1816." *Founders Online*, National Archives. Accessed April 11, 2019. https://founders.archives.gov/documents/Jefferson/03-10-02-0186. [Original source: *The Papers of Thomas Jefferson, Retirement Series*, vol. 10, May 1816 to 18 January 1817, ed. J. Jefferson Looney. Princeton: Princeton University Press, 2013, pp. 300–301.]
[142] Jefferson, Thomas. *Memoirs, Correspondence and Private Papers of Thomas Jefferson, Late President of the United States, Volume 4.* London: Colburn and Bentley, 1829. Pg. 249.
[143] Jefferson, Thomas. "From Thomas Jefferson to John Adams, 11 April 1823." *Founders Online*, National Archives. Accessed April 11, 2019. https://founders.archives.gov/documents/Jefferson/98-01-02-3446. [This is an Early

Access document from *The Papers of Thomas Jefferson: Retirement Series.* It is not an authoritative final version.]

[144] Jefferson, Thomas. *The Writings of Thomas Jefferson: Volumes 13-14.* Edited by Albert Ellery Bergh. Washington, D.C.: Thomas Jefferson Memorial Association of the United States, 1907. Pg. 71-72.

[145] Jefferson, Thomas. *The Writings of Thomas Jefferson: Volume 9.* Edited by Albert Ellery Bergh. Washington, D.C.: Thomas Jefferson Memorial Association of the United States, 1907. Pg. 237.

[146] Jefferson, Thomas. *Memoirs, Correspondence and Private Papers of Thomas Jefferson, Late President of the United States, Volume 4.* London: Colburn and Bentley, 1829. Pg. 141.

[147] See the Jefferson Bible on the Smithsonian web site here: http://americanhistory.si.edu/jeffersonbible

[148] Jefferson, Thomas. "The Papers of Thomas Jefferson Vol. 15, March to 7 October, 1788." Edited by Julian Parks Boyd, Lyman Henry Butterfield, Charles T. Cullen, John Catanzariti, Barbara Oberg. Princeton: Princeton University Press, 2008.

[149] Jefferson, Thomas. *The Works of Thomas Jefferson, Federal Edition.* New York and London: G.P. Putnam's Sons, 1904-5. Vol. 11. Chapter: "To Charles Thomson."

[150] Jefferson, Thomas. *The Works of Thomas Jefferson, Federal Edition.* New York and London: G.P. Putnam's Sons, 1904-5. Vol. 11. Chapter: "To Charles Thomson."

[151] America's Founding Fathers, Delegates to the Constitutional convention, Alexander Hamilton, New York, Archives.gov

[152] Hamilton, Alexander. "Letter to Theodore Sedgwick, May 10, 1800." In *The Works of Alexander Hamilton,* edited by Henry Cabot Lodge. Federal Edition. New York: G.P. Putnam's Sons, 1904. Vol. 10.

[153] Hamilton, Alexander. *The Revolutionary Writings of Alexander Hamilton,* Vol. XV, p. 117.

[154] Hamilton, Alexander. *The Works of Alexander Hamilton,* edited by Henry Cabot Lodge. Federal Edition. New York: G.P. Putnam's Sons, 1904. Vol. 6. Chapter: "The War in Europe."

[155] Jefferson, Thomas. *The Writings of Thomas Jefferson,* published by order of the Joint Committee of Congress on the Library. Washington, D.C.: Taylor & Maury, 1854.

[156] Mintz, Steven (INT) and Joy Hakim. *A History of US: Sourcebook and Index.* Oxford University Press, February 11, 2007. Pg. 92-93.

[157] Washington, George. "From George Washington to William White, 3 March 1797." *Founders Online,* National Archives. Accessed April 11, 2019. https://founders.archives.gov/documents/Washington/99-01-02-00390. [This is an Early Access document from *The Papers of George Washington.* It is not an authoritative final version.]

[158] Washington, George. *George Washington: A Collection,* compiled and edited by W.B. Allen. Indianapolis: Liberty Fund, 1988. Chap. 182, "To The Annual Meeting of Quakers."

[159] Washington, George. *The Writings of George Washington: Pt. V. Speeches and Messages to Congress, Proclamations and Addresses,* edited by Jared Sparks. Harper & Brothers, 1848, p. 155.

[160] Madison, James. *The Writings of James Madison,* edited by Gaillard Hunt, Library of Congress. Accessed February 21, 2011. http://memory.loc.gov/cgi-bin/query/r?ammem/mjmtext:@field(DOCID+@lit(jm090033)).

[161] *The American Enlightenment: The Shaping of the American Experiment and a Free Society.* New York: George Braziller, 1965, p. 93.

[162] Jefferson, Thomas. *Thomas Jefferson Papers Series 1, General Correspondence*, Library of Congress. Accessed February 21, 2011. http://hdl.loc.gov/loc.mss/mtj.mtjbib019322.
[163] Hamilton, Alexander. The Works of Alexander Hamilton, ed. Henry Cabot Lodge (Federal Edition) (New York: G.P. Putnam's Sons, 1904). In 12 vols. Vol. 4. Chapter: letter ii 1
[164]Jefferson, Thomas. *The Jeffersonian Cyclopedia: A Comprehensive Collection of the Views of Thomas Jefferson Classified and Arranged in Alphabetical Order Under Nine Thousand Titles Relating to Government, Politics, Law, Education, Political Economy, Finance, Science, Art, Literature, Religious Freedom, Morals, Etc.* Funk & Wagnalls Company, 1900, p. 559. Letter to Dr. Benjamin Rush, IV, 336. Ford Ed, VII, 460.
[165] Jefferson, Thomas. "V. To the Danbury Baptist Association, 1 January 1802." *Founders Online*, National Archives, accessed April 11, 2019. https://founders.archives.gov/documents/Jefferson/01-36-02-0152-0006. In *The Papers of Thomas Jefferson*, vol. 36, 1 December 1801–3 March 1802, edited by Barbara B. Oberg. Princeton: Princeton University Press, 2009, p. 258.
[166] Jefferson, Thomas. "I. Draft Reply to the Danbury Baptist Association, [on or before 31 December 1801]." *Founders Online*, National Archives, accessed April 11, 2019. https://founders.archives.gov/documents/Jefferson/01-36-02-0152-0002. In *The Papers of Thomas Jefferson*, vol. 36, 1 December 1801–3 March 1802, edited by Barbara B. Oberg. Princeton: Princeton University Press, 2009, pp. 254–256.
[167] Madison, James. "Presidential Proclamation, 4 March 1815." *Founders Online*, National Archives. https://founders.archives.gov/documents/Madison/03-09-02-0066. In *The Papers of James Madison, Presidential Series*, vol. 9, 19 February 1815–12 October 1815, edited by Angela Kreider et al. Charlottesville: University of Virginia Press, 2018, pp. 56–57.
[168] Madison, James. "Detatched Memoranda, ca. 31 January 1820." *Founders Online*, National Archives, accessed April 11, 2019. https://founders.archives.gov/documents/Madison/04-01-02-0549. In *The Papers of James Madison, Retirement Series*, vol. 1, 4 March 1817 – 31 January 1820, edited by David B. Mattern et al. Charlottesville: University of Virginia Press, 2009, pp. 600–627.
[169] Madison, James. "James Madison to Jasper Adams, September 1833." *Founders Online*, National Archives. https://founders.archives.gov/documents/Madison/99-02-02-2830. This is an Early Access document from *The Papers of James Madison.* It is not an authoritative final version.
[170] Adams, John. *The Works of John Adams*, vol. 4, *Novanglus, Thoughts on Government, Defence of the Constitution*, 1851. Accessed September 4, 2019. https://oll.libertyfund.org/titles/2102#Adams_1431-04_827.
[171] Yale Law School, The Avalon Project, Lillian Goldman Law Library, 2008. http://avalon.law.yale.edu/18th_century/bar1796t.asp.
[172] Madison, James. "From James Madison to William Bradford, 24 January 1774," posted on Founders.Archives.gov, accessed April 11, 2019, https://founders.archives.gov/documents/Madison/01-01-02-0029.
[173] Madison, James. "Memorial and Remonstrance against Religious Assessments, [ca. 20 June] 1785," Founders Online, National Archives, accessed April 11, 2019, https://founders.archives.gov/documents/Madison/01-08-02-0163. In *The Papers of James Madison*, edited by Robert A. Rutland and William M. E. Rachal, vol. 8, 10 March 1784 – 28 March 1786. Chicago: The University of Chicago Press, 1973, pp. 295-306.
[174] Library of Congress. Accessed February 21, 2011. http://www.loc.gov/exhibits/jefferson/images/vc66.jpg.
[175] Jefferson, Thomas. "Autobiography, 6 Jan.-29 July 1821," January 6, 1821. Founders Online, National Archives. Accessed April 11,

2019. https://founders.archives.gov/documents/Jefferson/98-01-02-1756. (This is an Early Access document from The Papers of Thomas Jefferson: Retirement Series. It is not an authoritative final version.)

[176] Madison, James. *The Writings of James Madison, comprising his Public Papers and his Private Correspondence, including his numerous letters and documents now for the first time printed,* ed. Gaillard Hunt (New York: G.P. Putnam's Sons, 1900). Vol. 9. Chapter: *To Edward Everett. mad. mss*

[177] U.S. Department of the Treasury. "About: History of 'In God We Trust'." Treasury.gov. Accessed July 19, 2012.

[178] Patterson, Richard S. and Richardson Dougall. *The Eagle and the Shield: A History of the Great Seal of the United States.* 1976. Office of the Historian, Bureau of Public Affairs, Department of State. Accessed February 21, 2011. http://www.greatseal.com/index.html.

[179] Boston, Rob. "Bible Riots." *Liberty Magazine*, May/June 1997. Accessed September 16, 2022. https://www.libertymagazine.org/article/bible-riots.

[180] Bellamy, Francis. "The Story of the Pledge of Allegiance to the Flag", *University of Rochester Library Bulletin,* Vol. VIII, Winter 1953.

[181] Federer, William J. *America's God and Country: Encyclopedia of Quotations.* 2000.

[182] Jefferson, Thomas. "SAXONS, CONSTITUTIONS, AND A CASE OF PIOUS FRAUD, To Major John Cartwright Monticello, June 5, 1824." In *Letters,* Electronic Text Center, University of Virginia Library. Accessed [date accessed]. Jefferson, Thomas, 1743-1826.

[183] Jefferson, Thomas. "CHRISTIANITY AND THE COMMON LAW, To Dr. Thomas Cooper from Thomas Jefferson, Monticello, February 10, 1814." In *Letters,* Electronic Text Center, University of Virginia Library. Accessed [date accessed]. Jefferson, Thomas, 1743-1826.

[184] "From James Madison to Thomas Jefferson, 17 October 1788." Founders Online, National Archives, accessed April 11, 2019, https://founders.archives.gov/documents/Madison/01-11-02-0218. [Original source: The Papers of James Madison, vol. 11, 7 March 1788–1 March 1789, ed. Robert A. Rutland and Charles F. Hobson. Charlottesville: University Press of Virginia, 1977, pp. 295–300.]

[185] "From Thomas Jefferson to John Jay, 25 January 1786," Founders Online, National Archives, accessed April 11, 2019, https://founders.archives.gov/documents/Jefferson/01-09-02-0190. [Original source: The Papers of Thomas Jefferson, vol. 9, 1 November 1785 – 22 June 1786, ed. Julian P. Boyd. Princeton: Princeton University Press, 1954, p. 215.]

[186] "Thomas Jefferson to Peter H. Wendover (Draft), 13 March 1815," Founders Online, National Archives, accessed April 11, 2019, https://founders.archives.gov/documents/Jefferson/03-08-02-0270-0002. [Original source: The Papers of Thomas Jefferson, Retirement Series, vol. 8, 1 October 1814 to 31 August 1815, ed. J. Jefferson Looney. Princeton: Princeton University Press, 2011, pp. 340–343.]

[187] "Silence Dogood, No. 8, 9 July 1722," Founders Online, National Archives, accessed April 11, 2019, https://founders.archives.gov/documents/Franklin/01-01-02-0015. [Original source: The Papers of Benjamin Franklin, vol. 1, January 6, 1706 through December 31, 1734, ed. Leonard W. Labaree. New Haven: Yale University Press, 1959, pp. 27–30.]

[188] "From George Washington to Officers of the Army, 15 March 1783," Founders Online, National Archives, accessed April 11, 2019, https://founders.archives.gov/documents/Washington/99-01-02-10840. [This is an Early Access document from The Papers of George Washington. It is not an authoritative final version.]

[189] Habeas Corpus: law a writ ordering a person to be brought before a court or judge, esp. so that the court may ascertain whether his detention is lawful. *Habeas Corpus*: "Habeas

Corpus." *Dictionary.com.* Collins English Dictionary - Complete & Unabridged 10th Edition. HarperCollins Publishers, 2009.

[190] Jefferson, Thomas. The Papers of Thomas Jefferson, Volume 33: 17 February to 30 April 1801
(Princeton University Press, 2006), 148-52; Originally printed in the National Intelligencer, 4 March 1801

[191] https://www.archives.gov/founding-docs/declaration/

[192] "V. "A Dissertation on the Canon and the Feudal Law," No. 3, 30 September 1765," Founders Online, National Archives, accessed April 11, 2019, https://founders.archives.gov/documents/Adams/06-01-02-0052-0006. [Original source: The Adams Papers, Papers of John Adams, vol. 1, September 1755 – October 1773, ed. Robert J. Taylor. Cambridge, MA: Harvard University Press, 1977, pp. 118–123.]

[193] Adams, John. The Works of John Adams, Second President of the United States: with a Life of the Author, Notes and Illustrations, by his Grandson Charles Francis Adams (Boston: Little, Brown and Co., 1856). 10 volumes. Vol. 10. Chapter: To Thomas Jefferson

[194] Vazquez, Maegan. "NY Gov. Andrew Cuomo says America was never great." *CNN*, August 16, 2018. Accessed May 8, 2020. https://www.cnn.com/2018/08/15/politics/andrew-cuomo-america-was-never-that-great/index.html.

[195] D'Souza, Dinesh. "What's Great About America?" Report Political Process, The Heritage Foundation, February 23, 2006. Accessed July 20, 2022. https://www.heritage.org/political-process/report/whats-great-about-america.

[196] Podhoretz, Norman. "Is America Exceptional?" *Imprimis*, October 2012, vol. 41, no. 10. Accessed July 19, 2022. https://imprimis.hillsdale.edu/is-america-exceptional/.

[197] Rand, Ayn. "The Monument Builders." 1962. In *The Virtue of Selfishness: A New Concept of Egoism*, edited by Nathaniel Braden, Penguin, 1964.

[198] Reuters. "'My rights were never read': Griner testifies in Russia." July 27, 2022. Accessed August 3, 2022. https://news.yahoo.com/rights-were-never-read-griner-172328049.html.

[199] "From Thomas Jefferson to James Monroe, 17 June 1785," Founders Online, National Archives, accessed April 11, 2019, https://founders.archives.gov/documents/Jefferson/01-08-02-0174. [Original source: The Papers of Thomas Jefferson, vol. 8, 25 February–31 October 1785, ed. Julian P. Boyd. Princeton: Princeton University Press, 1953, pp. 227–234.]

[200] Washington, George. The Writings of George Washington, collected and edited by Worthington Chauncey Ford (New York and London: G. P. Putnam's Sons, 1890). Vol. XII (1790-1794). Chapter: TO DAVID HUMPHREYS.

[201] Speech by the Rev. Martin Luther King at the "March on Washington", 1963; https://www.archives.gov/files/press/exhibits/dream-speech.pdf

[202] "For the National Gazette, 18 January 1792," Founders Online, National Archives, accessed April 11, 2019, https://founders.archives.gov/documents/Madison/01-14-02-0172. [Original source: The Papers of James Madison, vol. 14, 6 April 1791 – 16 March 1793, ed. Robert A. Rutland and Thomas A. Mason. Charlottesville: University Press of Virginia, 1983, pp. 191–192.]

[203] "VII. An Essay on Man's Lust for Power, with the Author's Comment in 1807," Founders Online, National Archives, accessed April 11, 2019, https://founders.archives.gov/documents/Adams/06-01-02-0045-0008. [Original source: The Adams Papers, Papers of John Adams, vol. 1, September 1755 – October 1773, ed. Robert J. Taylor. Cambridge, MA: Harvard University Press, 1977, pp. 81–84.]

[204] "From Thomas Jefferson to C. Hammond, 18 August 1821," Founders Online, National Archives, https://founders.archives.gov/documents/Jefferson/98-01-02-2260. [This is an Early Access document from The Papers of Thomas Jefferson: Retirement Series. It is not an authoritative final version.]

[205] "The Federalist No. 62, [27 February 1788]," Founders Online, National Archives, accessed April 11, 2019, https://founders.archives.gov/documents/Hamilton/01-04-02-0212. [Original source: The Papers of Alexander Hamilton, vol. 4, January 1787 – May 1788, ed. Harold C. Syrett. New York: Columbia University Press, 1962, pp. 555–561.]
[206] Hitler, Adolf. "Speech of April 12, 1922." Quoted in Hitler: Speeches and Proclamations 1932–1945: The Chronicle of a Dictatorship by Max Domarus. Nationalist.org. Accessed July 15, 2022.
[207] "New York Ratifying Convention. First Speech of June 21 (Francis Childs's Version), [21 June 1788]," Founders Online, National Archives, accessed April 11, 2019, https://founders.archives.gov/documents/Hamilton/01-05-02-0012-0011. [Original source: The Papers of Alexander Hamilton, vol. 5, June 1788 – November 1789, ed. Harold C. Syrett. New York: Columbia University Press, 1962, pp. 36–45.]
[208] "The Federalist Number 10, [22 November] 1787," Founders Online, National Archives, version of January 18, 2019, https://founders.archives.gov/documents/Madison/01-10-02-0178. [Original source: The Papers of James Madison, vol. 10, 27 May 1787–3 March 1788, ed. Robert A. Rutland, Charles F. Hobson, William M. E. Rachal, and Frederika J. Teute. Chicago: The University of Chicago Press, 1977, pp. 263–270.]
[209] "From James Madison to James Monroe, 5 October 1786," Founders Online, National Archives, accessed April 11, 2019, https://founders.archives.gov/documents/Madison/01-09-02-0054. [Original source: The Papers of James Madison, vol. 9, 9 April 1786 – 24 May 1787 and supplement 1781 – 1784, ed. Robert A. Rutland and William M. E. Rachal. Chicago: The University of Chicago Press, 1975, pp. 140–142.]
[210] "Speech in Virginia Convention, 2 December 1829," Founders Online, National Archives, accessed April 11, 2019, https://founders.archives.gov/documents/Madison/99-02-02-1924. [This is an Early Access document from The Papers of James Madison. It is not an authoritative final version.]
[211] "From George Washington to Patrick Henry, 9 October 1795," Founders Online, National Archives, https://founders.archives.gov/documents/Washington/05-19-02-0024. [Original source: The Papers of George Washington, Presidential Series, vol. 19, 1 October 1795-31 March 1796, ed. David R. Hoth. Charlottesville: University of Virginia Press, 2016, pp. 36–37.]
[212] Jefferson, Thomas. The Works of Thomas Jefferson, Federal Edition (New York and London, G.P. Putnam's Sons, 1904-5). Vol. 11. Chapter: To John Taylor
[213] Marshall, John. The Life of George Washington. Special Edition for Schools, ed. Robert Faulkner and Paul Carrese (Indianapolis: Liberty Fund, 2000). Chapter: V.: Farewell Address
[214] Jefferson, Thomas. The Works of Thomas Jefferson, Federal Edition (New York and London, G.P. Putnam's Sons, 1904-5). Vol. 9.
[215] "Proposals to Revise the Virginia Constitution: I. Thomas Jefferson to "Henry Tompkinson" (Samuel Kercheval), 12 July 1816," Founders Online, National Archives, https://founders.archives.gov/documents/Jefferson/03-10-02-0128-0002. [Original source: The Papers of Thomas Jefferson, Retirement Series, vol. 10, May 1816 to 18 January 1817, ed. J. Jefferson Looney. Princeton: Princeton University Press, 2013, pp. 222–228.]
[216] James Madison to United States House of Representatives, 3 March 1817, founders.archives.gov; https://founders.archives.gov/?q=%22insuperable%20difficulty%22%20Author%3A%22Madison%2C%20James%22&s=1111311113&sa=&r=4&sr=
[217] Hamilton, Alexander. Report of the Secretary of the Treasury to the United States on the subject of Manufactures presented to the House of Representatives, December 5, 1791.

http://ap.gilderlehrman.org/resource/hamilton%27s-report-subject-manufactures-1791?period=3
[218] "From Thomas Jefferson to George Washington, 23 May 1792," Founders Online, National Archives, accessed April 11, 2019, https://founders.archives.gov/documents/Jefferson/01-23-02-0491. [Original source: The Papers of Thomas Jefferson, vol. 23, 1 January–31 May 1792, ed. Charles T. Cullen. Princeton: Princeton University Press, 1990, pp. 535–541.]
[219] "From Thomas Jefferson to William Johnson, 12 June 1823," Founders Online, National Archives, accessed April 11, 2019, https://founders.archives.gov/documents/Jefferson/98-01-02-3562. [This is an Early Access document from The Papers of Thomas Jefferson: Retirement Series. It is not an authoritative final version.]
[220] Jefferson, Thomas. The Works of Thomas Jefferson, Federal Edition (New York and London, G.P. Putnam's Sons, 1904-5). Vol. 11. Chapter: To Doctor Benjamin Rush
[221] "Democratic-Republican Party." Editors of the Encyclopaedia Britannica, revised and updated by Jeff Wallenfeldt. https://www.britannica.com/topic/Democratic-Republican-Party
[222] "America's Founding Documents, US Bill of Rights," Archives.gov; accessed July 14, 2022; https://www.archives.gov/founding-docs/bill-of-rights/what-does-it-say
[223] "From Thomas Jefferson to Giovanni Fabbroni, 8 June 1778," Founders Online, National Archives, accessed April 11, 2019, https://founders.archives.gov/documents/Jefferson/01-02-02-0066. [Original source: The Papers of Thomas Jefferson, vol. 2, 1777 – 18 June 1779, ed. Julian P. Boyd. Princeton: Princeton University Press, 1950, pp. 195–198.]
[224] Washington, George. *The Writings of George Washington*. Vol. III (1775-1776). Chapter: To James Warren, Speaker etc. New York and London: G. P. Putnam's Sons, 1889.
[225] "From James Madison to David Rogerson Williams, 14 February 1816," Founders Online, National Archives, accessed April 11, 2019, https://founders.archives.gov/documents/Madison/99-01-02-4942. [This is an Early Access document from The Papers of James Madison. It is not an authoritative final version.]
[226] Henry, William Wirt. *Patrick Henry; Life, Correspondence and Speeches*, Vol. 3. Charles Scribner's Sons, 1891, Pg. 494.
[227] Wirt, William. *Sketches of the Life and Character of Patrick Henry*. Claxton, Remsen & Haffelfinger, 1878, pg. 141.
[228] Washington, George. George Washington: A Collection, compiled and edited by W.B. Allen (Indianapolis: Liberty Fund, 1988). Chapter: 169: First Annual Message
[229] "Circular to the Governors of the States, 25 February 1803," Founders Online, National Archives, accessed April 11, 2019, https://founders.archives.gov/documents/Jefferson/01-39-02-0488. [Original source: The Papers of Thomas Jefferson, vol. 39, 13 November 1802–3 March 1803, ed. Barbara B. Oberg. Princeton: Princeton University Press, 2012, pp. 579–580.]
[230] "From Thomas Jefferson to John Cartwright, 5 June 1824," Founders Online, National Archives, accessed April 11, 2019, https://founders.archives.gov/documents/Jefferson/98-01-02-4313. [This is an Early Access document from The Papers of Thomas Jefferson: Retirement Series. It is not an authoritative final version.]
[231] Thomas Jefferson to William Stephens Smith, The Works of Thomas Jefferson, Federal Edition (New York and London, G.P. Putnam's Sons, 1904-5). Vol. 5.
[232] "An Examination into the leading Principles of the Federal Constitution," in Paul Leicester Ford, ed., Pamphlets on the Constitution of the United States, published during its Discussion by the People, 1787-1788, edited with notes and a bibliography by Paul Leicester Ford (Brooklyn, N.Y., 1888).
[233] The Federalist Papers by "Anonymous". (Kessinger Publishing, 2004) No. 46, Pg. 235-236
[234] Mason, George. June 14, 1788, Virginia Ratifying Convention, Elliot p.3:379-380

[235] https://www.britannica.com/topic/militia; accessed 10/6/2019
[236] "Washington's Sentiments on a Peace Establishment, 1 May 1783," Founders Online, National Archives. Accessed April 11, 2019. https://founders.archives.gov/documents/Washington/99-01-02-11202. This is an Early Access document from *The Papers of George Washington.* It is not an authoritative final version.
[237] "From George Washington to George Mason, 5 April 1769," Founders Online, National Archives, accessed April 11, 2019, https://founders.archives.gov/documents/Washington/02-08-02-0132. [Original source: The Papers of George Washington, Colonial Series, vol. 8, 24 June 1767 – 25 December 1771, ed. W. W. Abbot and Dorothy Twohig. Charlottesville: University Press of Virginia, 1993, pp. 177–181.]
[238] Madison, James. Speech, Virginia Convention, December 1829. Published on Founders.Archives.gov. https://www.founders.archives.gov/?q=%22that%20persons%20and%20property%20are%20the%20two%20great%20subjects%22&s=1111311111&sa=&r=1&sr=
[239] "From James Madison to Thomas Jefferson, 24 October 1787," Founders Online, National Archives, version of January 18, 2019, https://founders.archives.gov/documents/Madison/01-10-02-0151. [Original source: The Papers of James Madison, vol. 10, 27 May 1787–3 March 1788, ed. Robert A. Rutland, Charles F. Hobson, William M. E. Rachal, and Frederika J. Teute. Chicago: The University of Chicago Press, 1977, pp. 205–220.]
[240] Adams, John. *The Works of John Adams, Second President of the United States: with a Life of the Author, Notes and Illustrations,* by his Grandson Charles Francis Adams. Boston: Little, Brown and Co., 1856. 10 volumes. Vol. 6. Chapter: First: Marchamont Nedham. The Right Constitution of a Commonwealth Examined.
[241] "For the National Gazette, 27 March 1792," Founders Online, National Archives. Accessed April 11, 2019. https://founders.archives.gov/documents/Madison/01-14-02-0238. Original source: *The Papers of James Madison,* vol. 14, 6 April 1791 – 16 March 1793, ed. Robert A. Rutland and Thomas A. Mason. Charlottesville: University Press of Virginia, 1983, pp. 266–268.
[242] The Federalist No. 62 by James Madison or Alexander Hamilton, February 27, 1788. https://founders.archives.gov/documents/Hamilton/01-04-02-0212
[243] Madison, James. *The Writings of James Madison, comprising his Public Papers and his Private Correspondence, including his numerous letters and documents now for the first time printed,* ed. Gaillard Hunt. New York: G.P. Putnam's Sons, 1900. Vol. 5. Chapter: Speeches in the First Congress—First Session.
[244] Washington, George. *The Writings of George Washington,* collected and edited by Worthington Chauncey Ford. Vol. XIII (1794-1798). Chapter: Farewell Address. New York and London: G. P. Putnam's Sons, 1890.
[245] Jefferson, Thomas. *The Works of Thomas Jefferson,* Federal Edition. Vol. 4. Chapter: Letter to John Adams, July 31, 1785. New York and London: G.P. Putnam's Sons, 1904-5.
[246] Cummings, William, and Aki Soga. "Bernie Sanders says he's a millionaire and 'If you write a best-selling book,' you can be one too." *USA TODAY,* April 10, 2019. https://www.usatoday.com/story/news/politics/elections/2019/04/10/bernie-sanders-millionaire-vows-release-10-years-tax-returns/3422903002/
[247] Orwell, George. *Nineteen Eighty-Four.* Harcourt, Inc., 1949.
[248] Orwell, George. *Down and Out in Paris and London.* 1933. Mariner Books. http://gutenberg.net.au/ebooks01/0100171h.html
[249] The White House, Office of the Press Secretary. https://obamawhitehouse.archives.gov/the-press-office/2012/07/13/remarks-president-campaign-event-roanoke-virginia

[250] Zitelmann, Rainer. "Hitler's Views on Private Property and Nationalization." Mises Institute, 2/24/22. Accessed 7/29/22. https://mises.org/wire/hitlers-views-private-property-and-nationalization

[251] Klein, Philip. "Amazing chart shows thanks to capitalism, global poverty is at its lowest rate in history." *Washington Examiner*, March 30, 2015. https://www.washingtonexaminer.com/amazing-chart-shows-thanks-to-capitalism-global-poverty-is-at-its-lowest-rate-in-history; Horwitz, Steven. "Capitalism Is Good for the Poor." Foundation for Economic Education, June 09, 2016. https://fee.org/articles/capitalism-is-good-for-the-poor/; https://ourworldindata.org/

[252] Bobbio, Norberto. *Left and Right: The Significance of a Political Distinction.* John Wiley & Sons, 2016. ISBN 978-1-5095-1412-0. https://books.google.com/books?id=8i7fCwAAQBAJ&q=National+Assembly&pg=PT112

[253] "2022 Index of Economic Freedom." Heritage.org. Accessed 7/8/22. https://www.heritage.org/index/ranking

[254] Vásquez, Ian, Fred McMahon, Ryan Murphy, and Guillermina Sutter Schneider. "The Human Freedom Index 2021." Accessed 7/8/22. https://www.cato.org/sites/cato.org/files/2022-03/human-freedom-index-2021-updated.pdf

[255] "Nationalism." Merriam-Webster dictionary. Accessed 8/5/22. https://www.merriam-webster.com/dictionary/nationalism

[256] "U.S. 'Party-switch' myth." Conservapedia.com. Accessed 7/11/22. https://www.conservapedia.com/U.S._%22Party-switch%22_myth

[257] "Debates over the Civil Rights Act of 1964." TeachingAmericanHistory.org. Accessed 7/11/22. https://teachingamericanhistory.org/document/the-civil-rights-act-1964/

[258] Charen, Mona. "Whitewashing the Democratic Party's History." Real Clear Politics, June 26, 2015. Accessed July 26, 2022. https://www.realclearpolitics.com/articles/2015/06/26/whitewashing_the_democratic_partys_history_127132.html#!

[259] Lyman, Brian. "Fact Check: Yes, Historians Do Teach That First Black Members of Congress Were Republicans." USA Today, June 18, 2020. Accessed August 6, 2022. https://www.usatoday.com/story/news/factcheck/2020/06/18/fact-check-democrats-republicans-and-complicated-history-race/3208378001/.

[260] Scott, Tim. "2020 Republican National Convention Speech." Channel 3000, August 25, 2020. Transcript accessed September 11, 2020. https://www.channel3000.com/i/transcript-tim-scotts-rnc-remarks/.

[261] "Hate crime hoaxes, like Jussie Smollett's alleged attack, are more common than you think." February 22, 2019. https://www.usatoday.com/story/opinion/2019/02/22/jussie-smollett-empire-attack-fired-cut-video-chicago-fox-column/2950146002/.

[262] Merriam-Webster. "Collectivism." Merriam-Webster Dictionary. Accessed April 24, 2019. https://www.merriam-webster.com/dictionary/collectivism.

[263] "Collectivism." Encyclopedia Britannica. Accessed July 14, 2022. https://www.britannica.com/topic/collectivism.

[264] The American Heritage Dictionary of the English Language, 5th Edition. Accessed July 14, 2022. Duck, Duck, Go search.

[265] "Authoritarianism." Britannica.com. Accessed July 14, 2022. https://www.britannica.com/topic/authoritarianism.

[266] Shaw, George Bernard. "Socialism." In Encyclopaedia Britannica, Thirteenth Edition. The Encyclopaedia Britannica Company, 1926.

267 Marx, Karl, and Friedrich Engels. "Manifesto of the Communist Party." Edited by Friedrich Engels and translated by Samuel Moore. Standard Socialist Series. Chicago: C. H. Kerr & Company, 1906.

268 Dagger, Richard, and Terence Ball. "Communism." Encyclopedia Britannica, November 13, 2019. Accessed August 11, 2022. https://www.britannica.com/topic/communism.

269 Engels, Friedrich. "The Principles of Communism." In Selected Works, Volume One, 81-97. Moscow: Progress Publishers, 1969.

270 Jefferson, Thomas. "Thomas Jefferson's Addition to Note for Destutt de Tracy's Treatise on Political Economy, [ca. 6 Apr. 1816]." Founders Online, National Archives. https://founders.archives.gov/documents/Jefferson/03-10-02-0035.

271 Adams, John. The Works of John Adams, Second President of the United States: with a Life of the Author, Notes and Illustrations, by his Grandson Charles Francis Adams. Vol. 6. Boston: Little, Brown and Co., 1856.

272 "United States Home Ownership Rate." Trading Economics. https://tradingeconomics.com/united-states/home-ownership-rate.

273 Madison, James. "The Federalist Number 10, [22 November 1787]." Founders Online, National Archives. Accessed January 18, 2019. https://founders.archives.gov/documents/Madison/01-10-02-0178.

274 Adams, Samuel. The Writings of Samuel Adams: 1764-1769. Edited by Harry Alonzo Cushing. Vol. 1. New York: G.P. Putnam's Sons, 1904.

275 Madison, James. "General Defense of the Constitution, [6 June 1788]." Founders Online, National Archives. Accessed April 11, 2019. https://founders.archives.gov/documents/Madison/01-11-02-0062.

276 Schwartz, Ian. "Hillary Clinton: Biden Did A 'Very Important Service To The Country' By Giving 'Strong And Necessary Speech'." Real Clear Politics, September 7, 2022. Accessed September 11, 2022. https://www.realclearpolitics.com/video/2022/09/07/hillary_clinton_biden_did_a_very_important_service_to_the_country_by_giving_strong_and_necessary_speech.html.

277 Ring, Edward. "California's Socialist Oligarchy: Who They Are." American Greatness, October 7, 2018. https://amgreatness.com/2018/10/07/californias-socialist-oligarchy-who-they-are-how-to-defeat-them/.

278 Franklin, Benjamin. The Writings of Benjamin Franklin. Vol. 5. New York: The Macmillan Company, 1906.

279 "George Bernard Shaw Reopens Capital Punishment Controversy." Paramount British Pictures, March 5, 1931. Video on YouTube. https://www.youtube.com/watch?v=B-Ljkoh_vmE.

280 Adams, John. The Works of John Adams, Second President of the United States: with a Life of the Author, Notes and Illustrations, by his Grandson Charles Francis Adams. Vol. 1. Boston: Little, Brown and Co., 1856.

281 Berry, Dr. Susan. "Daughters of Venezuela's Socialist Rulers Flaunt Their Substantial Assets as Nation Crumbles." Breitbart.com, February 5, 2019. https://pluralist.com/venezeula-rich-girls-flaunt-their-wealth-and-celebrity-lifestyle/.

282 Rapier, Robert. "How Venezuela Ruined Its Oil Industry." Forbes.com. Accessed February 20, 2020. https://www.forbes.com/sites/rrapier/2017/05/07/how-venezuela-ruined-its-oil-industry/#f3a65ad7399d.

283 Panné, Jean-Louis, et al. "The Black Book of Communism: Crimes, Terror, Repression." Edited by Mark Kramer. Translated by Jonathan Murphy. Cambridge: Harvard University Press, 1997.

284 Anton. "Debunking: 'Communism Killed More People than Nazism!'" August 24, 2017. Accessed June 26, 2022.

[285] Young, Adam. "Nazism is Socialism." Mises Institute, September 1, 2001. Accessed July 2, 2022. https://mises.org/library/nazism-socialism.
[286] Hitler, Adolf. "Speech of January 30, 1941." Quoted in My New Order. Nationalist.org. Accessed July 14, 2022.
[287] Dagger, Richard, and Terence Ball. "Communism." Encyclopedia Britannica, November 13, 2019. Accessed August 11, 2022. https://www.britannica.com/topic/communism.
[288] Zitelmann, Rainer. "Hitler's Views on Private Property and Nationalism." Mises Institute, February 24, 2022. Accessed July 15, 2022. https://mises.org/wire/hitlers-views-private-property-and-nationalization.
[289] Hitler, Adolf. "Speech of September 1, 1929." Quoted in Hitler: Speeches and Proclamations 1932–1945: The Chronicle of a Dictatorship by Max Domarus. Nationalist.org. Accessed July 15, 2022.
[290] Hitler, Adolf. "Speech of May 10, 1933." Quoted in My New Order. Nationalist.org. Accessed July 14, 2022.
[291] Hitler, Adolf. "Speech of July 15, 1932." Quoted in Hitler: Speeches and Proclamations 1932–1945: The Chronicle of a Dictatorship by Max Domarus. Nationalist.org. Accessed July 15, 2022.
[292] Hitler, Adolf. "Speech of October 5, 1937." Quoted in Hitler: Speeches and Proclamations 1932–1945: The Chronicle of a Dictatorship by Max Domarus. Nationalist.org. Accessed July 15, 2022.
[293] "Winterhilfswerk." Wikipedia. Accessed July 15, 2022. https://en.wikipedia.org/wiki/Winterhilfswerk.
[294] Hitler, Adolf. "Speech of April 17, 1934." Quoted in Hitler: Speeches and Proclamations 1932–1945: The Chronicle of a Dictatorship by Max Domarus. Nationalist.org. Accessed July 15, 2022.
[295] Hitler, Adolf. "Speech of April 12, 1922." Quoted in Hitler: Speeches and Proclamations 1932–1945: The Chronicle of a Dictatorship by Max Domarus. Nationalist.org. Accessed July 15, 2022.
[296] Somin, Ilya. "Remembering the Biggest Mass Murder in the History of the World." The Washington Post, August 3, 2016. Accessed February 11, 2020. https://www.washingtonpost.com/news/volokh-conspiracy/wp/2016/08/03/giving-historys-greatest-mass-murderer-his-due/
[297] History.com Editors. "Benito Mussolini." History.com. A&E Television Networks. Original Published October 29, 2009. Last Updated March 5, 2020. Access Date: June 25, 2022. https://www.history.com/topics/world-war-ii/benito-mussolini.
[298] "Fascism." Merriam-Webster.com Dictionary. Merriam-Webster. Accessed 1 Mar. 2020. https://www.merriam-webster.com/dictionary/fascism.
[299] Soucy, Robert. "Fascism." Britannica.com. Updated 1/2/20. Accessed 2/25/20. https://www.britannica.com/topic/fascism.
[300] Pope Pius XI. "Divini Redemptoris On Atheistic Communism." Papal Encyclicals Online. 1937. Accessed 9/18/20. https://www.papalencyclicals.net/pius11/p11divin.htm.
[301] Saint John Chrysostom, De Lazaro Concio, II, 6: PG 48, 992D; see next footnote.
[302] Pope Francis. "Apostolic Exhortation, Evangelii Gaudium." Nov. 24, 2013. Accessed 9/29/20. http://www.vatican.va/content/francesco/en/apost_exhortations/documents/papa-francesco_esortazione-ap_20131124_evangelii-gaudium.html#No_to_the_inequality_which_spawns_violence.
[303] Berry, Dr. Susan. "Jesuit-Led Parish Asks Parishioners to Take Pledge Affirming 'White Privilege' Must End." Breitbart.com. Sept. 5, 2020. Accessed 9/6/20. https://www.breitbart.com/politics/2020/09/05/jesuit-led-parish-asks-parishioners-to-take-pledge-affirming-white-privilege-must-end/.

---

[304] Hayek, Friedrich August. "The Road to Serfdom." University of Chicago Press. Sept. 1944.
[305] Hanson, Victor Davis. "The Other European Volcano: When Greece started to erupt, the volcanic ash spread over the social democrats' smug vision of a perfect European Union." National Review Online. May 14, 2010.
[306] Franklin, Benjamin. "Memoirs of the life and writings of Benjamin Franklin." Published by W. Colburn, 1818. Pg. 220.
[307] Addison, Kenneth N. "We Hold These Truths to be Self-evident—": An Interdisciplinary Analysis of the Roots of Racism and Slavery in America. United Press of America, 2009. Pg. 49-50, 55.
[308] Connolly, Katie. "What exactly is the Tea Party?" BBC News, Washington. Published: September 16, 2010. Accessed 7/27/22. https://www.bbc.com/news/world-us-canada-11317202.
[309] NBC News. "Countdown with Keith Olbermann." April 15, 2009. Accessed May 4, 2020. http://www.nbcnews.com/id/30249444/ns/msnbc-countdown_with_keith_olbermann/t/countdown-keith-olbermann-wednesday-april/.
[310] NBC News. "Countdown with Keith Olbermann." April 16, 2009. Accessed May 4, 2020. http://www.nbcnews.com/id/30264759/ns/msnbc-countdown_with_keith_olbermann/t/countdown-keith-olbermann-thursday-april/.
[311] Cesca, Bob. "The Tea Party Is All About Race." The Huffington Post, March 3, 2010. Accessed July 2, 2022. https://www.huffpost.com/entry/the-tea-party-is-all-abou_b_484229.
[312] Brooks, David. Column. New York Times, July 4, 2011.
[313] New York Historical Society. "A Conversation on Politics and Power in the 2012 Election," panel discussion hosted by the NY Historical Society, moderated by 60 Minutes journalist Lesley Stahl. Broadcast on C-SPAN TV, May 4, 2012. Reported by Scott Whitlock, senior news analyst for the Media Research Center, mrc.org, on May 16, 2012.
[314] Late Show with David Letterman. CBS, April 25, 2011. Transcript by Brent Baker, NewsBusters.org.
[315] The 9-12 Project. "The 9-12 Project was designed to bring America back to the unity that we experienced the day after the 9-11 terrorist attacks." Accessed from the912-project.com.
[316] FreedomWorks. "Founded in 1984, FreedomWorks is headquartered in Washington, DC, and has hundreds of thousands of grassroots volunteers nationwide. It is chaired by former U.S. House Majority Leader Dick Armey."
[317] Haislmaier, Edmund, and Abigail Slagle. "Obamacare Has Doubled the Cost of Individual Health Insurance." Heritage Foundation, March 21, 2021. Accessed July 27, 2022. https://www.heritage.org/health-care-reform/report/obamacare-has-doubled-the-cost-individual-health-insurance.
[318] Rich, Howard. "Obamacare Cost Skyrocket, Even Pre-launch." The Washington Times, March 14, 2012.
[319] Waldman, Deane. "An Objective, Evidence-Based Opposition to Obamacare." The Huffington Post, August 7, 2009. Accessed July 27, 2022. https://www.huffpost.com/entry/an-objective-evidence-bas_b_254184.
[320] Southern, Keiran. "Jim Carrey Takes Aim at Donald Trump in Extraordinary Awards Show Speech." Press Association Los Angeles Correspondent, October 27, 2018.
[321] Gehrke, Joel. "CBC Staff: Opposition to Obama is Racist." The Washington Examiner, June 11, 2012.
[322] Freeman, Morgan. "Morgan Freeman: Tea Party is Racist, They're Out to Get Obama." Interview with British TV host Piers Morgan. The Huffington Post, September 23, 2011. Updated December 6, 2017. Accessed April 29, 2020. https://www.huffpost.com/entry/morgan-freeman-tea-party-racist_n_978123.

---

[323] YouTube. "Watch Donald Trump Announce His Candidacy for U.S. President." Accessed April 27, 2020. https://www.youtube.com/watch?v=SpMJx0-HyOM.
[324] The Associated Press. "Cher Insults Trump, with Gusto, at Clinton Fundraiser." August 23, 2016. https://news3lv.com/news/entertainment/cher-insults-trump-with-gusto-at-clinton-fundraiser.
[325] Delaney, Brigid. "Fran Lebowitz: 'You Do Not Know Anyone as Stupid as Donald Trump'." March 2018.
[326] Streisand, Barbra. "Barbra Streisand on Why Trump Must Be Defeated in 2020." Variety, March 3, 2020. Accessed April 29, 2020. https://variety.com/2020/politics/news/barbra-streisand-trump-defeated-column-election-2020-1203521601/.
[327] The Guardian. "Robert De Niro Video Recorded for a 'Get Out the Vote' Initiative, but Considered Too Partisan to Include There." October 2016. https://www.theguardian.com/global/video/2016/oct/08/robert-de-niro-id-like-to-punch-donald-trump-in-the-face-video.
[328] Alterman, Eric. "Trumpism and the 'Liberal Elite'." The Nation, May 13, 2016. Accessed May 7, 2020. https://www.thenation.com/article/archive/trumpism-and-the-liberal-elite/.
[329] Heer, Jeet. "Donald Trump's Supporters Are Idiots." The New Republic. https://newrepublic.com/minutes/133447/donald-trumps-supporters-idiots.
[330] Politifact. "In Context: Donald Trump's 'Very Fine People on Both Sides' Remarks (Transcript)." April 26, 2019. Accessed May 9, 2020. https://www.politifact.com/article/2019/apr/26/context-trumps-very-fine-people-both-sides-remarks/.
[331] Sabia, Carmine. "Joy Behar Explodes on Trump Supporters: 'F*** the Kumbaya' ... Its Time to 'Go for the Jugular'." BPR Business and Politics, October 28, 2017. Accessed May 3, 2020. https://www.bizpacreview.com/2017/10/28/joy-behar-explodes-trump-supporters-f-kumbaya-time-go-jugular-554504.
[332] Reiner, Rob. "Tweet." July 29, 2019. Accessed April 29, 2020. Daily Mail.com. https://www.dailymail.co.uk/news/article-7301637/All-Donald-Trump-supporters-good-racists-says-Rob-Reiner.html.
[333] Alic, Haris. "Joe Biden Claims Trump Supporters Believe 'Mexicans Are Rapists,' 'All Muslims Are Bad'." Breitbart.com, April 16, 2020. Accessed May 3, 2020. https://www.breitbart.com/politics/2020/04/16/joe-biden-claims-trump-supporters-believe-mexicans-are-rapists-all-muslims-are-bad/.
[334] Ernst, Douglas. "Chuck Todd Blames Willfully Ignorant Voters for Trump's Election." The Washington Times, December 7, 2018. https://www.washingtontimes.com/news/2018/dec/7/chuck-todd-blames-willfully-ignorant-voters-for-tr/.
[335] Chait, Jonathan. "Here's the Real Reason Everybody Thought Trump Would Lose." The National Interest, May 11, 2016. NYmag.com. Accessed April 27, 2020. https://nymag.com/intelligencer/2016/05/heres-the-real-reason-we-all-underrated-trump.html.
[336] YouTube. "Lopez Tonight on TBS." October 26, 2010. https://www.youtube.com/watch?v=UnPSHFY4glc. Posted October 28, 2010.
[337] Reagan, Ron. "The Problem Isn't Just Trump. It's Our Ignorant Electorate." The Daily Beast, March 2018. https://www.thedailybeast.com/the-problem-isnt-just-trump-its-our-ignorant-electorate.
[338] Caplan, Joshua. "FBI Employee: 'Trump's Supporters Are All Poor, Uneducated, Lazy POS'." Breitbart.com, June 14, 2018. Accessed May 27, 2020. https://www.breitbart.com/politics/2018/06/14/fbi-employee-trump-supporters-poor-uneducated-lazy-pos/.

[339] Brennan, Jason. "Trump Won Because Voters Are Ignorant, Literally." November 10, 2016. Accessed April 29, 2020. https://foreignpolicy.com/2016/11/10/the-dance-of-the-dunces-trump-clinton-election-republican-democrat/.
[340] Weisberg, Jacob. "Blame the Childish, Ignorant American Public—not Politicians—for Our Political and Economic Crisis." Slate.com, February 5, 2010. https://slate.com/news-and-politics/2010/02/blame-the-childish-ignorant-american-public-not-politicians-for-our-political-and-economic-crisis.html.
[341] Barbato, Lauren. "Transcript of Clinton's 'Deplorables' Remark." *Bustle.com*, September 10, 2016. Accessed August 15, 2020. https://www.bustle.com/articles/183257-transcript-of-hillary-clintons-basket-of-deplorables-remark-gives-context-to-her-generalization.
[342] Howe, Caleb. "After Cheney Loss, James Carville Says Problem for GOP Is They Have 'Really Stupid, Evil' Voters." *MSN*, August 17, 2022. Accessed August 19, 2022. https://www.msn.com/en-us/news/politics/after-cheney-loss-james-carville-says-problem-for-gop-is-they-have-really-stupid-evil-voters/ar-AA10MnDK.
[343] Chaitin, Daniel. "Ex-CIA Chief Rates Today's Republicans as Most 'Dangerous' Political Force in History." *Washington Examiner*, August 17, 2022. Accessed August 22, 2022. https://www.washingtonexaminer.com/news/former-cia-director-michael-hayden-republicans-most-dangerous.
[344] Stephens, Bret. "I Was Wrong About Trump Voters." *New York Times*, July 21, 2022. Accessed August 20, 2022. www.nytimes.com/2022/07/opinion/bret-stephens-trump-voters.html.
[345] Trump, Donald. Campaign News Conference, Doral, Florida, July 27, 2016. https://www.youtube.com/watch?v=xFG5vBg45qs.
[346] Condon, Stephanie. "Hank Johnson Worries Guam Could 'Capsize' After Marine Buildup." *CBS News*, April 1, 2010. https://www.cbsnews.com/news/hank-johnson-worries-guam-could-capsize-after-marine-buildup/.
[347] Pararella, Emanuel L., Ph.D. "The Mass Dumbing Down of America: Donald Trump as the Canary in the Cave of Ignorance." *Ovi*, May 2016. http://www.ovimagazine.com/art/13052.
[348] Lemon, Don, Rick Wilson Republican Strategist, and Wajahat Ali CNN Contributor. *CNN Tonight*, January 25, 2020. Accessed May 6, 2020. http://transcripts.cnn.com/TRANSCRIPTS/2001/25/cnnt.01.html?mod=article_inline.
[349] Traub, James. "It's Time for the Elites to Rise Up Against the Ignorant Masses." *Foreign Policy*, June 28, 2016. https://foreignpolicy.com/2016/06/28/its-time-for-the-elites-to-rise-up-against-ignorant-masses-trump-2016-brexit/.
[350] Price, Greg. "Peter Strzok Was Asked 'What Does Trump Support Smell Like?' and If They're 'Hillbillies' During Wild House Hearing." *Newsweek*, July 12, 2018. Accessed August 15, 2020. https://www.newsweek.com/peter-strzok-trump-smell-hillbillies-1020892.
[351] Schwartz, Ian. "Sam Donaldson: Trump Core Supporters 'Ignorant', 'Don't Care About the Facts or Know About the Facts.'" *Real Clear Politics*, October 14, 2019. Accessed April 29,2020. https://www.realclearpolitics.com/video/2019/10/14/sam_donaldson_trump_core_supporters_ignorant_dont_care_about_the_facts_or_know_about_the_facts.html#!.
[352] Brzezinski, Mika. "MSNBC's Brzezinski: Trump Thinks He Can 'Control Exactly What People Think,' But That's 'Our Job.'" *Morning Joe*, MSNBC, February 22, 2017. Posted on February 22, 2017, by Tim Hains. Accessed May 6, 2020. https://www.realclearpolitics.com/video/2017/02/22/msnbcs_brzezinski_trump_thinks_he_can_control_exactly_what_people_think_but_thats_our_job.html#!.
[353] Pavlich, Katie. "Obamacare Architect: Yeah, We Lied to the 'Stupid' American People to Get It Passed." *Townhall.com*, November 10, 2014. Accessed May 26, 2020. https://townhall.com/tipsheet/katiepavlich/2014/11/10/obamacare-architect-yeah-we-

lied-to-the-stupid-american-people-n1916605.
[354] Fowler, Mayhill. "Obama: No Surprise that Hard-Pressed Pennsylvanians Turn Bitter." *HuffPost,* April 12, 2008. Accessed May 28, 2020. https://www.huffpost.com/entry/obama-no-surprise-that-ha_b_96188.
[355] Reiner, Rob. Twitter post, March 16, 2020. https://twitter.com/robreiner/status/1239556505013063680.
[356] Masciotra, David. "'Real Americans' vs. 'Coastal Elites': What Right-Wing Sneers at City Dwellers Really Mean." *Salon Magazine,* November 20, 2016. Accessed May 7, 2020. https://www.salon.com/2016/11/20/real-americans-vs-coastal-elites-what-right-wing-sneers-at-city-dwellers-really-mean/.
[357] Krugman, Paul. "What Happened on Election Day: The Economic Fallout." *New York Times,* November 2016. Accessed July 28, 2022. https://www.nytimes.com/interactive/projects/cp/opinion/election-night-2016/paul-krugman-the-economic-fallout.
[358] Attkisson, Sharyl. "25 Top Accomplishments of President Donald J. Trump." *Nation and State,* January 20, 2021. Accessed June 27, 2022. https://www.nationandstate.com/2021/01/20/25-top-accomplishments-of-president-donald-j-trump/.
[359] Schwartz, Ian. "Maher: I'm Hoping for a Crashing Economy So We Can Get Rid of Trump, Bring On the Recession." *Real Clear Politics,* June 9, 2018. Accessed April 30, 2020. https://www.realclearpolitics.com/video/2018/06/09/maher_im_hoping_for_a_crashing_economy_so_we_can_get_rid_of_trump_bring_on_the_recession.html#!.
[360] Hays, Gabriel. "With Inflation Worse Than He Predicted, NY Times' Krugman Admits: 'I Was Wrong', a 'Lesson in Humility.'" *Fox News,* July 21, 2022. Accessed July 28, 2022. https://www.foxnews.com/media/inflation-worse-he-predicted-ny-times-krugman-admits-i-wrong-lesson-humility.
[361] Fox News. "Rand Paul Shreds the Democrats' 'Ridiculously Juvenile Argument' on Kudlow." *Fox News,* March 22, 2022. Accessed August 24, 2022. https://video.foxbusiness.com/v/6301512804001#sp=show-clips.
[362] CNN Business. "US Stocks Rise After Fed Promises Low Rates for Years: September 16, 2020." *CNN Business.* Accessed August 24, 2022. https://www.cnn.com/business/live-news/stock-market-news-091520/h_f168cd760b9e74db3d83a59061bb707d.
[363] Feldman, Noah. "Trump's Fear of Experts Hurt the Coronavirus Response." *Bloomberg Opinion,* March 23, 2020. Accessed July 26, 2020. https://www.bloomberg.com/opinion/articles/2020-03-23/trump-coronavirus-response-was-kneecapped-by-his-fear-of-experts.
[364] Key, Pam. "Schumer on Coronavirus: 'We Are Very Worried About the President's Incompetence.'" *Breitbart.com,* March 10, 2020. Accessed May 27, 2020. https://www.breitbart.com/clips/2020/03/10/schumer-on-coronavirus-we-are-very-worried-about-the-presidents-incompetence/.
[365] CNN. "The Situation Room." *CNN,* April 13, 2020. Accessed June 28, 2020. http://transcripts.cnn.com/TRANSCRIPTS/2004/13/sitroom.01.html.
[366] Dorman, Sam. "Fauci Tells Fox He 'Didn't Get Any Sense' That Trump 'Was Distorting Anything' About Coronavirus." *Fox News,* September 9, 2020. Accessed September 20, 2021. https://www.foxnews.com/politics/dr-fauci-trump-woodward-downplay-covid-19.
[367] Howard, Jacqueline, and Veronica Stracqualursi. "Fauci Warns of 'Anti-Science Bias' Being a Problem in US." *CNN,* June 18, 2020. Accessed June 27, 2020. https://www.cnn.com/2020/06/18/politics/
[368] Newsmax. "Newsmax Interview with Dr. Anthony Fauci." January 21, 2020. Video, 6:28. Accessed June 28, 2020. https://www.youtube.com/watch?v=COqaUaQa9P8.

[369] Nelson, Steven. "CDC Director Downplays Claim that Coronavirus Spread is Inevitable." *New York Post,* February 27, 2020. Accessed June 28, 2020. https://nypost.com/2020/02/27/cdc-director-downplays-claim-that-coronavirus-spread-is-inevitable/.
[370] Asmelash, Leah. "The Surgeon General Wants Americans to Stop Buying Face Masks." *CNN,* March 2, 2020. Accessed June 29, 2020. https://www.cnn.com/2020/02/29/health/face-masks-coronavirus-surgeon-general-trnd/index.html.
[371] 60 Minutes. Interview with Dr. Anthony Fauci, May 8, 2020. https://www.instagram.com/p/CADc5BlFjEp/?utm_source=ig_embed&utm_campaign=embed_video_watch_again.
[372] Howard, Jacqueline. "WHO Stands by Recommendation to Not Wear Masks if You Are Not Sick or Not Caring for Someone Who Is Sick." *CNN,* March 31, 2020. Accessed August 22, 2022. https://www.cnn.com/2020/03/30/world/coronavirus-who-masks-recommendation-trnd/index.html.
[373] Gisondi, Victoria. "Fauci Endorses Double-Masking, Even After COVID Vaccine." *Life Site News,* January 26, 2021. Accessed June 28, 2022. https://www.lifesitenews.com/news/fauci-endorses-double-masking-even-after-covid-vaccine/.
[374] Klompas, Michael, Charles A. Morris, Julia Sinclair, Madelyn Pearson, and Erica S. Shenoy. "Universal Masking in Hospitals in the Covid-19 Era." *New England Journal of Medicine,* April 1, 2020. Accessed June 22, 2020. https://www.nejm.org/doi/full/10.1056/NEJMp2006372.
[375] White, Kaylee McGhee. "Do Masks Actually Work? The Best Studies Suggest They Don't." *Washington Examiner,* August 12, 2021. Accessed June 29, 2022. https://www.msn.com/en-us/health/medical/do-masks-actually-work-the-best-studies-suggest-they-don-t/ar-AANfurl.
[376] Aaro, David. "Wearing a Mask Cuts Own Risk of Novel Coronavirus by 65 Percent, Experts Say." *Fox News,* July 9, 2020. Accessed July 26, 2020. https://www.foxnews.com/health/wearing-mask-cuts-own-risk-novel-coronavirus-65-percent-experts-say.
[377] Alexander, Paul Elias. "More than 150 Comparative Studies and Articles on Mask Ineffectiveness and Harms." *Brownstone Institute,* December 20, 2021. Accessed August 22, 2022. https://brownstone.org/articles/more-than-150-comparative-studies-and-articles-on-mask-ineffectiveness-and-harms/.
[378] Prestigiacomo, Amanda. "Dr. Fauci: 10 Million Job Losses 'Inconvenient' But 'We Just Have to Do It'." *Daily Wire,* April 2, 2020. Accessed June 24, 2020. https://www.dailywire.com/news/dr-fauci-10-million-job-losses-inconvenient-but-we-just-have-to-do-it.
[379] Herby, Jonas, Lars Jonung, and Steve Hanke. "A Literature Review and Meta-Analysis of the Effects of Lockdowns on COVID-19 Mortality." John Hopkins Institute for Applied Economics, Global Health and the Study of Business Enterprise, January 2022. Accessed June 29, 2022. https://sites.krieger.jhu.edu/iae/files/2022/01/A-Literature-Review-and-Meta-Analysis-of-the-Effects-of-Lockdowns-on-COVID-19-Mortality.pdf.
[380] Ellis, Ralph. "Did Pandemic Lockdowns Do Little to Prevent COVID Deaths?" *WebMD,* February 4, 2022. Accessed June 29, 2022. https://www.webmd.com/lung/news/20220204/lockdowns-covid-deaths-study.
[381] Garcia, Victor. "Dr. Atlas: Coronavirus Lockdown is Killing People." *Fox News,* May 24, 2020. Accessed August 15, 2020. https://www.foxnews.com/media/dr-atlas-on-coronavirus-lockdowns-the-policy-is-killing-people.

[382] Williams, Thomas D., PH.D. "Stanford Physicians Suggest COVID-19 Could Have Lower Mortality Rate Than Flu." *Breitbart*, March 26, 2020. Accessed June 23, 2020. https://www.breitbart.com/health/2020/03/26/stanford-physicians-suggest-covid-19-could-have-lower-mortality-rate-than-flu/.
[383] Frieden, Tom. "When Will It Be Safe to Go Out Again?" *Washington Post*, March 25, 2020. Accessed July 27, 2020. https://www.washingtonpost.com/opinions/when-will-it-be-safe-to-go-out-again/2020/03/24/7cb2e488-6de1-11ea-aa80-c2470c6b2034_story.html.
[384] "Open Letter Advocating for an Anti-Racist Public Health Response to Demonstrations Against Systemic Injustice Occurring During the COVID-19 Pandemic." Signed by 1,288 public health professionals, infectious diseases professionals, and community stakeholders. Accessed July 27, 2020. https://drive.google.com/file/d/1Jyfn4Wd2i6bRi12ePghMHtX3ys1b7K1A/view
[385] Borchardt, Reuvain. "De Blasio: Only Protest Gatherings OK, Due to '400 Years of American Racism'." *Hamodia*, June 2, 2020. Accessed July 26, 2020. https://hamodia.com/2020/06/02/de-blasio-allowing-protesters-defy-social-distancing-due-angst-400-years-american-racism/.
[386] Mac Donald, Heather. "Four Months of Unprecedented Government Malfeasance." *Imprimis*, May/June 2020, Volume 49, Number 5/6. Hillsdale.edu. Accessed July 18, 2020. https://imprimis.hillsdale.edu/four-months-unprecedented-government-malfeasance/.
[387] Johnston, Lucy. "UK Lockdown was a 'Monumental Mistake' and Must Not Happen Again – Boris Scientist Says." *The Express UK*, August 26, 2020. Accessed August 29, 2020. https://www.express.co.uk/life-style/health/1320428/Coronavirus-news-lockdown-mistake-second-wave-Boris-Johnson.
[388] Fogery, Quint, and Josh Gertein. "Barr Calls Coronavirus Lockdowns the 'Greatest Intrusion on Civil Liberties' Since Slavery." *Politico*, September 17, 2020. Accessed September 18, 2020. https://www.msn.com/en-us/news/politics/barr-calls-coronavirus-lockdowns-the-greatest-intrusion-on-civil-liberties-since-slavery/ar-BB198L3z.
[389] Associated Press. "U.S. Attorney General Barr Likens Stay-at-Home Orders to Slavery, as Trump Derides Focus on Black History." *CBC News*, September 17, 2020. Accessed September 18, 2020. https://www.cbc.ca/news/world/us-barr-coronavirus-protests-1.5727693.
[390] Cult of Personality. Britannica.com. Accessed August 18, 2024; https://www.britannica.com/topic/personalismo
[391] Gerrans, Sam. "Soros to make a killing with European 'forced migration'", October 2, 2016. RT.com. Accessed August 18, 2024. https://www.rt.com/op-ed/361376-george-soros-investing-forced-immigration/
[392] Emba, Christine. "Why do Americans want guns? It comes down to one word." The Washington Post, May 15, 2023. Accessed August 18, 2024. https://www.washingtonpost.com/opinions/2023/05/15/gun-show-customers-fear-society
[393] Climate Depot. "Former Award-Winning NOAA Scientist Dr. Rex Fleming Declares His Climate Dissent, Converted from Warmist to Skeptic: Explains Why Climate Change Theory Is Bunk." Accessed July 30, 2019. https://www.climatedepot.com/2019/07/30/former-award-winning-noaa-scientist-dr-rex-fleming-declares-his-climate-dissent-converted-from-warmist-to-skeptic-explains-why-climate-change-theory-is-bunk/.
[394] Weise, Elizabeth. "End of Civilization: Climate Change Apocalypse Could Start by 2050 if We Don't Act, Report Warns." *USA Today*, June 5, 2020. Accessed September 6, 2020. https://www.usatoday.com/story/news/nation/2019/06/05/climate-change-apocalypse-could-start-2050-if-we-do-noting/1356865001/.

[395] CNSNews.com Staff. "Elizabeth Warren: 'Climate Change is an Existential Crisis'." *CNSNews.com,* August 30, 2019. Accessed September 6, 2020. https://www.cnsnews.com/blog/craig-bannister

[396]Cummings, William. "'The World Is Going to End in 12 Years if We Don't Address Climate Change,' Ocasio-Cortez." *USA Today,* January 22, 2019. Accessed September 6, 2020. https://www.usatoday.com/story/news/politics/onpolitics/2019/01/22/ocasio-cortez-climate-change-alarm/2642481002/.

[397] Gore, Al. "Leading the charge through earth's new normal." World Economic Forum, January 18, 2023. Davos, Switzerland. Full video accessed August 16, 2023. https://www.weforum.org/events/world-economic-forum-annual-meeting-2023/sessions/leading-the-charge-through-earths-new-normal/. Also see https://x.com/wideawake_media for more highlights of globalist speakers.

[398] McKitrick, Ross. "The Case for Pulling the U.S. Out of the Paris Climate Accord." *The Cato Institute,* April 26, 2017. Accessed July 25, 2022. https://www.cato.org/blog/case-pulling-us-out-paris-climate-accord.

[399] Lomborg, Bjorn. *False Alarm: How Climate Change Panic Cost Us Trillions, Hurts the Poor, and Failed to Fix the Planet.* Hoover Institute interview, July 14, 2020. Accessed August 3, 2020. https://www.hoover.org/research/bjorn-lomborg-false-alarm-how-climate-change-panic-costs-us-trillions-hurts-poor-and-fails.

[400] Doshi, Tilak. "The Dirty Secrets Of 'Clean' Electric Vehicles." *Forbes.com,* August 2, 2020. Accessed July 23, 2022. https://www.forbes.com/sites/tilakdoshi/2020/08/02/the-dirty-secrets-of-clean-electric-vehicles/?sh=5f60d9fe650b.

[401] Pan, Jing. "Bill Gates wants to 'fix the cows.'" Yahoo Finance. June 21, 2024. Accessed August 19, 2024. https://finance.yahoo.com/news/bill-gates-wants-fix-cows-102200934.html

[402] Accessed August 16, 2024. https://www.globalcitizen.org/en/content/climate-change-protests-action-creative-cop27/

[403] Kendall, Emily. "Cultural Appropriation." *Encyclopedia Britannica,* October 14, 2022. Accessed February 4, 2023. https://www.britannica.com/topic/cultural-appropriation.

[404] Brown, Lee. "School Defends 'Gender Rights' of Trans Teacher with Giant Prosthetic Breasts." *New York Post,* September 21, 2022. Accessed February 4, 2023. https://nypost.com/2022/09/21/canadian-school-backs-trans-teacher-with-giant-fake-boobs/.

[405] Taylor, Keeanga-Yamahtta. "The 'Free Speech' Hypocrisy of Right-Wing Media." *The New York Times,* August 14, 2017. Accessed August 10, 2020. https://www.nytimes.com/2017/08/14/opinion/the-free-speech-hypocrisy-of-right-wing-media.html.

[406] Pope Gregory XVI. *The Encyclical Letter of Pope Gregory XVI: Issued August 15, 1832. In which He Advocates Idolatry ... a Union of Church and State ... Exclusive Salvation ... Condemns Liberty of Conscience ... and Execrates the Liberty of the Press by the Catholic Church.* 1831-1846.

[407] Pope Leo XIII. *Immortale Dei: Encyclical of Pope Leo XIII on the Christian Constitution of States.* November 1, 1885. Vatican, Libreria Editrice Vaticana.

[408] Gibbon, Edward. *The History of the Decline and Fall of the Roman Empire,* Vol. 6, page 128. Methuen, 1898.

[409] Panné, Jean-Louis, Andrzej Paczkowski, Karel Bartosek, Jean-Louis Margolin, Nicolas Werth, Stéphane Courtois (Authors), Mark Kramer (Editor, Translator), Jonathan Murphy (Translator). *The Black Book of Communism: Crimes, Terror, Repression.* Harvard University Press, November 6, 1997.

[410] Moskowitz, P.E. "Everything You Think You Know About 'Free Speech' Is a Lie, How

far-right operatives manufactured the 'crisis' of free speech with books, think tanks—and billions of dollars." August 20, 2019. Accessed July 31, 2020.

[411] American Psychological Association. "Speaking of Psychology: Understanding your racial biases." Episode 31. Accessed August 2, 2020. https://www.apa.org/research/action/speaking-of-psychology/understanding-biases.

[412] Solomon, Danyelle. "Suppression: A Common Thread in American Democracy." *American Progress*, June 16, 2017. Accessed August 3, 2020. https://www.americanprogress.org/issues/race/news/2017/06/16/434561/suppression-common-thread-american-democracy/.

[413] Devega, Chauncey. "Trump's Darkness: White Supremacy, Christian Nationalism and the Coronavirus." *Salon.com*, April 15, 2020. Accessed August 3, 2020. https://www.salon.com/2020/04/15/trumps-darkness-white-supremacy-christian-nationalism-and-the-coronavirus/.

[414] Alberta Civil Liberties Research Centre. "Reverse Racism is a Myth." Accessed August 7, 2020. https://www.aclrc.com/myth-of-reverse-racism/.

[415] National Museum of African American History and Culture, Smithsonian. "Talking About Race: Whiteness." Accessed August 22, 2020. https://nmaahc.si.edu/learn/talking-about-race/topics/whiteness.

[416] Munro, Neil. "American Psychological Association Urges 'True Systemic Change in U.S. Culture'." *Breitbart*, September 3, 2020. Accessed September 4, 2020. https://www.breitbart.com/politics/2020/09/03/psychological-association-urges-true-systemic-change-us-culture/.

[417] Merriam-Webster. "White Supremacist, Definition of White Supremacist." Accessed August 6, 2020. https://www.merriam-webster.com/dictionary/white%20supremacist.

[418] Williams, Thomas D., Ph.D. "Journo: Anti-Looting Laws 'Inseparable from White Supremacy'." *Breitbart*, September 20, 2017. Accessed August 6, 2020. https://www.breitbart.com/politics/2017/09/20/journo-anti-looting-laws-inseparable-from-white-supremacy/.

[419] Smith, Karl W. "Trump's Economy Is Working for Minorities." *Bloomberg*, November 6, 2019. Accessed July 1, 2022. https://www.bloomberg.com/opinion/articles/2019-11-06/trump-s-economy-is-historically-good-for-minorities.

[420] "As opposed to the original definition of safe spaces as places of therapy and treatment for victims of violence."

[421] Crockett, Emily. "Safe Spaces, Explained." *Vox*, August 25, 2016. Accessed August 19, 2020. https://www.vox.com/2016/7/5/11949258/safe-spaces-explained.

[422] Uprety, Aastha, and Danyelle Solomon. "Combating Hate and White Nationalism in the Digital World." *Center for American Progress*, August 8, 2018. Accessed August 2, 2020. https://www.americanprogress.org/issues/race/reports/2018/08/08/454494/combating-hate-white-nationalism-digital-world/.

[423] Nelson, Sophia A. "From Emmett Till to Amy Cooper, Racism Eats Away at America." *The Daily Beast*, updated May 28, 2020, published May 26, 2020. Accessed September 14, 2020. https://www.thedailybeast.com/from-emmett-till-to-amy-cooper-racism-eats-away-at-america.

[424] Ford, Adam. "CNN's Van Jones: 'Even the Most Well-Intentioned White Person Has a Virus in His or Her Brain'." *Disrn*, May 30, 2020. https://disrn.com/news/cnns-van-jones-even-the-most-well-intentioned-white-person-has-a-virus-in-his-or-her-brain.

[425] Worland, Justin. "America's Long Overdue Awakening to Systemic Racism." *Time*, June 11, 2020. Accessed August 5, 2020. https://time.com/5851855/systemic-racism-america/.

[426] Kraychik, Robert. "Oprah Hosts White Guilt Session: 'Whiteness Gives You an Advantage No Matter What'." *Breitbart News*, August 3, 2020. Accessed August 5,

2020. https://www.breitbart.com/the-media/2020/08/03/oprah-hosts-white-guilt-session-whiteness-gives-you-an-advantage-no-matter-what/.
[427] Berry, Dr. Susan. "Jesuit-Led Parish Asks Parishioners to Take Pledge Affirming 'White Privilege' Must End." *Breitbart.com,* September 5, 2020. Accessed September 6, 2020. https://www.breitbart.com/politics/2020/09/05/jesuit-led-parish-asks-parishioners-to-take-pledge-affirming-white-privilege-must-end/.
[428] Montgomery, Jack. "WATCH: BBC Pushes 'White Privilege' Through Bitesize School Education Service." *Breitbart News,* August 5, 2020. Accessed August 5, 2020. https://www.breitbart.com/the-media/2020/08/05/bbc-pushes-white-privilege-through-its-bitesize-school-education-service/.
[429] Arora, Rav. "The Fallacy of White Privilege – and How It's Corroding Society." *New York Post,* July 11, 2020. Accessed August 6, 2020. https://nypost.com/2020/07/11/the-fallacy-of-white-privilege-and-how-its-corroding-society/.
[430] McIntosh, Peggy. "White Privilege and Male Privilege: A Personal Account of Coming to See Correspondences through Work in Women's Studies." 1988. Accessed August 6, 2020. https://www.racialequitytools.org/resourcefiles/mcintosh.pdf.
[431] National Museum of African American History and Culture, Smithsonian. "Talking About Race: Whiteness." Accessed August 22, 2020. https://nmaahc.si.edu/learn/talking-about-race/topics/whiteness.
[432] Nigatu, Heben. "21 Racial Microaggressions You Hear on a Daily Basis." *BuzzFeed,* posted December 9, 2013, updated August 14, 2020. Accessed September 12, 2020. https://www.buzzfeed.com/hnigatu/racial-microagressions-you-hear-on-a-daily-basis.
[433] Parrillo, Ali. "White Shame: How to Convert Guilt into Action." *Inverse,* June 17, 2020. Accessed August 11, 2020. https://www.inverse.com/mind-body/white-shame-anti-racism-efforts.
[434] Cohen, Seth. "An Overdue Debt – Why It's Finally Time to Pay Reparations to Black Americans." *Forbes,* June 21, 2020. Accessed September 4, 2020.
[435] Ghaffary, Shirin. "Civil Rights Leaders Are Still Fed Up with Facebook over Hate Speech: They Say Despite Repeated Promises Over the Years, Mark Zuckerberg Hasn't Stopped 'Vitriolic Hate' from Spreading on the Platform." *Vox,* July 7, 2020. Accessed July 30, 2020. https://www.vox.com/recode/2020/7/7/21316681/facebook-mark-zuckerberg-civil-rights-hate-speech-stop-hate-for-profit.
[436] Grimes, Daniel. "Should Hate Speech Be Banned on Campus?: Scholars Disagree." *Medill News Service,* October 16, 2018. Accessed July 29, 2020. https://dc.medill.northwestern.edu/blog/2018/10/16/hate-speech-banned-campus-scholars-disagree/.
[437] "The Matter of Marxism: Black Lives Matter Is Rooted in a Soulless Ideology." *The Washington Times,* June 29, 2020. Accessed September 14, 2020. https://www.washingtontimes.com/news/2020/jun/29/editorial-black-lives-matter-is-rooted-in-a-soulle/.
[438] Lakoff, George. "Why Hate Speech Is Not Free Speech." *FrameLab / Medium,* October 28, 2018. Accessed August 1, 2020. https://medium.com/@GeorgeLakoff/why-hate-speech-is-not-free-speech-428497fa616c.
[439] Steinmetz, Katy. "What Is Antifa? Anti-Fascist Protesters Draw Attention After Charlottesville." *Time,* August 14, 2017. https://time.com/4899658/charlottesville-antifa-protests/.
[440] "Hate." *Dictionary.com.* https://www.dictionary.com/browse/hate.
[441] "Hate Speech." *Dictionary.com.* https://www.dictionary.com/browse/hate-speech.
[442] Sadler, Kelly. "Top 10 recent examples of cancel culture." The Washington Times, February 16, 2021. Accessed August 19, 2024.

https://www.washingtontimes.com/news/2021/feb/16/top-10-recent-examples-cancel-culture/

[443] "Most of Facebook Censorship Board Has Ties to Leftwing Billionaire George Soros." *Judicial Watch*, May 29, 2020. Accessed August 29, 2020. https://www.judicialwatch.org/corruption-chronicles/most-of-facebook-censorship-board-has-ties-to-leftwing-billionaire-george-soros/.

[444] Goldsmith, Jack. "Internet Speech Will Never Go Back to Normal." *The Atlantic*, April 25, 2020. Accessed August 29, 2020. https://www.theatlantic.com/ideas/archive/2020/04/what-covid-revealed-about-internet/610549/.

[445] Nolan, Lucas. "5 of Big Tech's Most Serious Acts of Censorship." *Breitbart*, May 10, 2021. Accessed June 7, 2021. https://www.breitbart.com/tech/2021/05/10/5-of-big-techs-most-serious-acts-of-censorship/.

[446] Ahmari, Sohrab. "If Unreliable Is the Issue, Why Did Social Media Never Block Anti-Trump Stories?" *New York Post*, October 14, 2020. Accessed May 29, 2021. https://nypost.com/2020/10/14/if-unreliable-is-the-issue-why-did-social-media-never-block-anti-trump-stories/.

[447] Fox, Chris. "Twitter and Facebook's Action Over Joe Biden Article Reignites Bias Claims." *BBC*, accessed June 18, 2021. https://www.bbc.com/news/technology-54552101.

[448] Dorman, Sam, and Mike Emanuel. "Source on Alleged Hunter Biden Email Chain Verifies Message About Chinese Investment Firm." *Fox News*, October 16, 2020. Accessed June 18, 2021. https://www.foxnews.com/politics/hunter-biden-china-email-source-verifies.

[449] Bokhari, Allum. "Amazon Censors 'Killing Free Speech' Documentary About Censorship." *Breitbart*, June 22, 2020. Accessed August 29, 2020. https://www.breitbart.com/tech/2020/06/22/amazon-censors-killing-free-speech-documentary-about-censorship/.

[450] "Schools Are Teaching Gender and Sexual Identity." *The Heritage Foundation*, May 9, 2019. Accessed July 31, 2020. https://www.youtube.com/watch?v=G0SKtLrbZpU.

[451] O'Neil, Tyler. "Oregon Bakers Who Lost Their Livelihood Over a Gay Wedding Cake Make Appeal to the Supreme Court." *PJ Media*, October 22, 2018. Accessed August 20, 2020. https://pjmedia.com/news-and-politics/tyler-o-neil/2018/10/22/oregon-bakers-who-lost-their-livelihood-over-a-gay-wedding-cake-make-appeal-to-the-supreme-court-n61703.

[452] "President Trump's July 3 Mount Rushmore Speech." Transcript by *Newsmax*, posted July 4, 2020. Accessed August 21, 2020. https://www.newsmax.com/us/mount-rushmore-speech-transcript-july-3/2020/07/04/id/975688/.

[453] Prestigiacomo, Amanda. "WATCH: Leftist Mob Shows Up at Tucker Carlson's Home: 'You Are Not Safe.'" *The Daily Wire*, November 7, 2018. Accessed July 21, 2020. https://www.dailywire.com/news/watch-leftist-mob-shows-tucker-carlsons-home-you-amanda-prestigiacomo.

[454] Stelter, Brian. "The Inside Story of How ABC Fired Roseanne Barr." *CNN Business*, May 30, 2018. Accessed August 20, 2020. https://money.cnn.com/2018/05/29/media/abc-disney-roseanne-barr/index.html.

[455] Liwag Dixon, Christine-Marie, and Karen Miner. "What Really Happened to Paula Deen?" *Mashed*, August 22, 2018. Accessed September 8, 2020. https://www.mashed.com/131794/what-really-happened-to-paula-deen/.

[456] Visser, Nick. "Kevin Hart Says He's Stepped Down from Oscar Hosting Gig Amid Controversy Over Old Tweets." *HuffPost*, December 6, 2018. Accessed August 20, 2020. https://www.huffpost.com/entry/kevin-hart-homophobic-apology_n_5c09b9dfe4b0de79357b3b36.

[457] "A Letter on Justice and Open Debate." *Harper's Magazine*, July 7, 2020. Accessed August 20, 2020. https://harpers.org/a-letter-on-justice-and-open-debate/.
[458] Prager, Dennis. "PRAGER: The Lockdown, Evangelicals, and the Afterlife: A Response to Steven Pinker." *The Daily Wire*, May 30, 2020. Accessed September 1, 2020. https://www.dailywire.com/news/prager-the-lockdown-evangelicals-and-the-afterlife-a-response-to-steven-pinker.
[459] Hemingway, Mollie. "Media Falsely Claimed Violent Riots Were Peaceful and That Tear Gas Was Used Against Rioters." *The Federalist*, June 2, 2020. Accessed August 21, 2020. https://thefederalist.com/2020/06/02/media-falsely-claimed-violent-riots-were-peaceful-and-that-tear-gas-was-used-against-rioters/.
[460] Arama, Nick. "As CNN Reporter Claims 'Protests' 'Entirely Peaceful,' He Gets Proven Wrong Live on Air." *RedState*, May 30, 2020. Accessed August 21, 2020. https://www.redstate.com/nick-arama/2020/05/30/as-cnn-reporter-claims-protests-entirely-peaceful-he-gets-proven-wrong-live-on-air/.
[461] Birchall, Guy. "'Mostly Peaceful Riots'? Mainstream Media Has Given Up Any Shred of Objectivity Over BLM Violence. How Thick Do They Think We Are?" *RT*, June 12, 2020. Accessed August 21, 2020. https://www.rt.com/op-ed/491528-peaceful-protests-riots-black-lives-matter/.
[462] Garcia, Carlos. "CNN Faces Brutal Ridicule Over 'Mostly Peaceful' Chyron Message as City Burns in Background." *The Blaze*, August 27, 2020. Accessed September 4, 2020. https://www.theblaze.com/news/cnn-chyron-peaceful-protests-riots.
[463] Baker, Chris. "CNN Guy Calls These People a 'Merry Caravan' as They Throw Bottles at Him." *1110 KFAB News Radio*, May 30, 2020. Accessed August 22, 2020. https://kfab.iheart.com/content/2020-05-30-cnn-guy-calls-these-people-a-merry-caravan-as-they-throw-bottles-at-him/.
[464] Khazan, Olga. "Why People Loot." *The Atlantic*, June 2, 2020. Accessed August 22, 2020. https://www.theatlantic.com/health/archive/2020/06/why-people-loot/612577/.
[465] Trusdell, Brian. "Black Lives Matter Defends Chicago Looting as 'Reparations.'" *Newsmax*, August 11, 2020. Accessed August 21, 2020. https://www.newsmax.com/politics/chicago-looting-reparations-black-lives-matter/2020/08/11/id/981675/.
[466] Bauer, Scott, and Todd Richmond. "Wisconsin Governor Activates National Guard After Violence." *Associated Press*, June 25, 2020. Accessed August 30, 2020. https://abcnews.go.com/US/wireStory/crowds-tear-statues-attack-wisconsin-state-senator-71422820.
[467] Lapin, Tamar. "This Is What Seattle's CHOP Looks Like After Cops Oust Protesters." *New York Post*, July 1, 2020. Accessed August 21, 2020. https://nypost.com/2020/07/01/seattles-chop-full-of-destruction-after-cops-oust-protesters/.
[468] Lott, John R. Jr. "Liberal Politicians Who Order Police to Stand Down Are the Same People Who Want to Ban Guns." *The Washington Times*, June 3, 2020. Accessed July 24, 2020. https://www.washingtontimes.com/news/2020/jun/3/liberal-politicians-who-order-police-to-stand-down/.
[469] Wallace, Danielle. "Santa Monica Police Chief Faces Calls to Resign After Officers Watch Businesses Being Looted, Do Nothing." *Fox News*, June 2, 2020. Accessed August 21, 2020. https://www.foxnews.com/us/santa-monica-police-chief-petition-resign-looting.
[470] "Rioters Set Minneapolis Police Precinct on Fire as Protests Reignite Over George Floyd's Death." *FOX 9 Minneapolis*, Mayor Jacob Frey press conference, Published May 28, Updated May 29, 2020. Accessed July 24, 2020. https://www.fox9.com/news/rioters-set-minneapolis-police-precinct-on-fire-as-protests-reignite-over-george-floyds-death.

[471] Safi, Marlo. "15 People Died in the Protests and Riots Following George Floyd's Death. Here's Who They Are." *Daily Caller*, June 5, 2020. Accessed August 21, 2020. https://dailycaller.com/2020/06/05/15-people-died-protests-riots-george-floyd-death/.
[472] Pavlich, Katie. "BREAKING: Armed St. Louis Couple Has Been Charged for Defending Their Lives and Property." *Townhall*, July 20, 2020. Accessed August 21, 2020. https://townhall.com/tipsheet/katiepavlich/2020/07/20/breaking-mccloskey-family-has-been-charged-for-defending-their-lives-and-property-n2572800.
[473] Penrod, Josh, C.J. Sinner, and MaryJo Webster. "Buildings Damaged in Minneapolis, St. Paul After Riots, Twin Cities Restaurants and Retail Stores Were Hit the Hardest in the Rioting Following George Floyd's Killing." *Star Tribune*, July 13, 2020. Accessed August 21, 2020. https://www.startribune.com/minneapolis-st-paul-buildings-are-damaged-looted-after-george-floyd-protests-riots/569930671/.
[474] Selby, Nick. "Police Aren't Targeting and Killing Black Men." *National Review*, July 17, 2017. Accessed September 14, 2020. https://www.nationalreview.com/2017/07/police-shootings-black-men-race-not-reason-causal-effect/.
[475] "Propaganda." *Britannica.com.* Accessed June 4, 2021. https://www.britannica.com/topic/propaganda.
[476] "Congregation for the Propagation of the Faith." *Britannica.* Accessed June 4, 2021. https://www.britannica.com/topic/Congregation-for-the-Propagation-of-the-Faith.
[477] "Propaganda." *Online Etymology Dictionary.* Accessed August 15, 2022. https://www.etymonline.com/word/propaganda.
[478] "Hatred Going Viral in 'Dangerous Epidemic of Misinformation' During COVID-19 Pandemic." *UN News*, April 14, 2020. Accessed January 5, 2023. https://news.un.org/en/story/2020/04/1061682.
[479] Kornick, Lindsay. "The Mainstream Media's Top 10 Missteps in 2021." *Fox News*, December 30, 2021. Accessed November 13, 2022. https://www.foxnews.com/media/mainstream-media-top-10-2021.
[480] Ramaswamy, Vivek. Twitter Post. August 7, 2023. https://twitter.com/VivekGRamaswamy/status/1688343870407409664.
[481] Salzmann, Karl. "Flaskback: Biden Tells Migrans To Surge to the Border." The Free Beacon, May 10, 2023. Accessed August 19, 2024. https://freebeacon.com/biden-administration/flashback-biden-tells-migrants-to-surge-to-the-border/
[482] "About." *The Trilateral Commission.* Accessed January 12, 2023. https://www.trilateral.org/about/.
[483] Rockefeller, David. *Memoirs.* New York: Random House, 2002. Accessed December 26, 2022. https://www.goodreads.com/quotes/10465260-for-more-than-a-century-ideological-extremists-at-either-end.
[484] U.S. Congress. *Congressional Record.* February 9, 1917, 2947-2948. Transcribed from the Congressional record. https://www.congress.gov/bound-congressional-record/1917/02/09/house-section.
[485] Dodd, Norman. "The Dodd Report." Director of Research, Special Committee to Investigate Tax Exempt Foundations, May 10, 1954. The Long House Publishers, New York, NY. Accessed via Archive.org, January 11, 2023. https://ia600304.us.archive.org/19/items/DoddReportToTheReeceCommitteeOnFoundations-1954-RobberBaron/Dodd-Report-to-the-Reece-Committee-on-Foundations-1954.pdf.
[486] Dodd, Norman. Interview by G. Edward Griffin, 1982. https://www.youtube.com/watch?v=c5eHdTk5hjw&t=838s.
[487] Quigley, Carroll. *Tragedy and Hope: A History of the World in Our Time.* Volumes 1-8. New York: The Macmillan Company, 1966. https://archive.org/stream/tragedy-hope-a-

history-of-the-world-in-our-time-carroll-quigley/Tragedy%20%26%20Hope%20A%20History%20of%20the%20World%20in%20Our%20Time%20-%20Carroll-Quigley_djvu.txt.

[488] "Annual Meeting Davos 2023." *World Economic Forum.* Accessed January 12, 2023. https://www.weforum.org/agenda/2022/11/annual-meeting-davos-2023/.

[489] *Bilderberg Meetings.* Accessed January 12, 2023. https://www.bilderbergmeetings.org/.

[490] "Welcome to 2030: I Own Nothing, Have No Privacy, and Life Has Never Been Better." *Forbes*, November 10, 2016. https://www.forbes.com/sites/worldeconomicforum/2016/11/10/shopping-i-cant-really-remember-what-that-is-or-how-differently-well-live-in-2030/?sh=bbb04a317350.

[491] "What Is the Great Reset - and How Did It Get Hijacked by Conspiracy Theories?" *BBC*, June 24, 2021. https://www.bbc.com/news/blogs-trending-57532368.

[492] Wolverton, Joe II, J.D. "George Soros Funded by the House of Rothschild." *The New American*, May 2, 2011. Accessed January 13, 2023. https://thenewamerican.com/george-soros-funded-by-the-house-of-rothschild/.

[493] Ehrenfeld, Rachel, and Shawn Macomber. "George Soros: The 'God' Who Carries Around Some Dangerous Demons." *Los Angeles Times*, October 4, 2004. Accessed January 11, 2023. https://www.latimes.com/archives/la-xpm-2004-oct-04-oe-ehrenfeld4-story.html.

[494] Soros, George. "The Bubble of American Supremacy." *The Atlantic*, December 2003. Accessed December 27, 2022. https://www.theatlantic.com/magazine/archive/2003/12/the-bubble-of-american-supremacy/302851/.

[495] "Who We Are." *Open Society Foundations.* Accessed December 28, 2022. https://www.opensocietyfoundations.org/who-we-are.

[496] Soros, George. "The Capitalist Threat." *The Atlantic*, February 1997. Accessed December 28, 2022. https://www.theatlantic.com/magazine/archive/1997/02/the-capitalist-threat/376773/.

[497] Wilson, Woodrow. *The New Freedom.* 1913. Accessed January 11, 2023. https://www.blacklistednews.com/article/82521/dire-warnings-from-past-us-presidents-and-other-highprofile-leaders-about-an-invisible-government.html.

[498] Kennedy, John F. "Speech to the American Newspaper Publishers Association." April 27, 1961. Accessed January 11, 2023. https://www.blacklistednews.com/article/82521/dire-warnings-from-past-us-presidents-and-other-highprofile-leaders-about-an-invisible-government.html.

[499] Alfred Kinsey quote. Legacy Project Chicago. https://legacyprojectchicago.org/person/alfred-kinsey

[500] LibreTexts libraries. "Sociology: Socialization and Human Sexuality: Sexual Behavior: Kinsey's Study." Updated February 20, 2021. Accessed January 21, 2023. https://socialsci.libretexts.org/Bookshelves/Sociology/Introduction_to_Sociology/Book%3A_Sociology_(Boundless)/20%3A_Sexuality/20.01%3A_Socialization_and_Human_Sexuality/20.1B%3A_Sexual_Behavior-_Kinseys_Study.

[501] Kinsey, Alfred. "Sexual Behavior in the Human Male." 1948. Tables 30, 31, and 32. Reprinted on October 11, 2010, Reisman Institute. Accessed January 19, 2023. http://www.drjudithreisman.com/archives/2010/10/tables_30_31_32.html.

[502] Knight, Robert H., writer and director. "The Children of Table 34." Family Research Council production. Hosted by Efrem Zimbalist, Jr. Accessed January 20, 2023. http://drjudithreisman.com/broadcast.html#table34.

[503] The Phil Donahue Show. Episode with Judith Reisman. December 5, 1990. Accessed January 21, 2023. http://www.drjudithreisman.com/archives/2017/12/judith_reisman_14.html.

[504] Kinsey, Alfred. "Sexual Behavior in the Human Male." 1948. Pages 160-161. Posted October 11, 2010, Dr. Judith Reisman.com. Accessed January 20, 2023. http://www.drjudithreisman.com/archives/2010/10/pages_160-161.html.
[505] Reisman, Judith. "Kinsey: Crimes & Consequences." PhD, Chapter 7 "The Child Experiments." Accessed January 22, 2023. http://www.drjudithreisman.com/archives/chapter7.pdf.
[506] Raleigh, Helen. "Sri Lanka Crisis Shows the Damning Consequences of Western Elites' Green Revolution." *The Federalist*, July 15, 2022. Accessed July 25, 2022. https://thefederalist.com/2022/07/15/sri-lanka-crisis-shows-the-damning-consequences-of-western-elites-green-revolution/.
[507] Pryor, Steve. "A Partial List of the Over 6,000 Products Made from One Barrel of Oil (After Creating 19 Gallons of Gasoline)." Consultant Energy Asset Optimization & ETRM Projects, LinkedIn, July 26, 2016. Accessed July 22, 2022. https://www.linkedin.com/pulse/partial-list-over-6000-products-made-from-one-barrel-oil-steve-pryor/.
[508] Ables, Kelsey. "'15-minute city' planning is on the rise, experts say. Here's what to know." The Washington Post, March 3, 2023. Accessed August 19, 2024. https://www.washingtonpost.com/lifestyle/2023/03/03/15-minute-cities-faq/
[509] Cohen, Marshall. "The Steele Dossier: A Reckoning." CNN, November 18, 2021. Updated 7:19 PM ET. Accessed June 27, 2022. https://www.cnn.com/2021/11/18/politics/steele-dossier-reckoning/index.html. Strassel, Kimberley. "Inside the Clinton Dossier and the Con Behind the Russiagate Scandal." *New York Post*, November 5, 2021. Accessed June 27, 2022. https://nypost.com/2021/11/05/inside-the-clinton-dossier-and-the-con-behind-the-russiagate-scandal/.
[510] Williams, Pete, Julia Ainsley, and Gregg Birnbaum. "Mueller Finds No Proof of Trump Collusion with Russia; AG Barr Says Evidence 'Not Sufficient' to Prosecute." NBC News, March 24, 2019. Updated March 24, 2019, 5:14 PM CDT. Accessed June 27, 2022. https://www.nbcnews.com/politics/donald-trump/mueller-report-conclusions-trump-congress-attorney-general-william-barr-n986611.
[511] Durham, John. Special Counsel Report. Page 303, May 12, 2023. Accessed May 12, 2023. https://www.cbsnews.com/news/read-full-durham-report-here/.
[512] Stephens, Bret. "I Was Wrong About Trump Voters." *New York Times*, July 21, 2022. Accessed August 20, 2022. https://www.nytimes.com/2022/07/opinion/bret-stephens-trump-voters.html.
[513] Hutchison, Harry G. "FISA Memo Released and Fraud on the FISA Court Revealed." American Center for Law and Justice, February 2, 2018. Accessed August 22, 2022. https://aclj.org/government-corruption/fisa-memo-released-and-fraud-on-the-fisa-court-revealed.
[514] Attkisson, Sharyl. "What Would the Intelligence Community's 'Insurance Policy' Against Trump Look Like?" *The Hill*, August 9, 2018. Accessed August 22, 2022. https://thehill.com/opinion/white-house/401116-what-would-the-intelligence-communitys-insurance-policy-against-trump/.
[515] Biden, Joe. "Council for Foreign Relations Event in January 2018 Discussing the 2016 Firing of Ukrainian Prosecutor Viktor Shokin." YouTube. Accessed January 2018. https://www.youtube.com/watch?v=UXA--dj2-CY.; "Biden Reportedly Bragged About the Firing of a Prosecutor Who Was Investigating His Son's Firm." Law and Crime. Accessed January 2018. https://lawandcrime.com/high-profile/biden-reportedly-bragged-about-the-firing-of-a-prosecutor-who-was-investigating-his-sons-firm/.

[516] Carlson, Tucker. Interview with Devon Archer. Twitter, Episode 13, Part 2, August 4, 2023. https://twitter.com/TuckerCarlson?ref_src=twsrc%5Etfw%7Ctwcamp%5Etweetembed%7Ctwterm%5E1686799149109256192%7Ctwgr%5Ef8acc6176184ed035485db3d3d87f94f70be0983%7Ctwcon%5Es1_&ref_url=https%3A%2F%2Fredstate.com%2Fjenvanlaar%2F2023%2F08%2F02%2Fnew-tucker-carlson-interview-reveals-joe-biden-was-part-of-devon-archer-and-hunter-bidens-business-partnership-n786437.

[517] Ball, Molly. "The Secret History of the Shadow Campaign That Saved the 2020 Election." *Time*, February 4, 2021. Accessed July 1, 2021. https://time.com/5936036/secret-2020-election-campaign/.

[518] Moore, Mark. "CNN Staffer Boasts to Project Veritas That Network Peddled Anti-Trump 'Propaganda.'" *New York Post*, April 13, 2021. Accessed August 22, 2022. https://nypost.com/2021/04/13/cnns-charlie-chester-says-network-peddled-anti-trump-propaganda/.

[519] Schow, Ashe. "Reminder: These 50 Intelligence Officers Claimed, Without Evidence, That New York Post's Hunter Biden Story Was Russian Disinformation." *The Daily Wire*, March 19, 2022. Accessed August 20, 2022. https://www.dailywire.com/news/reminder-these-50-intelligence-officers-claimed-without-evidence-that-new-york-posts-hunter-biden-story-was-russian-disinformation.

[520] Justice, Tristan. "IRS Whistleblower Says Weiss Allowed Statute of Limitations to Expire in Hunter Biden Case." *The Federalist*, July 19, 2023. https://thefederalist.com/2023/07/19/irs-whistleblower-says-weiss-allowed-statute-of-limitations-to-expire-in-hunter-biden-case/.

[521] Crane, Emily. "FBI Brass Warned Agents Off Hunter Biden Laptop Due to 2020 Election: Whistleblowers." *New York Post*, August 24, 2022. Accessed September 11, 2022. https://nypost.com/2022/08/24/fbi-warned-agents-off-hunter-biden-laptop-due-to-election-whistleblowers/.

[522] Grassley, Chuck. "Letter to DOJ, FBI, Weiss." October 13, 2022. Accessed October 13, 2022. https://www.grassley.senate.gov/imo/media/doc/grassley_to_doj_fbi_weiss_political_bias_part_iii.pdf.

[523] Musk, Elon. Twitter Post. December 2, 2022. Accessed December 24, 2022. https://twitter.com/elonmusk/status/1598853708443357185.

[524] Ross, Chuck. "Twitter Blocked Hunter Laptop Story After Intelligence Officials Shared Hack 'Rumors.'" *Washington Free Beacon*, September 15, 2021. Accessed September 11, 2022. https://freebeacon.com/democrats/twitter-blocked-hunter-laptop-story-after-intelligence-officials-shared-hack-rumors/.

[525] Silverstein, Joe. "Podcaster Sam Harris: There Was a 'Conspiracy to Deny the Presidency to Donald Trump' in 2020." *Fox News*, August 18, 2022. Accessed August 19, 2022. https://www.foxnews.com/media/podcaster-sam-harris-there-conspiracy-deny-presidency-donald-trump-2020.

[526] Congress of the United States. "Letter." December 6, 2019. Accessed July 7, 2021. https://www.warren.senate.gov/imo/media/doc/H.I.G.%20McCarthy,%20&%20Staple%20Street%20letters.pdf.

[527] Zetter, Kim. "Exclusive: Critical U.S. Election Systems Have Been Left Exposed Online Despite Official Denials." *Vice*, August 8, 2019. Accessed July 2, 2021. https://www.vice.com/en/article/3kxzk9/exclusive-critical-us-election-systems-have-been-left-exposed-online-despite-official-denials.

[528] Bajak, Frank. "US Election Integrity Depends on Security-Challenged Firms." *Associated Press*, October 29, 2018. Accessed July 5, 2021. https://apnews.com/article/north-america-ne-state-wire-us-news-ap-top-news-elections-f6876669cb6b4e4c9850844f8e015b4c.

[529] Huseman, Jessica. "Voting by Mail Would Reduce Coronavirus Transmission but It Has Other Risks." March 24, 2020. Accessed July 3, 2021. https://www.propublica.org/article/voting-by-mail-would-reduce-coronavirus-transmission-but-it-has-other-risks.

[530] Commission on Federal Election Reform. Report issued in September 2005, led by Jimmy Carter and James A. Baker, III. Accessed July 6, 2021. https://www.foxnews.com/projects/pdf/election_reform_report.pdf.

[531] Flood, Brian. "New York Times Warned Readers About Vote by Mail Concerns in 2012, Now Claims That's a False Narrative." *Fox News*. September 17, 2020. Accessed July 6, 2021. https://www.foxnews.com/media/new-york-times-warned-readers-about-vote-by-mail-concerns-in-2012-now-claims-thats-a-false-narrative.

[532] Golinkin, Lev. "Trump's Denial Is the Second Big Lie." *NBC News*. November 7, 2022. Accessed November 29, 2022. https://www.nbcnews.com/think/opinion/trumps-denial-second-big-lie-ask-hillary-clinton-rcna55764.

[533] Swenson, Ali, and Amanda Seitz. "Fact Check: Trump Tweets Dominion Deleted Votes." *Associated Press*. November 12, 2020. https://www.boston.com/news/politics/2020/11/12/fact-check-trump-tweets-dominion-deleted-votes/.

[534] Prestigiacomo, Amanda. "Michigan: GOP Claims Software Glitch Switched 6,000 Republican Votes To Democrat, 47 Counties Used Same Software [UPDATE]." *The Daily Wire*. November 6, 2020. Accessed January 7, 2022. https://www.dailywire.com/news/michigan-gop-claims-software-glitch-switched-6000-republican-votes-to-democrat-47-counties-used-same-software.

[535] Baumann, Beth. "Here's What Was Discovered About Dominion Machines Used in a Swing State." *Townhall*. December 15, 2020. Accessed July 7, 2021. https://townhall.com/tipsheet/bethbaumann/2020/12/15/new-report-says-dominion-voting-systems-has-a-remarkably-high-error-rate-n2581624.

[536] Michigan Attorney General and Secretary of State. "Plaintiff's Report in Antrim County Election Lawsuit Demonstrates Lack of Credible Evidence of Widespread Fraud or Wrongdoing." December 14, 2020. https://www.michigan.gov/sos/0,4670,7-127--547432--,00.html.

[537] Layne, Nathan. "Exclusive: Trump-backed Michigan Attorney General Candidate Involved in Voting-system Breach, Documents Show." *Reuters*. August 8, 2022. Accessed August 20, 2022. https://www.reuters.com/world/us/exclusive-trump-backed-michigan-attorney-general-candidate-involved-voting-2022-08-07/.

[538] LaChance, Mike. "Senator Rand Paul Raises Questions About Voting Anomalies in Key Swing States." *The Gateway Pundit*. December 1, 2020. Accessed May 29, 2021. https://www.thegatewaypundit.com/2020/12/senator-rand-paul-raises-questions-voting-anomalies-key-swing-states/.

[539] Daniels, Corey. "Anomalies in Vote Counts and Their Effects on Election 2020." *New American Government*. November 30, 2020. Accessed October 6, 2022. https://newamericangovernment.org/anomalies-in-vote-counts-and-their-effects-on-election-2020/.

[540] Angelo, Carmen. "WATCH VIDEO! Ballot Count Irregularities in Atlanta?" *WTAM*. December 4, 2020. Accessed May 30, 2021. https://wtam.iheart.com/featured/mike-trivisonno/content/2020-12-04-watch-video-ballot-count-irregularities-in-atlanta/. "Video Shows Suitcases Filled with Ballots Pulled AFTER Supervisors Told Poll Workers to Leave." YouTube. Posted December 10, 2020. Accessed June 18, 2021. https://www.youtube.com/watch?v=aCenojrUwVM.

[541] "There is no evidence of widespread voter fraud in the 2020 US presidential election, government officials and election experts confirm." November 30, 2020. Summarization of various sources including ABC News, USA Today, NBC News. Accessed May 29, 2021. https://twitter.com/i/events/1308626736066617344?ref_src=twsrc%5Etfw%7Ctwcamp%5Etweetembed%7Ctwterm%5E1333145534765428737%7Ctwgr%5E%7Ctwcon%5Es1_&ref_url=https%3A%2F%2Fwww.thegatewaypundit.com%2F2020%2F12%2Fsenator-rand-paul-raises-questions-voting-anomalies-key-swing-states%2F.

[542] *Supreme Court of Wisconsin.* Case No. 2022AP91, 2022. Accessed August 23, 2022. https://www.wicourts.gov/sc/opinion/DisplayDocument.pdf?content=pdf&seqNo=542617.

[543] Donald J. Trump. January 2, 2024. "Summary of election fraud in the swing states." *Truth Social.* Accessed August 23, 2022. https://truthsocial.com/@realDonaldTrump/posts/111687076142669367.

[544] One repository of stories can be found here: https://debunkthis.eth.limo

[545] Associated Press. January 13, 2021. "Transcript of Trump's Speech at Rally Before US Capitol Riot." Accessed June 7, 2021.

[546] Beck, Glenn. "Did a Secret Service agent plant the Jan. 6 pipe bomb at the DNC?" August 19, 2024. Accessed August 20, 2024. https://www.glennbeck.com/radio/secret-service-jan6-bomb-dnc

[547] White, Jennie. January 11, 2021. "What I saw at the Save the America Rally." Accessed May 30, 2021. *The Federalist.* https://thefederalist.com/2021/01/11/what-i-saw-at-the-save-america-rally-in-washington-dc-on-jan-6/.

[548] The Associated Press. January 25, 2024. "Seattle: racial justice protesters who sued police win $10m payout." *The Guardian.* https://www.theguardian.com/us-news/2024/jan/25/seattle-police-settlement-protesters-george-floyd?ref=upstract.com.

[549] Marnin, Julia. February 24, 2021. "Fact Check: Was Capitol Police Officer Brian Sicknick Killed By Rioters?" Accessed June 5, 2021. *Newsweek.* https://www.newsweek.com/fact-check-was-capitol-police-officer-brian-sicknick-killed-rioters-1571891.

[550] Shiver, Phil. February 23, 2021. "Capitol Police Officer Brian Sicknick's mom says son died of a stroke, not a blow to the head — but authorities are staying mum." Accessed June 5, 2021. *The Blaze.* https://www.theblaze.com/news/brian-sicknick-possibly-died-of-stroke.

[551] Hermann, Peter, and Spencer S. Hsu. April 19, 2021. "Capitol Police officer Brian Sicknick, who engaged rioters, suffered two strokes and died of natural causes, officials say." Accessed June 28, 2021. *The Washington Post.* https://www.washingtonpost.com/local/public-safety/brian-sicknick-death-strokes/2021/04/19/36d2d310-617e-11eb-afbe-9a11a127d146_story.html.

[552] Massimo, Rick. April 19, 2021. "Medical examiner: Capitol Police officer Sicknick died of stroke; death ruled 'natural'." Accessed August 23, 2022. *WTOP News.* https://wtop.com/dc/2021/04/medical-examiner-capitol-police-officer-sicknick-died-of-stroke-death-ruled-natural/.

[553] King, Ryan. April 29, 2022. "Video shows officer striking motionless woman on ground during Capitol riot." *Washington Examiner.* Accessed August 23, 2022. https://www.washingtonexaminer.com/news/video-shows-officer-striking-motionless-woman-on-ground-during-capitol-riot.

[554] See Jake Lang, among others. https://x.com/JakeLangJ6

[555] Jansen, Bart. April 7, 2021. "Cause of death released for 4 of 5 people at Capitol riot - but not Officer Brian Sicknick." Accessed June 28, 2021. *USA Today.* https://www.usatoday.com/story/news/politics/2021/04/07/capitol-riot-deaths-cause-death-released-4-5-not-sicknick/7128040002/.

[556] *The National Pulse*. August 4, 2023. "'It Was Crawling With Feds' – Capitol Police Chief Confirms FBI, DHS Undercovers in Jan 6 Crowd." Accessed August 23, 2022. https://thenationalpulse.com/2023/08/04/exc-it-was-crawling-with-feds-capitol-police-chief-confirms-fbi-dhs-undercovers-in-jan-6-crowd/.

[557] Waller, J. Michael. January 14, 2021. "I Saw Provocateurs At The Capitol Riot On Jan. 6." *The Federalist*. Accessed June 23, 2021. https://thefederalist.com/2021/01/14/i-saw-provocateurs-at-the-capitol-riot-on-jan-6/.

[558] Vallejo, Justin. January 12, 2022. "Who is Ray Epps? The Capitol riot figure who disappeared from the FBI's wanted list." *Yahoo News*. Accessed December 24, 2022. https://news.yahoo.com/ray-epps-capitol-riot-figure-140228875.html?guccounter=1&guce_referrer=aHR0cHM6Ly9kdWNrZHVja2dvLmNvbS8&guce_referrer_sig=AQAAAF1aZUb9DxEsbkVxXQnlhc926vNWF71EUcI3BkbyPp9dGfm8nTccbzLnupiEa8MXf_5-spztpbdsZD7SnY0BewIUPSlCH8xUI88voz9w3DuGR9m4Hmwo69OVItxRShUrLAis_C2ihLllNjk9nGJXF2NC8CHZ-WAZh4bbbGZELU4H.

[559] Kaplan, Michael, and Cassidy McDonald. Updated June 4, 2021. "At least 17 police officers remain out of work with injuries from the Capitol attack." *CBS News*. Accessed August 23, 2022. https://www.cbsnews.com/news/capitol-police-injuries-riot/.

[560] Solomon, John. Updated June 8, 2022. "Trump Pentagon first offered National Guard to Capitol four days before Jan. 6 riots, memo shows." *Just the News*. Accessed August 23, 2022. https://justthenews.com/government/congress/trump-pentagon-first-offered-national-guard-capitol-four-days-jan-6-riots-memo.

[561] Cohen, Zachary. February 19, 2021. "US Capitol Police tells lawmakers that razor wire fencing should remain until September." *CNN*. Accessed June 5, 2021. https://www.cnn.com/2021/02/19/politics/us-capitol-police-fencing-extension-request/index.html.

[562] Folkenflik, David. June 8, 2022. "A former TV news executive is producing the Jan. 6 hearings." *NPR*. Accessed August 23, 2022. https://www.npr.org/2022/06/08/1103785079/a-former-tv-news-executive-is-producing-the-jan-6-hearings.

[563] Johnson, Ted. August 16, 2022. "Liz Cheney vows to do 'whatever it takes' to keep Donald Trump from 'anywhere near the Oval Office' as she concedes Wyoming primary race — Update." *Yahoo News*. Accessed August 17, 2022. https://news.yahoo.com/liz-cheney-loses-wyoming-primary-021706562.html?guccounter=1&guce_referrer=aHR0cHM6Ly9kdWNrZHVja2dvLmNvbS8&guce_referrer_sig=AQAAAFMSfRJaozxgg_oQTL7yznZkYAWPsCPLPOOOW3ymOKjc_z9i2ZsVL759tnmeg9Cqa7GSrf9eOUYciPWHPpiqgmNo3qCGFd9EQnX7ZlRefKjZ-2VwcQ-5pgUxGBwa8B4xqvnIwz22rf8MSW9hjomEmJ_pnY7D7T7anX5UlkDMMNlk.

[564] "Inauguration Day Protesters Clash in the Streets of DC." January 20, 2017. *World News Tonight, ABC*. Accessed August 23, 2022. https://www.youtube.com/watch?v=SCu2gxVZ4E8.

[565] Marks, Andrea. March 31, 2023. "Douglass Mackey found guilty of violating rights with 2016 memes telling Hillary fans to vote by text." *Rolling Stone*. Accessed August 23, 2022. https://www.rollingstone.com/culture/culture-news/douglass-mackey-trial-opening-trump-troll-disinformation-voting-rights-1234700422/.

[566] American Center for Law and Justice (ACLJ). June 12, 2024. Accessed August 23, 2022. https://aclj.org/government-corruption/confirmed-fbi-going-after-trump-supporters.

[567] "The Founding Fathers were right about foreign affairs." Rep. Ron Paul (R-TX). April 16, 2002. Posted on *Antiwar.com*. Accessed July 12, 2022. https://www.antiwar.com/paul/paul30.html.

[568] Jefferson, Thomas. *The Works of Thomas Jefferson, Federal Edition.* New York and London: G.P. Putnam's Sons, 1904-5. Vol. 4. "QUERY XVII The different religions received into that state?"
[569] Cheney, Dick. September 8, 2023. Accessed August 23, 2022. https://twitter.com/CollinRugg/status/1700140210837979248.

Made in United States
Orlando, FL
08 December 2024

55224160R00232